W9-BKQ-059

The World of Carnegie Hall

The World of Carnegie Hall

by Richard Schickel

JULIAN MESSNER, INC. · NEW YORK

Published by Julian Messner, Inc.
8 West 40 Street, New York 18

Published simultaneously in Canada
by The Copp Clark Publishing Co. Limited

Printed in the United States of America

Library of Congress Catalog Card No. 60-13802

This book is dedicated to no one in particular. Instead, it is for all those absent friends and good companions who, through the years, have offered aid, comfort and encouragement to a writer who herewith records his deepest gratitude.

Author's Note

It has been simply impossible to include within these pages an account of every important, interesting or amusing event that took place in Carnegie Hall during the seven decades of its existence. To have done so would have meant writing a book of unreadable length. Therefore, this book is necessarily a selective, or impressionistic, history of the hall. The selection of events covered here is, of course, one man's, and I take full responsibility for that selection. In the course of making it, I have found myself forced to blue pencil lengthy considerations of artists, compositions and personalities who are personal favorites of mine, and that grieves me. My purpose, however, was to record here events which have contributed most significantly to the artistic and intellectual currents of recent years. My criteria have always been: What is the larger meaning of this performance, this career, this speech? What is its contribution to the main current of American thought and art?

It is a pleasure to acknowledge the many debts I have contracted in the course of researching and writing this book. My fanatically loyal research assistants, Karen Shuter and Diane Walker Shaw, made it possible for me to get this book done within a limited time. Allen Hurlburt cast his cool professional eye over my picture selections and made all the good suggestions for their use. Susan Brady read a large portion of the manuscript and as a result my erring feet were placed in the path of righteousness. My editor, Lora Orrmont, dealt with unbelievable patience and skill with the eccentricities of both the writer's prose and personality. Arnold Arnstein combed the galleys looking for errors. My friend and agent Martha Winston held my hand through the whole long and difficult operation, and the Corporation of Yaddo, as it has before, gave me that rarest of all things in our society—a quiet place to work. Robert Kotlowitz of RCA Victor helped in a hundred ways.

A number of other people answered queries and placed research material at my disposal. Chief among them were Prof. Merle Curti, Frances Fuller of the American Academy of Dramatic Arts, Jack Frizzell of Columbia Records, Gilbert Millstein of *The New York Times*, jazz critic Robert Reisner, Raymond Rubinow of the J. M. Kaplan Fund, Iona Satescu and Leonora Shier of the Carnegie Hall staff, Prof. Burnet Tuthill, Prof. Joseph Wall and Rev. Carl Voss.

Three typists labored under forced draft, breaking many a fingernail, to get this book ready for the printer on time. I offer them—Barbara Bulkostein, Gail Deeb and Mrs. Lester Post—my admiring thanks.

Finally, I should like to make clear that the blanket dedication of this book includes my parents. Their support of my slightly bizarre career has meant a great deal to me.

All of these people—and many more—contributed to whatever merits this book has. Its faults are the faults of the writer and they are the result of, as Dr. Johnson classically put it, "ignorance, Madame, pure ignorance."

RICHARD SCHICKEL
New York City
August 25, 1960

Contents

Introduction
"Pursued by Visions" 3

One "A Platform for Good Causes" 15

Two "Amazing People, These Americans" 37

Three "Does Vanderbilt Get Sick of His Money?" 56

Four "The Center of the Musical World" 89

Five "To Raise Musical Standards" 133

Six "The Visions Which They Saw" 166

Seven "A Ghostly Rumble . . ." 193

Eight "Audacious Absurdity and Creativeness" 263

Nine "There Were Shadows" 315

Ten "Suddenly There Are Mass Markets . . ." 368

Index 418

The World of Carnegie Hall

“Music! What a splendid art, but what a sad profession.”

Georges Bizet

Introduction

"Pursued by Visions"

THIS BOOK IS A HISTORY OF THE MOST IMPORTANT CONCERT HALL IN America. When the cornerstone of that hall was laid, Andrew Carnegie, its principal backer, hoped aloud that Music Hall, as the building was originally called, would "intertwine itself with the history of our country." It did—and the result is that the historian of Carnegie Hall must necessarily be concerned with matters somewhat larger than the dates of debuts, the programs of premieres and the exact words spoken there by the oddly varied collection of spokesmen, special pleaders, faddists, fanatics and politicians.

Were one to concentrate only on the events that transpired inside the heavy masonry walls of Carnegie Hall, one would be forced to present an anthology of names and dates, having little significance to the general reader—and a rather confused and confusing anthology at that. I have tried, therefore, to stretch my rather detailed canvas on a frame of larger historical facts which I hope will give some hint as to the nature and direction of the very large world which has surrounded the very small world of Carnegie Hall.

Here, at the outset, I would like to state my operating assumptions about the history of the last seventy-odd years, the years during which Carnegie Hall has sat rather heavily upon the corner of Seventh Avenue and Fifty-seventh Street in Manhattan, New York City. I should also like to make clear my ideas about the relationship of music to the other intellectual and artistic currents of that period, for music has of course been the chief language spoken in Carnegie Hall.

One need only glance at the building itself to recognize the period in which it was born. Its exterior is ungraceful, vaguely reminiscent of the Italian Renaissance. This bespeaks, to the observer of American architectural taste, only one period, the Victorian, or "anything-you-can do-we-can-do-better," era. The interior of the main hall carries the impression further. There is a good deal of marble in its foyer, immense quantities of red plush in the appointments of the auditorium and liberal splashings of gilt. All this bespeaks the taste for elegance which was so important a part of the Victorian mentality. But when we speak of Victorianism, usually with a slight choke in our voices, we do not mean to include most of the inhabitants of that gold-plated era. We are speaking primarily of the upper classes and the middle-class professional groups—those terribly narrow and repressed people who controlled the thought, art and leisure of the age. It was for them that Carnegie Hall was erected and it was their tastes which its façade, and the programs presented behind it, reflected.

By 1891, when the hall was opened, they had made New York the center of the nation's business and financial establishment. Since culture goes where the money is, it was natural that Andrew Carnegie and his peers should decide that they needed a building which would be in effect what we now call a cultural center. It was more than a luxury to these people. It was a necessity. They had to prove that they were capable of nonmaterialistic activity, that the things of the spirit bulked as large in their minds as the latest market quotations. It may also be said that the newly wealthy, who had come to power in the years since the Civil War and who built the mighty industrial system on which the power of the United States today rests, had a need to prove that they were as culture-conscious as the older mercantile families which had ruled the nation since its founding. These people were builders on a gigantic scale, and when they turned their attention to the moribund cultural life of the nation they brought frantic energy to the task.

The depth of their devotion to cultural endeavors is, of course, suspect. Certainly it was not bred in their bones and certainly most of the "appreciating" was left to the ladies. The pianist Harold Bauer, who arrived in America for a tour in the decade after Carnegie Hall was built, did not notice any Medici-like devotion to the patronage of the arts. Instead, he observes in his autobiography that he had "no idea what work could really mean until I came to the United States. ... None of my friends and acquaintances [in the United States] ever seemed to enjoy any leisure or rest, and when they indulged in games or sports it was with the same terrific energy they employed in their business affairs. They were continuously pursued by visions of progress, expansion, increase of capacity, and increase of power resulting therefrom." The expansion of cultural opportunities was surely part of the vision which pursued these people, but it was a minor part—and a late starter in the race for their attention.

When Carnegie Hall was built the new rich stood at the zenith of their untrammeled power, at the height of their prestige. And it is one of the ironies of Carnegie Hall's history that it achieved landmark status during the half-century in which the thrust of American history was toward reform of the excesses committed by the very class that had erected it and was the chief support of the activities which took place in it. Even as it was being built a great restlessness born of vast social and economic pressures was coming over the nation.

In 1892, a year after Carnegie Hall was opened, the Populist Party, representing the economically disenfranchised elements of the society, was declaring in its platform that it convened "in the midst of a nation brought to the verge of moral, political and material ruin. Corruption dominates the ballot box, the legislatures, the Congress, and touches even the ermine of the bench. The people are demoralized. ... The newspapers are largely subsidized or muzzled, public opinion silenced, business prostrated, homes covered with mortgages, labor impoverished and the land concentrated in the hands of capitalists. The urban workmen are denied the right to organize for self-protection, imported pauperized labor beats down their wages, a hireling standing army unrecognized by our laws, is established to shoot them down, and they are rapidly degenerating into European conditions. The fruits of the toil of millions are boldly stolen to build up colossal fortunes for a few, unprecedented in the history of mankind; and the possessors of these, in turn, despise the Republic and endanger liberty." Things may not have been quite that bad—after all this was a campaign document—but the Populists did speak for millions who felt that *their* vision of the American dream was being despoiled.

During the ten years that followed, great fissures opened between the various class groups. "Serious fault lines ran between the large and small manufacturer, between capital and labor, between the masses of the new immigrants and the older population, between the city and the farm," according to the historian George Mowry. In the years before the Spanish-American War tensions erupted in violent labor disputes, in the angry words of agrarians, who saw power slipping from them to the urban masses, and in prejudice directed against the politically malleable new immigrants by the descendants of older settlers. The war temporarily covered these differences, but by 1900 America was ready for its first great period of political progressivism. In these years the first liberal consensus of the twentieth century was formed. The impulse to reform was confined to no particular class or socio-economic group. Instead, it was, in the words of Richard Hofstadter, "a rather widespread and remarkably good-natured effort of the greater part of society to achieve some not very clearly specified self-reformation. Its general theme was the effort to restore a type of economic individualism and political democracy that was widely believed to have existed earlier in America and to have been destroyed by the great corporation and the corrupt political machine; and with that restoration to bring back a kind of morality and civic purity that was also believed to have been lost."

Culturally the period had a profound effect on the great mass of people. They were no longer certain that all virtue resided with those who had made the most money; they began to realize that their own tastes and opinions were, in a democracy, as good as anyone else's. But politically and economically, for all the antitrust laws and pure food and drug acts, the progressive period accomplished little in terms of a genuine redistribution of power. That "damned cowboy," Theodore Roosevelt, spoke the epitaph of the reform era when he remarked that it was impossible to unscramble the eggs. The upshot was that the controlling classes were reminded that other people did exist and that if they wished to retain their power they had better use it with a little more circumspection.

America's entrance into World War I again bound up the wounds of class struggle. The aftermath of the war was disgust—disgust with political solutions, the whole dirty game of politics, domestic and international. The intellectuals and their fellow-travelers, the taste-makers, turned from political to aesthetic activism. All the nonpolitical values of the prewar society—moral, sexual, religious, social—were called into question in an atmosphere of artistic and intellectual questing in the Twenties.

Among the values called into question were the tastes that had prevailed for the first twenty-nine years of Carnegie Hall's existence. The sort of music accepted there had remained standardized. Beethoven ruled supreme and Wagner was regarded as his modern heir, the last important innovator. It fact, it might be said that the upper-class American musical audience accepted no music written before 1800 (the year of Beethoven's First Symphony) or after 1882 (the date of the *Parsifal* premiere). Bach and Mozart were virtually unplayed, Brahms was grudgingly accepted, the sounds of such barbarians outside the gates as Richard Strauss, Mahler, Bruckner, even Debussy were ignored in the hope that they would cease.

Despite the eagerness of professional musicians and intellectuals to play and listen to new sounds, there was still reluctance on the part of the majority audience to accept the new and this had a rather disastrous effect on music in the Twenties. Just before World War I two European gentlemen began fooling around with new sounds. One was Igor Stravinsky and his brand of modern music came to be called neoclassicism. The other was Arnold Schönberg and his work and that of his disciples was known as atonalism. Between members of the warring camps who rallied around "the two heap big chiefs" of modern music, there was—and is—naturally, a certain enmity. But between traditionalists and the members of the two modernist camps there is a dislike so intense as to almost preclude communication.

The result of the introduction, in the Twenties, of neoclassicism and atonalism to America was a widened gap between the professionals and the musical amateurs who form their audience. Of all the arts, music has the most highly developed special language. Through the ages only a small number of people—nearly all of them direct participants in the art (composers, performers, critics)—have acquired proficiency in the language. To some extent, this is true of all the arts. But the intelligent amateur can acquire, with minimum effort, some technical knowledge about writing merely by reading, about painting merely by looking. But it takes years of concentrated effort to acquire the standards of judgment that must precede any intelligent musical appreciation and it cannot be learned merely by listening. Even to acquire the amateur's knowledge, of the sort that enhances the common reader's pleasure, takes more time and effort than most people care to invest. No one except the professionals writes music and no sane person entertains even the vaguest hope that he can join that particular priesthood. Hence the dominance of the performer—for the world is full of people who have taken piano lessons, and therefore have some criteria for the critical consideration of performance.

Musical composition has been, more than any other art, peculiarly dependent on the raw emotional response of its audience for its existence. When the modern composers decided to sacrifice the appeal to the emotions in favor of the purity of technical and intellectual virtuosity, they lost most of the audience for contemporary music. Of course, not everyone abandoned them. Some of the intellectuals hung around to see what was going to happen, and a few musical lion hunters continued to invite the composers to drop in for drinks after the concert. A few people even found that the new music could quicken and sharpen—and even express—their emotional response to the anxiety-ridden existence of our century. Basically, however, the only people who care greatly for modern music are the people who compose and play it. The average music lover simply ignores it. He continues to listen to the music of the nineteenth century.

This is a curious phenomenon. In literature the romantic movement is as extinct as its contemporary, the carrier pigeon. In painting the misty, musty pastorals of the romantic movement have been relegated to the less-frequented rooms of our museums. In all the arts, the sentimental, the sweet, the self-consciously beautiful have been gratefully passed on to the mass communicators to use at will in the selling of soap and insurance policies. Among composers, the romantic style is a live item only among the writers of popular songs, musical comedies and movie scores.

It is only in the concert hall that the romantic music of a century ago is regarded as a living tradition. A handful of modern pieces have wormed their way into the repertory, it is true, chief among them a few pieces by Stravinsky. But by and large competent critics are agreed that the repertory of today is basically the repertory of the turn of the century. Within it there has been some movement, as of stocks on a carefully controlled exchange. Mozart and Bach have shown the steadiest upward trend since 1920 and Berlioz has enjoyed a late rally. Tchaikovsky's stock, along with that of Liszt, Mendelssohn and Dvořák has been depressed for some time, although some trading in these items continues. Wagner has come back slightly as the association of his music with Nazism has faded. Steady at the top of the list are music's blue chip composers—Beethoven and Brahms. Of the moderns only Strauss, Debussy, Ravel and Rachmaninoff, modern carriers of the romantic torch, have achieved listing on music's big board. They are joined by other composers of this century only when the round-numbered anniversary of a composer's birth or death occurs, but this causes no more than a brief flurry, a fraudulent revival that expires in a year or two.

Of the men composing in a truly modern idiom little is heard. They get occasional playings, of course, and everyone agrees that something ought to be done for them. Conductors, for the most part, are quite dedicated to the new, correctly believing that there is no vitality in an art unless there is lively interest in its current manifestations. The recitalists share this dedication, perhaps to a slightly lesser extent. The men of the orchestra, bored beyond description by endless repetitions of the standard pieces usually welcome a chance to try something new. Critics tend to look with favor, these days, on new enterprises, and even managers and boards of directors, sadly recognizing that it takes all kinds to make a world, don't mind scheduling a few moderns to see if the eggheads can't be enticed away from their hi-fi sets and into the concert hall.

But because the response of the audience is so predictably negative, no one's heart is really in it. Quite simply, it has been demonstrated over and over again, since the heyday of the new music in the Twenties, that most people don't care to hear it. Musicians, it is true, have been struggling against this indifference, but their fight is a difficult one. The struggle of Wagner and his disciples against the conservatives was a brilliantly conducted duel with what seemed to all contestants nothing less than the future of the art at stake. The trouble today is that the modernists can't even get a good argument going. The majority of the musical audience merely shrugs its shoulders and turns up the volume of the Beethoven a little louder.

Briefly, in the Thirties, the composers, inspired by various notions of proletarian solidarity—not to mention the great new popular audience which radio and records had opened up to them—made a distinct effort to seek a *rapprochement* with a larger audience. In effect, they were appealing over the heads of the average symphony subscription audiences to the larger musical audience they thought they detected outside the concert hall. The effect was a brief moment in time in which it looked as if certain folkish variations on modern music might break through the wall of indifference. Even the people in the concert rooms seemed to be sitting up and taking notice. But with the coming of the post-World War II era, with the sense of national purpose and unity suddenly destroyed and the vaguely liberal consensus of modern American welfare democracy an accepted—and slightly boring—fact, the composers as well as other artists and intellectuals have retreated into themselves again and once again the gap has opened between creator and audience.

There is, however, one difference between the modern musical audience and the one of the Twenties. It is larger. To some degree this is a result of the liberal, reformist thrust of modern American history which we spoke of earlier. To some extent it is the result of technology. But mostly it is a by-product of a rising birth rate.

After the politically dolorous decade between 1919 and 1929, and after the business community's prestige suffered its most crushing defeat in 1929, America once again turned to reform. This time it was more thorough-going than it had been before. Perhaps the ultimate centers of power remained undisturbed, but, after the first awful years of depression, it became apparent that the common man (whose century it was alleged to be) was going to have more bread (and more circuses, too) than ever before. His rights to economic security and social security (in the broadest sense) were guaranteed by the government. The result was a shift, after World War II had completed for America its task of economic recovery, from an economy of scarcity to an economy of abundance—to the affluent society. This affluence has meant that nearly everyone has the money to purchase a ticket to Carnegie Hall—and a stereophonic hi-fi set to boot. It has also meant that more people than ever before have the leisure to acquire a taste for the good things of life and the leisure to exercise those tastes.

The small, closed society that built Carnegie Hall as well as dozens of other early cultural institutions in this country, and who had once talked vaguely of the stewardship of wealth and of allowing some of the good things they enjoyed to trickle down to the masses, suddenly found themselves surrounded on all sides by a milling mob of people who were intent on having cultural parity as a logical extension of the economic and social gains made since 1932.

The older, upper-class audience for music seems to feel an understandable resentment of this poaching on what had once been its private preserve. Whatever their motivations, it was they who had supported music in America through long years when the mass audience demonstrated nothing but indifference to high culture of any kind. During the period when music was under the stewardship of wealth it grew from the tiniest seed to great size as a cultural establishment. When Carnegie Hall was built there was only one truly professional symphony orchestra in this country and virtually no American musicians and composers. There were no places in this country where a young artist could develop his skills. By the middle of the twentieth century all that had changed. There were at least a dozen first-class orchestras in the country, America had begun to develop young artists and composers, it had built a large music education establishment, and the eagerness of the small audience for good music had caused the economic center of power to shift from Europe to America. It was here that the major artists came to receive the cash-on-the-line support they needed. In the same period the technical powers of performers began to reach the heights we now accept as minimal professional standards.

Today, no man who is not a technical virtuoso dares to appear on the stage of Carnegie Hall or any other major concert platform. For the financial support which made all this possible, the vast modern musical public owes a debt of gratitude to the relatively small audience which underwrote music during its pioneering days in this country.

The day in which the iron whims of that small audience ruled the musical fate of the nation is without question gone. Our history of Carnegie Hall ends with the creation of the new Lincoln Center for the Performing Arts and with the passing of Carnegie Hall itself from private to public ownership. And there is one highly symbolic fact about the Lincoln Center concert hall: it has no boxes, those traditional refuges of the cultural ruling class from the *canaille.* In its advertisements and publicity releases the Lincoln Center speaks of itself as a symbol of "America's cultural maturity." It will, its directors promise, "speak for all the nation to all the world." In short, it is evidence of a new American cultural consensus, a consensus which states quite emphatically that our cultural life belongs to everyone, not simply to a privileged few. It seems to state also that the majority of our people believe that their government should take a larger role in providing cultural opportunities for everyone. Carnegie Hall itself would today be a parking lot if this consensus had not been operative, for it was saved as a result of action by the governments of New York City and New York State.

But there would be no such wide consensus had not a foundation for it been laid by the small group of people who, in the 1890's, turned their attention—for purely selfish reasons—to the building of a cultural establishment to equal the economic establishment they had already created. If they had not done so, the majority of our citizens would never have discovered what they were missing.

Their eventual loss of control of America's cultural establishment was implicit in its very founding by the wealthy class. The same may be said of their founding of our gigantic industrial power. They will never totally lose control of either, but they will never again be able to operate without paying considerable attention to the wishes of the majority, which through the pressure of public opinion on government now exerts a strong countervailing power against them.

To borrow Theodore Roosevelt's early metaphor, this is the new omelet, and it cannot be unscrambled either. We can only wonder, standing at the beginning of the era of mass democracy and mass culture whether the stewardship of the majority will be any wiser—or even as wise—as the stewardship of the minority. And we can observe, through the microcosm of institutions like Carnegie Hall, the shift of the power center of American life from class to mass. Musical history is our metaphor, but we would be imperceptive indeed if we did not see that it can be applied to questions that range far from the concert hall.

One

"A Platform for Good Causes"

LIKE NEARLY EVERYTHING ELSE IN AMERICA, INTEREST IN MUSIC GREW with tremendous speed in the decades following the Civil War. A basic economic change was taking place. The nation was transforming itself from an agrarian nation into a mighty industrial power, the mightiest the world has ever seen. The basic product of this change was an unparalleled organization for the production of goods. The primary by-product of that organization was wealth. This wealth was concentrated in the hands of a very few people. And where there is wealth, there follows a desire for that most elusive of all status symbols—culture. From this desire there developed, by the turn of the century, a fairly well-endowed cultural establishment. By the end of the nineteenth century, museums, art galleries, universities, auditoriums proliferated in America. By and large, they were supported by only a small group of people—those who had the leisure and the inclination to acquire at least rudimentary knowledge of the arts and taste.

Culture was kept in the grip of a small group—one no larger than ten per cent of the population, if that. And these people had a problem. They had been—and continued to be—preoccupied with the economic world. They had no training in taste, and although they had a desire for the snobbish concomitants of art patronage, they were innocents when they entered that arcane world.

But they were Americans. And that meant that they brought feverish energy to any task they undertook. They made some laughable mistakes when they tried to build a cultural institution to equal their economic establishment, and they passed by much of quality in their haste. In fairness, it must be said that for most of them high culture remained basically irrelevant to their most basic needs and drives. It was an afterthought, grafted onto the American consciousness late in the game.

But, thanks to the work of a few dedicated artist-pioneers, there was a fair amount of quality on the cultural scene and, more importantly, there was a desire to learn, to appreciate, on the part of the small society which had suddenly learned that there were values in life besides getting and spending. The performing artists, for example, were beginning, by the 1880's, to have some success with the doctrine that the work of artists was in a different category from the work of circus performers.

It had not always been so. Before the Civil War there was little interest in such distinctions. Musicians, for example, were regarded as oddities of nature, and it was no accident that Jenny Lind, the first great European singer to tour extensively in the United States, was managed by P. T. Barnum. Nor was it regarded as anything but good showmanship for a pianist, playing a piece about sleighing, to attach bells to his legs and jingle them at appropriate moments while an assistant offstage cracked a whip. Another pianist advertised his ability to play with fists, elbows and even a cane. Still another "guaranteed" his audiences four hundred notes in one measure while a singer offered six hundred words and three hundred bars of music in four minutes. Jullien, a European conductor who eventually went mad, was wont, in moments of ecstasy, to sink into a throne-like velvet chair, always handy to his podium, when his emotions quite overpowered him. In a more joyous vein he was apt to whip a piccolo out of his pocket and accompany his orchestra with it. And before he conducted Beethoven, a pair of immaculate white gloves was always borne to him on a golden platter—presumably so he would not soil the Master's work.

But Jullien, as well as the small Germania orchestra which toured here (many of whose members eventually settled here and populated the leading latter-day orchestras), did create the first small audience for symphonic music. And in pre-Civil War days America discovered its first native-born musical genius, a young man named Louis Gottschalk. Contemporary audiences still hear his music, arranged by Hershy Kay, as the score for the ballet, *Cakewalk*. A pianist, he toured Spain and France, and when he returned to this country his reception was at least the equal of Jenny Lind's. Thus a typical American pattern was established—one which would repeat itself time and again, even down to the days of Van Cliburn. Quite simply, an American artist needed, and still needs, the stamp of European approval before his own country will trust itself to praise him.

After the war between North and South, American musical taste shifted from the ridiculous to the grandiose. When, for example, the "Anvil Chorus" was played in Boston at the Peace Festival of 1869, someone saw to it that one hundred red-shirted firemen banged away at one hundred anvils at the appropriate moments. At the same festival a chorus of ten thousand, assisted by an orchestra of one thousand, regaled a gigantic audience, while at its 1872 successor, no less a personage than Johann Strauss the younger was required to conduct forces twice that size. "How would the business start, how would it end?" he asked himself. The answer was not long in coming. "Suddenly a cannon-shot rang out, a gentle hint for us twenty thousand to begin playing 'The Blue Danube.' I gave the signal, my hundred assistant conductors followed me as quickly and as well as they could, and then there broke out an unholy row such as I shall never forget. As we had begun more or less simultaneously, I concentrated my whole attention on seeing that we should finish together too! Thank Heaven, I managed even that. It was all that was humanly possible." Four years later, at the Philadelphia Centennial Exposition, booming cannons were regarded as a requisite for a successful performance of Handel's *The Messiah*.

But a handful of musicians were doing "all that was humanly possible" on another level to introduce music not as vaudeville or spectacle, but as music, to America. Hans von Bülow and Anton Rubinstein both toured here and played seriously and well (although the latter sometimes enlivened his concerts with variations on "Yankee Doodle"). And they were only two among many.

Orchestrally, however, the country was poverty-stricken. To be sure, the New York Philharmonic had been founded in 1842, as a cooperative orchestra whose sixty-or-so members split the tiny profits on a three to six concert season. Despite the able direction of Carl Bergmann, America's first important conductor, profits remained low (less than a thousand dollars a year) and were never enough to build a permanent—and first-class—orchestra. The members of the orchestra looked to the pits of theaters and opera houses for steady salaries and were perfectly content to send over substitutes if a Philharmonic concert interfered with more profitable pursuits.

It was Theodore Thomas who was to begin the orchestral revolution in this country. He had come here from Germany as a boy of ten, toured as a violin prodigy and played in Jullien's orchestra. A chance to substitute as a conductor for the opera, then playing at the Academy of Music on New York's Fourteenth Street, opened a new world to him and it was not long before he had formed his own orchestra which was almost permanently on tour. "I decided," he later wrote, "to devote my energies to the cultivation of public taste in music." Thomas had much the spirit of the builders of the industrial establishment. For twenty years he toured with his orchestra, giving his men blessedly steady work, giving the nation an opportunity to hear an orchestra composed of men who had a chance to work together constantly. Between tours Thomas often conducted the Philharmonic, bringing it the first solid profits, as well as the first solid musicianship, of its career.

He was an arrogant man. As David Ewen put it, "He brushed aside criticism, antagonism, opposition in his determination to bring his audiences into contact with the best in music." Audiences were often apathetic, often openly hostile to new and complex music. Once, in New York, they were noisily critical of his presentation of Liszt's "The Mephisto Waltz." He simply pulled out his watch and gave the dissenters five minutes to leave the hall before he continued. After that, he said he would play the piece regardless of the audience's attitude. Amidst a shocked silence he did just that.

Thomas was an egotist, but more than any other man, in the decades following the Civil War, he created an atmosphere in which music could be listened to. And there is no doubt that his tours did much to encourage cities like St. Louis, Cincinnati and Pittsburgh

Theodore Thomas, America's great orchestral pioneer, left New York the year of Carnegie Hall's opening to found the Chicago Symphony orchestra.

Brown Brothers

to form their own orchestras. In 1891 he himself created, at the invitation of wealthy patrons, the Chicago Symphony Orchestra.

When he died in 1905 *The New York Times* editorialized: "It is hard to estimate the debt that this country owes to Theodore Thomas. It is the debt of a pupil to a teacher; it is the debt of a people led out of the wilderness by the prophet who has shown them a sight of the promised land. . . . To an amazing persistency in the face of repeated discouragement and piled-up difficulties he joined the fine and catholic taste, and most of all, the willingness to make his propaganda gradually, that were precisely the qualities necessary for his success. . . ." In short, his was a spirit that commended itself to a nation engaged in one of history's busiest building periods, a nation committed to belief in progress and the inevitability of success through perseverance.

There were others, on a local level, who manifested the same spirit, creating a climate of opinion favorable to music amid the simultaneously—and paradoxically—gaudy and genteel excesses of The Gilded Age. The most influential of them was Leopold Damrosch, who came to New York from Germany in 1871, where he had had a distinguished career as a violinist, composer and, finally, as a conductor. He had been a friend of Wagner and Liszt, playing in the great orchestra the latter founded at Weimar. He had gone on to found his own orchestra in Breslau, and he came to New York to lead the concerts of the Arion

Society. It is with him that the history of Carnegie Hall properly begins, for it was he who first had the vision to see, and to communicate, the need for it. The atmosphere, which he found here despite the existence of only one genuine conductorial competitor, was hardly encouraging to Damrosch. Thomas encountered him in a music store one day and welcomed a man who was to be, in a larger sense, his ally in the battle for music by saying, "I hear, Dr. Damrosch, that you are a very fine musician, but I want to tell you one thing: whoever crosses my path I crush." Thomas may have been honestly convinced that there was room for only one conductor in America, but more likely he was intent upon protecting what he regarded as his private property from trespassers. This, too, was in the spirit of the times, and one can imagine a Carnegie or a Morgan or a Rockefeller regarding his attitude as perfectly justifiable.

But Damrosch did not frighten easily. If Thomas had an orchestra, he would have one too. In 1873, at the suggestion of Anton Rubinstein, he formed a tiny oratorio society with eighteen singers. Out of this, in 1877, grew his own orchestra, the New York Symphony. His son, Walter, has described the ensuing orchestra war between his father and Thomas in his autobiography. Thomas, entirely American educated, "had always striven for great cleanliness of execution, a metronomical accuracy and rigidity of tempo, and a strict and literal (and therefore rather mechanical) observance of the signs put down by the composers. . . . My father had been educated in a more modern school of interpretation, and his readings were emotionally more intense. . . .

"Both conductors had their violent partisans and, as they were at that time literally the only orchestral conductors in America, feeling ran very high. My father was the last comer, and Thomas was well fortified in the field, with a group of wealthy men to support him. The first years for my father were very hard and a portion of the New York papers assailed him bitterly, continuously and with vindictive enmity. . . ."

But Leopold Damrosch was as tough and as stubborn as Thomas. A warmhearted and gregarious soul, he was "by nature a romanticist, his head was often in the clouds. He could dream bold dreams, unhampered by sound practical considerations." Damrosch's single season at the helm of the Philharmonic (1876-1877), in which he gave the first American production of Act III of Wagner's *Siegfried*, had been a failure. The public had not yet developed a taste for Wagner and the other late romantics. Thomas' friends were intent on easing Damrosch out and Thomas into the director's post. But Damrosch was not to be put down. In 1879 he gave New York its first truly satisfying taste of Berlioz, conducting a full-scale festival of that composer's works in Steinway Hall. The same year, with the aid of a patron, he stole the American premiere of Brahms's First Symphony right out from under Thomas. Damrosch inquired about the score at Schirmer's music store and was told that it had indeed arrived, but that Thomas had reserved it and intended to produce it. Damrosch communicated his disappointment to Mrs. James Neilson, one of his patrons. She promptly went to the store, bought the piano reduction of the score and sent it to Damrosch. He immediately set three coypists to work making approximations of the orchestral parts, and with a frantic effort managed to get some sort of performance on ahead of Thomas.

In 1881 Damrosch staged New York's first gigantic musical festival, conducting an orchestra of three hundred and a chorus of twelve hundred in a week of great music at the Seventh Regiment Armory. But it was difficult for him to keep both the Symphony and the Oratorio Society going. As his son wrote: "Orchestral conditions were bad compared with today. There was no such thing as a 'permanent orchestra.' . . . And yet, in spite of this disheartening condition, my father succeeded in infusing the orchestra with such emotional intensity, and in imparting so lofty an interpretation to them, that the audiences of that day were often roused to the greatest enthusiasm."

This occasional enthusiasm, however, only underlined the difficulties encountered by America's musical pioneers. "There was," as the younger Damrosch understated, "as yet but a small public for the higher forms of music." Indeed, audiences were so small that his father time and again thought that he would have to abandon his orchestra and chorus.

Not the least of the problems was the willingness, even the eagerness, of the American male to abandon "culture" to his wife while he devoted himself to what he regarded as more masculine pursuits. Nowhere was this more apparent than in the work of the Oratorio Society which suffered chronically from a lack of male voices, especially tenors. "The terribly one-sided condition of musical development in our country, proceeding almost exclusively on feminine lines, showed itself markedly in this branch of the art," Damrosch writes. "Many of the men singers who in one way or another had been cajoled or coerced into joining a choral society, had often to be drilled in their parts like children, though without a child's quickness of perception. The result was that the labor of training was incessant and the mistakes of one year repeated themselves inevitably the next."

But Leopold Damrosch, like Theodore Thomas, persevered, and if the improvement in the state of orchestral music in America was sometimes so gradual as to be almost unnoticeable, he was at least able to build his own name to a point where it truly rivaled that of Thomas—at least in New York. Thus, when a group of *nouveau-riche* opera patrons were frozen out of the directorate—and the boxes—of the company at the Academy of Music by the older money, they formed their own company, the Metropolitan, and when that company's first season turned out to be disastrous financially, it was natural for them in the 1884-1885 season to turn to Damrosch. He was engaged to conduct a season of Wagner. He worked himself and his company unmercifully, but the results must have been extremely gratifying to all concerned. America, apparently, was finally ready to accept Wagner, and the season was both artistically and financially rewarding. Unfortunately, Leopold Damrosch did not live it out fully. Weakened by overwork, he collapsed at a rehearsal in February, 1885, and died shortly thereafter of pneumonia. His son, Walter, then only twenty-three, finished the season in his father's place and even conducted the Metropolitan on its first tour. The following season he took over the direction of both the New York Symphony and the Oratorio Society and continued to conduct German opera at the Met, but as an assistant.

By this time the value of permanency, both artistic and financial, had been dramatically demonstrated by the Boston Symphony Orchestra. Founded in 1881 by Colonel Henry Lee Higginson, it was, by the end of the decade, able to provide its players with thirty weeks of

The Bettmann Archive

Leopold Damrosch and his son, Walter. Leopold, the friend of Liszt and Wagner, came to New York in 1871 and founded the New York Symphony and the Oratorio Society. On his death, Walter succeeded him and conducted the orchestra until 1928.

steady work, and was setting a standard of orchestral playing such as America had never heard. Walter Damrosch did his best to keep his orchestra on a par with the Boston group. But he had no wealthy patrons. Although he used the New York Symphony in the pit whenever he conducted at the Met and successfully sought work for it as accompanist to touring recitalists, and although in later decades he would take the orchestra on tours rivaling Thomas' in length, his difficulties were not solved until he was able, after the turn of the century, to attract extremely generous patronage from Harry Harkness Flagler.

By the spring of 1887, Walter Damrosch, with two seasons of leadership behind him, was deeply conscious of the seriousness of his problems. There was, for example, no good hall for orchestral and choral music. The new Metropolitan Opera House was inadequate acoustically for orchestral performances, as the Philharmonic was proving; Steinway and Chickering Halls were really suitable only for recitals, and the theaters did not provide the right atmosphere. Damrosch's Oratorio Society was still giving its concerts in the showrooms of a piano store. In addition, there was the lack of a broad base of support for music, a problem that has still not been totally solved in America. It was with these problems—as well as his own conductorial inadequacies—that Damrosch sailed for Europe for a summer of study with Hans von Bülow, the great German conductor. He also planned to resort to that great nineteenth-century cure-all, a session in the baths at one of the Continent's fashionable spas.

Unknown to Damrosch, another dissatisfied man was to be a passenger on his voyage. He was Andrew Carnegie, who had risen from telegrapher to control of the nation's largest steel mill. By 1887 this Scottish immigrant had acquired a personal fortune of some $30 million, not huge by Robber Baron standards, but enough for his modest wants. He had also acquired a young wife, the former Louise Whitfield, and he was taking her to a somewhat excessive honeymoon cottage—Kilgraston, his castle near Perth, Scotland. There is evidence that he, like Damrosch, was anxious to use his vacation for a thoughtful consideration of the problem of where he was heading and what it all meant.

He had already begun the trickle of philanthropic giving which was to grow to a $350 million torrent by the time he died in 1919. His program of donating libraries to communities—if they agreed to support them after his initial benefaction—had begun, and he was also well along in his career as an essayist and apologist on the subject of wealth and its responsibilities.

A close student of Carnegie's career, Professor Joseph Wall, whose definitive biography of him will appear shortly, comments that "Carnegie was too vain a man to think it necessary to create in the eyes of the public a particular image. Unlike Rockefeller, I doubt if the idea ever occurred to him. He was much too secure in his own high estimate of what the public thought of him to even raise the question." Rather, his benefactions represented an attempt, consciously or unconsciously, to justify his own career to himself, not in terms of conscience . . . but in terms of lasting value. In addition they represented the quite amazing breadth of the interests he had acquired in the course of his self-education. In a larger sense, Carnegie's donations symbolized a great transition in the attitudes of the wealthy. He was the first multimillionaire to turn the major share of his attention from getting to spending. "This," he wrote, ". . . is held to be the duty of the man of wealth: To set an example of modest, unostentatious living, shunning display or extravagance; to provide moderately for the legitimate wants of those dependent upon him; and, after doing so, to consider all surplus revenues which come to him simply as trust funds, which he is called upon to administer . . . in the manner which, in his judgment, is best calculated to produce the most beneficial results for the community—the man of wealth thus becoming the mere trustee and agent for his poorer brethren, bringing to their service his superior wisdom, experience and ability to administer, doing for them better than they would or could do for themselves."

Just what made Andrew Carnegie so certain that he—and other men of wealth and power—actually possessed "superior wisdom" is not quite clear, but there is no doubt that the accumulation of great wealth seemed to bring with it sure conviction of moral and mental superiority in the nineteenth century. (That this was not necessarily true is borne out by Roger Fry's characterization of the tastes of J. P. Morgan, to whom Carnegie sold his steel interests in 1901 for $300 million. Fry, who helped Morgan build his fabulous art collection, gleefully sneered that "a crude historical imagination was the only flaw in his otherwise perfect insensibility.") Indeed, the arrant snobbery of Carnegie, along with his divine contempt for the intellectual abilities of those less well-off than himself, was never far from the surface. Nor was his sublime conviction that he and his equals, alone among men, had the ability to administer the fate of the world intelligently ever shaken. His essays are studded with remarks like: "It were better for mankind that the millions of the rich were thrown into the sea than so spent as to encourage the slothful, the drunken, unworthy. Of every thousand dollars spent in so-called charity today, it is probable that nine hundred and fifty dollars is unwisely spent." And: ". . . wealth, passing through the hands of the few, can be made a much more potent force for the elevation of our race than if distributed in small sums to the people themselves." This last, incidentally, was the rationale for the low wages he paid in his mills. There followed from this confidence in his own abilities an innocent conviction that the system which produced him and his friends was, naturally, perfect.

But dour as were his convictions about the ability of the poor to master their own destinies, and firm as he was in his belief that he was a leading citizen of the best of all possible worlds, Andrew Carnegie must be credited at least with a desire to make that world still better. And within his very limited terms, he did contribute his cubit to that betterment. For reasons that can only be guessed at, he was determined, if he could not take it with him, to oversee personally the distribution of his wealth while he was here. He was no man to leave that task to strangers after he was gone.

Finding ways to aid the common good was therefore, in 1887, a challenge to Carnegie. And finding ways to promote music, distinctly an infant industry in need of protection, was much on the mind of his shipboard companion, Walter Damrosch. It was perfectly natural for the two to come together, for Carnegie had served on the board of the Oratorio Society and had come to know and like Damrosch's father. Indeed, he regarded the modest encouragement of music to be a part of the common good. "He prided himself," says Wall, "on

Culver Service

Andrew Carnegie. He wanted to be remembered for what he persuaded others to give. Tchaikovsky thought he looked like the Russian playwright, Ostrovsky.

his good taste in music, but at the same time he prided himself on being properly suspicious of musicians as businessmen." Alas, Andrew Carnegie's taste in music ran to bagpipes and to organs (he donated 8,182 of them to various institutions and for several years paid a church organist to awaken him by playing Scotch folk tunes and hymns in his home). His suspicion of the musician's business abilities was to lead to a rather peculiar, but not totally impractical, method of financing Carnegie Hall.

This, of course, was all in the future. Walter Damrosch, a young man with a shrewd eye for the main chance and an all-consuming ambition to make music a vital part of the American scene, was a self-appointed ambassador of musical good will to the masses. He was determined to sell music to the country and, although he was never a truly great conductor, he devoted himself with endless patience and energy to his educational job—and did it well. His meeting with another man who, in a different way and from different motives, shared his desire to elevate and educate, was a chance for him to enlist a valuable ally in his cause.

Happily, Carnegie took a liking to this eager young man and invited him to visit Kilgraston when he had completed his brief immersion in his studies and the baths. In due course Damrosch found himself in Scotland, participating in the genteel pleasures of nineteenth-century upper-class country life—there were musical evenings (with the emphasis, of course, on Scotch folk music), picnics, walks and fishing trips. It was on the fishing trips that "Mr. Carnegie talked continuously and freely about his plans to better the world through liberal benefactions. . . . He told of his poverty and craving for education. His imagination would kindle at the opportunities libraries would give to youth. Constant optimism as to the future of the world seemed to direct his plans. . . . It was at these times and at others and in the evenings at Kilgrasten that the need of a hall large enough for a chorus as large as the Oratorio Society began to take shape in Mr. Carnegie's mind."

The idea, one may be certain, did not come from the blue: Leopold Damrosch's vision of a large musical hall in New York had been passed on to his son. There was no question that New York in the Eighties needed not only a music hall but what we would now call a cultural center. Although no final decisions were reached at Kilgrasten, that need was firmly implanted in Carnegie's thinking, and the necessary beginnings of a beginning were made.

Simultaneously, Damrosch was making another beginning. For among the guests at Kilgraston were Senator James G. Blaine, the narrowly defeated Republican presidential nominee in 1884, and his daughter, Margaret. Damrosch's liking for her was immediate and he pursued her with his customary energy (and with Carnegie's blessing) not only that summer but the following one, and eventually married her.

His campaign for her hand, indeed, continued through the period of his campaign for the hall, and although in retrospect neither issue seems ever to have been in serious doubt, there were problems. It was not until 1889 that Carnegie finally formed a corporation to construct the hall. Damrosch writes that "while Mr. Carnegie had a real admiration for music in the simpler forms, this never crystallized into so great a conviction regarding its importance in life as that which he had regarding the importance of science or literature, and though always generous in its support, his benefactions never became as great as in other directions. He could understand that a library, a school or a hospital could not and should not be self-supporting, but I could not convince him that music should fall into the same category. He always insisted that the greatest patronage of music should come from a paying public rather than from private endowment. He built Carnegie Hall in order to give New York a proper home for its musical activities, but he did not look upon this as a philanthropy and expected to have the Hall support itself and give a fair return upon the capital invested."

Carnegie was obviously tempering his enthusiasm for Damrosch's project with the businessman's traditional distrust of the artist and suspicion of the value of his work. His plan for the development of Music Hall (as it was first called) was consistent with the pattern of giving he had already successfully established in his library program. He refused to endow any benefaction beyond an initial gift. It was up to the community to maintain and expand the institution provided by his gift. "I do not wish to be remembered," Carnegie once said, "for what I have given, but for that which I have persuaded others to give."

Although the pattern was generally successful, it did not work well in connection with Carnegie Hall. For years Carnegie was forced to underwrite—not without a good deal of complaining—the hall's yearly operating deficits. One year, shortly after the turn of the century, he revolted and told his secretary to get some other wealthy person to put up half the needed amount. It was, he pointed out at some length, healthy for a broad base of support to be built for the hall. The secretary obediently went off on his errand and in a matter of a few hours returned with the necessary amount. Carnegie chortled happily as he wrote out his matching check, made a small lecture on how easy it was to get money if you just asked, then inquired who the foresighted and generous donor was. "Mrs. Carnegie, sir," said the secretary, heading for the door.

From the beginning, Carnegie attempted to keep the hall on a business basis. He organized a stock company which, at its second meeting in May, 1889, elected officers and a board of directors. Both Carnegie and Damrosch were on the board, and the president, Morris Reno, as well as the other officers and directors were, with one exception, representatives of the business community.

The exception was William Burnet Tuthill, who had been appointed chief architect for the hall, and was therefore included among the directors. Tuthill, who was later to be active in the Society for the Publication of American Music and the International Society for Contemporary Music, was a happy choice for the job. His interest in music was life-long, and it was his membership on the board of the Oratorio Society which had brought him to the attention of Carnegie and Damrosch. His interest in acoustics fitted well with his musical interests and, indeed, became one of his chief preoccupations. He lectured on the subject at several universities and was capable of making practical, as well as theoretical, contributions, as for example when he tuned the chimes for the Society's performance of *Parsifal* and even constructed the special hammer with which they were struck. Although the science of acoustics was then—as now—an extremely accidental one, Tuthill, perhaps better than any of his contemporaries, was the man to reduce the accidental factors to their minimum. For him, Carnegie Hall was a labor of love as well as the most important building of his career. His son recalls that his "one feeling of dissatisfaction about the hall was that he was forced to take quite a number of thousands of dollars' worth of stock at par value as payment of his fee. . . . A number of years later, when the hall was not paying, Mr. Carnegie took advantage of the situation and bought in the outstanding stock (including my father's) at twenty-five cents on the dollar."

Since Tuthill continued to collect fees for designing renovations and additions to the hall, he probably did not suffer unduly from Carnegie's shrewdness and, in any case, Carnegie was carrying the heaviest portion of the financial burden of the unprofitable hall, and he was probably justified in wanting to share it. He purchased the land on which the main hall was eventually to stand and then transferred it, in 1891, to the Music Hall Company, seeing to it that he was reimbursed with shares of stock in the company, just as he was when he advanced the largest share of the money for construction. He received mortgages for later additions which he financed.

When plans for Music Hall were announced in 1889, its welcome was not as warm as Carnegie and his associates might have expected. The *Times* was merely hopeful. It asked those responsible to remember that the hall should educate, not simply entertain, and hoped that the musical advancement of the *entire* city—not just the wealthy—was its goal. This, it said, "should be kept steadily in view in the planning and arrangement of the new concert hall, which should contemplate at every point the greatest good of the greatest number and the establishment of a veritable 'People's Palace' for enjoyment and instruction."

Even less sanguine were William Steinway and Charles F. Chickering, piano manufacturers and proprietors of the two major existing halls. Said Steinway: "Mr. Carnegie's hall will never pay. Take our present Philharmonic concerts, for instance . . . increase the number of these high-class concerts to twelve and financial disaster would be certain. The public can only stand a certain amount of this sort of music. . . . As to educating the masses to a pocket appreciation of high-class music, that cannot be done to such an extent as to encourage unendowed enterprise to go into business. . . ." Chickering was equally positive: "I have never known an instance of a person being turned away from Chickering Hall on the occasion of any first-class concert because that person could not get a good seat. First-class concerts have always gone a-begging in Chickering Hall, with a seating capacity of fifteen hundred." He, like Steinway, was especially concerned because Music Hall was not the only large competitor on the scene. There was talk of a summer garden at Madison Avenue and Fifty-ninth Street and the promoters of the second of the three Madison Square Gardens (opened in 1890) were also active. It looked as if the city was about to have too many halls instead of too few.

But Theodore Thomas had a ready reply to the doubters. He said: "At present New York has no place in which orchestral concerts can be effectively given. Steinway Hall is well enough as far as it goes, but it is not large enough and is ill-appointed besides. The Metropolitan is utterly inadequate for the purposes of great concert music. The finest effects of the orchestra are lost in the vast recesses of the stage. . . . With a perfect music hall we shall be able to reach that part of the public which does not at present go to hear music from a sense of duty. Something more is required to musically evangelize the people than mere music."

That "more," he felt, was "comfort—even luxury." Damrosch, too, was inclined to take a grandiose view of the building's function. "The new hall . . . will be a veritable temple of music," he said. But he offered a very practical argument in its favor: a man would not have to declare allegiance to a piano company to play in it, as the pianists at Steinway and Chickering halls were forced to do.

Added to the doubts about the need for the hall were some doubts about its location on Fifty-seventh Street and Seventh Avenue which was "'Uptown" in the late Eighties. These were easily answered, for although the theater district was still centered around Union Square, there was evidence of a northward trend in the city. Fifth Avenue above Fifty-ninth Street was, in 1889, a street of fashionable residences, if not quite yet the "solid mile and a half of millionaires' residences, practically without a break, except where a vacant spot awaits the coming of still another Croesus" that it would be in ten years. And both the upper East and West Sides were developing into fashionable residential districts. It was obvious to all but the most churlish that the location of the hall on the corner of Seventh Avenue and Fifty-seventh Street was convenient to most of its potential audience and that it would become more so.

The neighborhood itself, when excavation began for the main building in the summer of 1889, was unprepossessing. The site was surrounded by blacksmith shops and a number of saloons. The latter were an offense to the eyes of the teetotaling Carnegie. They became more so after construction began, for he saw that the quitting whistle started a stampede of his workmen toward the watering places. He dealt with the chief offender—a bar run by a brewery on Fifty-sixth Street—in a straightforward fashion. He simply bought the property and shut the tavern down.

The land on which the hall stood was acquired in several parcels between 1889 and 1892 and the hall as it stands today was constructed piecemeal over seven years. The basic structure housing the main hall and the basement "lyceum," aptly described by one writer as a "fat, brown-and-buff Romanesque pile," was considered quite à la mode in late-nineteenth-century America. The nation was then in an architecturally eclectic humor, scattering gothic castles and classic temples over the landscape in gaudy—and inappropriate—profusion. Carnegie Hall was, to its credit, a rather restrained, even tasteful, example of the tendency to look to European styles of other centuries for models. A contemporary promotion booklet spoke of its exterior design as "stately, rich and dignified in an architectural style easily and simply expressing the public purposes for which the structure is intended. . . . Its location, its conscientious, thorough and perfect construction, its fullness of accommodation, the flexibility with which it will lend itself to the differing requirements that are essential to the purposes of its varying tenants, the completeness of its scientific features, its richness, beauty of decoration . . . surely place 'Music Hall' . . . at the very forefront of concert halls." In short, it was a serenely confident manifestation of a prosperous and certain age which, in this case, built well, if somewhat heavily and eccentrically.

The heaviness of the building can be accounted for by the prevalent methods of construction. Music Hall was built several years before advanced methods of structural-steel construction enabled us to turn our cities into ranges of skyscrapers. Therefore the full weight of the building had to be carried by its masonry walls which are several feet thick in order to bear the load. The same limitations may account for the odd method of building the hall. For it is not one building, but three, cunningly interconnected to appear as one. Next to the main hall is the so-called "lateral" building which contains, besides studios, the recital hall and the chapter room, intended originally as a meeting place for fraternal organizations. The third building runs along the back of these two on Fifty-sixth Street. In 1894, this building was extended to the corner of Seventh Avenue, and in 1896 the mansard roof came off the entire six-story structure to be replaced by a studio floor, while a ten-story tower was added to the lateral building. This somewhat haphazard method of construction is responsible for the building's most intriguing architectural anomaly—the running together of the eighth floor of one unit with the tenth floor of another, to this day confusing casual visitors.

Certainly in one sense—the acoustic—Tuthill and his associates were to build better than they knew. And in this connection the nineteenth century taste for elegance served a useful purpose. For the velvet with which Tuthill liberally adorned the hall acted as an excellent absorbent for unwanted reverberations and echoes, while the sweeping curve of the boxes, designed to give the groundlings the best possible view of the occupants, protected one and all from the sharp angles which cause sound to bounce about in annoying fashion. Finally, the avoidance of a domed ceiling and of unnecessary gingerbread—certainly a tribute to Tuthill's taste—were probably dictated by acoustical considerations as well.

A little more than a year after plans for the new building had been announced, its cornerstone was laid. On May 13, 1890, a goodly delegation from the musical, social and economic elite turned out to witness the launching of the city's latest cultural vessel. "All the musical organizations were well represented," the *Times* reported. "The Oratorio Society turned out in almost full force. There was a large delegation from the Philharmonic Society, the parent organization in advanced musical culture in this city." In addition, "Brooklyn and New Jersey societies sent representatives and the boxholders at the Opera House were out in good numbers."

Morris Reno spoke for the Music Hall Company and E. Francis Hyde, president of the Philharmonic Society, spoke, with some small satisfaction, on recent strides made by music in the city.

Then, escorted by Walter Damrosch, Mrs. Carnegie "advanced to the cornerstone and patted the mortar around its edges with a bright metal trowel while the band played the castle air from *Das Rheingold*." Beneath the stone, in a copper box, reposed "accounts of recent great musical events, a history of the inception of the Music Hall enterprises, the names of the officers of the various musical societies of the city and kindred matter."

The day's masonry work completed, Reno introduced Carnegie, who summed up his hopes for the hall in the following terms: "Who shall venture to paint its history or its end? It is built to stand for ages, and during these ages it is probable that this hall will intertwine itself with the history of our country. All good causes may find here a platform; here may be celebrated the triumphs—I trust only the peaceful triumphs—of the Republic. Here may the benefactor of the country be hailed; and here also may the death of the great be mourned. From this platform men may be spurred to aims that end not with the miserable self; here an idea may be promulgated which will affect the world or here a good cause may be promoted."

Carnegie's peroration contained no reference to the joys of music or to its consoling qualities. In his preference for the more direct forms of communication over the insinuating subtleties of musical statement, he shared a fairly widespread American prejudice: Music may be a source of innocent merriment, but it is not part of the mainstream of our existence. Indeed, it is doubtful that Carnegie, despite the best efforts of Damrosch, would have built his hall at all were it not for its subsidiary value as a lecture platform and the pressure exerted on him by his wife to build it. (In fact, when the board of directors decided in 1890 to acknowledge New York's indebtedness to Carnegie by making the full name of the building "Music Hall, founded by

Andrew Carnegie," Carnegie, apprised of the honor done him, declared himself "satisfied that the hall is worthy of association with any name" and added that the action deeply gratified his wife, "who has the cause of music and its future home very much at heart.")

The cornerstone laid, construction proceeded smoothly, Carnegie having vetoed the slightly radical notion that an elevator should be installed for the benefit of the lower classes who would inhabit the upper galleries. Undoubtedly he believed the climb would do them good.

The board felt justified, in December, 1890, in turning to the pleasant task of planning a suitable inaugural for the new hall. Walter Damrosch was placed in charge of arrangements and he proceeded to recruit forces for a five-day, six-concert festival. Three days before Christmas, he received permission "to engage the Russian composer Tchaikovsky, and other solo artists for the music festival on the best terms possible." Damrosch had already seen to it that his orchestra and his chorus would have the week of work which the festival represented to musicians. He signed up Tchaikovsky for the reasonable sum of $2500, and proceeded to arrange a moderately ambitious program built around the talents of his famous guest.

There was some carping over the plans for the opening. H. E. Krehbiel, the *Tribune*'s crusty and independent critic, wrote that "the series is to be called a Festival, which compels a new interpretation of that much abused term," but conceded that "the acquisition of so beautiful a temple of music is fit cause for rejoicing." The *Times*, maintaining its policy of damning the whole project with faint hope, commented that it was ironic that "Mr. Theodore Thomas, who has without question done more for the advancement of music in this country than any other man in it, is just leaving New York for lack of such popular support as would enable him to continue his work." But doubts were not allowed to spoil an occasion that was undoubtedly the event of the season, if not the decade, for New York society. It is doubtful if The Four Hundred ever reveled more typically—or more healthily—than during those five days when Carnegie flung open the doors of his new hall and invited his peers to share his pleasure in it.

Two

"Amazing People, These Americans"

THE FIRST MAN TO PLAY IN CARNEGIE HALL WAS NEITHER A RICHLY publicized European genius nor an exciting new American star. Rather, he was a mediocre and familiar pianist named Franz Rummel, who booked the basement lyceum hall for a series of "farewell" concerts in the month preceding the formal opening. He gave his first recital on the first of April, and his rendition of Beethoven and Chopin sonatas received moderate praise from the press, which was more intent on appraising his surroundings than on listening to him. The man from the *Times* found the hall comfortable and well ventilated even though it was in the basement, but complained of "reverberations" and the sound of hammering coming from other parts of the building.

Five days later a group of New York chapters of the Grand Army of the Republic hired the same hall and were regaled by speeches on "Fraternity and Charity," the story of Shiloh, and "The Influence of the Grand Army of the Republic on the Future of the Republic." In addition, there was martial music, and while "Marching Through Georgia" was being played and sung, a guard formed of members of the Lafayette Camp and a youth auxiliary, "bore forward to the platform the colors which covered the coffin of General Sherman on its journey from New York to St. Louis."

On the seventh of April, Arthur Friedheim, the pianist, was heard in "a programme making the severest demands upon the technical skills of a player." His management found it prudent to insert a note in the program respectfully requesting "the indulgence of the audience for the inconvenience caused by the noises incidental to the completion of the main hall of this building, it being a matter entirely out of its control."

The noises of construction undoubtedly interfered with the other concerts of that opening month, which included two appearances by Leopold Godowsky, the affable and extremely intelligent pianist who was to figure so prominently in the history of the main hall. But to those in the audience the sounds of construction must have been as sounding brass and tinkling cymbal, harbingers of richer resonances to come. For musical New York was in a proper swivet over the opening festival. Two days before Tchaikovsky, the somewhat moody lion of the occasion, was due to arrive, tickets were virtually impossible to get. Their par value was not exorbitant. A box for the entire evening series cost eighty dollars, a single box seat cost fifteen dollars for the five evenings, an orchestra seat ten dollars, dress circle eight dollars and balcony five. Only ten boxes were reserved for the board of directors and their guests, and the only other drain on the ticket supply was those given to escorts of ladies singing in the chorus. But demand far exceeded supply, and the scalpers were active. One perturbed gentleman wrote to the *Times* that he arrived some ten minutes before the box office placed tickets for single concerts on sale and found, in addition to about sixty legitimate purchasers, "a cloud of speculators in attendance—not the usual guerrillas, but apparently a well-disciplined and officered force. By what means these speculators cornered the best seats or what their relations are to the management of the hall I do not know, although I can imagine," he muttered darkly.

This, however, was nowhere near as annoying as the free enterprise of the ushers inside the hall, who, once the festival was under way, took to selling unoccupied seats for a dollar or a dollar and a half, and, what was worse, ushering the lucky purchasers to their seats while music was being played.

But such mundane matters were far from the minds of the welcoming committee that stood on the dock late in the afternoon of April 26th to welcome Peter Ilyitch Tchaikovsky to the New World.

This included Morris Reno, E. Francis Hyde, Ferdinand Mayer, a representative of the Knabe Piano Company, Reno's daughter Alice and "some young man," undoubtedly one of Alice's suitors.

The man they were welcoming was, of course, one of the musical giants of the time. At this point much of his great work was behind him. Five symphonies, three piano concertos, the great Piano Trio, sundry suites and overtures, the wonderful ballets, the opera *Eugene Onegin* had all been written. Still to come was perhaps his greatest creation, the Sixth Symphony. Musically, Tchaikovsky was not regarded as one of the master innovators of his time. Liszt, Wagner, Brahms, among his contemporaries were the real musical trend setters. But Tchaikovsky's undisciplined gift for appealing melody had brought him fame, and comfortable, if not great, fortune. Given the musical tastes of the time in America it is easy to see why he was extended an invitation to come here. What is not so easy to understand is why he accepted. It is true that the patronage of his famous pen-pal, Nadejda von Meck, whom he never met but from whom he received around $3,000 a year, had suddenly come to an end. But he had a modest pension from the government and was in no great need of funds. Another man might have been motivated by a simple desire to travel, but there was nothing simple about Tchaikovsky. Whenever he left Russia he was homesick. Whenever he returned home he wanted to flee again. The same ambivalence was apparent in his personal life. He craved affection but he convinced himself that he was misjudged and misunderstood. A suppressed homosexual, he had embarked on a disastrous marriage which lasted but nine weeks (he never saw his equally neurotic wife again), then tried to kill himself.

In those pre-Freudian times, however, his ambivalences, his terrible gropings and his moodiness merely contributed to a personal image which was the very model of what the romantic movement hoped an artist would be. In addition, there was a basic sweetness and kindness in the Tchaikovsky nature which made people respond to him with considerable warmth. Only when considering the works of fellow composers did he allow a certain testiness to show through, and he carried on a number of quite splendid bickerings with such worthies as Brahms and Moussorgsky.

The group waiting on the pier to welcome the honored guest was in a festive mood, naturally enough. Little did they know that one of his moods was upon Tchaikovsky. "The nearer we came to New York, the greater grew my fear and homesickness," he wrote in his diary, "and I regretted ever having undertaken this insane voyage. When it is all over," he added doubtfully, "I may look back to it with pleasure, but at present it is not without suffering."

The welcoming committee helped Tchaikovsky with the formalities of landing and drove him to the Hotel Normandie. He was pleased to be seated next to "the pretty Miss Alice" and surprised himself by carrying on "an unbelievably amiable and incredibly animated conversation (as though I were pleased with all that was happening)."

Tchaikovsky's moodiness stemmed from several causes. Just before leaving for America, he had read quite accidentally in a Paris newspaper of the death of his sister. In addition, he was not comfortable away from Russia. It is no wonder, therefore, that "in my soul there was despair and a desire to flee from them to the world's end." No wonder, also, that as soon as he was alone in his comfortable suite, he put first things first as follows: "First of all, I wept rather long. Then took a bath, changed and went downstairs to the restaurant." The rest of the evening was equally bleak: a cheerless dinner, a walk down Broadway, where he was surprised by the number of Negroes he saw, and then home where he "took to whimpering again several times," then "slept excellently."

The next day he got his first glimpse of Music Hall, which he thought "magnificent." He found Damrosch rehearsing the orchestra in Beethoven's Fifth Symphony and was amazed to see him conducting the rehearsal without wearing a frock coat as was the European custom. After an ovation from the orchestra, he took over the baton to conduct his own Third Suite, after which he was relieved to pronounce the orchestra splendid.

That night he dined with Damrosch and his wife and found that "both host and hostess are very charming." Damrosch later wrote that "in all my many years of experience I have never met a great composer so gentle, so modest—almost diffident—as he. We all loved him from the first moment—my wife and I, the chorus, the orchestra, the employees of the hotel where he lived and of course the public." After dinner Damrosch took him to meet Carnegie, whom Tchaikovsky thought bore an uncanny resemblance to the Russian playwright Ostrovsky. "I liked him very much," he writes in his diary, "mainly because he adores Moscow, which he visited two years ago. No less than Moscow, he loves Scottish songs, and Damrosch played a considerable number of them for him on an excellent Steinway." A visit to an athletic club with Damrosch completed his first full day in America. "Is it necessary to say that I was completely exhausted?" he asked his diary just before tumbling into bed.

It was costing Tchaikovsky a strenuous effort to retain his melancholy demeanor against the onslaughts of American hospitality. The next day he wrote: "Amazing people, these Americans! Compared with Paris, where at every approach, in every stranger's kindness, one feels an attempt at exploitation, the frankness, sincerity and generosity of this city, its hospitality without hidden motives, and its eagerness to oblige and win approval are simply astonishing and, at the same time, touching. This, and indeed, American customs, American manners and habits generally are very attractive to me—but I enjoy all this like a person sitting at a table set with marvels of gastronomy, devoid of appetite. Only the prospect of returning to Russia can awaken an appetite within me."

In the days that followed Tchaikovsky was to have many more tempting morsels set before him, and although some of them fell as flat as a bride's first cake, many of them greatly delighted him, and one detects throughout his diary a bemused—and shrewd—interest in this strange new land. A trip to the *atelier* of photographer Napoleon Sarony, who "amused me with some almost clownish tricks" and who was "unusually likable and genial . . . in the American way," was a highpoint, as was a trip to Central Park which Tchaikovsky found "young but grand." A less successful entertainment was a performance at the Metropolitan Opera of *The Captivity*, an oratorio by one Max Vogrich. "More banal and poor music I have never yet heard," Tchaikovsky growled. "The boredom was terrible."

A dinner at Reno's the following evening interested him in an anthropological way, but proved to be something of a strain. "The dinner started at seven-thirty o'clock and finished exactly at eleven. I write this without the least exaggeration; such is the custom here. To recount all the courses is impossible. In the middle of the dinner ices were served in some kind of small boxes to which were attached small slates, with pencils and sponges, on which excerpts from my works were finely written in pencil. Then I had to write my autograph on these slates." As Damrosch noted, Tchaikovsky was the first truly great composer to visit America, and society was at pains to make the most of the occasion. This time their elaborate attempt at entertainment was a little too much for the visitor. "At eleven o'clock, tortured by the need of smoking and nauseated by the endless eating," he asked permission to rise and thereby broke up the somewhat excessive rites of the lion hunters.

Next day, Tchaikovsky was prevailed upon to write an article for the New York *Morning Journal* by Ivy Ross, first in the long line of Cholly Knickerbockers; then he rehearsed the chorus at Music Hall, met Tuthill and his assistant, Waldemar Stark, with whom Tchaikovsky conversed in Russian, which pleased him no end. Having "wept, as usual" he got a good night's sleep and then proceeded, on May 1st, to a day which took him, physically and socially, to the highest and lowest levels of the city.

His sightseeing began in the Wall Street area, where he found the buildings "ridiculously colossal." He was taken to the top of one of them by the ubiquitous Mayer, whom Tchaikovsky could never persuade to leave him alone. "The view from there is glorious," he thought, "but I felt dizzy looking down on the Broadway pavement." From the heights to the depths—the next stop was the vault of the subtreasury building where Tchaikovsky was allowed to hold in his hand a package of bills valued at $10 million, and was surprised to find out that "Americans prefer the soiled, disagreeable bank bills to metal, finding them more convenient and practical." Lunch with E. Francis Hyde, who besides being president of the Philharmonic was vice-president of the Central Trust Company, provided a second opportunity to examine at close hand "mountains of valuable bank notes," while the postprandial entertainment was a trip to the Stock

Brown Brothers

This is the photograph of Tchaikovsky taken in New York by Napoleon Sarony when the composer came to conduct at the Carnegie Hall opening festival in 1891.

Exchange, which seemed quieter to Tchaikovsky than the *Bourse* in Paris.

Having investigated the workings of capitalism during the day, Tchaikovsky encountered, quite accidentally, the activity of its opposition while out for an evening stroll. For this, remember, was May Day, and some five thousand socialists had massed on upper Broadway. Wearing red caps and shouting slogans, they carried huge lanterns and banners reading, according to Tchaikovsky, "We are slaves in free America! We do not want to work more than eight hours." The whole demonstration, the composer thought, "seemed to me like some buffoonery; indeed, I believe the people here look at it that way also, judging by the fact that few appeared interested and folks moved about just as on any other day." This was a fairly acute summation of the impact of radical political ideas on the nation at that time, although it reflected Tchaikovsky's own indifference to politics perhaps more than it did his abilities as a political observer.

The next morning Tchaikovsky attempted to conduct a rehearsal of his Third Suite, his *Marche Solennelle* and the orchestral part of his First Piano Concerto "amidst the noise of workers, the knocking of hammers and the excitement of the managers." He was irritated by all this, as well by the fact that the orchestra was spread widely across the stage, causing an uneven tone. Feeling "a rage coming on and a desire to drop everything indignantly and run away," he conducted "carelessly" and dropped the rehearsal of the concerto after the first movement. "He was not," as Damrosch said, "a conductor by profession and in consequence the technique of it, the rehearsals and concerts, fatigued him excessively; but he knew what he wanted and the atmosphere that emanated from him was so sympathetic and love-compelling that all executants strove with double eagerness to divine his intentions and to carry them out."

Whatever the effects of fatigue and melancholy, Tchaikovsky worked as hard as he could in the days before and during the festival to perfect the performances of his works, striving to get the coarseness out of Adele Aus der Ohe's performance of his concerto, burying his impatience with Damrosch, who seemed to him to be monopolizing the rehearsal time of the orchestra when it was at its freshest, and maintaining the heavy schedule of social demands which his eager hosts pressed on him in profusion. "One must give credit to American hospitality," he sighed, "only in our own country would one encounter anything like it."

Of course, the hosts were hardly at their relaxed best as the time of the first performance on May 5th drew near. Reno had to give a speech on opening night and "the poor man was terribly excited" by that awesome prospect. There were a thousand and one details to attend to, ranging from finishing the hall to making sure no one was slighted in the seating arrangements. No one, in short, was in a position to offer much genuine comfort to Tchaikovsky, homesick, nervous and sad. A stroll in the park, a game of cards with Alice Reno, these offered him brief moments of respite, but they were more than offset by a series of petty annoyances added to the larger anxieties. Franz Rummel kept pestering him to conduct—at no fee—one of his concerts. A shipboard acquaintance attempted to touch him for a loan. The newspapers had mistaken Alice Reno for his wife when she had been seen entering a cab with him at the dock, so he was continually barraged with questions about how his "young and pretty wife" liked New York.

Thus, it was with some relief that Tchaikovsky, accompanied by Reno's brother-in-law, boarded a crowded trolley at seven-thirty on May 5th and set out for the inaugural concert in the salmon-colored main auditorium of Music Hall. At last the long period of irrelevant activity was coming to an end and he was about to begin the primary task of his American visit.

While Tchaikovsky was making his way to the hall, "carriage after carriage rolled up to the broad entrance and deposited its precious freight." At the height of the rush, a row of rigs stretched a quarter of a mile down Fifty-seventh Street. For once in its life, society was determined to be on time. As a result, "the hall was completely filled before the time set for the opening," the *Sun* reported, noting that "crowds of men and women bought admission tickets at the door and stood up wherever they could find room."

"The gathering was exceptionally brilliant in color and general appearance and finer in general effect than an average opera audience, although the women were not in full dress," the paper noted, while the *World* found that "to mention those in the orchestra stalls would necessitate a list of nearly every New Yorker prominent in literature and music." The *Times* called the audience "large, brilliant and enthusiastic." And the *Herald* was highly pleased by the decorum of the occasion which a later writer termed "an authentic saturnalia of Victorian propriety." It was, in short, "most interesting as a study of music lovers not under the pressure of the mandates of fashion. . . . There was no idea of chatter. . . . There was no coming and going of dandies and mouthpieces. . . . All was quite, dignified, soft, slow and noiseless, as became the dedication of a great temple." Among the dignified and noiseless in the boxes were the consuls of various nations along with Mr. and Mrs. William C. Whitney, John D. Rockefeller, W. C. Frick, William Sloan, William Abbott and, of course, Carnegie and his wife and Damrosch's in-laws, the Blaines. Eying them, the man from the *World* noted that for "the display of gowns, its [Music Hall's] advantages are greater than those of the Metropolitan Opera House, and its facilities for conversation are certainly no less."

Indeed, the hall in general drew extremely good notices. The *Times* found it "ample, well-placed, well-planned and well-equipped," although it questioned "whether the roof might not wisely have been made invisible. What is seen of it is, in effect, a blunt mansard, though still very steep and unbroken. The spectator feels that there should be either more or less of it. It might be enlarged and developed into a really crowning feature, or it might have been left out of sight altogether." But perhaps had it been "a really crowning feature" the audience would have been less pleased by the sounds they heard: That would have been too bad, for all agreed the acoustics were wonderfully mellow. The *Herald*, indeed, thought they "were perfect; there was no echo and no undue reverberation. Each note was heard. The orchestral combinations were not blurred or exaggerated. . . ." This was a typical voice in the swelling chorus of praise that greeted architect Tuthill's creation.

He, unfortunately, was not on hand to hear most of it. Standing backstage before the concert began, his eye happened to stray toward the gallery. With all seats taken and standees crowding behind them,

Culver Service

Carnegie Hall as it looked to an artist on the night it opened, May 5, 1891.

the slender steel columns supporting it suddenly looked extremely frail to the understandably anxious Tuthill. Without further ado, he slipped hastily out of the hall and went home where he sat up far into the night recalculating his estimates of stress and strain on those columns. He did not go to sleep until he was certain that all his figures were correct.

But for everyone else connected with the construction of the hall, the night was an unmixed triumph. When Andrew Carnegie entered his rose-garlanded box, number thirty-three, the chorus, some four hundred strong and already massed on stage behind the orchestra, applauded him.

Promptly at eight Damrosch raised his baton and the strains of "Old Hundred," that favorite war horse of Christian soldiers, filled the house. "The audience arose . . . as if by impulse and many joined in the grand old hymn." Then it was the nervous Reno's turn. His chief function was to introduce Bishop Henry Codman Potter, who was to deliver the dedicatory address, but he took the occasion to note that, "founded with the loftiest purposes, free from all disturbing private interests, devoted solely to the highest ideals of art, such is Music Hall, and such, we fondly hope, may it remain forever."

Then he presented Bishop Potter. "His grace was attired in a shawl roll . . . dress coat, an Episcopal waistcoat buttoned to the chin, and ordinary bags." The good bishop was of a mood to be flowery and lengthy that evening, and the man from the *Herald* noted tartly that "beauty beamed and culture yawned while the Bishop explained the end and purpose of the temple."

The Bishop quite rightly supposed that the world "would little note nor long remember what we say here" and pointed out, unexceptionally, that "through the long vista of tune-filled days and nights which open from this hour it will be others who are to make it vocal with song and resonant with melody and harmony." These others, he thought, would "dedicate and rededicate this noble building to those noble uses to which this evening is set apart."

The *Herald's* reporter thought that "the modest little man in Mr. Blaine's box who bore that name so often mispronounced—call it Carnaggie, if you please—and had borne all the burdens of erecting the splendid hall in which we were seated, must have felt his ears tingle as the Bishop, in his well-chosen periods and precise and courtly manner proceeded to extoll a munificence and love of art which is as rare of conception among our millionaires as it has proven to be, in this instance, beautiful in creation."

The Bishop, for his part, was happy to point the capitalistic moral he found in Carnegie's gift, a highly appropriate sentiment given his audience and his times, which feared "alien doctrine" almost as much as they did beer on Sunday. "In other countries, and under other governments," he said, "such things are largely done by subsidies and through the intervention of the state. It is a happy omen for New York that a single individual can do so princely a thing in so modest a way."

"Happy the man who can use his wealth to widen human happiness," declared the Bishop as he wound his delighted way through the jungles of his own prose, pausing to sniff contentedly at each eulogistic flower he plucked from the tangled vines. By the time he finished, everyone connected with the project had received his benign attention.

Up in Reno's box, Tchaikovsky found his restlessness increasing as he listening to the "long, and they say, unusually boring speech." But at last the Bishop reached his peroration: "Men and women of New York, we bring this finished work to you. Generously cherish, conserve and use it for its highest ends. In the name and in behalf of the president and directors of the Music Hall of New York, I pronounce this building open, and henceforth dedicate and set it apart to the noble ends for which it was erected."

Then, at last, the concert proper got under way with the playing of "America," followed immediately by Beethoven's *Leonora Overture No. 3*, conducted by Damrosch and "performed very well," Tchaikovsky thought. During its playing a reporter noted that "Mrs. Damrosch kept her glasses fixed on the swaying body of her leader; a poor little girl who chanced to sneeze was regarded as a fiend incarnate, and at last Mr. Carnegie realized his own dream of perfect music, perfectly rendered in a perfectly beautiful and appropriate setting."

"Intermission. Went downstairs. Excitement. My turn. Was welcomed very loudly. The March went off excellently. A big success. Listened to the remaining part of the concert in Hyde's box. Berlioz *Te Deum* is somewhat boring; only toward the end did I find great enjoyment in it. The Renos carried me away with them. An impromptu supper. Slept like a dead man." So Tchaikovsky summed up the remainder of the evening. The great Berlioz work, although received respectfully by the critics on this, its first New York performance, was less interesting in their eyes than Tchaikovsky, "the lion and hero of the hour," conducting his own, comparatively minor, *Marche Solennelle.* To his great distress, they lavished as much space on his appearance and mannerisms as they did on his music. "Tchaikovsky is a genial looking and very gentlemanly appearing man," wrote the *Sun*, "with a bright complexion, gray hair and beard and a quick, decided manner, which is emphasized and accentuated when he is conducting."

"He seems a trifle embarrassed, and responds to the applause by a succession of brusque and jerky bows. But as soon as he grasps the baton his self-confidence returns," another paper noted. Little did anyone know that Tchaikovsky suffered acutely when conducting, often imagining that his head was falling off. In earlier years he had been in the habit of gripping it with one hand to prevent that happening.

"It angers me when they write not only about the music but also about my personality," Tchaikovsky confided to his diary. "Cannot bear it when my embarrassment is noticed." But he could console himself with the *World*'s dazzled review: "The musicians followed him involuntarily. There is no mistaking his meaning." And the *Musical Courier's*: "The Beethoven overture received a very loose reading. Everybody, including Mr. Damrosch, was evidently too excited to play smoothly. When Mr. Peter Tchaikovsky took the band in hand this was changed. The great Russian's beat is firm, forcible, a little harsh, but as to its effectiveness there can be no doubt, for the orchestra followed him implicitly, and not he the orchestra."

But more important than the reception of the music was the reception of the hall. Everyone agreed that the real significance of the occasion was the fact that at long last New York—by then a city of two and one-half million citizens—had a concert hall large enough and magnificent enough to support its claims to being one of the capital cities of the world. "It Stood the Test Well" said the *Times* headline over the story of the opening night. And the *World*, speaking editorially, caught the essence of the intelligent music-lover's opinion of the occasion: ". . . no one will grudge Mr. Carnegie the credit of giving New York one of the finest concert halls in the world, even if it be some years ahead of the musical development which it suggests. That New York could not afford to keep the greatest of our conductors is a fair indication of how much the society that calls itself musical is ready to do for the support of the highest art. All the more necessary it is, therefore, that some man with a large bank account and a habit of giving should set the example of endowing music with the indispensable resources. Music Hall is a magnificent start to what it is hoped will be a long course of liberality in a similar direction."

The program to which Peter Ilyitch Tchaikovsky lent the necessary glamour, represented the beginnings of what everyone hoped would be America's musical coming-of-age. Those most intimately connected with music recognized that it could go no further in the United States until it received institutional encouragement and protection. On the night Music Hall opened, its proprietors had only a handful of rentals lined up for the following season. But the very existence, at long last, of a suitable hall, would cause that handful to grow steadily during the next few decades, even though it was not until after World War II that the hall had enough bookings to make it consistently profitable. The essential point is that there was finally a hall that *needed*—that cried out—to be filled, and that empty it was a vacuum irresistibly attractive to musicians and their managers. The need to fill the hall was to cause its owners to encourage new musical and cultural activity as they sought out attractions to keep the new house lighted. America's musical interests needed to be focused and defined.

But all of this, of course, mattered very little to Tchaikovsky who, having survived his first public ordeal, now had to face up to more concerts. Happily, May 6th was a light day for him. He conducted another rehearsal of his Third Suite in the morning, was embarrassed to have to converse after it with Mrs. Reno while "drenched with perspiration" from his work, but pleased at the enthusiasm of the musicians who shouted "something like *Hoch*" when he finished. That evening he listened politely to a spectacular performance of Mendelssohn's *Elijah* with a chorus of six hundred at the second concert of the festival. He found it "an excellent work but somewhat long and drawn out." At intermission Tchaikovsky found himself "dragged to the boxes of the various bigwigs here," a chore he found tedious, except for his chat with Carnegie—"charming millionaire."

By the following day Tchaikovsky found his suffering reaching what he termed a "crescendo" despite a birthday gift of "lots of flowers" from Mrs. Reno. "Never, it seems, have I been so afraid. Is it not because they scrutinize my outward appearance here and therefore my shyness will be noticeable?" Whatever the reasons, he spent "several painful hours" waiting to appear at the first afternoon concert, where he was to conduct his suite, which was sandwiched into an afternoon of operatic excerpts. But again, he was "splendidly greeted, and created, as it said in today's newspapers, a 'sensation.'" Indeed it was. Wrote the *Times*: "... the star of the afternoon was certainly Tchaikovsky. The eminent composer's Third Suite has been heard here several times, but it is safe to say that on none of these occasions was it played so brilliantly as it was yesterday under his inspiring guidance. . . . His suite is a masterly work and he conducted it in a masterly manner."

Happily, there was no concert that evening, so Tchaikovsky could avoid invitations and get to sleep early, for Friday was to prove a heavy day. There were "visitors without end," among them a correspondent for a pair of Russian papers. "Since it was the first time that I had had occasion to indulge in a heart-to-heart talk with a Russian woman, a shameful thing happened. Suddenly tears came, my voice trembled, and I could not keep from sobbing. Ran into the other room and did not come out for a long time. Burn with shame to recall this unexpected incident." A nap cooled the shame of the neurasthenic composer, and he was able to conduct that evening an *a cappella* choral rendition of two of his songs, "Our Father" and "Legend." The featured works were the first American performance of Henrich Schütz' seventeenth-century cantata, *The Seven Words of Our Savior*, which the leading singer "sang persistently out of tune" and, as a special tribute to the man who had first had the vision of Music Hall, Leopold Damrosch's oratorio, *Sulamith*, which Tchaikovsky pronounced "splendid" and the *Herald* found "shocking in its baldness" and hardly less so in its "eroticism." A rival paper, however, said it was written "in a mellifluous, sentimental style, which is quite appropriate to the words."

Afterwards there was the inevitable dinner party, which acted as a further depressant on Tchaikovsky. The group was surprised to learn that he was only fifty-one. "Have I aged during recent years?" he asked himself. "Extremely possible," he answered, adding another straw or two to his already overburdened psyche. "I feel that something within me is crushed ... influenced by the conversation ... I had horrible dreams all night. Along a gigantic, rocky descent, I was tumbling down irresistibly into the sea and was clinging to a small projection of rock."

The following afternoon, calm before a performance for the first time, Tchaikovsky listened to Damrosch conduct the Beethoven Fifth Symphony, had a green room conversation with Mrs. Carl Alves, who sang one of his songs and one of Damrosch's, and then went forth to conduct a triumphant performance of his First Piano Concerto. It was his last New York appearance and "the enthusiasm was such as I never succeeded in arousing even in Russia. They called me out endlessly, shouted 'upwards,' [sic] waved handkerchiefs—in a word, it was evident that I had really pleased the Americans. But especially dear to me was the enthusiasm of the orchestra."

Tchaikovsky was particularly pleased by the work of Adele Aus der Ohe, his soloist in the piano concerto, in private life the wife of conductor Anton Seidl, who had just been engaged to lead the Philharmonic. Tchaikovsky was amazed to learn that she had come here "without a penny" four years earlier to play with the Symphony Society, had been well received and, after a series of successful tours, "she possesses a fortune of *one half million marks*" (about $120,000). "That's what America is!" he exclaimed, giving further credence to the European myth about life in the new world. For her part, she showed "the most charming modesty and tact in her refusal to accept any of the applause for herself" after playing the concerto with Tchaikovsky. Truly, it was a superlative climax for the Russian who, drenched by his exertions, had to hurry home to bathe and change without hearing the conclusion of the concert, Damrosch's rendition of excerpts from *Parsifal.*

Then it was back to Music Hall for Tchaikovsky to hear the final concert of the opening festival, Handel's oratorio, *Israel in Egypt*, conducted by Damrosch. "The performance was distinguished," Tchaikovsky thought, but the critics remained consistent in their lukewarm reactions to Damrosch's work. It is sadly significant that, a few days later, he asked Tchaikovsky to take him on as a pupil, a request which embarrassed the Russian immensely.

The post-concert supper that night was held at the Manhattan Club, the renowned cuisine of which Tchaikovsky found "repugnant." But if the food was repugnant, the company certainly was not. His dinner partner was Carl Schurz, Senator, Secretary of the Interior, liberal and intellectual. A towering figure in an age of political pygmyism, Schurz impressed Tchaikovsky as "a man truly very wise, cultured and interesting. He sat next to me and talked very much about Tolstoi, Turgenev and Dostoevski. The supper went off very gaily. . . ." Looking back on Tchaikovsky's stay in New York, spent mostly amidst the very rich and the very genteel, one cannot help but be relieved that he met at least one great figure from the American intellectual world.

The following day Tchaikovsky encountered a minor facet of American life in the Victorian era which irritated him considerably. After spending the afternoon visiting Russian acquaintances, he set forth hurriedly for his hotel to change for the farewell dinner Carnegie had arranged. "On account of its being Sunday, all the cafés were closed. Inasmuch as they are the only places where (1) one may buy cigarettes and (2) satisfy nature's little need, and I being in extreme want of the one and the other, one can imagine how great were my sufferings until at last I reached home. These remnants of English Puritanism . . . make me very indignant. It is said that the legislators who made this law in New York State are themselves awful drunkards."

Much more pleasant was his final encounter with Carnegie, who had been trying to persuade Tchaikovsky to return to America the following year for a more extensive tour (he later received an offer of $4000 for twenty concerts). Tchaikovsky liked Carnegie, "who has remained simple, modest and not in the least turning up his nose at people. . . ." The steel magnate was in an unusually ebullient and expansive mood that night, and he displayed his affection for Tchaikovsky in a particularly high-spirited way throughout the course of the entire evening: "He grasped my hands, declaring that I am the uncrowned but true king of music; embraced me (without kissing—here men never kiss), expressed my greatness by standing on tiptoe and raising his hands up high, and finally threw the entire company into raptures by showing how I conduct. He did it so seriously, so well, so similarly, that I myself was delighted."

But Tchaikovsky's delight was never allowed to linger long, so his final summation of this last evening of his association with Music Hall's sponsors was that it "was pleasant but, at the same time, somehow embarrassing to me. I was very glad to start for home at eleven o'clock."

The next day Tchaikovsky set forth on an excursion to Niagara Falls, returning briefly to New York two days later before going on to engagements in Baltimore and Washington. It was then that he discovered why Mayer, the man from Knabe, had been so persistently helpful in handling the details of his trip. He wanted Tchaikovsky to write a testimonial on the virtues of his firm's pianos. Tchaikovsky grudgingly agreed to do so, but rejected a wording which implied that he thought they were America's best. He liked the Steinway better, despite "the comparative unfriendliness of its representative." He returned to New York on May 19th, attended a concert in his honor at the Metropolitan Opera House ("one lady threw a gorgeous bouquet of roses straight into my face") and sailed from New York on the 21st. He was seasick during part of his crossing, bored with his fellow-passengers and "inexpressibly tense and nervous." He wondered, at the height of the storm that marred his passage, whether it was possible he would "decide on torture like this once more." He never did.

In his diaries he failed to sum up the meaning of his American stay. But in a letter to a friend, he expressed his mixed feelings about his visit, balancing his pleasure at his welcome—and his fame—against the pressures it heaped upon his sensitive psyche: "New York, American customs, American hospitality—all their comforts and arrangements—everything, in fact, is to my taste. If only I were younger I should very much enjoy my visit to this interesting and youthful country. But now I just tolerate everything as if it were a slight punishment mitigated by many pleasant things. All my thoughts, all my aspirations tend toward Home, Home!!! I am convinced that I am ten times more famous in America than in Europe. . . . Several of my works which are unknown even in Moscow are frequently played here. Is not that curious?"

But if Tchaikovsky's feelings about the visit were mixed, New York's reaction to him and to the hall he had helped dedicate were not (although the musical details of the opening festival were subject to considerable debate). There was no doubt in anyone's mind that the musical millennium was at hand.

Three

"Does Vanderbilt Get Sick of His Money?"

THE EVENING OF NOVEMBER 17TH, 1891, WAS AN EVENING OF MANY beginnings. That night a legend began, and a trend, and a tradition. A young Polish pianist named Ignace Jan Paderewski played the first American concert of his career. At the time, no one fully realized the importance of what was happening. It is true that an excellent European reputation had preceded Paderewski to this country and that there was a modicum of curiosity about the newcomer. But the gross that night was only $500 and the enthusiasm of the critics, while in the main generous, was not unbounded. But on that night, and on the nights that followed, Paderewski managed to set a chord reverberating in the hearts and minds of his audience, a chord that all artists seek to touch but rarely find. Once it is found and strummed, a communion—magical, mystical, romanticize it as you will—is established which assures response, enthusiasm, affection, even a kind of love, for all the years to come.

The legendary quality of what Paderewski accomplished on his first tour did not become wholly apparent for years; it was not until he had become a beloved humanitarian and political leader, one of the last spokesmen for freedom on the grand romantic scale, that the full reverberations of that November night in Mr. Carnegie's new auditorium reached their climax. But the immediate consequences of his first American tour could be observed quickly. One of the results was the identification of the new hall as the American summit that had to be conquered if the new artist, or visiting virtuoso, was to achieve full financial and artistic success here. It was the largest, the most elegant and most important hall in the most important city in America. Until it existed, New York had lacked only the proper setting for the musical jewels it displayed. Once that setting existed, New York's musical status was assured, and Paderewski was the first to learn of its tremendous value. His triumph there began a musical trend that was to bemuse the American musical public for at least three decades (and that continues, in somewhat diminished form, today). In the years that followed, the visiting virtuoso, his portmanteau bulging with European encomiums, became a common figure on the concert stage, and, indeed, in the train stations and hotel lobbies of the nation. After Paderewski the temper of the American musical world was tuned to the virtuoso, particularly the pianist and the violinist.

It can be argued that this predilection was no different in kind from that which led to the excesses of Barnumism that had accompanied earlier touring artists in the years between 1840 and 1890, but it is obvious that the appeal of Paderewski and his fellows were more subtle and more musically valid. Masters of what a later critic would call the "wow" technique, lush stylists, romantics in tone, temperament and technique, uncompromising in their musicianship, they were not entertainers or freaks. Their appeal, certainly not austere and mathematical, and not always popular among musical purists, was based on solid—and often amazing—ability. The people came to *see* their concerts as much as to *hear* these new masters, but without the sheer technical ability with which they played, their concerts would merely have been shows, empty experiences in the techniques of salesmanship of inferior musical products, rather than the totally involving emotional experiences they, from all accounts, were.

Just how hard the virtuoso had to work to achieve the technical proficiency on which his appeal was built was demonstrated by the experience of Paderewski before his American debut. With dazzling European successes behind him, with a contract guaranteeing him $30,000 for eighty concerts in his pocket and with the highest of hopes, he embarked on his first voyage to America. That contract and those hopes came to seem vain indeed as his passage wore on. For it was a rough November crossing of the North Atlantic, one which remained for Paderewski "one of his memory's nightmares," and by the time he landed he was ill and exhausted. Facing a grueling series of concerts in which he would have to play six concertos in one week, he had had virtually no opportunity to practice on his voyage and what was left of his confidence was shattered by the greeting of the man from Steinway's who was in charge of booking his tour and who met him at the dock.

"We hear you have had brilliant successes in London and Paris," the man said. "But let me tell you, Mr. Paderewski, you need not expect anything like that in America. We have heard them all, all the pianists, all the great ones, and our demands are very exacting. We are not easily pleased here . . . we have a certain standard which is very difficult to overcome. . . . You should not . . . expect extraordinary houses. Although I have done my best for you, it is nothing very remarkable." Indeed, his most unremarkable services included papering the house with free tickets, so sure was he that Paderewski could not draw an audience here.

This was arrogant musical provincialism at its worst. The truth was that America had by no means "heard them all" at this point, that it had virtually no standards beyond showmanship with which to judge a pianist, and that the reflexes of an American audience, living in a society with little or no vital musical ability, were largely conditioned by the European reputation of the artist, which took years to become widely circulated currency here.

But the thirty-year-old Paderewski did not know all this, and the man from Steinway succeeded in unnerving him completely. As the final straw, the hotel in which the Steinway people housed him was dirty and uncomfortable, his bed crawled with bugs, mice scurried in the wall, and the next day he was forced to cut short his practice to move to the more palatable Windsor Hotel.

That night he came on stage, "a picturesque young man, very slim, very nervous, very awkward, with a colorless face surmounted by a shock of tawny reddish hair, made his way to the front of the stage and bowed again and again in answer to the warm welcome of the audience."

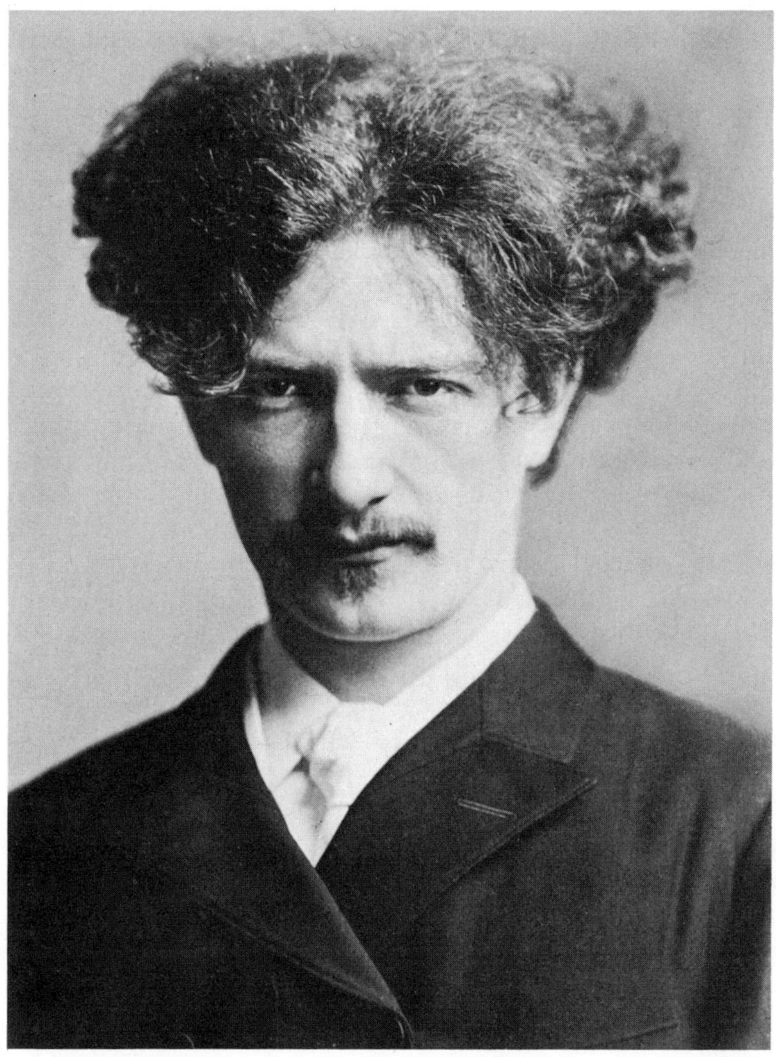

Culver Service

Ignace Jan Paderewski made his first American debut at Carnegie Hall on November 17, 1891. His first reviews were only moderately good, but by the time of his third concert, critics and public were wildly enthusiastic.

"He began by disappointing some of his auditors," said the *Times*, "next he interested them and finally he conquered them." The *Sun* described his technique by saying that he "coaxes, persuades and fascinates the piano to give forth the most varied and beautiful tones, to compel it to yield up its whole soul in immense volumes of sound." The critics liked his work in the unaccompanied Chopin group better than they did his playing of the Saint-Saëns C minor Concerto or his own First Piano Concerto which he played with Damrosch and the Symphony Society orchestra. His notices were moderately favorable, but in every review there was some reservation not always subtly stated. The *Times*, for instance, said: "He is not the ideal pianist."

So the first concert was no more than a modest success, a mixed blessing. And Paderewski realized this without waiting for the reviews. At the end of the particularly long concert, he went directly to his hotel, and began to practice the works scheduled for his next appearance, the *Emperor* Concerto, Schumann's A minor Concerto and the Liszt *Hungarian Fantasia*. He was hard at work when the hotel manager tapped on his door. No piano playing, he was told. It disturbs the guests. But Paderewski had to practice. Mulling over his problem, he remembered the dozens of pianos he had been shown at the Steinway warehouse. Routing out his secretary, the two men plunged out into an extremely chilly November night, hurried downtown to Fourteenth Street, pounded on the door until the night watchman heard them and let them in. Then, by the light of two candles placed on the top of a piano, Paderewski practiced in the unheated warehouse until dawn, managed to be on time for a 10:00 A.M. rehearsal with the orchestra and was rewarded that evening with a rush to the stage by the audience (a favorite method, in those days, of demonstrating approval) and by a headline in the *Times*: "The Success of Ignace Jan Paderewski Is Assured."

And indeed it was. The next afternoon, after seventeen hours of practice within the previous twenty-four, he played concertos by Chopin and Anton Rubinstein. The auditorium was packed, there were scores of standees, and "the ladies, having heard that he could play scales faster than anybody else, turned out in full force and feather." If anything his reception exceeded the one of the previous evening, and now there was no longer any question of a need to paper the house. The demand for Paderewski far exceeded the supply of music he could provide. Steinway hastily added eighteen concerts to his itinerary (at increased fees) and the pianist looked confidently forward to resounding financial success at a series of New York solo recitals.

But, alas, the unconfident Steinway people had booked only one of them in Music Hall. The rest were scheduled for the small hall in the old Madison Square Garden. Paderewski was furious, and his protest resulted in the transfer of several of them to the larger hall where his receipts were as high as $3000 a concert. By the time that series of six recitals was over, the Paderewski legend, as well as the Paderewski career, was well launched, and America had found a European virtuoso to replace Anton Rubinstein in its high and romantic regard.

When he returned to New York after his tour, Paderewski was an attraction of unprecedented drawing power. Playing with the Brodsky string quartet, his name alone filled the hall for a chamber music recital, something few artists before or since have managed. "Paderewski can make anything interesting and heaven-storming, even a Brahms chamber music work," wrote a musical journal, reflecting the discount at which Brahms was commonly held at the time in this country. His solo recitals also amazed the critics who regarded it as remarkable that he could hold a full house silent while he played a solo recital. By the time he played a farewell concert he was able to bring $6390 into the box office, "the largest receipts ever realized by a piano recital in this or probably any other country."

But if Paderewski's concerts were a major triumph, the rest of the season at Music Hall was not. The Philharmonic was still playing at the Met because its boxes were "superior in size, location and number" to Music Hall's. The number of recitals was amazingly low, and the small number of bookings at the hall a source of concern to the board of directors. All told, the main hall had less than fifty bookings for the season, chief among them a dozen concerts by the Symphony Society and eight by the Oratorio Society, which did Brahms' *German Requiem* and the third portion of Schumann's musical setting of *Faust*.

The most interesting of that season's bookings, and the most typical of an age that placed high value on the educational value of the lecture platform, was a series of scientific lectures. The first, "A Trip to the Moon," billed as a "celestial drama," had been seen by Morris Reno in Berlin. He brought it to New York, along with a companion feature called "From Chaos to Man." It regaled Victorian New York for most of the winter. The "trip" consisted mainly of slides of paintings which showed various eclipses, sunsets and lunar landscapes, all accompanied by a lecture. "The whole series of views," the *Times* thought, "is stilted and sounds as if written for German philosophical children who asked for a fairy story. . . . With all respect to the gravity of the subject, the lecture should be made more colloquial in style, and the reader should not act as if he believed himself inspired." The *Herald* was more succinct: "A large number of the people who gathered stayed until it was all over. The fortitude they displayed was the most interesting sight of the evening." But within a month, the flop had turned into a hit. A new lecturer named Garrett P. Servios was at the lectern, and suddenly, wonder of wonders, the pictures moved. By a complicated and ingenious arrangement of lights and screens, the moon and the sun were made to move when eclipses were shown, and as a final fillip, "the moon was made to rise out of the blue surface of a lake, and the landscape was gradually illuminated as it climbed up the blue sky and the stars began to disappear. The effect was marvelous, and the spectators burst into applause."

"From Chaos to Man" was even more spectacular. It included mechanical scenery which reproduced erupting volcanos—complete with real steam hissing out over the audience—thunder, lightning, clouds and sunsets, along with views of prehistoric man. To the startled and entranced eyes of audiences which shared the nineteenth-century faith in, and wonder at, the new scientific age, it was a revelation more awesome—and perhaps more relevant to their interests—than the work of a musician. For here was living proof of the miraculous age in which they were living, and a taste of the wonders yet to come. The naïve —and rather touching—faith of the nineteenth century in progress through science was demonstrated and renewed again. It was, as they were fond of saying, "a great age"—and the future seemed to promise even greater things.

The following season was to provide evidence of progress on the musical scene, an area which sometimes seemed to be exempt from the general faith in the inevitable upward trend of life, art and intellect. For in that year Antonín Dvořák arrived to assume the direction of the National Conservatory of Music. The conservatory itself was one of the most hopeful signs of serious interest in serious music. Founded in 1885 by a wealthy and indefatigable music lover, Jeanette Thurber, it was not the first such institution, but because of the brilliant faculty she gathered for it, it became the most important conservatory of its time, instrumental, with its sister institutions, in increasing the number of professional musicians in America by some 300 per cent in the last fifteen years of the nineteenth century. Unfortunately, American instruction was still regarded as inferior to European study, and the musician desiring to build a major career in his native land had to acquire the cachets of European teaching and approval before daring to venture onto the concert or opera stage here. An even more galling lack in the musical life of the times was the absence of American composers and an American compositional idiom. The few writers of music were mainly anemic and genteel imitators of European traditions, lacking boldness of innovation—and technique. It was to increase the prestige of American musical instruction and to inject some life into the compositional field that the conservatory engaged the celebrated Dvořák. To launch him, a Carnegie Hall concert was arranged with Anton Seidl, then beginning his second season with the Philharmonic, as conductor. The event was, in every sense, gala. Colonel Higginson, founder of the Boston Symphony and therefore a considerable figure in the musical awakening, came down to deliver a pre-concert oration on "Two New Worlds—The New World of Columbus and the New World of Music," and then the concert began with orchestra and chorus singing "America" while "Dr. Dvořák stood at the door leading to the stage regarding the spectacle with interest. He seemed unconscious that every soul in that vast audience was principally concerned with a mental inventory of his own personality."

When he advanced to the podium he received a rousing reception. The orchestra rose as one man and played a *tusch*, while the audience cheered and even the more sedate occupants of the boxes waved their handkerchiefs in greeting.

He conducted two American premieres of his own works, the *Te Deum* and a triple overture, "Nature, Life and Love." The *Herald* thought he handled the orchestra "with a brilliancy attained by few living composers. . . . As a leader Dr. Dvořák does excellent work, keeping his forces well in hand and obtaining a nice gradation of time."

The *Times*, on the other hand, thought him "an extremely bad conductor. His beat is so uncertain that it is impossible to see how any body of players or singers could follow it with confidence."

In fact, the *Times* was distinctly irritable about the whole business, beginning with the playing of "America" which it thought any institution calling itself a *National* Conservatory should know was not officially the hymn of the republic. "It ought moreover to know—and if it does not it should be made to know—that the people of the United States will not accept as their national hymn any masquerading version of 'God Save the Queen.' "

Nor could the paper see any excuse for Higginson's speech. "Speech making is altogether too common an offense," it opined, "and when it is so tenuous in thought, so platitudinous in style and so lachrymose in delivery as the oration of the eminent Bostonian . . . it is altogether a weariness to the flesh." All in all, the occasion was presumptuous and pretentious in the eyes of the great newspaper. "To give Dr. Dvořák's engagement as the director of a local music school the appearance of a national event was beyond all question a piece of impudence," it summarized, "and could have been attempted only by persons conversant with the great truth, established by Mr. Barnum, that the American public loves to be humbugged."

But the *Times* had to admit that whether or not Dvořák was involved in a public relations stunt, whether or not he was a good conductor, was not really important. "So long as he will continue to pour forth music from his fertile brain men and women will be found to sing and play it well." Within a year that fertile brain was to pour forth a brilliant piece of work and the value of his tenure at the National Conservatory was to be placed in a category beyond question.

In the meantime, the Philharmonic was well along in what James

Gibbons Huneker has called "a new era . . . not only of material prosperity but of increased artistic endeavor and accomplishment." For the conductorship of Anton Seidl was, without question, proving to be a success. By the time the Philharmonic gave the first Carnegie Hall concerts in its history, on November 18th and 19th, 1892, he had succeeded in totally assuaging New York's grief over the loss of Theodore Thomas to Chicago. He was the perfect conductor for the period, his heavily romantic taste in perfect keeping with the tastes of an audience which had been completely won over to the style of the late Romantics —Wagner, Liszt, Tchaikovsky and their contemporaries. Before taking over the Philharmonic he had been the principal conductor of Wagnerian opera at the Met, a post he had come to with the unreserved recommendation of his teacher and master, Richard Wagner.

But he was far from a well-balanced conductor. "It may truthfully be said," wrote Huneker, "that he conducted certain classic compositions for the first time in his career at the Philharmonic Society concerts. This is not surmise, but fact." Such imbalance has been the undoing of many a conductor, and tampering with the classics, a favorite Seidl occupation, has undone many another. Indeed, Gustav Mahler lost his job and his health—perhaps even his life—for offenses far less grievous and certainly more intelligent and more interesting, when he directed the Philharmonic less than twenty years later. The difference between the fates of the two men undoubtedly was a result of the difference in their personalities. Mahler was nervous and neurotic, incapable of dealing with critics, the public, the boards of directors. Seidl was his opposite. "There was elemental power in this man with the picturesque head . . . his fiery Hungarian temperament made venerable bones rattle. Seidl was nothing if not dramatic."

His readings of Beethoven in general, and of Bach and Mozart on occasion (neither was much played in those days) created storms of controversy over his "irreverence." But Seidl had his excuses and his apologists. "He absorbed from Wagner revolutionary theories as to the interpretation of the master symphonies. Liszt had taught him the beauty of orchestral coloring and the superiority of the symphonic poem. Is it any wonder that he saw as if with freshly annointed eyes; saw that the old had been superseded by the new; and that even a

Beethoven symphony might be mended out of all resemblance to its original shape and gait?" These, remember, were the great days of "interpretation." It was years before Toscanini was to make fashionable the view that the conductor's job was primarily to realize the composer's intentions and that this arduous task was work enough for a man. To be sure, there were intelligent music-goers who clung to this view against all the importunings of the Wagnerian cohorts, and they grumbled incessantly about Seidl until he at last realized that "a cathedral may be repaired, but not a symphony." At the time of his death (which came suddenly in 1898) his once startling methods had rather mellowed, or else quite vanished.

But whatever his way with the classics, everyone was agreed that his work "in the domain of the dramatic, in the more spacious music of Wagner, Liszt, Berlioz, Tchaikovsky and Strauss" was perfectly splendid, as was his interest in modern music. During his first Carnegie Hall season he programmed Paul Gilson's symphonic sketches, "The Sea," Templeton Strong's Second Symphony and, on his very first program in the new hall, songs from Dvořák's *The Spectre's Bride* shared the program with Tchaikovsky, Saint-Saëns and Wagner. A month later he played the American premiere of Dvořák's First Symphony. The two men were close friends and Seidl remained an ardent champion of Dvořák's work.

A year after the premiere of the First Symphony, it was Seidl and the Philharmonic who gave the world premiere—the first important one in Carnegie Hall's history—of Dvořák's Fifth (*From the New World*) Symphony, an event which gladdened the hearts of those who were anxious to hear American themes joined with the older European symphonic tradition.

His American competitors had pooh-poohed Dvořák's claim that a legitimate American folk music existed, that it was the most exciting and vital music in the country and that he intended to tap this rich lode for a new symphony. So there was high interest when it was announced that the new symphony would be presented, from manuscript, at Music Hall.

After two movements, the audience was completely won over and

The Bettmann Archive

Culver Service

Museum of the City of New York

The score of Dvořák's Fifth Symphony, From the New World *(top), which Anton Seidl (above) and the Philharmonic premiered at Carnegie Hall in 1893 with the composer (left) present.*

the applause reached the proportions of an ovation (it is a comparatively recent custom not to applaud between movements of a symphony, and there was considerable protest in musical circles when conductors began asking for restraint of applause in the middle of a work). "The applause," according to one newspaper, "swelled to a perfect tumult. Every face was turned in the direction in which Anton Seidl was looking. Every neck was craned so that it might be discovered to whom he was motioning so energetically. . . . At last a broad-shouldered individual of medium height, and as straight as one of the pines in the forests of which his music whispered so eloquently, is descried by the eager watchers. A murmur sweeps through the hall. 'Dvořák! Dvořák!' is the word that passes from mouth to mouth." Dark, with a short graying beard, Dvořák seemed to at least one viewer to be a happy sort of man, with just the right touch of pathos about him. "The face," he wrote, "is honest, kindly and with a general expression of a perfectly guileless nature."

Of the music created by this perfectly guileless nature there was unanimity of opinion. "He has written a beautiful symphony, which throbs with American feeling," wrote the *Times*, which thought that it detected in the music hints of "the final subjection" of our land through "the tremendous activity of the most energetic of all peoples." It further felt that "we Americans should thank and honor the Bohemian master who has shown us how to build our national school of music." "It is," the paper said in another edition, "an altogether unique and notable event that one of the world's greatest composers . . . should produce a new work written in America, for Americans, before Americans."

That it required a visiting Middle European to show us the richness of American musical possibilities was, apparently, an irony lost on one and all. Everyone was simply too blushingly pleased that one of the greatest living composers had attempted to immortalize the American experience musically to question the work of the handful of American composers, notably Edward MacDowell, who steadfastly turned to European models for their inspiration. Nor would anyone, until the late 1950's, deign to consider the work of Charles Ives, the first great

American composer, who used folk material with far greater daring, originality and force than Dvořák.

For weeks after the debut the musical world debated whether Dvořák's work would significantly influence the growth of a national school of composers. To which question Victor Herbert finally addressed himself: he summed up the situation admirably when he answered, "Yes, if the composers are Dr. Dvořáks." The truth was that there were no American composers of the stature of Dvořák and that it would be years before we developed any. So, despite a longing for a music to express the forcefulness and energy of a nation which was in an intensely proud and patriotic mood, arrogantly sure of its virtue and of its mission to democratize the world, musically America remained curiously passive. Eagerly receiving the artists and compositions of Europe, but still too unsure of itself to create its own music, or even its own artists, it took the best the world had to offer, eager to prove its ability to appreciate, but unable and unwilling to make payments on its musical debt to the Old World.

Typical of American musical activity of the time was the career of Victor Herbert, Irish by birth, but a citizen since childhood of the United States. Herbert was by way of being the Leonard Bernstein of the age—a composer of both serious music and of the light operas that are his chief claim to immortality, a workmanlike conductor and the leading American cello virtuoso of his day. He was a true jack of all musical trades, but like others of his type he never found his true voice. Seidl was glad to premiere Herbert's Second Cello Concerto in the spring of 1894. The critics found the piece technically proficient, ambitious, but only occasionally interesting. "It is a pity that the gods did not bless him with a violin," wrote one critic, while a colleague doubted that "the concerto is what Mr. Herbert fondly intended it to be." The *Times* dealt in particularly stern fashion with Herbert: "When a man is a composer by natural gift, and a cello player by choice," it said, "he will write concertos for his favorite instrument, and it is not possible to prevent him from doing so. But it does seem that the exercise of a little resolution and a gentle force might prevent a man from playing them in public."

So, despite the efforts to encourage native compositional talent, the results were far from satisfying. The efforts to broaden the audience for serious music, however, seemed to be bearing modest fruit. Walter Damrosch, working hard to maintain his orchestra on a permanent basis without the aid of subsidy, would try anything to get an audience. He and his men got most of the best accompanying jobs when visiting virtuosos played here, went on tours rivaling those of Theodore Thomas in length and began a series of Sunday concerts of light music because "Sunday was the one day of the week when men were not immersed in business cares and . . . on that day they and their families would be more susceptible to the appreciation of . . . music." He was also fond of presenting operas in concert version, at one point even engaging Lillian Russell to sing *The Daughter of the Regiment.* She backed out at the last moment but Marie Tempest, another musical comedy favorite, substituted more than adequately. He, too, conducted a large number of premieres, beginning with the first American performance of Tchaikovsky's Sixth Symphony, permission for which he had obtained from the composer when they happened to be seated together at a dinner in England. The score arrived in Damrosch's mail only days after word of the composer's death (of cholera) had been received here. Moved by this posthumous display of loyalty ("It was like a message from the dead"), Damrosch conducted late in 1893 an epitaph to the composer who had had nightmares of his death while visiting New York two years previously.

During the Dvořák year, Damrosch programmed his works frequently, giving the American premiere of the Bohemian's Violin Concerto. In that same season, he decided to revive what seemed to be a waning interest in Wagnerian opera. His father had been a Wagnerite, he himself had been Seidl's assistant in the German repertory at the Met and the success of a concert version of *Götterdämmerung* in 1894 encouraged him to form his own Wagnerian company the following season. He sold his home to finance it, and in his first season made $53,000 on the project. Andrew Carnegie warned him to broaden his repertory for a second season, but he didn't. The result was a $43,000 loss, and it was only the addition of Italian and French works, along with the presence of stars like Calvé and Melba, that saved the venture.

But his musicians had steady work (he used them as the pit orchestra) and it added excitement to the opera season.

Not, really, that it needed it. For public interest in opera at this time was far higher than it was in symphonic music. These were the dawning days of opera's golden age, and it was in this realm that American artists (particularly women) were making the first major breakthrough to acceptance. Emma Eames and Lillian Nordica, among others, built reputations in Europe and returned home to conquer American audiences. More were to follow them in the years to come. Their road was not easy, for they could not get the fees their European peers received here. But most of them waged a constant war with managers and critics for equal status. Nordica, for example, turned down a bid to sing with the Philharmonic because it refused to pay a fee she considered proper ($1500). "What's sauce for the foreign goose should be sauce for the domestic gander," said a musical journal, correctly, if inelegantly.

But there was no American opera for these ladies to sing, and although the lack was hardly a matter of primary concern, there was a good deal of hope that one would come along. In the season of 1894-1895 Damrosch attempted to satisfy that dream. He performed a concert version of an opera of his own, which at least had the virtue of an American theme, no less a one, indeed, than Hawthorne's *The Scarlet Letter.* Nordica was cast as Hester Prynne and everyone was duly surprised and impressed by the enterprise. Though the critics found the musical style more Wagnerian than American, everyone was politely encouraging about the work.

Musically it was a dull season, even though in other ways it was a significant year for the hall. For one thing, it acquired a new name. Music Hall had proved to be a bad choice for an unthought-of reason. On the Continent music halls denoted vaudeville halls, and when European artists were invited to appear in a place with that name, visions of sharing the bill with jugglers and trained seals danced in their fantasies, and they refused to compromise their prestige (the day of the fading opera star on the two-a-day bills at the Palace was still a few years off). So the board informally changed the name to

Carnegie Hall, which is what a lot of people had been calling it anyway.

In the same year the first major additions to the hall, in the form of more studios, were placed under construction and when the Philharmonic opened its season on November 16th the *Times* reported that "the most interesting features . . . were the fall of some plaster in the gallery and the appearance of Eugène Ysaÿe, the Belgian violinist, on the stage. The former almost destroyed the effectiveness of the latter's cantabile playing, because it frightened a good many people, whose nerves were already irritated by the half-muffled hammerings and scrapings that accompany all afternoon concerts in the Carnegie Hall as it is now called."

The additions were necessary if the financial health of the hall was to improve, and they apparently did not unduly upset Ysaÿe, whose "powerful artistic personality" and "interesting" technique were widely praised in this, his American debut. Indeed, Ysaÿe's appearances as a recitalist and as soloist with the Damrosch orchestra in the American premiere of fellow violinist Joseph Joachim's *Theme and Variations* were the chief items of musical interest that season, even though his first recital was marred by bad weather which made itself felt in his intonation several times, and certainly made itself felt in the region of his pocketbook, by limiting the size of his audience. Among the novelties of the season were Edward MacDowell's Second Piano Concerto, which was received with a good deal of enthusiasm, and some minor Dvořák.

The 1895-1896 season was equally lackluster. The only major premiere was the Philharmonic's presentation of Tchaikovsky's First Symphony, subtitled *A Winter Journey.* One critic opined that "the slush must have been ankle deep." The chief success among the Carnegie Hall recitalists that year was Rafael Joseffy, who had debuted in New York in 1879 and who came out of his retirement in Tarrytown to recapture the imagination of New Yorkers—and the critics—in an appearance at a Liederkranz Society concert. The audience, according to one observer, waited restlessly through a dull reading of the *Eroica.* "Presently a small man, with short, curly hair, and a little mustache walked from the door toward the front of the stage. Young people who have reached the concert-going age in recent years sat up and said to their older friends: 'Is that really Joseffy?' " Indeed it was, and it soon became apparent that he had been practicing during these years of exile and that the old form, much admired in former years, was very much intact. His was but a small triumph in the larger sweep of Carnegie Hall's history, but it loomed large in a year singularly lacking in triumphs of any kind.

But if 1895-1896 was a thin season, 1896-1897 was a vintage year in the hall's history. To begin with, it acquired the most famous and the most long-lived of its tenants, the American Academy of Dramatic Arts, which after several changes of name and address was at last settling down in the place it would call home until 1951. The Academy was one of the true cultural pioneers in this country, the first school of drama to invade a theatrical world in which birth or early service as a backstage errand boy were regarded as the only fit ways to enter the profession. When the school was founded in 1884 there were only three other dramatic academies in the world, the most notable being the one affiliated with the Comédie Française.

The school was the idea of Franklin Haven Sargent, who had been an early disciple of Steele MacKaye, a leading theoretician of the theater (and inventor of the folding theater seat). MacKaye, in turn, was a disciple of François Delsarte, founder of a school of acting that depended heavily on pantomimic training and believed firmly that an actor could be taught a mathematical control of voice and body to project mechanically whatever mood and action a role demanded. Delsarte thoughtfully devised a complete selection of exercises to secure these ends, and they were the basis of the Academy's early curriculum.

MacKaye was not long for the world of teaching. Indeed, he never actually instructed a class, a fact which caused the student body of the school to strike during the first term of the school. But ten years later, the school, having impressed various theatrical magnates with the caliber of its graduates, was on a firm foundation, and was ready to expand its curriculum, facilities and student body. So, it moved into Carnegie Hall. Among the advantages of the new location was the lyceum theater in the basement which the school obtained for student productions and rehearsals. In addition, an early catalog announced that "this location, high above the din and dust of the city and flooded with sunlight, is an ideal one for students' work. From its windows one overlooks Central Park, the Hudson and America's metropolis. This famous building is made absolutely fireproof and safe, with all the conveniences of an electrical age."

In the new setting, and with a former student named Charles Jehlinger, the chief intellectual force in the school, turning its teaching methods away from Delsarte and toward subjective naturalism, the Academy became an important influence on theatrical style, helping to lead it away, over the years, from the declamatory style which was then fashionable to an increased use of the actor's inner resources. Passionately anonymous, Jehlinger developed, but never recorded, a system of acting that was allegedly very similar to Stanislavski's, of whom, at the time, he had not heard. Said Jehlinger, who was a martinet of a teacher: "The hardest thing is to get a student to overcome himself. I can't put talent into them, but I can draw it out if they will respond." Said Cecil B. De Mille, an early (1898-1900) student: "The only man in my life of whom I was ever afraid was Charles Jehlinger."

De Mille, unlike many of his fellow students, and contrary to the official version of his career, found Jehlinger anything but inspirational, his methods dictatorial rather than liberating. "I respected the tough fiber of Jehlinger's character and teaching . . . but . . . he believed in imposing upon actors his own conception of a role, making them do, in every detail of voice, movement and business, exactly what he thought they should. That is one way to get a well-articulated performance out of a cast. It is not the way to teach the art of acting."

The roster of the school's graduates is impressive and includes Walter Abel, Jim Backus, Lauren Bacall, Anne Bancroft, Hume Cronyn, Robert Cummings, Kirk Douglas, Betty Field, Nina Foch, Martin Gabel, Margalo Gillmore, Jennifer Jones, Garson Kanin, Grace Kelly, Sam Levene, Howard Lindsay, Guthrie McClintic, Agnes Moorehead, Don Murray, Pat O'Brien, Tom Poston, William Powell, Thelma Ritter, Jason Robards, Sr., Jason Robards, Jr., Edward G. Robinson, Rosalind Russell, Joseph Schildkraut, Ezra Stone, Spencer Tracy, and

Graduation photos of students of the American Academy of Dramatic Arts which maintained studios in Carnegie Hall from 1896 to 1951. Courtesy of American Academy of Dramatic Arts.

Cecil B. DeMille

Edward G. Robinson

Spencer Tracy

Agnes Morehead

Rosalind Russell

Kirk Douglas

a man who applied his dramatic education in another field, Dale Carnegie.

But if the beginning of a long and honorable theatrical tradition in the new studio tower was the most important Carnegie Hall event of 1896, the return of Moriz Rosenthal, on November 10th, after an absence of ten years, was the event which most excited musical New York. A quotation from one review suffices to sum up the phenomenal welcome he received: "Carnegie Hall last night was the scene of one of those uncontrolled, spontaneous, half-insane outbursts that give color to Lombroso's theories about mob mania and the physical impulse of the crowd. Rosenthal the unique, Rosenthal with fingers of steel shod in velvet, Rosenthal whose playing may be compared to a rose, to a cyclone, Moritz Rosenthal, the world's greatest piano virtuoso, made his reappearance . . . and made us forget Rubinstein. "He played like a god from the Olympus of pianists, and little wonder the people strove frantically to salute him after he had finished the well-worn *Hungarian Fantasia.*"

The sensation of Rosenthal's first appearance had hardly died down when there was a new sensation, of quite a different kind. Its cause was a child prodigy named Bronislaw Hubermann, who was engaged to play his violin with the Philharmonic. He chose the first movement of Mendelssohn's Violin Concerto for his debut, and it was wonderingly noted that "if a musical hearer, unacquainted beforehand with the nature of the occasion, had turned his back to the stage a few minutes after Seidl's orchestra had done playing Dvořák's overture at Carnegie Hall last evening . . . his conclusion would have been that some hitherto unknown but very individual violinist was giving his own interpretation, at many points, of the familiar classic." He would never have believed, according to this critic, that such mature musicianship could be demonstrated by a boy of thirteen.

The nineteenth century was, if anything, more susceptible to child prodigies than our own time. The magic which a precocious talent exercised on that age was totally unmarred by speculation about its ill effects on the delicate developing of the personality. That question, much on the lips of a psychologically-oriented modern audience, never came up for discussion, while naïve wonder at the miracle of it all was often expressed—and there was no doubt that Master Hubermann was something of a miracle. As an adult he never quite equaled his childhood accomplishments, but in the golden days of his youth, a musical public, not far removed from the days of its confusion between genius and freakishness, welcomed him wholeheartedly.

It was not long, however, before critical reaction to this overgenerous enthusiasm took place. The notices for Hubermann's first solo recital were quite churlish. "Bronislaw Hubermann," stated the *Times*, ". . . suffers from overadvertising and underdressing. There really is no good reason why Hubermann should be advertised as a mature artist," the paper said, contradicting its earlier review of his appearance with the Philharmonic, "nor is there good reason for dressing him in knee trousers, loose silk shirts and long hair."

Two mature artists, both pianists, fared better than Hubermann in the next few months. Martinus Sieveking, the Dutch pianist, played a well received New York debut at Carnegie Hall, and despite an upset during the first half of his program due to trouble with the piano lid, received excellent notices. More sensational was the Carnegie Hall debut of Teresa Carreño, former child prodigy, sometime opera singer, the pupil of Anton Rubinstein and the teacher of Edward MacDowell. She was an object of great popular interest because of her stormy marriage to Eugene d'Albert, the composer, and because of her forceful, masculine style. A lady pianist, especially one who could play like a male virtuoso, was a rarity, and one musical journal was entranced by the discovery that her hands were, in the eyes of those who knew, "the exact counterpart of Rubinstein's."

The reaction to her debut—in which she played Rubinstein's Second Piano Concerto—were mixed, but excited. The *World* angered her by heading its review "The Lioness of the Piano" and noting that "she has lost the feminine tenderness, the poetic feeling, the suavity which were once elements in her playing. She has become purely a bravura player—almost brutal. . . . She was once magnetic, but she has lost that quality in spite of the still potent charms of beauty and grace."

Other critics, however, liked the very quality which the *World* condemned. "She is a strong woman, playing her instrument strongly," wrote the man from the *Advertiser*. "She either stands revealed in the glare of midday, or you hear her clear cry in the tropical jungle at midnight [a reference to her Venezuelan birth], while nearby two burning points tell of something lurking and feline."

These qualities were to make her a prime American favorite—a crowd-pleaser—for almost twenty seasons until her death in 1918. She was fortunate. The force and vitality which were the very center of her art did not diminish. Not so fortunate was a lady who followed her to the stage of Carnegie Hall that same month—January, 1897.

Lilli Lehmann was then almost fifty and her great voice was only a memory. A true soprano in her prime, she was now singing songs mainly from the mezzo repertory. "In a word," wrote the *Musical Courier*, "Lilli Lehmann should not be singing in public, but the indomitable money-getting propensity of the woman . . . made her risk her past reputation for a few thousand dollars." The *Courier* was not a particularly reputable source, for it was in the habit of giving bad notices to singers who would not buy advertisements in its pages, but in this case criticism and commerce appear to have coincided, for the rest of the critics were equally disappointed with Lehmann, who, undaunted, continued to sing for several more seasons. But the concerts in 1897 were the beginning of the end for her reputation.

The reputation of another kind of vocalist—William Jennings Bryan—was also at a low ebb when he appeared in Carnegie Hall during the same season. He had just been defeated for the presidency by William McKinley, and now, although far from finished in politics, he was on the commercial lecture circuit, still pleading the case for cheap money and against the gold standard. But the crowds that had cheered the Great Commoner during the heady days of the fall campaign were now small. Only the galleries of the hall were filled, and it was from there that the applause came when he declared that "we are fighting a battle between aggregated wealth and humanity, between the money power and the common people," and, "if you made those who make the tramps feed the tramps, they would stop making them." But, as the *Herald* said, he was appearing "in the role of a fallen idol," and although he looked well, he had lost a good deal of the magic which had surrounded him in the days immediately following the "Cross of

Gold" speech. He was never again to regain the force that had made him such an appealing figure in his first campaign.

The 1897-1898 season opened with Ysaÿe coming back to America to repeat, and, indeed, to extend and deepen, his previous triumphs. "... Even greater, even broader, even more magnetic is this Belgian virtuoso, with the mane of a lion and a heart as tender and naïve as a child's," rhapsodized one critic after the concert with the Philharmonic. He spoke for nearly everyone and the orchestra's season, which was to end tragically, opened propitiously. Seidl brought forward a handful of novelties of some interest: MacDowell's *Indian Suite*, a Rousseau-like evocation of the more pleasant aspects of life among America's first citizen; Alexander Glazunov's Fifth Symphony; and Siegfried Wagner's symphonic poem, *Sehnsucht*. The son of Richard Wagner, Siegfried was making a brave attempt to follow in his father's footsteps, and Seidl, undoubtedly influenced by respect for his *lieber Meister*, programmed the thing, to everyone's consternation. Siegfried, alas, simply did not have it.

Somewhat more encouraging to those interested in the development of new musical talent was a recital by the pupils of a teacher named Alexander Lambert who headed a music school of the same name. Damrosch and his orchestra accompanied them, and a musical journal noted with pleasure that "this concert was indeed an indisputable proof that a musical education of the most thorough nature can be obtained in New York." Lambert, himself, was crowned with laurel leaves by his faculty, received a silver loving cup from the students and a bouquet of roses from Mme. Marcella Sembrich, the singer.

Late in the year Josef Hofmann, after appearing in recital at the Met, moved to Carnegie Hall for two concerts, and "women and men fought one another, trampled upon each other and behaved in a generally barbarous way, so as to gain admission to the hall." The description may have been hyperbolic, but there was no doubt that the public loved its virtuosos and that, among them, none was more respected than Hofmann. This wild enthusiasm for the matinee idols of the concert stage undoubtedly interfered to a considerable extent with the appreciation of symphonic music. Until the virtuoso conductor replaced the recitalists—or at least was able to compete on an equal plane—in the esteem of the public, the orchestra remained secondary in musical life and the average conductor was regarded primarily as a time-beater.

The chief exception to this rule was Theodore Thomas. When he brought his Chicago Orchestra to Carnegie Hall for the first time in March, 1898, the orchestra, in the words of one critic, "covered itself with glory," and once again the legion of Thomas supporters in New York rent the air with wails over his defection to the Middlewestern wilderness. Thomas played a program of Franck, Berlioz and Saint-Saëns, with Raoul Pugno as soloist in the latter's Fifth Piano Concerto. He was "in magnificent form" and the concerto, new to New York, was "brilliant, impetuous, the passage work consisting of glancing scales and rapid chord flights."

But if a certain percentage of the musical public was envious of Chicago's good fortune, there were changes, as yet unseen, on the way. The first was the result of misfortune, for on March 28th, Anton Seidl died suddenly of a heart attack at the home of a friend, while a group of distinguished musicians, among them Ysaÿe, Pugno and Gerardy, awaited him at his own home. The last Philharmonic concert of the season was turned into a memorial program for Seidl and the Philharmonic's loyal patrons genuinely mourned the death of a controversial, competent—and often exciting—leader.

The replacement chosen for him by the orchestra (the Philharmonic was still a cooperative society governed by its players) was Emil Paur, whose reign at the Boston Symphony had been in the nature of a competently ruled interregnum, between the glamorous Arthur Nikisch and the return of the polished Wilhelm Gericke. According to that orchestra's biographer, Mary A. de Wolfe Howe, "the great things which he brought to pass were those which consorted best with the qualities represented in his very personality—a large Teutonic sincerity and robustness. The polish and the subtleties sought and wrought by his two predecessors were less attainable at his hands than a vigor and largeness hitherto unknown."

Paur's critics, both in Boston and New York, were often offended by the heavily stomping foot with which he beat time and which could often be heard thumping away above the sounds of the orchestra. He was not an inspiring conductor, but his reign at Boston was slightly more successful than his period of constitutional monarchy at the Philharmonic only because the Boston was a better orchestra. He himself had said, when taking over the Boston orchestra in 1893: "It is the best orchestra in the world." And he, like many another observer, could tell the reason why. It was the permanency of the orchestra, the lengthy period of steady employment that kept the men together, welding them into a smoothly functioning unit. He also noted the wisdom of "the absolute power given to the manager, in all business matters, and to the conductor in all artistic matters, both *only* responsible to the owner of the orchestra." The success of this combination of policies was readily apparent to inhabitants of the anarchical orchestral world of New York, and undoubtedly there was hope that the coming of Paur would somehow magically transform anarchy into the order necessary for great symphonic music.

Musical America, newly founded, and answering the need for a reliable and honest musical journal, summed up the situation aptly when it wrote that "the conditions that have existed here during the last decade were not calculated to foster the public's interest in purely orchestral music. We have become accustomed to expect only mediocre performances of our local players, and the more serious music lovers have looked upon the annual visits of the matchless Boston Symphony Orchestra as the only revelations in the way of orchestral concerts."

But Paur, no more than his predecessors, could bring about the conditions necessary for greatness. He did his best, and his championship of Richard Strauss's new—and to many ears, barbaric—music was a valuable service. But it was not long before his stomping foot was irritating New Yorkers as much as it had Bostonians. His inability to remedy the impossible conditions under which he was forced to work, and his weakness in the classic repertory, doomed his tenure to just four seasons. Walter Damrosch, sturdy pioneer that he was, simply did not have the conductorial skills and temperament to bring great music to New York. His constant economic struggles as he went his unsubsidized way didn't help, either, so it was really not until the Twenties, if then, that New York had an orchestra in a class with the Boston Symphony, which in 1898 moved its New York subscription series into Carnegie Hall, where it has continued uninterrupted to the present day.

The soloist on that inaugural occasion was Moriz Rosenthal, and he was in the midst of a fine critical flap, touched off by Huneker, the *Times* critic. It was his opinion that while technically Rosenthal had no peer, he had stopped growing emotionally. Huneker found it ludicrous that Rosenthal's best work was in inferior showpieces, works that called for technical fireworks but which were not great music. Some of Huneker's colleagues, like Krehbiel, thought that in works calling more for sensitivity than bravura, such as the Chopin B minor Sonata, he played "in plain truth, very badly indeed." But Rosenthal's devoted audience barraged his attackers with irate letters and their pressure finally forced Huneker to a defense of his position in which he quoted a German musician, saying, "Himmel! You would think there were six men at the piano. But I wouldn't want to hear him again." The trouble was that the public wanted to hear him again and again and again. This caused some of the critics to turn their attention to the audience. One found it "disheartening" that it was pieces like Liszt's "monstrous perversion of themes from *Don Giovanni*" that "called out the loudest thunders of applause."

"There is not any room for doubt that this public likes to hear Moritz Rosenthal play upon the piano," Huneker finally conceded, having witnessed a capacity audience trying to applaud him to more and more encores until the lights had to be turned out. And he also conceded that "he behaves with the most charming modesty under the stress of adulation," but he stuck to his critical guns.

Rosenthal never replied directly, but someone did think to ask him if he ever got sick of all the talk about his technical powers. His reply set the ironic coda to the whole controversy. "Does Vanderbilt," he asked, "get sick of his money?"

In December, Walter Damrosch's *Manila Te Deum*, composed in honor of Admiral Dewey's victory over the Spanish at Manila Bay, was premiered at Carnegie Hall by the Oratorio Society. The performance was under the direction of Damrosch's brother, Frank, and it was his debut in a post he would hold for decades. Dewey's success occasioned a great patriotic outburst and convinced practically everyone that America at last was a first-class military power, even though the quality of the opposition was such that Dewey's only casualty was a stoker who keeled over in the heat of his boiler room. Damrosch's piece used bugle calls and "The Star-Spangled Banner" as a *cantus firmus*, and was, by all accounts, fully as naïve as his countrymen's enthusiasm over Dewey's feat of arms. But it was momentarily so successful that the organizers of a campaign to construct a victory arch in the Admiral's honor asked the society to repeat the performance at a fund-raising concert. The Admiral himself was to be present, and New York's governor, one Theodore Roosevelt, was to be the speaker of the evening. Everyone expected the man who was shortly to emphasize the role of the navy as the chief instrument of national prestige and who was to use it to force America's way into the highest ranks of world power, to make a rousing declamation on the global significance of Dewey's victory. But that night the Rough Rider had other fish to fry. His chief topics were the duty of everyone to vote in the primaries and the need for a first-rate sanitation department in New York. The victory arch, incidentally, was never built.

At least as unsuccessful as the plans for the victory arch was the "farewell" appearance of Madame Blanche Marchesi. Once again the chief tormentor was Huneker. She, like Lehmann, was near the end of her career. And since filling Carnegie Hall was now an accepted need of everyone who desired to become, or to be remembered as, great, she had a go at it. The hall was not more than half filled, and "a good many of those who were in it seemed to be a little chilled either by the condition of the outer air or by the air which they heard inside," Huneker, who was admirably warm to his task, wrote. "Mme. Marchesi," he continued, "indulged in audible strokes of the glottis, in disjointed and irrational phrasing, in a remarkable emission of the upper tones, in singing out of tune and in some indistinct enunciation. None of these things are generally regarded as graces of song, yet the admirers of Mme. Marchesi always expect that others . . . will overlook these things because of the dramatic interpretation which she possesses."

Huneker, however, was no man to be taken in by the stratagems of a fading star. "The fact that she knows what her songs mean and that she tries to make the meaning clear to her hearers is really not especially remarkable," he said blandly. "A goodly number of singers have given evidence of human intelligence and it is now expected even of those trained in Italy."

The following season, during which the century turned, there was new evidence of America's increasing concern for the world beyond its shores. Most Americans were on the side of the Boers in their bloody war for independence from the British, so when a rally in favor of the underdogs was held at Carnegie Hall, there was a full house to hear one W. Bourke Cockran sarcastically denounce British colonialism, propose that the United States reinvigorate its old dispute with Canada over the Alaskan boundary, and, most significantly of all, ask for a wider participation in world affairs by the United States. His speech was one of a growing number of manifestations of the end of America's post-colonial preoccupation with its internal affairs, of the beginnings of a desire for a status in world affairs comparable to its ever growing power.

The meeting was a stormy one. A British sympathizer, waving a Union Jack and shouting "Rule Britannia" had the flag torn from his hands and had to be rescued by a policeman from his irate neighbors. A heckler from the gallery, described by the *Tribune* in the egregious idiom of the day as "such a hostile 'nigger heaven' as has probably never before confronted a speaker in Carnegie Hall," received a stinging rebuke from Cockran who told the audience not to hiss the man or ask his removal. "Accept him rather as a fit representative of his sentiments."

The upshot of the meeting was a resolution calling on the government to apply all possible pressure on Britain to end the South African struggle and a decision to appoint a committee to disseminate pro-Boer propaganda throughout the United States.

The meeting was certainly more stimulating than the memorial service for the evangelist Dwight L. Moody, who had been a frequent speaker at Carnegie Hall. The eulogies for the departed spirit were at least as emotion-laden as any of Moody's own harangues, one colleague stating flatly that "the greatest preacher the modern world has known has gone to his reward. If I were called upon to point out the names of the two greatest Americans of the nineteenth century, two figures which every youth in this country should follow the example of, I would say without hesitation, Abraham Lincoln and Dwight L. Moody."

Musically, the season was interesting, if not overly impressive. Paderewski was back, receiving his accustomed encomiums. Alexander Petschnikoff, the Russian violinist, made his American debut at the first concert of the Philharmonic season in a highly poetic rendition of the Tchaikovsky Piano Concerto ranging from "the mad to the melancholic," then played a joint recital with pianist Mark Hambourg which attracted a standing-room audience and good notices. Paur introduced *Ein Heldenleben* to America, scandalizing some and entrancing others. The outrage over Strauss's work, which was to reach a climax with the presentation of *Salome* at the Met in 1907, was still only a murmur, not the remarkable roar that it was to become. The reigning *enfant terrible* of the musical world, Strauss was easily the most widely debated composer of the prewar period, and curiosity over his work was immense. "Customary aesthetic standards must be resolutely put aside for here is music that is a law unto itself," one critic wrote. He had taken the symphonic poem for his own, the critic said, "and raising its emotional power to a pitch of intensity undreamed of by his predecessors, he attempted to dower it with an articulate expression that at first seemed sheer madness."

Still muted also was the laughter over the comic-and-tragic platform behavior of Vladimir de Pachmann, beginning the series of farewell concerts that were to persist into the late Twenties, with increasingly mad behavior attending them.

More encouraging than any other musical event of the season was the first New York appearance of the newly-formed Pittsburgh Symphony Orchestra at the hall. Victor Herbert, up from a job as a regimental band master, a background which his critics never let him forget and which, among other factors, probably cost him the leadership of the Philharmonic in 1902, was the conductor. Although the critics were somewhat patronizing, everyone was pleased that the Steel Town now had a real symphony orchestra. It showed that America was becoming

Brown Brothers

Lillian Nordica, one of America's first great opera singers. At the turn of the century she predicted that America was about to become "a musical Atlantis."

a first-rate power musically as well as politically. And indeed, the formation of new orchestras during the period 1890-1910 was one of the signs of genuine musical awakening in the land, even if the motivation was more often the pursuit of civic status rather than real love of music.

Herbert played a program simultaneously ambitious and popular, including Berlioz' *Roman Carnival* Overture, Tchaikovsky's Fifth Symphony, Liszt's "Mephisto Waltz," and the prelude to *Die Meistersinger*. Huneker thought the performance" not one to call forth expressions of ecstasy." The orchestra, he felt, lacked solidity of tone and attack. Krehbiel of the *Tribune* was more generous, ranking the new orchestra with those of Boston, New York, Cincinnati and Chicago. And Henry Finck of the *Post* had high praise for Herbert. He thought his work showed "thorough knowledge, sympathy, confidence and above all, enthusiasm. He is the embodiment of buoyancy itself, and as his players are young like himself, they 'just made things hum.' "

At the second performance, later in February, the same orchestra, playing a new symphonic suite, *Episodes Amoureuses*, by its conductor, got the same kind of mixed notices, Krehbiel again leading the chorus of praise and Huneker hitting below the belt. For if Herbert the conductor was plagued by his low past as a band master, Herbert the composer was equally plagued by his burgeoning future as a composer of light opera. Wrote the *Times*' man: "The recent labors of

Brown Brothers

Madame Schumann-Heink. In 1900 she and Nordica sang a concert together at Carnegie Hall symbolizing the joining of a new musical tradition with the old.

the composer in the field of light opera have shown him the easy path to popular approval and he has not been slow to tread it." So much for his suite. The world of music had certain rules of behavior for its citizens, and transgressions, particularly over the boundary toward popularity, were serious matters. Undoubtedly, Herbert's talents did not lie in the direction of the larger musical forms, but he was a craftsman in all that he attempted, a remarkably gifted man in many ways. He probably deserved a kinder critical fate.

The final season of the nineteenth century and the first of the twentieth came to an appropriate end with a joint recital of Madame Schumann-Heink and Lillian Nordica (the New World and the Old, the new times and the old sharing a platform). At that point America could look back on its humble musical beginnings and forward to an exuberant musical adolescence. There were surprises in store for those prophets who predicted a wastrel future for the somewhat eccentric and disturbed youth. For willy-nilly, the hopeless case was about to grow into a powerful force—economically, at least—on the world musical scene, and before the next century was half finished it was to be as powerful, and generally as benign, a figure in that area as it was in the political and social realm. The American Century was beginning, and its events were to be more stirring, and more stimulating, than the wildest jingoes of the nineteenth century ever predicted. Even its failures were on a magnificent scale, as were the attempts to rectify them.

Four

"The Center of the Musical World"

THE GREAT MUSICAL QUESTION OF THE TWENTIETH CENTURY'S FIRST decade, formulated and reformulated a hundred times, was whether America could build a musical culture of its own, reflecting accurately the American ambience, the qualities peculiar to the land and the time. In matters of high culture America was naïve and self-conscious, rather like a low-born and newly-rich industrialist's wife, afraid she might use the wrong fork for the salad and afraid to speak to her dinner companions for fear she would make some terrible *gaffe*, yet conscious, also, that her husband could buy and sell everyone at the table.

In her goodhearted way, she was anxious to make a genuine contribution to the larger cultural conversation in which, for reasons not always readily apparent, she seemed to be included. She wanted that quite desperately, for what was the use of economic power if she could not buy happiness with it? And the security which comes from certain knowledge of—and belief in—self. What she needed, now, more than anything else, were deeds demonstrating her virtues. She needed to show her strength to herself and to her visitors.

Visitors were legion in her great new democratic *salon.* They came, they saw—and they commented, usually with a politeness which surprised and delighted their hostess. Gustav Mahler, for instance, enjoying huge success as an opera conductor at the Met in 1907, was "impressed at every turn by the interest you show in art. . . . I have become convinced that those who speak ill of it have only themselves to blame for what they grumble at." Mahler actually spoke too soon. Within a few years he was to be a victim of his hosts' cultural insecurity and the experience would break him.

Closer to the truth was a rebellious daughter named Mary Garden, who although never an absolutely first-rate singer, was a delightful ornament on the musical scene, beautiful, fiery and determined to awaken her country's interest in new, post-romantic music. "Our people are not musically educated and are incapable of being their own judges. They have been submissive so long that they have fallen away from the thought that original opinions in such matters will and can be tolerated." For the nonce, she noted with inelegant asperity, "they are still going to broken-down old operas which nobody goes to hear in Europe."

Vincent d'Indy, the French composer, who visited here, was only slightly less critical of the American predilection for ambling amiably along behind the European pathfinders. He even pointed out that the cultural sharpsters of the Old World were making a very good thing of our naïveté. He thought American musicians would do better to study at home instead of being sent "by the hundreds to European professors who care more for the dollars of their pupils than anything else, and who generally send them back home unsuccessful virtuosos instead of the good plain artists . . . they might have become." His certainty that the best Americans could hope to be were orchestra players and chorus singers was annoying, but he was nevertheless on solid ground when he declared that "these migratory artists are just so much strength lost to America, and to art, and how much more desirable it would have been if they had become what it was intended they should be both by nature and by temperament." The obvious need in America at the time was for a broad base of competent musicians, as well as for an intelligent audience.

The trouble was that America was in a terrible hurry to catch up with a culture that had been developing for several centuries. D'Indy found this borne out by the American music which he read here. "Most of the young composers . . . were in too much haste. Here and there a touch of beauty showed what might have been produced if the author had only studied his art thoroughly," he said, urging them to slow down. For he recognized that haste makes not only waste but imitation. Our composers imitated European styles, the performers learned their techniques from European masters and worst of all, the audience for music was concerned mainly with aping the tastes of European audiences.

But there is no point in passing judgment on these sad facts. The period was probably a necessary one in the formation of a musical culture, and it demonstrated an important fact that Lillian Nordica (who had changed her name from Norton in an attempt to get ahead faster in the Europeanized musical world of her native land) pointed out as the decade drew to a close. "The keynote of the national condition," she said, returning from a lengthy tour, "is the strong desire, the steady unvacillating desire of the people at large to make for themselves a musical Atlantis, which unlike that fated city, will not sink beneath the ocean's surge, but will stand as a monument memorial in the onward sweep of the centuries."

Her metaphor may have been gaudy, and she may have overestimated the desire of "the people at large" for music, but the fact was that Americans were spending vast quantities of money on music, and the willingness of the upper and middle classes to do so was having an inexorable economic effect on the world musical scene. Call it economic determinism, or just plain determination, but the truth was that this powerful economic magnet was transforming the nation from a cultural colony into a cultural capital. As Olin Downes said, "In the first quarter of this century New York became the musical center of the world. Nowhere else was to be met in the course of a season so many commanding personalities, interpretive and creative, of the period."

At the center of the center stood Carnegie Hall, its very existence a key factor in the creation of the new cultural balance of power. If the first season or two of the new century were no more exciting than the better seasons of the hall's first decade, it is clear in retrospect that the days of musical undernourishment were gone forever and that although a rich diet of European truffles and trifles was not the best way to prepare for a healthy adulthood, the nation was building an appetite that, by the middle of the century, would give it at least the outward appearance of health.

In November, 1900, two musical giants came to Carnegie Hall for the first time. One was Ernö Dohnányi, who made his American debut at the Met, then came to Fifty-seventh Street to play his own Piano Concerto in E for the first time in America, with the Boston Symphony Orchestra. The concerto was described variously as "too long," "bizarre," "weak," and as "a vigorous work with passion and dash." But about Dohnányi's playing there was no debate at all. "Mr. Dohnányi played his work with superb skill. In the crashing finale he rose to unusual heights, and he left the audience in a state of exaltation, which earned for him half a dozen enthusiastic recalls." At his recital two days later, "he played like a young Apollo," according to the *Times*, which thought "he is the first pianist made known to this public since Paderewski who has whetted the musical appetite."

The *Times* was soon to back away from that statement, but not before it had severely criticized a second piano virtuoso, Ossip Gabrilowitsch, who came to the hall only a day after the Dohnányi recital. The young Russian, one of the most warmly generous and openhearted musical personalities of recent times, was hardly welcomed with open arms when he played the Tchaikovsky concerto with Damrosch's orchestra. Altogether too much "extravagant nonsense" had been written about him, thought the *Times*, which found him a competent technician, but neither an "opulent nor varied" colorist and, in general, "talented but unripe." It is, of course, true that this was the golden age of the piano player, with more flashy keyboard geniuses performing than at any time since, but the *Times* was wrong about Gabrilowitsch, who was solid and had staying power.

His concert was not a total failure by any means, and personally, it was an occasion of real happiness for Gabrilowitsch. Two years earlier, in Vienna, he had met Clara Clemens, Mark Twain's daughter, who was studying voice in Europe (and who was to have a modest little concert career). They fell in love and when Clara and her family left, Ossip resolved to come to America as soon as possible. He was

Museum of the City of New York

Pianist Ossip Gabrilowitsch debuted in America at Carnegie Hall, later married Mark Twain's daughter Clara and was founder-conductor of the Detroit Symphony Orchestra.

a punctilious young man who, before pressing his suit with Clara, had drawn her aside and "with great dignity" said: "I wish you to know something about me that you may not have heard. You and I are not of the same race. I descend from the Jewish people." Recalling the incident later, Clara wrote, "He would not run the risk of my being ignorant of anything connected with himself which, if I knew it, could possible cause a shadow in my thoughts."

But the affair did not prosper when Ossip first arrived in America. Clara was soon referring to him as "that Cossack"—a most inappropriate phrase for a Russian Jew—and finally Ossip wrote her a one-line note: "I renounce our friendship."

Happily, Clara was in no mood for renunciation. At his debut, "following in the footsteps of . . . Grecian ladies who had lived and suffered centuries before me," she sent a large laurel wreath which was delivered to Gabrilowitsch across the footlights. This restored their friendship, but it was nine years before they married. They were separated by their careers, Clara's mother was ill and required her attention, and Gabrilowitsch was not sure that he could make anyone happy. But in 1909 Clara heard by chance that Ossip was dying in a New York hospital. She rushed to his side and in a while, aided by her presence, he recovered from the severe mastoid infection that had threatened him. She brought him home to Hartford with her to convalesce and they were married there on October 6, 1909. Ossip spoiled their honeymoon by coming down with appendicitis, but by that time he had become "the poet of the piano," and their future was secure.

December, 1900, was another good month in Carnegie Hall. Paur brought forward two new pieces, one of them the First Symphony of Joseph Suk, Dvořák's most apt pupil (and eventually his son-in-law). Although it lacked noteworthy themes, it was commended for its brilliance of orchestration and detail. A couple of weeks later Fritz Kreisler made his New York debut as an adult (he had had an indifferent New York reception as a child prodigy some years before). He was perhaps underrated because he shared the program with a new composition. It was to the new work, not the violinist, that the critics bent their ears.

The first year of the new century in Carnegie Hall ended with

Teddy Roosevelt speaking his philosophy of charity to a YMCA meeting: "Every man of us needs help at some time, and each of us should be glad to stretch out his hand to a brother who stumbles. But no man can afford to let himself be carried, and it is worth no man's while to try thus to carry someone else." It was to be only a very short time before Theodore Roosevelt was acting out his philosophy on a wider stage than Carnegie Hall.

A month later another man who was destined to act on a far larger stage arrived at the Carnegie Hall rostrum to give the final speech in an American tour on which he earned $10,000. The young man was Winston Churchill, and he had been elected to Parliament in the famed Khaki Election of 1900, in which the vote of soldiers returned from the Boer War contributed largely to a conservative—and, therefore, imperialist—landslide. Churchill was armed with stereopticon slides taken by the dashing Richard Harding Davis and with a worldwide reputation gained as a journalist who had been captured, escaped and returned to England a hero. He needed money and reputation to get into Parliament, and more money to keep him there in style. Two books and a lecture swing through England had obtained the first, and his American tour insured the second. He later remarked to a correspondent who had unfortunately overslept and therefore missed the armored train off which Churchill had been plucked that "if I had not been caught I would not have escaped, and my imprisonment and escape provided me with the materials for lectures and a book which brought me enough money to get into Parliament."

In pro-Boer America Churchill won over his audiences by forthrightness. He reminded his listeners that it was the Boers who had declared war, been the first to invade territories not their own and to break off peace negotiations. He convinced audiences of his belief that history would justify the policies of Great Britain. One scene thrown on the screen was of the British review in front of the Government House in Pretoria. Churchill said that as an Englishman he had rejoiced to see the British flag raised on the building, but he would not wish to have it remain there unless it meant constitutional freedom, representative government, purity of administration and equal rights to all under the law. "The sentiment was applauded vigorously," according to one newspaper.

Applause of equal vigor was waiting for the next significant musical figure to make his American debut. Twenty-one-year-old Jan Kubelik, riding a wave of tremendous European acclaim (including a command performance in England) found, during his initial series of concerts the following December, that "whether he played well or ill, salvos of tremendous applause were his invariable reward, and when he finished a cheap but glittering paraphrase of the sextet in *Lucia di Lammermoor* smarting hands no longer sufficed. It was necessary to use the voice. The seeker of sensations, who had been repressing his emotions for several years, has found a long desired idol in this young Czech, and is going to make hay while the sun shines."

Kubelik was fortunate in appearance, manner and style. He gave an impression of suffering sensitivity which went well with the ladies who could make or break a concert artist at the box office. "He is small for his years . . . slender, narrow-shouldered with the stoop of an old man. He walks with a step which suggests the lisp of speech, holding his arms angularly. His face is rugged, with colorless skin, absolutely expressionless. His hair is thick and falls over his head like the mane of a horse," one description read. He was also fortunate in having a publicity-conscious manager who beat the drum for him so assiduously that the *Tribune* found it necessary to criticize the publicity as much as the artist: "It is a pretty appreciation of the notion that the world of today, in spite of all that is seen, said and written of its sordid commercialism, is still fond of a hero and needs only to be told with sufficient assiduity and emphasis that the hero is arrived to believe the statement and adopt the attitude of adoration. There is nothing essentially vicious in the doctrine and much that is essentially amiable when the object has phenomenal qualities. . . ."

Kubelik was a master fiddler who was perhaps too adroit for his own good. "He dazzled," according to the *Times*, which thought "it was all exceedingly clever, but it was not new and, still worse, it was not music."

The nice question of whether or not he was a great musician the

Culver Service

Two popular violinists of the early twentieth century—the romantic Jan Kubelik (left) and the incomparable Eugène Ysaÿe.

The Bettmann Archive

public left to the critics. They reveled in the demonstrations of his technique and were perfectly happy to hold in abeyance consideration of his ultimate musical ability. In this case, the public's lingering taste for the spectacular in music proved more or less correct. In the next years Kubelik won over many of his critical foes and came to be one of the chief ornaments of an age of fiddlers that was almost as great as the much discussed golden age of pianists.

The concerns of the weeks following Kubelik's appearance were many. There was the debut of a new American piece, which received polite notices, a symphonic prologue to Sophocles' *Oedipus Rex* by Ernest Schelling, who later became the much-beloved conductor of the Philharmonic's series of children's concerts. There was another appearance by Fritz Kreisler, who scored another modest triumph, and a performance by Eduard Zeldenrust, a Dutch pianist, who, it was noted, "hurls himself upon the instrument, which rings brilliantly under his virile attack." There was also concern over the career of Mme. Marcella Sembrich, a frequent commuter from the opera stage to Carnegie Hall, who was the victim of a sneeze. It ruptured a blood vessel in her neck, and there was doubt that she would sing again. After a month's convalescence, however, she relieved her admirers by singing a splendid program of German lieder. Later in the month Paur brought forward yet another Strauss snippet, an orchestral version of a scene from his latest opera, *Feuersnot.*

Perhaps the most interesting recital of the year came in mid-April, when Kreisler, Jean Gerardy, the cellist who had appeared earlier with the Boston Orchestra, and Josef Hofmann, who had opened the Philharmonic season playing a Rubinstein concerto, combined forces to play the Beethoven Trio in B flat in Carnegie Hall. It proved to be the sort of music unadapted to presentation in the hall, since chamber music requires a chamber not a cavern, and that fact was noted by all the critics, who thought the subtle interplay of instruments was lost in the large hall.

A different kind of failure was recorded a month later in the Carnegie Hall Chapter Room, which was inhabited periodically in this era by a ladies' group known as the Rainy Day Club. Devoted to innocent—and charitable—merriment, they provided many a fair example of the manner in which people liked to spend their time at the turn of the century. None was more typical than the cocoon dance which the ladies announced as the *chef-d'oeuvre* of their May 14th tea. Out of a cocoon, they promised, a butterfly would emerge. "Mere men came, as expected, in hordes," wrote one newspaperman, "to see the Rainy Daisies emerge in airy butterfly costumes. All their expectations were blasted in one fell swoop." The trouble was that the children of members—it was they who were supposed to don the diaphanous—had failed to get the dance ready in time for public inspection. Therefore, a lone professional dancer was engaged. But again the male onlookers were doomed to disappointment. She emerged from behind a screen, "looked witheringly" at the club's leaders, "evidently thinking that even an unsophisticated Daisy might know that no right-minded butterfly would dance without music. Then she folded her wings and silently stole away." But charity was still a winner, for behind a partition members of the club were "putting paint on cardboard in such a way as to suggest butterflies to a gifted imagination" and these objects were on sale, along with other "gorgeous things" made of tinsel and crepe paper.

The era of social good feeling was obviously in full swing. But in the smaller world of orchestral music, it was about to come to an end. Under Paur, attendance at the Philharmonic concerts had fallen off 50 per cent, and the orchestra was in serious difficulties. Still governed, as it had been since its founding, by its players, it simply could not compete with the Boston Symphony, or even with such newer entries as the Chicago and Cincinnati orchestras, as a first-rate instrument. Its directors therefore took a radical step. They engaged Damrosch, leader of the only serious local rival, as conductor, perhaps on the can't-lick-'em-join-'em theory, and Damrosch set about trying to make the orchestra over.

Opening the 1902-1903 season, he received good personal notices. Richard Aldrich, beginning his twenty-year career as music critic of the *Times*, noted that Damrosch "has worked hard for his experience . . . and largely through his own industry, courage and determination to profit by the opportunities that have been set before him, he has made himself a conductor of real power and authority." He found hope for the Philharmonic's future in Damrosch's reading of the Tchaikovsky Fifth Symphony, and warned that even the Philharmonic's best friends "cannot conceal from themselves the fact that it has had to face more criticism in recent years than ever before . . . and criticism that has been quite justified."

This statement was but the first of many tremors that would shake the orchestra for the rest of the decade. Its problems were many, and although rooted in the orchestra's peculiar method of organization, they extended in several directions. "I found to my amazement," Damrosch wrote, "that of the hundred players at the concerts less than fifty were actual members of the organization, the rest being engaged from the outside, and often changed from one concert to another. Some of the members were old men who should no longer have played in the orchestra at all . . . but . . . they naturally would not vote themselves out of office."

As Damrosch struggled with the problem of molding this orchestra into a true symphonic unit, a new orchestra appeared on the scene. Organized by Hermann Hans Wetzler, with its purpose "nothing else than the establishment of a new series of symphony concerts," the orchestra seemed to Aldrich and others to fill "no musical need now existing . . . except the need that Mr. Wetzler himself feels of exploiting his own powers as a conductor."

The opening concert, with Gabrilowitsch as soloist in Beethoven's Fourth Piano Concerto and Elsa Ruegger the soloist in Rubinstein's D minor Cello Concerto, was greeted with little enthusiasm except by a few who were intent on sounding a premature death knell for the Philharmonic. Aldrich thought the orchestra's accompaniments lacked "steadiness and elasticity" and that in general, its leader and founder "has a long road to traverse." The road was cut short, for the band persisted only two seasons. A year later, when Richard Strauss led it during his visit here, the orchestra broke down completely during a performance and there was so much bickering at rehearsals that when Strauss later encountered a contentious player in Boston he asked the man if by any chance he was from New York.

But the foundation of this orchestra, and of the Russian Symphony Orchestra two years later, as well as the sudden appearance in New York of the new Philadelphia Orchestra under Fritz Scheel, indicated growing interest in, and dissatisfaction with, the orchestral situation in the city. The Philadelphia Orchestra's debut was a highly successful one. "There is very little in its playing to indicate that it is of so recent establishment," wrote Aldrich after the November debut with Mark Hambourg as soloist in the Tchaikovsky Piano Concerto and a limpid reading of the Brahms First as the high points of the evening. In the latter, "Mr. Scheel and his men showed their powers in the best light," said Aldrich who found Scheel's readings penetrating and intellectually powerful.

Meantime, the Boston Symphony Orchestra sailed serenely on, secure in its position as the nation's one great orchestra. It had an opportunity to demonstrate its superlative qualities in December, 1902, when, toward the end of the last movement of a Schumann symphony, all the lights in Carnegie Hall suddenly went out. The orchestra finished the beat and a half which concluded the phrase they were playing, "paused composedly as if for a hyper-eloquent rest," then resumed the instant the lights were turned back on. Gericke and his men received a well-deserved ovation, for such discipline, as Damrosch was finding out, was rare in American orchestras.

Damrosch decided to attempt a radical cure. He gathered a group of wealthy patrons and urged them to subsidize the orchestra, putting up $50,000 for each of the next four seasons, the funds earmarked for the building of a permanent, salaried orchestra, and administered for the society by a board of nonplaying directors. The present orchestra would be the nucleus for a new Philharmonic, but there was no doubt that the men would no longer control the affairs of the orchestra, and that many would lose their jobs if a conductor was actually allowed to run the orchestra. Damrosch made it clear to the men that he was not seeking control of the orchestra and that he would step aside for anyone the board decided to name as conductor. At first the men liked the idea of steady salaries and the hope that, just possibly, they could, through a permanent orchestra, escape the theater pits. But in the end the older hands, those most likely to lose power and jobs, prevailed. Their letter, rejecting the offer, stated that the new plan "would so change the nature of the society as to seriously interfere with the control of its affairs by its members which has always been its vital principle, and that the future prosperity of the society would thereby be impaired."

The society tried to stave off the inevitable. For the next three seasons they indulged themselves in the anarchy of guest conductors, some good, some indifferent, then hired a good-natured but not particularly distinguished permanent conductor, and finally capitulated to a group of determined women who succeeded in reorganizing the society on precisely the lines Damrosch had suggested.

He, as usual, landed on his feet after what he himself termed the "blunder" of his season with the Philharmonic. Among the men who had agreed to underwrite the reorganization scheme was Harry Harkness Flagler, a symphony buff of long standing. Shortly after the members of the orchestra rejected the Damrosch plan, Flagler got in touch with the conductor, and offered to back Damrosch's own Symphony Society and to help raise funds for it among his friends. He did this for a decade, then took over full subsidization all by himself, principally because he found it easier to give all the money himself than to be constantly proselytizing his friends for aid. He was a rare figure among the wealthy of the time—a man to whom music was not mere duty, but sheer pleasure. He had even bothered to cultivate a fairly intelligent taste for it, something most of his fellow Americans had failed miserably to do.

Precisely how unsophisticated American musical tastes were in this era was discovered by Victor Herbert when he polled his Sunday matinee audience on their favorite music. Their choices were: Suppé's *Poet and Peasant* Overture, the March from Raff's *Lenore* Symphony, Rubinstein's *Melody in F*, Massenet's *Neapolitan Scenes*, and selections from Herbert's own operettas. Not a single symphony was chosen, not a single work by the acknowledged classic or romantic masters. A similar poll in St. Louis found Liszt's Second *Hungarian Rhapsody* heading the list, and the highest ranking symphony—Beethoven's Fifth—in twenty-eighth place.

The sort of new music that attracted the most serious attention was typified by the Carnegie Hall reception of Edward Elgar's cantata, *The Dream of Gerontius*, a work which had rescued its composer from obscurity when it was first produced in England in 1900. It then received great acclaim in Europe, and a hardly less enthusiastic reception when Frank Damrosch and the Oratorio Society offered it on March 27, 1903.

This last labored gasp of the great tradition of English choral writing, with its emotional climaxes of allegedly "indescribable power," was a *fin de siècle* success, pleasing critics and audiences alike. For this was a profoundly conservative musical public, frightened of even such tentatively transitional figures as Strauss and Mahler, anxious for the imitators of the great romantic tradition to reassure them that their taste for the romantic, for the self-consciously beautiful, was still viable.

Happily, the Elgar fad was short-lived, and the presentation of his next oratorio, *The Apostles*, the following year marked the beginning of enthusiasm's end, as critics sought to rationalize their approval of *The Dream* and their dislike of its successor, in which Elgar "wandered into many trackless paths of harmony.... There are long stretches of dullness and tediousness. . . . Sometimes the composer seems as one overcome and hampered by the very vastness of his apparatus. More often he seems to have little to say and to be saying it laboriously...."

But, of course, it is unfair to categorize an age totally. There was an audience for fine performances in a different tradition. The artistic success of Franz Kneisel's quartet, "one of the greatest forces for good in the musical history of this country," was an example of a countervailing force. Founded by Colonel Higginson and composed of members of his orchestra, it had, since 1885, been playing an austere program of excellent chamber music, the only such group on a high professional level in the country. It frequently played the smaller halls in Carnegie Hall as well as other New York halls, and it succeeded in making attendance at its concerts a *cachet* of musical sophistication. In 1903 the quartet moved to New York, where its early economic trials were severe. Only the intervention of a handful of its most devoted admirers prevented it from moving elsewhere when support for its activities failed to rise above the marginal level.

Undoubtedly one factor that kept it before the New York public was that there was no place else for the quartet to go. On its tours it encountered bottomless ignorance and indifference. It received requests for all-Wagner programs and commiseration because its leader could not afford a full orchestra instead of only four players.

The first season (1903-1904) the Kneisel Quartet spent in New York was a season of considerable orchestral and vocal excitement in Carnegie Hall, but before the musical season began, the hall withstood—while the city rebuffed—an invasion by the renowned evangelist, John Dowie. Three thousand of his followers from Zion, Illinois, arrived on eight special trains, intent on turning the big city from its wicked ways. Dowie had his troubles, beginning with the reluctance of his own flock to submit themselves to the possible temptations of the metropolis. He had to issue an ultimatum to pry them out of Zion.

A message heralded his arrival and announced his plans for great mass meetings in Madison Square Garden and Carnegie Hall. "Beneath the banner of the Christian Catholic Church and the Stars and Stripes," he promised to proclaim in addition to the "everlasting gospel of the Kingdom of God," "repentance, restitution, salvation, healing and holy living . . . obedience, the eleven commandments and [sic] the law of love, Christian union and cooperation in church, home, business and state, the downfall of all forms of apostasy, secrecy and tyranny," and, in case he had left anything out, "the restoration of all things."

But as it had to so many of his ilk before and after him, the great city turned a deaf ear to him. The Madison Square Garden meetings were a flop and by the time Dowie hit Carnegie Hall his audiences were small enough to fit into the basement lyceum, and the newspapers were proclaiming him a failure.

The assault of a famous singer on the sensibilities of New Yorkers was equally disastrous. Adelina Patti, the Baronesse Cederström, sixty years old and the owner of something like a hundred canary birds, was greeted by a vast crowd when she gave her first recital in

Carnegie Hall, some forty-four years after she had first captured the city. "It would have been," the *Tribune* reported, "a moment to warm the hearts of her old admirers, who were as numerous as the lovers of artistic song in the olden days, had there not weighed upon them the memories of a decade ago when last she said farewell to them, and a woeful apprehension that old ideals must be shattered and their fond belief in their idol be turned into mockery and derision. The apprehension had a bitter realization."

The great voice was gone, and nearly everyone regretted with Aldrich of the *Times* that she had chosen to come back and spoil their memories. As encores she chose "The Last Rose of Summer," "Home Sweet Home," and "as an additional boon, an unspeakably vulgar sentimental song, written especially for her, fitted for the artistic plane of the vaudeville stage, called 'The Last Farewell.'"

This last sally drew an angry letter from the song's composer, who said there was not a vulgar word in it and that he and the singer were deeply insulted. The *Times* clarified: it had not meant the song was coarse, just dull. All of which must have worried Mme. Patti all the way to the bank. In the middle of the season when she was due to set forth on her lengthy tour of the nation, singing mainly American and English ballads, along with a few familiar arias, it was announced that her fee was to be $5,000 per concert and that she would sing only two songs plus encores, on each program. That was about all she could manage; one critic noted that she even became short of breath singing "Home Sweet Home."

Much more successful were the recitals of Marcella Sembrich and Nellie Melba. The former's program moved Aldrich to a rare pitch of enthusiasm: "Such an occasion does honor alike to the public and to the great singer, signifying the potency of her consummate art and the appreciation of its fine and gracious qualities, an understanding of their inestimable value and rarity." It was not the quality of her voice alone which accounted for Sembrich's greatness. Aldrich mentioned, among other qualities, "the deeply musical feeling that Providence so often withholds with its gift of voice, the high intelligence, the swift prescience, the wide sympathy with music of many different kinds, periods and nationalities, and the enthusiasm and zeal that prompt to study great voices and perfect vocalism. . . ."

Melba, singing her farewell for the season in New York, received similar acclaim. The *Times* noted that "her runs, trills and staccato notes glittered and scintillated, [and] especially in the aria from *Lucia* she compelled a new admiration for the marvelous vocal mechanism over which she has such absolute command, and which has not its superior at the present day."

On that evening (December 18th) she was recalled at least eight times, finally ran out of encores and was forced to sit down at the piano and accompany herself in "Comin' Through the Rye." "Even then her delighted admirers seemed loath to leave her and remained massed in the aisles near the stage, applauding her, and some calling out, as this was her farewell concert of the season—'Good-by' which was drowned out with cries from others—'no, no, only au revoir!' At last the prima donna bade them all good night and withdrew, after which the gathering slowly left the auditorium."

Equally successful with the public (hundreds of them cheerfully shared the stage with her), if not with the critics, was Mme. Ernestine Schumann-Heink. She was aging, but "the power, range and richness of her contralto voice seemed as great as they ever were," to many critics. But others questioned her forcing in the lower range, and her unsteadiness and tendency to stray off pitch in the upper tones. Some even found "a certain monotony in the color of her voice." But the harshest critic had to admit that "there are very few people who can fill Carnegie Hall with such a throng of enthusiastic admirers by their sole, unaided efforts."

If Schumann-Heink represented the best of the musical old guard, a young poet who came to Carnegie Hall during the middle of the musical season represented the best of a rising literary generation. William Butler Yeats spoke, on no less a subject than the need for revolution, at a meeting presided over by the ubiquitous Cockran, who was making a career out of plaguing the British. Yeats was on tour to propagandize Irish nationalism, and after paying polite tribute to the aid of his host country to his cause, he declared that "it now remains for us to see to it that Irish poetry of the remote past is kept

Culver Service

William Butler Yeats. The Irish poet came to New York in 1904 to plead the cause of Irish independence, spoke of calling up "phantom armies" to guard the nation.

alive and that the sacrifices of Ireland's dead patriots were not in vain. It has been said that all one needs in order to create a nation is a cemetery and a library, and the intellectual improvement of Ireland was begun some years ago with the idea of creating that library. We must never forget that it rests with us to call up the phantom armies of the past and to ask them to guard our future. If these phantom armies will answer our calls, we need have no fear for the future of our nation." There was much of the essential Yeats in that statement, his romanticism, his national fervor, even his mysticism, although it created but a small stir in New York at the time.

Less successful than Yeats (who at least drew some favorable newspaper attention) was a young cellist named Pablo Casals. He was simply too austere for America's half-formed taste. His audiences were small and often bored by programs that were heavy-laden with the severely beautiful works of Bach. They were also put off by Casals' rather forbidding mannerisms, or rather his lack of mannerisms. Since he lacked the lengthy locks which Paderewski was wont to shake, or the idiosyncrasies of a de Pachmann, or the gaudy style of a Kubelik, his manager suggested that he might at least manage a smile or two. Casals thought so little of the notion that he changed managers. Years later, counting a packed house come to hear him play the Bach which an earlier age had rejected, he commented grimly: "And I'm still not smiling."

While all this was proceeding, the orchestral season, from its opening, had proved to be rather more successful than anyone had dared hope. Jacques Thibaud, the violinist, debuted with the Wetzler orchestra and was enthusiastically greeted as "an artist of the finest fiber." The premiere, by the Boston Orchestra, of Alexander Glazunov's Fourth Symphony was also praised. One critic was relieved to discover that he was not "a Russian of the untamed bear variety. His paw is shod in velvet and he dances to every tune but the tartar."

More importantly, the Philharmonic was actually managing to have an interesting season. The public was responding to the opportunity to compare various conductors and, by and large, the season was "free of the sins" of virtuoso conducting. Although none of the conductors "really made a complete exposition of himself and his art or

Culver Service

Pablo Casals. His playing was too austere for the American public when he debuted in 1904. He fired a manager who suggested that his receipts would be better if he smiled more often.

[showed] what his highest capacities [were]," there were some highly gratifying concerts. The first visitor to show his wares was the Frenchman Edouard Colonne who, perhaps seeing a chance to snare a permanent position, took the trouble to bring minutely marked orchestral scores with him. He was well received, but he made the mistake of playing Berlioz' *Symphonie Fantastique.* One critic, demonstrating the peculiar tastes of the age, thought it was "unfortunate that the Philharmonic's public had no opportunity to hear the famous French conductor in music of more substantial quality and greater value as music. . . ."

Victor Herbert, conducting Schubert's Eighth Symphony, his own *Hero and Leander* Suite and Liszt's Second Piano Concerto, with Alfred Reisenauer making his New York debut as soloist, fared no better and no worse than Colonne. Far more successful was Felix Weingartner. He conducted, among other pieces, his own symphonic poem, *King Lear*, and was so popular that a special matinee concert had to be arranged to give his audience an extra opportunity to hear him. "His keenly analytical power and divination of the essential spirit of the music he had in hand . . . his sympathy and glowing enthusiasm were always foremost in his readings; and with these his remarkable mastery of detail and his feeling for proportion, made for some of the most remarkable performances of the season."

But even more remarkable was the appearance of a dark horse in the race for popular approval, one Wassily Safonoff, who was barely known outside of his native Moscow. He was a floridly romantic musician, but he was a splendid showman, among the first modern conductors to dispense with the baton, and New York's matrons fell in love with the graceful patterns he traced with his expressive hands. "It doubtless came as a surprise that the man least known to the public should have made the deepest impression," wrote Aldrich. "The scenes that were witnessed at Mr. Safonoff's concerts were such as have had few parallels in the Philharmonic Society's history." After conducting works by Tchaikovsky, Beethoven, Rubinstein, and Glazunov, at his first appearance, "he was recalled a dozen times, cheered, pelted with flowers and made so much of generally that . . . his eyes filled with tears, presumably of happiness."

The reception of Richard Strauss, who conducted three concerts of the Wetzler orchestra, as well as the premiere of his *Sinfonia Domestica* with the Philharmonic, was far more controversial. He was "the man of the hour in the musical world," a stormy petrel with a shrewd business eye, and he intrigued New York as a personality, even though his podium manner was extremely reserved.

"He is a young man of unpretentious appearance," one newspaper wrote, "slim, loose-jointed as he threads his way among the orchestra to the front of the platform, singularly lacking in distinction of presence. His face, smooth except for an almost imperceptible mustache and surmounted by a remarkably high forehead, is grave and impassive; and not withstanding the bald spot in evidence as he turns toward the orchestra, he looks his youth. His methods as a conductor are extremely reserved. His beat is quiet, but firm; he has few significant gestures except at some of the most important climaxes, when he summons the power of the bass instruments through an insistent beckoning with his left hand, of which otherwise he makes little use."

At his first concert Wetzler conducted *Also sprach Zarathustra,* tenor David Bispham sang three Strauss songs, then the composer conducted *Ein Heldenleben.* At the next concert Strauss's wife sang more of his songs and he conducted *Enoch Arden* while Bispham recited the poem. And at the third concert he repeated *Ein Heldenleben,* did *Don Quixote* and accompanied his wife in seven of his own songs.

All of which set the stage for the debut of the *Sinfonia Domestica.* Intended as a depiction of a day in the life of the composer and his family, it was one of Strauss's less happy inspirations. One critic complained that program music had to be based on recognizable subject matter if the listener was to make sense out of it. Since no one was privy to the domestic arrangements of the Strauss household, it was difficult to figure out what it all meant. This was surely obtuse criticism, since Strauss's intent was to use his home symbolically, not realistically. More germane was the statement of another critic that the piece ranged from naïve simplicity in some passages to needless complexities in others and that the whole thing was disproportionate in construction. On the whole, the premiere was not a successful one, and, indeed, Strauss's entire visit was a matter for much conjecture in the press, which seems, in retrospect, to have made his music seem needlessly difficult. "That the composer has succeeded in the larger purpose he had in view cannot at present be successfully maintained. . . . How far Dr. Strauss himself can succeed in seeking it remains to be seen. The power and beauty of much of his music is felt as well as its ugliness."

The last point, these days, seems a strange one. For his dissonances were mild compared to those which were to come after him only a few years later. The prevailing opinion was that Strauss, who now seems so transparent, so easily approachable, was just too intellectual, too indirect in his appeal, and too advanced generally to find wide public approval.

The season of 1904-1905 was one of returns and renewals. A number of favorites returned to Carnegie Hall, among them Josef Hofmann, Ysaÿe and Paderewski. Hofmann and Paderewski disappointed, in differing degrees, because they insisted on pleasing the crowd rather than the critics. Ysaÿe, however, received full recognition as the master he was. Another who returned, after an absence of four years, was Fritz Kreisler. This violinist did not travel an easy road to recognition; his early appearances as a prodigy in 1888 had been merely promising, and his recitals early in the decade had been only modestly successful. But now, at last, the promise that the more astute observers had heard in his playing was delivered. When he appeared with the Damrosch orchestra, playing concertos by Beethoven and Brahms, Aldrich remarked that each time Kreisler returned in the years since his American debut he showed "steady progress, the result of rich endowment in talent and unwearied industry. Now he . . . makes it clear that he has attained a position incontestably among the great ones of his art."

Two debuts by pianists that season are of interest because of factors unrelated to their technical powers. The first was the appearance, accompanied by Damrosch's orchestra, of Rudolf Friml, who had first come to New York as Kubelik's accompanist and who played some of his own pieces on a lengthy program. "As a composer he has little to offer," one critic remarked, adding that "his conception of the pianist's

Richard Strauss conducted his own controversial compositions in a series of concerts at Carnegie Hall in 1904.

The Bettmann Archive

art is . . . one in which technical brilliancy, crude and garish contrasts of crashing resonances and purring pianissimos prevail. He expects continually to dazzle and excite his hearers and has little concern with the inner spirit of beauty. . . . It is all extremely unimportant from an artistic point of view. . . ." The trouble, of course, was that Friml had not yet found his *métier*. When he turned to composition for the musical stage his talents for showmanship and unimportance were to pay off handsomely.

The case of Olga Samaroff who, despite her exotic name, was an American girl from Texas, was somewhat different. She was the first American woman to achieve any sort of reputation at all as a concert pianist. A girl of remarkable power and endurance, a sort of native Teresa Carreño, she proved to be "painstaking and resolute" but failed to "make it clear that she possessed the temperament or the poetic feeling to fill . . . music with the breath of life." She shortly became the wife of a rising young conductor named Leopold Stokowski.

The orchestral season was, with one exception, a duplicate of the preceding one. Damrosch brought forward two important novelties on the same program, Elgar's symphonic overture, *In the South*, and Gustav Mahler's Fourth Symphony, and neither was particularly well received. The Philharmonic proceeded on its comparatively prosperous way with guest conductors Safonoff receiving the public adulation and Weingartner the critical acclaim. Perhaps the most interesting of the society's concerts was the one on January 24th, 1905, at which Eugène Ysaÿe and Eugene d'Albert appeared as soloists in their own works with each man conducting the orchestra for the other's accompaniment. They also had a go at the *Kreutzer* Sonata together but were defeated by the vast reaches of the hall.

The exception to the orchestral routine of the season was the appearance of a new orchestra, the Russian Symphony, conducted by Modeste Altschuler. Founded to present the works of gifted young Russian composers, it was a vitalizing force in American music. Rachmaninoff, Scriabin, Mischa Elman and Josef Lhévinne were among the soloists who made their first appearances here with the orchestra. In its on-and-off existence during the next fifteen seasons it probably presented more new works than any other orchestra playing regularly in New

York. The only trouble was that most of the new pieces were not very important. The idea of bringing to America the works of the obscure —and distinctly minor—Russian contemporaries was ultimately self-defeating, for they were simply not weighty enough composers on which to found a solid repertory. The group's very first concert indicated this. Honoring the 100th anniversary of the birth of Glinka, Altschuler programmed excerpts from his *A Life for the Czar*, distinctly minor music that called forth critical warnings to Altschuler to mend his ways. But he was an inventive program maker, and the gimmicks he thought up to build interest in the orchestra were, for the most part, pleasant and good fun. In his first season, for example, he prevailed on Safonoff to play the celeste part in excerpts from the *Nutcracker* Suite, and the delight of the audience in seeing a conductor being conducted, particularly in such charming music, forced the orchestra to repeat the piece not once, but twice.

The season of 1905-1906 was more interesting than its predecessor, from the first concert of the Philharmonic to the farewell of the esteemed Gericke from the Boston podium. The Philharmonic opening was the American debut of Willem Mengelberg, the conductor who was to write his name so large in the history of that organization in the Twenties. His program, the afternoon of November 10th, included Schumann's Fourth Symphony, Brahms's Violin Concerto and *Ein Heldenleben.* "Seldom," wrote Aldrich, "has the Philharmonic played with more vivifying spirit, and seldom have its players been more thoroughly controlled by the purposes of the conductor." Nowhere did Mengelberg show his mettle more advantageously than in the Strauss work, but, unfortunately, the audiences began walking out in the middle of it. The appearance of a young English violinist named Otie Chew also dulled what should have been an illustrious occasion. "It would be a mournful task to enumerate the defects of her playing," wrote one critic, who hoped they were the results of nervousness or illness rather than lack of talent. Another, representing a minority, was so affronted by the concert, and his review was so scathing, that Carnegie Hall's management took the unprecedented step of barring him from the hall.

The return of Jan Kubelik, later in the month, was an occasion for much excited talk by a public which was avid for details of life in his castle in Bohemia, his aristocratic connections, the insured value of his fingers, even his new-born twins. His fans were out in force at his concerts, applauding eagerly, "sometimes in the wrong place," and, in general, throwing obstacles in his path to critical recognition with terrible abandon. But this time even the critics had to admit that he was a talented violinist, something more than a mere dazzler.

The appearance, shortly thereafter, of Vincent d'Indy at the head of the Boston Symphony, the first time anyone other than its titular leader conducted it on tour, caused nowhere near the excitement of, say, a Strauss or even a virtuoso instrumentalist. He led the orchestra in a program of modern French music, including his own Second Symphony and works by Fauré and Dukas. Some "doubted whether he presented a more intelligible performance of his own symphony than Mr. Gericke gave last January." Besides, the piece was not particularly well-liked. "An unmeaning cacaphony . . . a deliberate seeking for effects that have never entered the ken of musicians of the older days," wrote one critic, who thought the modern Frenchman wanted to "reconstitute our ears and force the acceptance of these sounds that now seem to most so grating."

Much the same attitude greeted a young pianist who came to America for the first time a month later, preceded by tales of "past and present greatness," according to which he had been a child prodigy who had been preserved from the special hell reserved for artists who force their talents too early. Now, it was said, he was a mature artist, however youthful in appearance. The young man's name was Arthur Rubinstein (the "h" was later dropped from his first name) and the reviews of his debut with the Philadelphia Orchestra and a subsequent recital were at best mixed. Everyone conceded his talent, but his austere virtuosity ran counter to the current of the time. Critics and public alike thought he lacked the ability to poeticize. That this judgment was unfair to the young artist has been borne out by the passage of time—and much bitterness on the part of Rubinstein who after this tour, and again after a tour in the Twenties, foreswore an America which refused to recognize his greatness as the rest of the world did. It was not until 1938 that we at long last elevated him to the pianistic pantheon where he belonged.

Surely, he had good reason for bitterness. Rarely has an artist received a more patronizing review than he got from one musical magazine which suggested a remarkable cure for his virtuosity. "Let the next five years bring him some genuine heartache, such as befalls the majority of us," it suggested. "Let some American girl twist his heartstrings around her dainty little finger and then break the alleged seat of affection and—Arthur Rubinstein will be the greatest of all pianists."

There were also invidious comparisons of Rubinstein to Josef Lhévinne, who made his debut later in the same month with the Russian Symphony Orchestra. Henry T. Finck of the *Post* called the Russian's debut "an immediate and a really sensational success. An attempt has been made lately to introduce a new [Anton] 'Rubinstein' to local audiences, but the real Rubinstein II is Mr. Lhévinne. He has the great Anton's technique, his dash and bravura, his brilliancy and a good deal of his leonine power. He can make a piano sing, too." There was general concurrence in this and perhaps a historical lesson for the modern observer. The taste of the age ran toward the big game. It demanded as well a great deal of raw emotionality. Lhévinne could communicate this emotionality; Rubinstein whom Thomas Mann called "that civilized man," could not, although modern listeners find no lack of sensitivity in his prodigious technique. In a sense, it took the American audience thirty years to grow up to him.

In the month of Rubinstein's debut, Mark Twain came to the hall to speak in behalf of a fund-raising drive for Booker T. Washington's Tuskegee Institute. He was impressed by Washington whom he called, in his *Autobiography*, "a most remarkable man" and "a fervent and effective speaker on the platform." The old writer's comment on the meeting dealt not with its more serious aspects, but with the crowd that pressed around him after his speech. "It always happens," he wrote. "I shake hands with people who used to know my mother intimately in Arkansas, in New Jersey, in California, in Jericho—and I have to seem glad and so happy to meet these persons. . . . And this is the kind of thing that . . . turns a person into a polite liar and deceiver, for my mother was never in any of those places."

Orchestrally the year saw a beginning and an ending. Wilhelm Gericke, unable to come to terms on a new contract with Colonel Higginson, decided to leave the Boston Symphony Orchestra. At one of his last New York concerts he conducted the local premiere of Mahler's Fifth Symphony which met a typically mixed, but generally unfavorable reception. H. E. Krehbiel spoke for most of its hearers when he wrote that Mahler "has moments of frank and simple utterances but . . . he is obsessed by the prevalent conviction that when an ounce of inspiration cannot be commanded, a pound of reflection and labor will serve as well." A month after conducting this concert Gericke gave his last New York farewell and was presented with the usual large laurel wreath as a parting gift.

Meantime, the Philharmonic had found a new permanent conductor. Wassily Safonoff had returned for still another popular triumph and a group of ladies finally decided they could not bear to live without him for another moment. They therefore raised $45,000 to buy him for the Philharmonic. His price was $15,000 more than they had in hand, but they scurried around and raised the additional money. In effect he would receive a thousand dollars per concert, "the highest fee ever paid to a conductor anywhere," according to *Musical America*, which noted with some wonder that it was as much as the top singers at the Metropolitan were getting. In opera-mad New York this was a phenomenon, perhaps the first sign of a rise in the status of orchestral music to a point of parity with opera.

Safonoff returned to Russia for a rest, then came back to New York exuding an affable confidence in the future. "I find the people very musical," he said of his new audience. "And yet they are too practical to concentrate themselves sufficiently on artistic matters to produce great creative spirits, but that will come."

His confidence was not without reason, for the 1906-1907 season was a success. Oscar Hammerstein I was launching his new opera company, challenging the domain of the Metropolitan with such stars as Melba, Edouard de Reszke, Tetrazzini and Lilli Lehmann, and with productions of the works—mostly French—which the Met had been ignoring in favor of the Italian and Wagnerian repertory. These were beginning to bore the public, as were the moth-eaten mountings of Met productions. For the next few seasons, until Hammerstein was bought off by the Met's wealthy board of directors, his opera was to provide New York's major musical excitement, with new productions, new stars (like Geraldine Farrar and Mary Garden), even new operas (*Hänsel und Gretel* and *The Girl of the Golden West* among others).

With opera dominating the musical scene it was natural that the Carnegie Hall season began with the appearance of Ruggiero Leoncavallo and an orchestra said to belong to La Scala, but which, the moment it played, proved to be a pick-up band. The singers Leoncavallo brought with him proved to be almost as inept as he was as a conductor. Wrote Krehbiel: ". . . an evening of operatic tune, long drawn out and made hot and wearisome by the style of the singers. In a way the concert was an object lesson in the passionate melody of the younger . . . school of Italian opera composers—its origin, development into a tiresome formulary and its decay."

The formal opening of the orchestral season came a month later. Walter Damrosch's New York Symphony Society had as its guest on that occasion the venerable French composer Camille Saint-Saëns. "Short of stature, but robust in figure, of quick and rather precise movements, gray bearded but darkly thatched except for an oncoming bald spot, whose face, with its startling aquiline nose, has long been familiar from his portraits," the seventy-two-year-old composer's reception "lacked nothing in warmth and enthusiasm," including the inevitable floral tribute. In the course of three concerts the old gentleman soloed in all five of his piano concertos and, as Damrosch said, "his extraordinary vitality and the fluency of his playing amazed us all. . . . We had heard many stories from French musicians of his 'nasty temper' at rehearsals and his caustic comments on this or that phrasing. . . . We were all very agreeably disappointed in finding him genial, cheerful and grateful for what we were able to give him. He even insisted on playing the organ himself at my performance of his Symphony No. 3. . . ."

A week after Saint-Saëns' American debut, Karl Muck brought the Boston Symphony Orchestra to Carnegie Hall for his New York debut as its leader. He divided his program between Beethoven's Fifth Symphony and some shorter Wagnerian selections; it was "a performance . . . that at every point compelled admiration." Muck, who was to suffer much in this country during World War I, was tall and spare, almost ascetic looking. His manner toward the orchestra was straightforward and explicit and he had the classical merit of knowing what he wanted and getting it.

A superb technician, one of the first of the late-nineteenth- and early-twentieth-century leaders to submerge his personality in the music, to make the attempt to unlock the message of the composer from the notes of his score, Muck was one of the great conductors and under him the Boston Symphony reached new heights of precision of ensemble, of balance of tone, of orchestral color.

Quite a different sort was Wassily Safonoff who opened his first season as director of the Philharmonic on November 16th, with Josef Lhévinne as soloist in the Rubinstein D minor Concerto. Beethoven's *Coriolanus* Overture, Tchaikovsky's Fifth Symphony and Mozart's *Eine Kleine Nachtmusik*, previously unplayed in New York, made up the rest of the program. Safonoff, according to one observer, "still clutches, whirls, slits and pokes the atmosphere with his hands in a way that is disturbing to the eye but must be condoned if it is necessary to the attainment of his purposes." In Russian music the batonless one was at his best and there was general agreement, on the opening night, that his Tchaikovsky was superb, his Beethoven all right and the Mozart piece indifferent.

Almost simultaneous with the Safonoff debut, Moritz Rosenthal returned to Carnegie Hall to "a reception seldom equaled in the degree of enthusiasm manifested." Accompanied by the Damrosch orchestra, he played works by Chopin, Liszt and Brahms, stirred at least a thousand of his hearers to rush the stage at the end of the concert. No wonder, following such adulation, that he told an interviewer that "the Americans are very musical, vastly more so than the English. They have more temperament, more nerves, and therefore they enjoy music more, since it appeals primarily to the nerves. . . ."

As for his own nerves, they were apparently set on edge by modern music. He conceded that composers "have the desire and the will to

Brown Brothers

Camille Saint-Saëns was soloist in his own piano compositions with Walter Damrosch and the New York Symphony in 1906. He insisted on playing the organ part of his Third Symphony. His response to New York was "genial, cheerful and grateful."

do something great, something not in accordance with the accepted idea . . . but the trouble is they are not big enough to do it." One of those not quite big enough for the tastes of people like Rosenthal was Bruckner, whose Seventh Symphony was on Karl Muck's second Boston Symphony program at Carnegie Hall. It was damned with the mildest sort of praise.

Another modern who fared indifferently in the same month was Alexander Scriabin, who performed with the Russian Symphony under Safonoff. He was soloist in his own piano concerto. His compositions, which received frequent playings by himself and by the Russian Orchestra throughout the season, were thought to be quite expressive of his personality—"charmingly fluent and melodious"—but nearly everyone agreed that his was a distinctly minor talent. It was nowhere near as minor as that of George Chadwick, an American composer who essayed a symphonic poem on no less a subject than *Cleopatra*, a work which received the noncommittal notices that New York critics especially reserved for American works, when Karl Muck, beginning the great Boston tradition of searching out American pieces to play, presented it in January.

The appearance of Ossip Gabrilowitsch playing the Tchaikovsky Piano Concerto was much more warmly greeted. There was agreement that he had "materially advanced and ripened in his art since he was last here, and to all his fire and impetuosity he had added breadth of style and repose." He, like Fritz Kreisler, had built his career slowly, but well, and he was on his way to lasting regard in the minds of critics and public.

The orchestral and recital season was unusually good in 1906-1907, and so was the choral season, usually the weakest part of New York's musical life. The appearance of the huge (220 voices) Mendelssohn Choir of Montreal with the Pittsburgh Symphony under Emil Paur, in a program of incredible length, was its chief ornament. The chorus received excellent notices, although it quite drowned out the orchestra at several points in the Beethoven Ninth Symphony. An audience used to the rather loose work of the Oratorio Society was impressed by the "precision and accuracy" of a group so large.

The appearance of Edward Elgar with the Oratorio Society, conducting his own works, *The Apostles* and *The Kingdom* (the latter was a premiere), proved disappointing. The new work was pronounced "irretrievably dull," and the old one did not seem to improve with greater familiarity. Elgar proved to be a competent conductor of his own works, but he was composing in a form which not even his employment of all the newer musical resources could rescue.

The year in Carnegie Hall came to an end with an exercise in futility of far greater magnitude than Elgar's oratorios. This was the peace conference organized and directed by Andrew Carnegie. Three thousand delegates from all over the world assembled in Carnegie Hall on April 15th to explore together, for a month, ways and means to promote peace. They were a distinguished lot and throughout the month they listened to speech after speech extolling the virtues of peace, and speaking hopefully, even confidently, of a warless future.

The address made by Mayor McClellan of New York was typical. "That a movement for universal peace is considered seriously, that many practical men believe that it may in God's good time and in God's own way come to fruition is because of a new spirit that influences mankind," he said. "Your duty, as that of everyone who knows the difference between national honor and national land-lust, between true courage and swash-buckling, is to convince the world that man has a higher, nobler mission than to be forever at his brother's throat; that war should be resorted to only as a last, desperate remedy for injustices and oppression. The task which you have set yourselves, and which can be accomplished, is to cultivate a spirit of sober common sense among men, a sense which will cause them to think twice before going to extremes, and to hesitate before glorifying the war spirit. To such a public spirit governments must bow."

But the government in Washington, personified by Teddy Roosevelt, was having no part in such do-goodism. He sent a message to the opening session which must have come as a shock to those gentle souls who were giving nineteenth-century optimism a final outing before packing it away in the attic with mankind's prettier souvenirs. T.R. thought it might be a good idea if they considered the paradox of peace through strength. Busy building a foreign policy whose object was to enmesh us firmly in foreign entanglements, he wrote a statement which sounds as if it could have come out of Washington, circa 1960. Wrote the man with the big stick: "Harm and not good would result if the most advanced nations, those in which the most freedom for the individual is combined with the most efficiency in securing orderly justice as between individuals, should by agreement disarm and place themselves at the mercy of other peoples less advanced, of other peoples still in the stage of military barbarism or military despotism. Anything in the nature of a general disarmament would do harm and not good if it left the civilized and peace-loving peoples, those with the highest standards of municipal and international obligation and duty unable to check the other peoples who have no such standards, who acknowledge no such obligations."

Andrew Carnegie's meeting was harmless enough—it passed any number of unexceptionable resolutions which betrayed a total lack of healthy pessimism about the nature of man—and then disbanded, having done a good thing. Undoubtedly it was one of the few occasions which it is correct to see through a pale golden haze of genuine nostalgia, for such innocent optimism was shortly to be destroyed forever.

Late in the next (1907-1908) season, Karl Muck and the Boston Symphony Orchestra offered a unique concert—the first of its kind by a major orchestra in New York. They presented a complete program of American music. It was not until 1939 that a similar program was again presented (and again by the Boston Symphony). The pieces programmed by Muck, who was shortly to return to Germany, were none of them notable. Works by Frederick S. Converse and Charles Martin Loeffler preceded a performance of Edward MacDowell's *Indian Suite.* The performance of the latter was brought about by tragic circumstances—the death of the composer after three years of severe mental illness in which he regressed to a childlike state. His death, on January 23rd, had brought about more performances of his work than had ever before been heard in one season in New York.

At the time many attempts to assess the meaning and ultimate value of his work had been made, and the circumstances of his break with

Columbia University, whose music department he headed for some years and had tried to make over into a more vitally creative institution, were extensively reviewed. His attempt to rout a spirit of sterile academicism from the department had been defeated by Nicholas Murray Butler and the university's board of trustees, and there is no doubt that the tensions resulting from this fracas, which unfortunately got into the papers, contributed to his breakdown. Nor could there be much doubt that his gentle and sensitive personality was unsuited to a career as a composer in a country that was almost totally uninterested in the creation of new music. He had consciously turned away from an attempt to create a national music, saying, "Nationalism is the common property of all the world, not the vital part of it. Music goes so quickly that ten years leave nationalism behind and out of the question." A disciple of Joachim Raff and the romantic school, he turned away also from any sort of literalism or realism in music. His themes today, reflected in such titles as *Forest Stillness, In Autumn, Hamlet and Ophelia,* and *Lancelot and Elaine* seem mistily quaint and pretty rather than very exciting or interesting. It was his misfortune to be a pioneer in a time which demanded, and which unconsciously shaped in its artists, a devastating genteelism.

Quite simply, music came of age in America at the wrong time. An artist living in this period, if he wished to be a part of its mainstream, could not ply his craft with rude strength, could not seek the dangerously novel. The career of Mark Twain proves a perfect example of this. Not only did he turn from the rude and lusty frontier humor which built his early fame, he actually managed to convince himself that works like *The Prince and the Pauper* and *A Connecticut Yankee* were superior to *Huckleberry Finn.* The same syndrome undoubtedly affected MacDowell. For the wealthy Eastern tastemakers were terribly insecure; as a result they were terribly conservative, afraid to trust their judgment on new works and quickly offended by pieces which could not be fitted into their limited—and defensive—aesthetic.

The repressions they forced on the artist are clearly apparent in MacDowell's work. Writing long after his death, Olin Downes noted that "in pages of his sonatas there hover great shapes and the lightnings of mighty dreams. The music is prescient with them." MacDowell did not live long enough to unlock these "great forms" from the prison of his times, and one wonders if he could have done so had he lived. Yet he was, as Downes said, "the man who marks the beginning of the epoch of serious American musical composition . . . the one whose imagination projected farther in the realm of the seen and the unseen than that of any of his fellows." Coming at the end of a great musical tradition, the product of a society committed to the preservation of that tradition against the encroachments of an onrushing new era, his entrapment was as great a tragedy as his death, and he remains, despite unquestioned talent, merely an important historical figure, dependent on the whims of historical fashion for his tenuous position in the archives of achievement.

Such reflections were far from the minds of those who paid him honor during the early months of 1908. Wassily Safonoff conducted an *Eroica* in his memory, then, shortly after Muck's concert, presented an all MacDowell program in which Teresa Carreño, his piano teacher, played his Second Piano Concerto and his Concert Etude; David Bispham sang songs like "Tyrant's Love," "False Spring," and "A Maid Sings Light"; and May Muckle, an English cellist who was having a successful American tour that season, played her own arrangements of such MacDowell songs as "A Merry Song and a Chorus Brave." Corinne Rider-Kelsey sang "Merry Maiden Spring," "Long Ago," and "Blue Bell." The orchestra, playing before a laurel-wreathed bust of the composer, played his arrangement of "Clair de Lune" and the *Woodland Suite*. The very titles of his works, recited now, have a ring of comic sadness to them, convey a sense of talent wasted on minor matters.

The season's new music was equally small in scope and spirit, with the possible exception of the American premiere of Sibelius' Third Symphony by the Russian Symphony which was dismissed as powerless. Vincent d'Indy's *Jour d'été à la montagne* was received with equal indifference, while Walter Damrosch's ambitious concert version of Tchaikovsky's *Eugene Onegin*, the beginning of a series of such events and only the third hearing the opera had had in the United States, was rudely dismissed, despite the fact that there was little chance at that time of hearing the opera anywhere but on the concert stage.

Damrosch was much more successful with a season-ending Beethoven cycle, termed "the most important thing Mr. Damrosch has done this season."

By far the most successful new work of the season was Josef Hofmann's premiere of his own Third Piano Concerto. It was the first time any of his five concertos was performed in public. Since he was in the midst of a remarkably successful season here the piece received far better reviews than it probably deserved. Wrote Krehbiel: "Plainly Mr. Hofmann is an artist gifted with that rare but extremely valuable intellectual quality, self-criticism. We fancy that it was not of his own volition that his concerto was given a place in yesterday's list; yet it was right that his admirers should be privileged to hear it. . . . It contains evidences of an artistic nature that are gratifying in these days of shifting ideals, laborious groping and vicious pretense."

In short, Hofmann had written a safely conservative piece, well suited to his bravura style, and all was therefore temporarily right with the world. But ideals were beginning to shift, and there were genuine gropings toward new ideas, new forms in music as well as in the other arts. Theodore Dreiser, one-time (1903) resident in Carnegie Hall's smallest apartment was in the forefront of a determined shift in American literature away from tradition to a bald naturalism that was as exciting to some as it was disconcerting to others. There was a genuine mood of social protest in political circles which was to culminate four years later in the formation of Teddy Roosevelt's Bull Moose party and in the election of a liberal intellectual of reformist tendencies named Woodrow Wilson to the White House. The art world was still five years away from the Armory show of 1913 at which a nude would descend a staircase and end forever the dominance of Watteau-like painting in America. Already a scandal had given the musical world a shocking taste of modernity to come. That was the Met's production of *Salome*, which it previewed one Sunday in 1907, right after church, a bit of inept timing which caused the assorted Christians on the board of directors to react more violently than necessary to the harshness of the music and to the daring dance of the seven veils, not to mention an all-too-realistic representation of John the Baptist's head on a platter. Pressures were applied by the board, and the management hastily withdrew the production. It remained for the competition, Hammerstein's Manhattan Opera Company, to establish the work in the repertory (with the lovely Mary Garden in the title role) where it continued as a matter of controversy for years.

Despite the *Salome* scandal, the surface of the musical scene seemed serene as the 1908-1909 season began, but before it ended a major revolution was to shake the Philharmonic to the core and a new era was to begin.

The Philadelphia Orchestra, opening the season, accompanied Emil Sauer on the first leg of his farewell tour. He had last played in New York ten years before, and now he played his own piano concerto "with great éclat," according to Reginald DeKoven, the light opera composer who was then the *World's* music critic. He thought it a "musicianly work," but, like his confreres, he was not unduly impressed by it. Nor did the opening of Safonoff's last season with the Philharmonic particularly excite anyone. Arthur Hartmann, an American violinist, played one of the Saint-Saëns violin concertos. The conservatives, as usual, were upset by Safonoff's reading of *Also Sprach Zarathustra*. Thus spake *Musical America*: "The composition is an effort to carry music into a realm where no music may enter and retain a sane form and content. . . . The audience evidently did not appreciate this experiment with their musical taste, for they quite forgot to applaud with their usual enthusiasm." Things, obviously, were quite normal.

The debut of Albert Spalding, son of the eminent baseball manufacturer, caused hardly a ripple, perhaps because he too had a go at a Saint-Saëns concerto, one of the works of which the public was beginning to tire, at long last, in his debut with Walter Damrosch's orchestra. He was thought to lack the requisite lushness of tone for a major career, although everyone was quite pleasant about his efforts.

A similar greeting awaited Karl Muck's successor when he brought the Boston Symphony Orchestra to town for the first time. Polite indifference ruled the reception of Max Fiedler, who was familiar to New York audiences as a result of his brief stints as guest conductor during the Philharmonic's leaderless years. "He is a well-equipped musician in the technical details of his art and entirely at home on the conductor's stand," one critic conceded, but he thought that he "did not convey the impression that his is a deeply poetical or musically stimulating nature." It was not to be many years before Muck was back on the Boston podium.

The season picked up considerable interest when Mischa Elman appeared in New York. He gave his first concert at the Metropolitan Opera House, then repaired to the more congenial atmosphere of Carnegie Hall where the critics were divided on the nature of the seventeen-year-old's talents. Aldrich praised his technical equipment, but thought "this extraordinary talent has unfortunately been diverted from a sound and normal artistic development into fields where it counts for less than it might and should as an artistic force. . . . There are serious defects in his playing, upon the purely musical side, that prevent him, at any rate at present, from taking the position of a really great artist." DeKoven, on the other hand, said that "not since Ysaÿe have I heard such a broad, mellow and sympathetic tone or greater dash and enthusiasm, which an occasional lapse in correct intonation hardly mars." He was utterly convinced that the young man would shortly take his place among the handful of great violinists. The audience must have agreed, for when he returned later in the year to play the Beethoven Violin Concerto with the Boston Orchestra, he played to a packed house and to enthusiasm reserved only for the best.

But as the musical season wended its accustomed way to its conclusion, with standard repertory dominating such experiments as the Bruckner Eighth Symphony presented by Fiedler, Ernest Schelling's Fantastic Suite for Piano and Orchestra (into which themes from "Dixie" and "Swanee River" were worked), and the remarkably well-received Altschuler premiere of Rachmaninoff's Second Symphony, there was a great stirring not too far beneath the surface.

The first public announcement of it was in a December letter to the *Times* from Mrs. George R. Sheldon. She declared that "there is now not only willingness but desire on the part of the Philharmonic Society for radical changes in its organization and methods." These changes, she said, included giving up its cooperative basis, bringing its discipline and methods into line with modern practices, the creation of a board of trustees to govern the orchestra, the absolute control of conductor over orchestra and the playing of more concerts. All this, of course, required money, but that was available. In addition, Mrs. Sheldon and her friends also had a very good idea of whom they wanted to conduct the new orchestra. Their man was Gustav Mahler, who had come to New York the previous season to conduct German opera at the Met and had scored a great success here. In addition, of course, he had a superb reputation based on his work as an opera conductor in Vienna where he had completely remade the moribund Court Opera Company, creating perhaps the finest—and certainly the most exciting—opera company in Europe. Antisemitism and his own moody, mystical and difficult personality had cost him that job. Had the ladies cared to look closely, they could have seen the workings of that personality before they committed themselves to Mahler.

In November he took over Damrosch's orchestra for a series of three concerts. He conducted Schumann's *Spring* Symphony, the Prelude to *Die Meistersinger*, and the *Coriolanus* and *Bartered Bride* Overtures. The reviews were ecstatic. "As a conductor Mr. Mahler scorns to cultivate any devices, picturesque or otherwise, to attract attention to his personality. . . . He conducts with the utmost simplicity of gesture, but at the same time he exerts an influence almost hypnotic. . . . His readings were those of a master musician in whom highly developed intellectuality, keen appreciation of the subtlest phases of emotion and forceful dramatic feeling are combined in extraordinarily well-balanced proportion."

But Mahler was unhappy. He complained bitterly—and publicly—about Damrosch's orchestra. The men, he said, didn't come to rehearsal and when they did come they didn't stay as long as he wanted them to. Conducting under such conditions, he said, was "a farce." At his second concert the reviewers spoke of his "rough handling" of the Beethoven Fifth. One said the orchestra was not up to its customary quality under Damrosch because "the men . . . like the audience, were evidently worked up to a high pitch of tension and concentration." This, of course, was Mahler's way. He demanded that his men give as much to the work as he did. As for the "rough handling" of Beethoven, musical historians are fairly generally agreed that the raw power of his symphonies had been smoothed down considerably by the conductors of the genteel age. Mahler was attempting, probably successfully, to restore the original vitality to the work. Such accusations, however, were to be leveled at him time and time again during the coming years. For whatever his neuroses, whatever the difficulties of character and disposition which were to mar his relations with people, Mahler was first and foremost a great and austere musician, fanatically devoted to his personal vision of his art. He would tolerate no interference with that vision. The success of Mahler's final concert, at which he conducted his own massive Second Symphony—and got good reviews—quelled the trouble. But the good ladies, intent on reorganizing the Philharmonic and equally intent on getting the musician who was currently most fashionable among New York music lovers, should have pondered the small outburst of temperament which surrounded Mahler's appearance with the Symphony Society. They should have realized that they were about to sign a musician too radical for their public's taste and one whom they could not dominate.

Instead they signed him in February, such worthies as J. P. Morgan, August Belmont and Joseph Pulitzer having put up the necessary money. They guaranteed in their announcement of his signing a twenty-three-week season (currently it was only eight weeks) as well as the underwriting of all deficits for the next three seasons. At long last the men were to go on a regular-salary basis.

But controversy continued through the latter part of the season. Frank Damrosch charged that the $100,000 raised by the guarantors of the new Philharmonic was a direct affront to his brother and his work. This was hastily denied by one and all, and Walter Damrosch avoided direct comment on the activity of his competitors, concentrating on a Mendelssohn Festival. It included a performance of that composer's incidental music for *A Midsummer Night's Dream* which accompanied the first dramatic performance ever to take place on the Carnegie Hall stage, in which a little troupe known as the Ben Greet Players performed a shortened version of Shakespeare's play.

By the end of the season things were calm enough for the Philharmonic to bid a dignified farewell to Safonoff, who had continued his amiable way throughout the season without so much as a comment on the reorganization of his orchestra. On March 27th, at the society's final concert, Andrew Carnegie himself stepped forward after the final number to present Safonoff with a laurel wreath and to tell the Muscovite that "you have been a power among music lovers and have made a host of friends . . . you have enthralled your audience . . . you have filled the community with memories which this generation at least can never forget."

Safonoff, "honored that one of your prominent citizens has felt it his duty to speak here," declared that "the memory of the emotions of this evening will remain with me all the days of my life. The sympathy of the American audiences at my first efforts here were such as to make me almost forget my own home."

This little drama concluded, Carnegie then called forth Richard Arnold, the venerable concertmaster of the orchestra, and leader of the conservative faction which had fought off all previous attempts at change. Calling him "the beloved Nestor" of the orchestra, Carnegie presented the retiring violinist with a loving cup and assured him that he "could not get away from the society if [he] wanted to." He had been kicked upstairs to the manager's office, for Mahler wanted no opposition sitting on his left hand as he mounted his new podium. Arnold, however, was equally bothersome in an executive capacity, and within a year he was out of that job, too.

There remained only the formal induction of Mahler into office, and that came on March 31st, at a special concert in which he led Wagner's "Siegfried Idyl" and the overture to *Tannhäuser*, the Beethoven Seventh and the *Manfred* Overture of Schumann.

All was sweetness, light and optimism. A new era was beginning. And no one saw the hand-sized clouds scudding low across the musical horizon.

Five

"To Raise Musical Standards"

AFTER THE SPECIAL APRIL CONCERT, MAHLER RETURNED ALMOST IMmediately to Europe to rest, to plan his new season and to work on the Tenth Symphony, which remained unfinished at the time of his death. He was convinced that the fates were aligned against him. Dismissal from his opera post in Vienna, the result of years of scheming by an anti-Mahler cabal, still hurt deeply. An even worse blow was the sudden death of his beloved eldest son at almost the same time. In addition, he was now convinced of the imminence of his own death, his serious heart condition having been discovered. A resigned fatalism now dominated Mahler's thoughts—and his music.

Despite this, however, Mahler returned to New York in the fall of 1909 full of confidence. Two-thirds of his musicians were new, and although the musician's union had prevented him from hiring European replacements for the lame, halt and aged among the pre-Mahler players, he had succeeded in engaging good American players and had every reason to make satisfied sounds to an interviewer. "To raise popular musical standards and make the New York Philharmonic orchestra the best in the country and the equal of any in the world is what I am striving for," he said. "If hard work can accomplish that ambition, accomplished it surely will be."

"The great thing," he added, "will be to weld the orchestra into an effective instrument. This can only be done by constant practice in the best of the world's music and that is what the reorganization will make possible." He intended, he said, to educate the orchestra and the public by programming historical cycles and cycles of composers. It was an austere program, and not one calculated to endear the conductor to his audience, conditioned to the old-shoe, old-hat comfort of Philharmonic programs. He warned the public that he wouldn't play novelties, or indeed, anything, just because they asked him to do so. He tempered this statement by promising to play the public's choice "provided the music is worthy and even though I may not personally like the composition. But if the music is not worthy, then I shall not play it." Since the final arbiter of music's worthiness was to be Gustav Mahler, a man with a tolerance for mediocrity as short as his public's was long, the new season obviously promised a certain interest beyond the merely musical. "It will be my aim" Mahler said, "to educate the public . . . and that education will be made gradually and in a manner which will enable those who may not have a taste for the best later to appreciate it."

But before his stringent educational process could begin, Carnegie Hall was to witness the beginning of quite a different educational effort.

On October 3rd, Dr. Stephen Wise conducted Rosh Hashana services in Carnegie Hall and thereby inaugurated thirty years of tenancy there by his famous Free Synagogue. His use of the hall provided him with the largest auditorium regularly used by a clergyman of his faith. The great political and spiritual liberal needed all the seating capacity he could get, for he was a dynamic and forceful speaker who refused to avoid comment on any issue, social, religious or humanitarian. Through the years he launched many a good crusade from his Carnegie Hall pulpit. From it, he fought for social reforms of all kinds and against the sundry forms of repression and tyranny endemic to the twentieth century. From it also he led the fight for Zionism as well as for better understanding between Christians and Jews, and for reformed Judaism, which was represented by him as a sort of "Unitarianism modified by Jewish observances."

Wise had returned to New York from Portland, Oregon, in 1907, where his "prophetic ministry" had attracted nation-wide attention. He had been offered the pulpit at Temple Emanu-El, perhaps the most important post of his faith in New York. But he refused the call when the board of trustees insisted that his utterances must be subject to its control.

In an open reply to the board, Dr. Wise said: "The chief office of the minister, I take it, is not to represent the view of the congregation but to proclaim the truth as he sees it. How can he serve a congregation as a teacher save as he quickens the minds of his hearers by the vitality and independence of his utterances? . . . In pursuit of the duties of his office the minister may from time to time be under the necessity of giving expression to views at variance with the views of some, or even many, members of the congregation. Far from such difference proving the pulpit to be wrong, it may be and ofttimes is, found to signify that the pulpit has done its duty in calling evil evil and good good, in abhorring the moral wrong of putting light for darkness and darkness for light."

It was on this rock that Rabbi Wise founded his temple and through the years of his ministry, which coincided almost precisely with the rise of liberalism to the status of a basic political consensus in this country, this freedom of speech enabled him to speak out on all issues, and allowed him to be one of the great forces in the shaping of the liberal sensibility.

It was no great coincidence that in the same month that Rabbi Wise began his ministry in Carnegie Hall, another reform group also hired the hall. Politically and socially this was a time of great restlessness in the United States. The first wave of reform, which had culminated in the election of Theodore Roosevelt, had passed and the White House was occupied by an affable "Modern Republican" named William Howard Taft. His term was merely an interregnum while the nation gathered energy for a second period of reform during Woodrow Wilson's first term. During these years nothing more exercised the land than the question of votes for women. Thus, When Mrs. O. H. P. Belmont's Political Equality League for Self-Supporting Women announced that it had engaged a notable speaker for its Tuesday evening meeting, considerable polite excitement was engendered. Mrs. Emmeline Pankhurst was very nearly the most famous feminist of all time, a tiny, angry lady who had been hooted by antifeminist mobs, thrown out of the House of Commons, stoned, dragged through the streets by police and sent to jail twice for her activities on behalf of female suffrage. Her first appearance in America was a rousing occasion.

Long before the doors of Carnegie Hall were opened, the crowd was lined up four abreast all the way to Fifty-ninth Street and a police detachment of 125 men was on hand to keep order. They were not needed, for as their captain told an inquiring reporter, "The ladies are behaving as well as possible and the gentlemen are behaving like perfect ladies."

On the platform with Mrs. Pankhurst, who was dressed in purple, green and white, the colors of her Social and Political Union, were scores of conspicuously self-supporting women, including three tattooed Maori ladies currently appearing in a spectacle at the Hippodrome (they had voted in New Zealand, which gave women the franchise in 1893), an explorer, six dentists, an architect, two sculptresses and sixteen authoresses. In the audience were quantities of society ladies who were anything but self-supporting, but who would just as soon vote as not.

The night's revels began with the singing—to the tune of the "Marseillaise," naturally—of a song which urged the ladies to "March on, march on/ List to the dawn, the dawn of liberty." Then it was Mrs. Pankhurst's turn. "I know you have not all come here tonight because you are interested in suffrage," she began. "You have come to see what a militant suffragette looks like and to what a hooligan woman is like."

Having made her little joke, she pressed on to more serious matters, declaring in ringing tones that "not a woman but is willing to face fasting and even death to force the government to action. We are willing to be prisoners for life, to lose citizenship for life if they will give the franchise to the peaceful women."

This, she warned, had better be done immediately, "before worse things come. We have pleaded and got nothing. Now we are fighting and we are going to win. We are taxed like men, punished like men and we claim the rights and privileges of men. And we are going to win very soon, to win freedom for the men also." No one in the audience, "exalted, amazed and affrighted by turns," dared to disagree.

Culver Service

Tiny, furious Emmaline Pankhurst brought her tireless crusade for female suffrage to Carnegie Hall in 1909. She knew her audience was less interested in her crusade than they were in seeing what "a hooligan woman" looked like.

The debut of the revamped Philharmonic—the result of a determined feminine effort by Mrs. Sheldon and her friends that would have gladdened Mrs. Pankhurst's heart—occured on November 4, 1909. The program opened, appropriately, with Beethoven's *Consecration of the House* Overture, and included, in addition, his *Eroica* Symphony, *Till Eulenspiegel* and Liszt's symphonic poem, *Mazeppa.*

Mahler and his men received the most hopeful set of reviews of the era. Aldrich of the *Times*, providing indirect comment on the standards which had gone before, wrote that "scarcely within the memory of man have the wind choirs played so nearly in tune and with such brilliancy and precision." He was convinced that when Mahler had completed his transformation of the orchestra it would be "an extremely fine one." Henry T. Finck of the *Post* agreed. "Not that its playing is as yet flawless," he said, "but the ensemble . . . was admirable and indicated that great treats are in store for music lovers." W. J. Henderson of the *Sun* was also encouraged by evidence that the ensemble playing "has emerged from the mists which surrounded it last season," and found the entire evening "an encouraging demonstration of the achievement of a good conductor in the matter of dynamics, attack and nuance."

So the season was well launched. And no attacks were forthcoming during the rest of its first month. Instead, Carnegie Hall patrons were treated almost simultaneously to the ridiculous and the sublime in piano playing.

The ridiculous was provided by Master Pepito Arriola, a twelve-year-old prodigy whom the critics thought nothing short of marvelous—for a child. "Of course no humane person would measure his playing by the same foot rule that is applied to grown men," one hastily added. But the wee one, in his lacy shirts and short pants, was button-eyed and bug cute, and he was, until puberty caught up with him, an interesting spectacle, made no less so by the frighteningly bright interviews he gave out to the newspapers. "Chopin," he said on one occasion, "has not spoiled my taste for toy soldiers and Schumann does not interfere with me when I want to row, bicycle or play ball. There is nothing like broad-mindedness for the artist."

Alas, some did not share his belief in broad-mindedness. Among them was H. E. Krehbiel. That crusty critic, who was capable of being monstrously unfair, as we shall shortly see, marched firmly out of one of the prodigy's recitals after hearing his disastrous attack on one of Beethoven's sonatas. The boy genius' manager, Robert E. Johnston, promptly struck him from the free list for writing a "roasting" review based on this rather limited acquaintance with the lad's talent. Krehbiel didn't mind at all, and he was proved correct by the quick fading of the Arriola reputation when he outgrew his velvet knee-pants. Pepito, however, was not the only pianist in New York that season. On November 13th, Sergei Rachmaninoff debuted with Max Fiedler's Boston Symphony, playing his own Second Piano Concerto.

With his close-cropped hair, worn in what we would now call a crew-cut, with sharply-defined features and a tall, strongly-built, somewhat angular figure, he looked so unlike a professional pianist as to seem almost out of place on a concert platform. But the Rachmaninoff style, strong, masculine, yet passionate and technically brilliant, soon convinced his hearers that you did not have to look like a virtuoso to play like one. It was the beginning of a long and distinguished career of American concertizing by Rachmaninoff, who, after the revolution of 1917, made his home here.

Rachmaninoff himself was not delighted with his life in the United States. Replying to a young cousin who had written him, he said, "You know, in this accursed country, when you're surrounded by nothing but Americans and the 'business,' 'business' they are forever doing, clutching you from all sides and driving you on—it is terribly pleasant to receive a letter from a Russian girl."

In the end, he found his tour extremely fatiguing, and on his return to his homeland he told an interviewer: "America was a strain. Imagine giving an almost daily concert for three whole months. . . . The audiences are astonishingly cold, spoiled by the tours of first-class artists and forever looking for novelty, for something they've never had before. Local papers are obliged to note the number of times you are recalled to the stage, and the public regards this as a yardstick of your talent."

The one artistic experience he truly enjoyed was playing his Third Piano Concerto with Mahler and the Philharmonic in Carnegie Hall.

His recollection of that performance gives an excellent insight into Mahler's conductorial methods: "... Mahler was the only conductor whom I considered worthy to be classed with Nikisch. He devoted himself to the concerto until the accompaniment, which is rather complicated, had been practiced to the point of perfection, although he had already gone through another long rehearsal. According to Mahler every detail of the score was important—an attitude too rare amongst conductors. Though the rehearsal was scheduled to end at 12:30, we played and played, far beyond this hour, and when Mahler announced that the first movement would be rehearsed again, I expected some protest or scene from the musicians, but I did not notice a single sign of annoyance. The orchestra played the first movement with a keen or perhaps even closer appreciation than the previous time."

By the time of the Rachmaninoff performance the pattern of Mahler's conductorship had already been established by two December performances. The first, which included the American premiere of his own First Symphony drew mixed appraisals. Some, like W. J. Henderson, found the work approachable and enjoyable: "neither the subject matter nor the manner of its treatment will tax the analytical power of the average listener. The subject matter indeed is thoroughly melodious, unaffectedly simple and directly presented." But another, sensing the mood of the audience, pointed out that "the old subscribers of the society, recognizing in the work a very radical departure from its traditions, received it with what might be described as courteous applause, much dubious shaking of heads and no small amount of grumblings."

These grumblings increased when, a couple of days later, Mahler led a stirring performance of the Beethoven Fifth Symphony. A headline in a musical journal read: "Disconcerting Performance..." and the review said that "Mr. Mahler's liberty with the Beethoven seemed to approach the domain of sheer license or even whimsicality and at times to take him from the spirit of Beethoven's intent."

This was the first in a long series of criticisms which followed this line. Its basis was Mahler's determination to bring to his listeners the spirit of the composer. The modern conductor tries to give us the raw, rebellious challenge Beethoven flung at the fates in his music. But the prevailing interpretation of the Master's works, particularly in New York during this period, was one in which their crude force was cast over by a pale romantic mist. It was not, in short, the spirit of Beethoven that Mahler offended, but the spirit of his time.

Mahler's disciple, Bruno Walter, has written of his conductorial methods: "Intimate knowledge strengthened Mahler's wonder and admiration for works 'beyond description glorious' . . . He approached them like a lover, constantly wooing; he was always ready to reconsider, improve, plumb new depths. Nothing was routine in his performances. . . ."

But this search was always based on a reverence for the score that approached the fanatical. Demanding absolute musical clarity, "the precision of his exemplary beat was never impaired by emotion, however strong," Walter notes. "But one never had the impression of mechanical precision. . . . With him precision was a means to an end, the end being to bring the work to life."

It was his Beethoven, his supreme achievement, which caused the most widespread public complaint against him, but he could have survived that, had he been a bit more approachable as a human being, not quite so fanatic, not quite so withdrawn in personality. Mediocrity distrusts genius, and Mahler was indubitably a genius, the first to conduct the Philharmonic, and with the exception of Toscanini, probably the last. Those simple, wealthy ladies with little knowledge of music and no real love of it, representatives of a million would-be patrons of all the arts, were simply not the people to deal with such a temperament. For them, music was merely a pleasurable social activity, in a category with charity balls and shopping expeditions as a means of passing time. For Mahler, as for any artist truly engaged in his work, it was his very life. He would not tolerate their infuriatingly stupid demands, any more than he bothered to care about the public's reaction to his work. He played, as does any artist, to please himself. If he thereby pleased others, well and good; if not, they were the losers, not he.

In defense of the indefensible, it may be observed that as the ladies (and gentlemen) of his board of directors would not tolerate a surly caterer at one of their parties, so they would not tolerate a difficult conductor. The root of their problem was in not being able to differentiate between a caterer and a conductor. It is a problem that persists.

Mahler's season was one of mounting frustration. A performance of his own *Kindertotenlieder*, its first in New York, was received with no particular understanding despite a shrewd bit of programming. The solo voice, customarily a mezzo-soprano's, on this occasion belonged to Dr. Ludwig Wüllner, who had been one of the surprises of this and the previous musical season. Without much of a voice, this aging singer was able to fill Carnegie, as well as other halls, with his recitals of German lieder. Most of the critics were favorably disposed to the educational nature of his work, for lieder has never been precisely good box office, and they were pleased to proclaim the value of his missionary work. For he was a magnificent actor, and even if he could not hit all the notes, he could convey to the audiences the emotional nuances of his songs. Henderson of the *Sun* remarked shrewdly that an audience went to Dr. Wüllner as it would go to a father confessor because he expressed the things with which the millions were throbbing, and for which they had no outlet in expression. Granting that "he is more themselves than they are," he nevertheless thought Wüllner's style bad art and a worse example to young singers. Given his popularity he was the very man to introduce the *Kindertotenlieder*, but even he could not conquer New York's indifference.

Meantime, Mahler was suffering a series of minor crises. First there was the business of the Tchaikovsky Sixth. His first performance of it was disastrous. He played the piece only at the insistence of his board, then got perfectly dreadful reviews. He scheduled it again, trying his best to do it in a way that would please himself as well as his audience. The results were slightly improved, but still not up to par.

Then there was the unpleasantness with Josef Weiss. Mahler and Weiss were friends, and he had brought the pianist over from Germany especially to play the Schumann Concerto in A minor. At a rehearsal things went along all right until at one point the oboes entered, to Mahler's entire satisfaction, but to the discomfiture of the pianist, who complained. They tried the section again, and again Weiss complained.

"Will you please confine your attention to your own instrument?" Mahler asked after Weiss's second outburst. Whereupon Weiss threw his score at Mahler, and told him he was as good a pianist as Mahler was a conductor, and, as coequal in the enterprise, had a right to his views. When Mahler refused to change his interpretation, Weiss stalked out of the rehearsal.

Mahler forthwith hired a substitute, Yolanda Mérö, who practiced and practiced and practiced—until she sprained a tendon in her right arm on the morning of the concert. There was nothing to do but get another pianist. Luckily Paolo Gallico knew the piece and played it with some success.

Weiss turned up at Carnegie Hall just before the scheduled time of the concert. For purposes of a law suit he was planning, he announced himself ready, willing and eager to play. No thank you, said Mahler.

Weiss then released a statement to the press: "Mr. Mahler was my closest friend, and I think he still is. But I came from Germany for this concert and I didn't play. . . . If I am not paid I will have to go to court, and of that, too, I will be very sorry."

The affair was quieted down, and although such an incident could hardly be fatal in such a high-strung business, it certainly did not endear Mahler to his board.

Neither did an incident late in the season, when Mahler and another pianist, Busoni, decided to "clean up" the *Emperor* Concerto. The piece had acquired, over the years, any number of interpretive accretions, and the two artists decided they would try to play it as written for a change.

Unfortunately, some of the ladies from the directorate decided to drop down to rehearsals on the day they were playing through the work. It just didn't sound right to them, and they said so—at length. Finally one of them ended the painful session by stomping out of the rehearsal room crying, "No, Mr. Mahler, this will never do." Mahler's reply is left to the imagination, which undoubtedly cannot conjure up anything worse than what he actually said to the busybody.

Actually, the version did very well, probably due to the presence of Busoni, a favorite being welcomed back to the scene of past triumphs. The reviews were excellent, and Busoni went on to two recital triumphs, at the last of which the audience stayed to applaud until the lights had to be turned out.

But the incident brought into the open the tensions existing within the Philharmonic organization, and as the season drew to an end, there were rumors that Mahler would not be asked to return to the orchestra. The deficit was large, $75,000 for his first season; critics and audiences were less enthusiastic than had been hoped, and the obvious strains in the relationship between conductor and board were common knowledge. But in due course there was an announcement that the board was "satisfied" with the artistic results of the season and that Mahler would be back next year.

This announcement came, however, just as a program of moderns including Bruckner, Richard Strauss and Pfitzner was drawing "the smallest audience at a Philharmonic concert in fifty years." This confirmation of the board's musical prejudices was partially offset by the performance of Beethoven's Ninth Symphony which ended the season. Mahler's reading received the usual set of controversial reviews: a few strong dissents, the majority hedging, and one or two highly laudatory ones.

There were just enough people in New York, people who could listen with a fresh ear, an ear unclogged by musical clichés, for Mahler to feel that his work was not a total failure. He bravely pronounced himself "much pleased with the results of my season's work here," before departing for Europe and a summer of success, particularly in Munich, where his *Das Lied von der Erde* was warmly welcomed.

Mahler's first concert of the 1910-11 season was well received. On the program were Schubert's mighty Symphony in C major, *Also Sprach Zarathustra* and two Bach Suites which Mahler had arranged for orchestra and conducted from the piano.

But although the first months of the season passed with a surface serenity, there was no calm between Mahler and his board of directors. Increasingly, the ladies of that board attempted to bend the conductor to their will, especially in the matter of his programs. The orchestra, too, was suddenly hostile. One charge was that Mahler had placed a spy among the second violins. He allegedly reported the gossip of the players to the conductor. Alas, the spy was no figment of imagination

The Bettmann Archive

Gustav Mahler conducted the New York Philharmonic for two seasons, literally hastening his death in 1911.

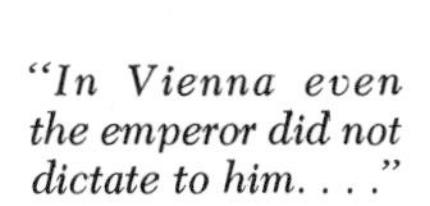

"In Vienna even the emperor did not dictate to him. . . ."

The Bettmann Archive

or malice. Even Mahler's wife, Alma, admitted his reality—"a sycophant who had been Mahler's choice and managed to keep his backing."

This was a tactical error of major proportions. As long as Mahler had the confidence of his men, the board had no strong weapon to use against him. Their differences with him in matters of musical taste was hardly sufficient excuse to fire him, especially if they were forced to justify his dismissal in public. Dissension in the ranks, however, gave them the means to beg the real issue and to bring forth an unexceptionable excuse for letting him go.

By mid-January it was being reported that at least half a dozen conductors were being informally approached with offers to take over Mahler's baton for the following season. The leading candidate at the moment was Franz Kneisel, the eminent violinist and quartet leader.

Meantime, Mahler's programs, if anything, were more interesting, especially in the matter of new music, than they had been during the previous season. On one January program he offered no less than three European novelties, an Enesco Suite, Debussy's *Iberian Suite* and Chabrier's "Ode to Music." But the works were not well received, and neither were Schumann's Third Symphony and a Bizet Suite, a couple of weeks later.

An early February program of Berlioz, Strauss and Beethoven received an excellent welcome, by and large, by a public that was becoming a bit more accustomed to Mahler's exciting ways with standard works. But a noisy minority, led by the indomitable Krehbiel, rose up wrathfully, as it had on past occasions, over a new "desecration" of Beethoven's Seventh. It seems Mahler doubled some of the woodwind scoring to achieve a better balance for the modern orchestra. It was the kind of sensible tampering that many conductors often do in order to bring out the spirit of works composed before the orchestra had grown to its modern size. Such things often go unmarked. But Mahler, in his precarious position, could do nothing without being observed and chastised.

Several concerts which featured recent American works, including Chadwick's *Melpomene* and works by Henry Hadley, Charles Martin Loeffler and MacDowell, all popular and respectable American composers, very much in favor with New York audiences, did nothing to placate Mahler's critics, and in mid-February the situation came to a head.

He was summoned to the home of one of the ladies of the board and forced to defend himself against a multitude of charges. Defend himself he did, perhaps not very politely, and then the ladies administered the *coup de grâce.* One of them flung aside a curtain to reveal a lawyer taking notes of everything Mahler had said to them. That broke him and he surrendered. He left the apartment after signing an agreement to fire the "spy" and giving the ladies full rights to veto any piece he wished to program. He returned home from the meeting shivering and furious. Next day he suffered chills, fever and a sore throat, but there was a series of concerts to conduct that week, and against his doctor's orders, he conducted them.

On the twenty-first day of February, Mahler gave his last performance with the Philharmonic. It was to be a program in his series of concerts based on the musical heritage of various nations. This one was the Italian concert, and it featured a new work by Mahler's friend Busoni, *Berceuse Elégiaque* which was called "gruesome . . . a scheme of aciduous dissonance that few ultra-moderns could improve upon."

By the time the reviews were out, Mahler was past caring about them. During the intermission of the concert he had complained of a headache and weariness. He insisted on finishing, and even seemed to feel better as a result. When he returned home his temperature was back to normal and he joked about conducting as a cure.

But the cure was only temporary. Severe tonsillitis placed a heavy strain on a congenitally weak heart. His resistance to disease was low, a result of the nervous strain of the past few months, and he never fully recovered from the infection.

The orchestra was placed in the hands of Mahler's concertmaster, Theodore Spiering, who led it for the rest of the season, while rumors about Mahler's absence from the podium continued to circulate. Many thought the announcement of his illness merely a politely agreed-upon fiction to save face for all concerned while a new conductor was sought.

To her credit, Mrs. Sheldon attempted to smooth things over. "We had only one ideal, that of giving good concerts," she told reporters, adding that she personally felt Mahler was "the greatest conductor either in Europe or America today, and I feel further that we have been fortunate in keeping him as long as we have."

She even went so far as to say that although the matter was not yet settled, she believed he would stay with the orchestra at least one more year. This, of course, was nonsense. As far as the ladies of the Philharmonic were concerned, his illness was providential. It gave them a perfect excuse for politely dropping him.

Unable to rally from his sickness, Mahler and his wife left for Vienna in the early spring. In Paris he became too ill to travel farther, and early in May Mrs. Mahler gave an interview to reporter Charles Henry Meltzer, in which she laid the whole story before the public. "You cannot imagine what Mr. Mahler has suffered," she said. "In Vienna my husband was all powerful. Even the emperor did not dictate to him, but in New York he had ten ladies ordering him about like a puppet. He hoped, however, by hard work and success, to rid himself of his tormentors. Meanwhile he lost health and strength. . . . Heaven knows how it will all end."

Even as she was speaking, the Philharmonic board was hiring a replacement for Mahler. They had attempted to find a great conductorial name, but word about the difficulties of working with the ladies had gone around the musical world and no man of reputation would take the job. They finally reached low in the barrel of talent and came up with a nonentity named Josef Stransky, who was to hold the post for nine unexciting years.

Shortly thereafter, Mahler and his wife reached Vienna where, in a sanitarium, he finally succumbed on May 18th, 1911. His last words were "Alma" and "Mozart." He had tried, in his wife's words, "to give God the slip." Beethoven had died after completing his Ninth Symphony, Bruckner had died in the midst of his Ninth. Therefore, Mahler titled, rather than numbered, his ninth (*Das Lied von der Erde*), finished his tenth and numbered it nine, then passed on to number ten which, in reality was his eleventh. God, however, was not to be fooled any longer and Mahler died with his last work unfinished and without ever having heard *Das Lied von der Erde*, perhaps his crowning masterpiece.

But that was not quite the end of the story of Mahler's New York career. Although most of the obituary notices were polite and respectful, one was not. Henry E. Krehbiel took the opportunity to launch a vitriolic attack on Mahler's musicianship, warming over the charges of tampering with scores, and accusing Mahler of being "willing wantonly to insult the people's intelligence and taste." Krehbiel's attack was shocking in its own gratuitous wantonness. But such were the emotions that Mahler stirred among his enemies.

Mahler's friends, however, were at least as dedicated as his enemies, and one of them, Ossip Gabrilowitsch, rushed into print with a warmly-felt and brilliant defense of Mahler. He rebutted Krehbiel's charges with ease, pointing out that Mahler had done nothing without precedent, that he had brought greatness to a place ridden with banality. He ended with a tribute to an artist of the highest integrity: "Mahler is to me the very incarnation of the highest ideals, artistic and human. I did not believe that such ideals could ever be realized till I met him. To have known him made life seem nobler, more worth while living. He had the kind of limitless devotion to a high cause that only a saint has. He was the only artist I have ever known to whom personal success meant nothing. Not one atom of vanity was in his disposition. His was the childlike naïveté of true genius. . . . He knew that in order to give a work his full eloquence the reproducing artist must be able to recreate the composition as if it were flesh of his flesh and blood of his blood. This he did, and that is why he presented works of the standard repertory with such spontaniety, such freshness, that one seemed never to have heard them before."

Such was a musician's epitaph, and beside the story of his trial, the other events of his final season on earth seem insignificant.

But there were others who came to the Carnegie Hall stage and brought with them a vision of the new. Like Mahler only in his devotion to his highly personal view of the condition of the world, a Midwestern politician named Robert M. La Follette, Sr., in January gave the eastern seaboard a first-hand glimpse of the liberal movement which was stirring the distant prairies. La Follette was being prominently mentioned as a Republican presidential possibility. The progressive wing of the party, anxious to secure the nomination for a liberal, was divided between Theodore Roosevelt and the Wisconsin senator, who had virtually remade his conservative state as governor, and then become the leading liberal spokesman in Washington. The New York speech was an important test for the Midwesterner. He had Republican support throughout the West, but the East was Roosevelt territory, and he had to impress New York if he was to have a chance for the nomination.

He was impressive. When he drove up to the hall he faced a crowd of a thousand people who had not been able to find seats inside. Standing in his car, he had to make two brief speeches before the zealots would let him go inside to make his formal address.

He was introduced by the great liberal and conservationist, Gifford Pinchot, who spoke warmly of La Follette's contributions to the causes closest to Pinchot's heart. La Follette rose to face "tier after tier of well-dressed men and women reaching from the footlights to the last seat in the top gallery." Very quickly he got on good terms with the audience and threw aside his prepared speech, telling his audience they were "just like Wisconsin folk." One of the great political orators (he had almost become an actor instead of a politician) he spoke and answered questions ad lib for more than two hours, then spent more than an hour shaking hands with the hundreds of people who crowded about the stage to meet him.

The meeting was a success, but Roosevelt, whom the progressives finally decided to back, lost the nomination to Taft, bolted the party to form his own Progressive party, thereby giving the election to Wilson. The career of Bob La Follette, however, was not over. He was one of the "small group of willful men" who fought to keep America out of World War I, and just six years after he came out of the West to receive the cheers of the Carnegie Hall crowd he was denounced from the same platform as a traitor. Yet the traitor would, six years after that, be a candidate for president on the Progressive ticket and would receive one out of every six votes cast for the presidency, one of the most impressive showings ever made by a third party presidential candidate.

If La Follette was the great spokesman of a new political vision, one which would guide the future of American liberalism—particularly during the depression decade—an enchanted and enchanting young lady named Isadora Duncan was the great spokesman of a new vision of personal freedom—a vision which would become reality before La Follette's.

Isadora Duncan had been in New York before. She and her family, imbued with a romantic vision of what the life of the artist should be, had come to the city at the turn of the century—and had very nearly starved to death in Isadora's Carnegie Hall studio. They stuck it out for several years while Isadora was making the small beginnings of a career, which refused to flourish. Whereupon she went off to Europe. There she found success, artistically and in the realm of publicity. Students in Berlin, Budapest, Vienna and Munich hauled her carriage through the streets. She bore the children of Edward Gordon Craig, the theatrical designer, and Paris Singer, the sewing machine heir, without bothering to marry either. She toured Russia and danced at dawn at the Acropolis. In short, she lived, lived, lived—and took precautions that the world should know precisely how much and where.

When she returned to Carnegie Hall on February 11th, there was not a seat to be had, and "the American girl who is directly responsible for the train of barefoot dancers who have spread themselves like a craze over two continents in the last five years" was warmly, eagerly greeted. She did not disappoint either her devoted, almost fanatical, admirers or those who wanted simply to see her in her celebrated diaphanous costumes. Her accompanists were no less than Walter Damrosch and his orchestra, her music had been written for slightly different purposes by Bach and Wagner, and her setting was a semicircle of bare floor, rose-lighted, her backdrop folds of green velvet drapery.

Her opening number was the Bach Suite in D, and she entered as the violinists took up the celebrated slow movement of the suite. "Miss Duncan waved her arms and posed during this movement but did not do much of what is conventionally called dancing," Carl Van Vechten, writing anonymously in the *Times*, reported. But in the two gavottes and gigue which followed she "flitted about the stage in her early Greek way and gave vivid imitations of what one may see on the spherical bodies of Greek vases."

Following an intermission, she returned to dance various Wagnerian snippets. Reginald DeKoven, who had previously observed that her "draperies [left] nothing to the imagination in regard to a pair of legs not so graceful as formerly," now noted that she performed the *Tannhäuser* Bacchanale "almost without raiment of any kind." The dance, which combined pantomime and conventional dance steps did not particularly please the critics; the tempestuousness which might properly have been associated with the music was apparently missing.

The evening's *chef-d'oeuvre* was Isadora's interpretation of the "Liebestod" from *Tristan.* Before beginning it Walter Damrosch made a brief announcement. He said the dance had not been on the program—although it had been rumored for days that Duncan would attempt it—but that at a rehearsal he had decided the public should have a chance to see it, even though "whatever she does now must be largely experimental." He then told the audience that "as there are a great many people here to whom the idea of giving pantomimic expression to the 'Liebestod' would be horrifying, I am putting it last on the program, so that those who do not wish to see it may leave." Naturally, not a creature stirred—except Isadora—as the piece began. It was not a success. The breathless beheld nothing more exciting than Isadora going through "most of the motions which the operatic artists make over the dead body of Tristan," according to Krehbiel, who was out of patience with the whole business. Van Vechten merely noted that "she puzzled those who knew the music drama, and did not interest those who did not. Therefore one may ask, why?"

Why? One is tempted to ask it about Isadora's entire life. For in retrospect her dances seem terribly arty and pretentious. Undoubtedly she was a fresh breeze blowing through a stuffy post-Victorian living room, one of those great characters who delightfully enliven the dullness of American cultural history. But beyond her own beauty and a certain grace, her work seems fatally flawed by the ludicrous conceptions of her not very brilliant mind. Yet, true as all this may seem, brilliant as John Dos Passos' comic-tragic portrait of her in *U.S.A.* seems, there is no doubt that Isadora, for all her foolishness, was a valuable person. She would be laughed off the stage today, but in those easily-shocked times, she was anything but a harmless eccentric.

Brown Brothers

Isadora Duncan was a fresh breeze blowing through the Victorian Parlor which was American culture in 1911.

She was the incarnation of a new sexual and social freedom which would shortly sweep the world. The very obviousness of her revolt was a danger to the established order. Its single concrete result was to free the dance from the restraints of the time. From her work sprang a new dance tradition. Beyond that, she was a wonderfully absurd figure, one of the few of her time who had the courage of her absurdity, and if she had done nothing else, she would deserve reverence for being a free spirit in a repressed and repressive time, an individual who was absolutely unafraid to make a damn fool of herself. Her contemporaries could have learned a lesson from that. They waited, and posterity did the job for them.

Writing years later of the impact of Isadora's Carnegie Hall debut, Walter Terry noted that she had "upset" music lovers by daring to dance "an extremely personal interpretation of the emotional qualities she found in the music, and by daring to use an entire symphony orchestra as an accompanist to her one-woman show." But her real crime, in the eyes of the conservatives, was her abbreviated costumes. "Many in the audience probably understood the greatness of this woman," he writes, "but one of the symphony's directors disapproved of this 'barefoot' dancer, and further performances were forbidden." It was years before the barefoot dancer again appeared on the Carnegie Hall stage. But by that time the world had turned over so radically that Ted Shawn could shortly follow her, dancing his historically significant "Death of Adonis," clad only in conventional fig leaf. After him, came the deluge of modern dancers. Shawn and his wife, Ruth St. Denis, with their Denishawn dancers, Martha Graham, Doris Humphrey and Hanya Holm all trod in their variously graceful ways the boards which Isadora had tested and made ready for them in years before the time of modern dance had come.

Another lady, who, like Isadora, was a newsman's delight came to Carnegie Hall in 1911, to make her concert debut. She was Mary Garden, perhaps the most beautiful opera singer in the history of that overstuffed institution. She too was a free spirit, but she always retained a kind of girl-next-door mischievousness and high spirits. Not a truly great singer, she was obviously a delight to have around. Clad in "a wild and wonderful costume" she was in high spirits and obvi-

The Bettmann Archive

Mary Garden was not a great singer, but she was a great musical personality. She was first presented to America by opera impresario Oscar Hammerstein I but sang her first New York recital "in a wild and wonderful costume" at Carnegie Hall.

ously enjoyed the reception she was given, one of indulgent delight in the success of a neighborhood youngster. The critics were discreet, and unangry. How could you ask such a nice girl to be a great artist, too? One wrote: "Miss Garden gave a concert yesterday afternoon... in full imitation of Mme. Johanna Gadski, Mme. Marcella Sembrich and other persistent and successful recitalists. How did she sing? Well, she was deliciously dressed in nothing but black and a ta-ra-ra-boom-de-ay round her sacred head."

Mary Garden was spunky, a sharp contrast to the new conductor of the Philharmonic, who showed his true mettle not long after her concert. Interviewed in Paris by a reporter from the *Herald,* he said he thought his new job would be "comparatively easy for . . . certain works specified by the committee of the Philharmonic accord naturally with my own preference, belonging as they do among the noblest compositions in musical literature. Consequently I venture to hope that the set of programs I have submitted will suffer only minor changes. Naturally, they must be regarded as in a certain sense as tentative and subject to the final judgment of the manager and the executive board." In short, there was no question that the board had made an excellent choice. At last they had a conductor whom they could treat like a caterer.

His opening concert, on November 2, 1911, received rather better notices than one might have expected. For on the podium Stransky gave up his passivity and conducted like a lion. Richard Aldrich wrote that he "possessed... abundant energy and self-possession; he is a man of authority, of commanding presence, possessed of clearly-defined intentions which he is capable of imparting and his decisive beat, sometimes tending to the picturesque molding of phrases and the ostentatious indication of entrances, was followed by his men with evident enthusiasm."

There was significance to the occasion of Stransky's debut beyond the beginning of one of the longest reigns in the orchestra's history. For on the program that night was a young violinist named Efrem Zimbalist, making his first American appearance, playing the Glazunov Violin Concerto in A minor. W. J. Henderson thought the twenty-two-year-old fiddler "one of the most excellent violinists heard in recent years. His playing is intrinsically musical and is governed by fine taste. His technic is great . . ." The other critics agreed, Aldrich noting that "his appearance was fraught with more significance than any other violinist who has visited New York in a good many years. . . . He is already a virtuoso . . . a mature artist who can stir feelings that it is not given to many to touch."

Among those who were impressed by the artistry of the young violinist and who saw the commercial possibilities inherent in his rave reviews was a young hardware salesman not long from Russia. He prevailed upon Zimbalist to play for a socialist meeting in Brownsville for which he was booking the entertainment, and even managed to get him at a reduced fee.

It was the first time S. Hurok presented anybody, and emboldened by his success, Hurok got permission from the artist to manage a Carnegie Hall recital debut. The name he chose for his new management firm was the Von Hugo Musical Society. The "h" and "u" came from Hurok's name, the "go" from his partner Goldberg's name, and the "Von" was the contribution of Ludwig "von" Beethoven.

Hurok prudently hung on to his hardware job until he saw what the results of his first managerial enterprise were. The house was sold out and 250 people took seats upon the stage. The latter interested Hurok's boss from the hardware business. "I suppose those people on the stage are the members of your society," he said to the incipient impresario. "Yes, of course," replied Hurok, hiding a smile and his intention to leave more rational pursuits for full time impresario status. The receipts from the first Zimbalist recital, and a second which was hastily arranged, launched the career that has launched a thousand other careers.

Meantime, Stransky's career was also flourishing. An all-Wagner concert was a great success, as was a Mahler Memorial Concert which the Philharmonic blandly arranged. By January, with still more successes behind him, the Philharmonic presented him with a three-year contract doubling his salary to $20,000 a year and preserving him from the Vienna Opera which had approached him with an offer.

In fairness, it must be said that Stransky's first season was a reasonably interesting one. He exhibited several novelties, including Bruckner's

Rabbi Stephen Wise launched many a good liberal crusade from Carnegie Hall which was his pulpit for many years.

Culver Service

Fifth Symphony and Felix Weingartner's Third, neither of which was well received, programmed the latest work of Frederick Delius, "In a Summer Garden," which was regarded, probably correctly, as pretty, rather poetic and innocuous music, and debuted Siegfried Wagner's overture to *Bruder Lustig* which got the sort of reviews poor Siegfried must have been getting used to by then.

As far as the critics were concerned, Hector Berlioz was in the same class with Siegfried Wagner, and when Stransky, who was a disciple of the great romantic, did the *Harold in Italy*, he received a thorough chastisement from the critics, who thought that Berlioz' ambitions outran his abilities. "One feels behind it all a powerful will striving . . . to create something out of nothing, but one ends by becoming keenly sensitive to the impotence of this striving," one critic wrote.

Despite the failure of all his novelties, the critics and public were pleased with Stransky's first season. Krehbiel, naturally, led the chorus of praise, terming him "a fine handicraftsman, a sensitive, highly appreciative artist, a musician of large and generous sympathies." Henry T. Finck shrewdly noted that the new man "has what New Yorkers enjoy most, rhythmic energy, dramatic impulses and the art of bringing out emotional climaxes." At the season's end the orchestra received a bequest from Joseph Pulitzer, which eventually totalled

Museum of the City of New York

Efrem Zimbalist made his Carnegie Hall debut in 1911. His concert then was the first ever presented by a young, would-be impresario named Sol Hurok.

$900,000 and which was contingent on its finding 1000 subscribers giving ten dollars per season. This necessitated some reorganization of the orchestra's board of directors.

The rest of the 1911-1912 season at Carnegie Hall was dominated by visiting orchestras. Besides Zimbalist, there were few recitalists, instrumental or vocal, who made significant debuts, but many of the old hands, especially pianists, were back. In fact, there were so many of them in New York that winter that it seemed to many that a renaissance of an art which had lately been neglected was at hand. Virtually lost in the shuffle, which included Josef Lhévinne, Josef Hofmann, de Pachmann, Goodson, Bauer, Shattuck, was a young pianist's pianist named Wilhelm Bachaus. He did not debut at Carnegie Hall, but came there for his first solo recital. Among Bachaus' listeners, a tiny group, were both Hofmann and Lhévinne, who applauded their colleague with an enthusiasm that was more than professional courtesy. The critics found Bachaus an artist of commanding intellect rather than profoundly emotional characteristics. Like Rubinstein, his lack of the big game doomed him to failure in this country, until after World War II when as an old man, his fame spread by his phonograph records, he finally found the acclaim which he had deserved much earlier.

But if most of the pianists who returned to Carnegie Hall were familiar figures, the orchestras which visited were virtual strangers. The first of them was the Chicago Symphony, under Frederick Stock. It had not been in New York since 1898, and it received a good, but by no means ecstatic, reception. Almost everyone agreed with Krehbiel that "Chicago has an orchestra deserving of being ranked with the principal local ones." The critics would have liked more brilliancy of tone and less sonority, and the program, featuring Albert Spalding playing the local debut of Elgar's long and unrewarding Violin Concerto, was not of the best. Of the concerto one critic wrote: "Why so much pother should have been raised over it or why its publishers should demand fancy prices for its performances is puzzling."

If anything, New York critics found the Carnegie Hall debut of another Midwestern orchestra, the Minneapolis Symphony, more exciting than the reappearance of the Chicago group. The Minneapolis Orchestra was newer, it came from a city a bit farther off the cultural map than Chicago and its existence was therefore encouraging evidence of the spread of music to the wilds of America. Charles Henry Meltzer of the *American* stated flatly that "no body of musicians in this country . . . has excelled the Minneapolis Society. But for local pride I might be tempted to add—none has equalled it." All in all, the performances of the Minneapolis Symphony under Emil Oberhoffer represented a triumph over the insularity of its home setting and a triumph over the insularity of the eastern seaboard which tended then, as now, to believe that it had a corner on culture.

Equally elevating, in a different way, was the week-long Brahms festival which Walter and Frank Damrosch and the New York Symphony and the Oratorio Society provided at the end of the New York season. It included all the symphonies and concertos, the *German Requiem*, and songs, overtures and other minor pieces. Bachaus and Zimbalist were the soloists, along with soprano Florence Hinkle and baritone Gwilym Miles, and their efforts provided something of a revelation to New York. Brahms's career here had been an odd one. At first considered variously as decadent or radical, his work had, in the past several years, been virtually ignored. The piano and violin concertos could not compete in popularity with the works of Saint-Saëns and the now almost forgotten show pieces of Anton Rubinstein. The symphonies were heard only occasionally, the German repertory being completely dominated by Beethoven and Wagner. The great *Requiem* had had but two performances in twenty years before the festival. Apparently after the early failure of his work in New York, no one was willing to campaign for it, despite evidence that the musical tastes of the time might easily accommodate, and even welcome, it.

The Brahms festival began to redress the balance in Brahms' favor. After it, his pieces found a higher place in the symphonic repertory. One critic summed up the import of the festival this way: "The day when Brahms was a mystery to the masses has evidently passed. Both Walter and Frank Damrosch are to be highly commended for their preparation of the present festival; it is fitting that the compositions of a giant in the tone world should be fully appreciated, and this festival will go far to make his music better loved and his name even more highly reverenced."

But interesting and successful as the Brahms festival was, and important as the successes of the provincial orchestras were to America's sense of pride in its musical growth, there is no doubt that the high point of the orchestral season was the appearance of the London Symphony Orchestra under Arthur Nikisch, reigning prima donna of the podium. The orchestra, a cooperative society, was a good one, "highly thought of by Londoners, and deservedly so. . . . The strings are numerous and have a fine solidarity and power. . . . The woodwinds are uncommonly good. . . . The orchestra on the whole is exceedingly responsive to the conductor. . . ."

But it was by no means a perfect orchestra, no better than the Boston Symphony or a dozen other first-class organizations throughout the world. Critics found its attack, particularly in the ensemble playing, ragged and although they appreciated the orchestra, they were at a loss to explain the wild enthusiasm it aroused on purely musical grounds.

The secret of its success lay in the personality of its leader. Nikisch was a thousand-dollar-a-night conductor, and his poetic good looks, even including his fingertips, were the subject of much prose poetry. He was embraced on the street and mobbed after his concerts. Krehbiel summed up his impact admirably when he wrote that "we used to have prima donnas in New York whose names on a program insured financial success for the performance. . . . For prima donna . . . read the conductor, and a parallel is established in orchestral art which is even more humiliating than that pervading our opera houses."

Once again, New York was exercising its naïveté for all to see, and it was embarrassing to some of its better trained ears.

The next season, 1912-1913, the audience was given a chance to mend its ways. Karl Muck was back on the podium of the Boston Symphony, and Eugène Ysaÿe, after an eight-year absence, was back on the concert stage rescuing the public, in Krehbiel's image, from "sidewise excursions into primrose paths," bringing them back "into the great classic highway and expounding for them the cardinal principles of artistic beauty."

A similar service was performed by Leopold Godowsky, back in New York after a dozen years away. He appeared with the Philharmonic playing a Brahms piano concerto, following the Stransky debut of Bruckner's Sixth Symphony. "The audience," according to one observer, "enjoyed its opportunity to applaud all the more because the Bruckner symphony . . . had plunged the vast majority into a mood of profound apathy and boredom."

The man who came back from the longest distance to appear at Carnegie Hall was Captain Roald Amundsen, whose claims to discovery of the South Pole had lately been substantiated against the similar claims of Captain Frederick Cook, who had previously spoken at the hall. The dispute had been one of the chief items of journalistic interest at the time, and there was a good house on hand to see Amundsen receive a gold medal from the National Geographic Society honoring his many chilly achievements, to hear him tell of the sundry hardships he and his men had suffered in the cause of science and to see his lantern slides of arctic wastes.

An announcement by Stransky, who had been visiting Europe over the summer, that the "Mahler cult" on the continent was passing must have cheered his employers greatly as the season of 1913-1914 began. The reason adduced by Stransky for this was simple: "Mahler's lack of originality cannot be concealed," he said. "He tried to delude himself to hide his deficiency under a staggering mass of externals." This "business-as-usual" statement was an appropriate way to begin the last season of "normalcy" in New York.

The Paderewski cult also showed signs of waning strength. "Perhaps the most amazing feature of Paderewski's playing today is its disconcerting lack of poise," one critic wrote. His audience remained large and enthusiastic, but purely musical enthusiasm for his work had been fading a little on each of his return visits in recent years. It is possible that Paderewski, about to be forced by world events to begin a new career as humanitarian, statesman and eloquent defender of freedom, sensed the import of onrushing events in Europe and was distracted from concentration on the small world of the keyboard.

If he was preoccupied by affairs in Europe, the rest of the musical world, isolated in a nation delusively certain that it had no stake in European politics, was not. Even so, there was little of interest in the new season. Karl Muck brought a pair of interesting programs to Carnegie Hall, one composed of eighteenth-century music, the other featuring a new work by Florent Schmitt, a suite based on the Salome legend and impressionistic in style. Ysaÿe, Godowsky and Jean Gerardy, back in the country for the first time in six years, combined forces for a pair of chamber music concerts in the hall, but came a cropper on its unsuitability to such music and on the fact that three virtuosos do not necessarily add up to a fine chamber group.

Historically, the event of the year was Leopold Stokowski's debut in New York as conductor of the Philadelphia Orchestra. He had been organist at St. Bartholomew's Church in New York just nine years before, had gone on to make the Cincinnati Orchestra into a major symphonic organization and had now come to Philadelphia to rebuild the languishing orchestra there. In a program of Mozart, Brahms and Richard Strauss, as well as some operatic arias sung by Alma Gluck, he was able to demonstrate the versatility, even the adventurousness, of his taste and ability (for Mozart, like Brahms, was a virtual stranger to the American concert platform, and Strauss was still a radical). Those who have witnessed the Stokowski hands swoop and soar like a pair of unloosed swallows in recent years will be surprised to learn that at that time the Stokowski stage attitude was "devoid of mannerisms, his attention . . . concentrated on his work." They will be equally surprised to learn that the man who was shortly to become the very model of the modern conductor was not highly rated by the critics. "While Mr. Stokowski is not at present to be accounted a great conductor," Richard Aldrich wrote, "he is an interesting one and showed unquestionable talent and native gift that ought to take him far."

How far he went is part of modern musical history, for this boldly imaginative innovator was equally a supreme showman and devoted importer of the novel and the shocking. He had to wait two years, however, before Manhattan would take to him. Then, in April 1916, he brought his orchestra to the Metropolitan Opera House and presented the massive Mahler Eighth Symphony, "the symphony of a thousand," to the startled and then beguiled ears of New Yorkers, and launched the reputation which was to be the most glamorous, if not, ultimately, the solidest, in American orchestral history.

But in 1914, his time—the Twenties—was yet to come. The world had to be made over before it was to be ready for a Stokowski, though the processes of remaking were already in motion at the time of his debut.

By the time the next season began, a certain minor prince had been murdered in the streets of a distant Balkan city, and the forces which had for so long been boiling beneath the determinedly placid surface of the twentieth century's first decade-and-a-half were set free. The good years, the innocent years, the years of American isolation were over, and all the efforts to recapture them would come to nought. The larger world was never to be the same again; neither was the small world of music.

Six

"The Visions Which They Saw"

THE IMPACT OF THE EUROPEAN WAR WAS FELT IMMEDIATELY IN THE American musical world. As the first summer and fall of conflict wore on, worried announcements began to appear in the musical press. In August, *Musical America* reported that the start of the season would undoubtedly be delayed because so many stars of the concert and opera stage were marooned on the continent. No one, for example, was quite certain where Josef Stransky was. There was knowledge of the whereabouts of Josef Hofmann and his wife, Marcella Sembrich. They were holed up with Paderewski at his villa, along with dozens of other refugees who were camped, in tents, on the Paderewski lawn. Stokowski and his wife, Olga Samaroff, were trapped in Munich. Since Stokowski was a British subject, it was necessary for them to escape clandestinely—which they did.

All of these people along with many others who were in Europe for the festival season eventually found transportation to America, but concern for their safety and the sudden knowledge that the war seemed about to cause its first shortage—a shortage of talent—were overriding concerns in the musical world.

Nothing brought the meaning of the war home more dramatically than the report that Fritz Kreisler had been killed in action against the Russians in the battle of Lemberg. A reserve captain in the Austrian army, Kreisler had been mobilized at the outbreak of the war.

Unconfirmed reports indicated that he had been killed in a cavalry charge against Austrian entrenchments. An anxious month passed, then his wife wrote to let his American friends know that although he had been severely wounded—ridden down by a horse and lanced by a Russian spear—he was recuperating. There was still some doubt about his ability to play again. But that was resolved by the end of October when it was announced that his bow arm was not, after all, permanently disabled.

By this time Stransky had been found in Switzerland and *Musical America* could relievedly report that the war would cause few changes in programs. At the same time, the Boston Symphony Orchestra, which had been forced to cancel its early fall tour reported that Karl Muck would be returning shortly—as soon as he had rounded up those members of his orchestra who were missing on the continent.

Kreisler and his wife arrived aboard the *Rotterdam* in late November. He was using a cane and limping when he came down the gangplank. But he was able to report that he had been declared permanently disabled and would not have to return to the front. He planned to spend the war in America, a decision that was to lead to needless hardship for him after our entry into the war. At the moment, however, he was obviously relieved to be here and Americans, despite their sympathy with the Allied cause, were relieved to have him here.

He issued a hopeful statement: "It is to the artist that we must look, first of all, I think, as the true diplomat, the true missionary of peace, and in that service that will come to us it is my great hope to do my part."

Unfortunately, he was not allowed to play an active role for very long. Prejudice against German and Austrian music and musicians was rising, and once America entered the war, Kreisler was to be forced into temporary retirement. But not before he received one of the most heart-warming receptions in Carnegie Hall's history when he returned to the concert platform.

There had been considerable speculation as to what sort of reception a former Austrian soldier might receive in pro-Allied America. But when he came on stage, doing his best to minimize his limp, to face a capacity audience, including standees and some 300 people seated on the stage, "he was given a long continued, enthusiastic and warmly demonstrative welcome," according to the *Times*. The *Post* reported that "Since the hall was opened . . . it has held many crowded and enthusiastic audiences, but none more so than that which greeted him . . . All united in bestowing on him plaudits that rose in crescendos like storm winds, both when he first appeared and after each of his numbers."

Many in the audience were aware that Kreisler was doing his best to act the role of "true diplomat, the true missionary of peace," in trying almost single-handedly to support the orphans of comrades killed beside him and of men who had died in the hospital where his wife had acted as a nurse. In addition, he was extending what help he could to some 1500 European artists who were in dire economic straits due to the war. So there were clear and compelling reasons for giving him a warm reception as he played such familiar Kreisler standbys as the "Devil's Trill" sonata and the chaconne from Bach's solo Sonata in D minor. It is unfortunate that America could not continue to extend the spirit of fair play and decency which it gave to Kreisler as the war continued.

In the case of Kreisler and other artists as well, the effects of superpatriotism would not be felt for a couple of years. For the moment, the war's effect on the musical audience was demonstrated only in small ways. For instance, there was the case of the clicking needles. In the first winter of the war a number of the ladies who attended matinees, an easily distracted audience at best, began to bring their Red Cross knitting projects along with them to the concerts. Several hundred pairs of needles going simultaneously can cause a fearful racket, and it finally became a subject for editorialists. "The concert hall," humphed one, "is not the place for such activity. The conductor of an orchestra, or any individual artist giving a recital, has the right to demand of his audience its undivided attention." In due course a sign appeared in the hall's lobby requesting the ladies to quell their humanitarian ardor long enough for a concert to proceed in relative peace.

Among the artists who benefited from the new—and typically American—rule of concert etiquette were Kreisler and John McCormack who gave recitals in the hall along with Busoni and, most interestingly, Casals and Harold Bauer who gave a joint recital that "was a delight from beginning to end." It was Casals' first trip to New York since the unhappy experience of 1904. This time, although still not a great favorite with the public, he was fortunate at least in being able to work with Bauer, perhaps the greatest exponent of ensemble playing of his time. It was not the first—and certainly not the last—time that Bauer's fine musicianship, excellent taste and willingness to share, rather than dominate, a platform served the cause of chamber music well.

The year was not notable for new orchestral music at Carnegie Hall. Stransky programmed no novelties of importance; Damrosch, who had not been a regular tenant of the hall since the Philharmonic reorganization, was playing most of his concerts elsewhere, and the Boston Symphony was curtailing its travel because of the war. Perhaps the most interesting orchestral concert was the last concert of the Russian Symphony Orchestra's season at which Modeste Altschuler presented the first New York performance of Scriabin's *Prometheus.* Not only was this the first New York performance, he claimed, but the first performance anywhere of the work in its entirety. What its other performers had left out was the portion scored by the composer for *clavier à lumières*—or color organ. Directions for the use of this instrument, a sort of giant electronic kaleidoscope, were as detailed as any other part in the score.

The piece was performed in total darkness, the orchestra seated before a large screen, in back of which was the infernal machine which was to disconcert the conservatives and enchant the naïve. As the piece progressed colored lights on the screen merged into one another, shifting and changing in kaleidoscopic fashion. "The composition which is in one movement but is not brief, was given twice in order that the listeners, or the spectators, might have an opportunity to take in fully the revolutionary significance of it," Aldrich noted sourly. "As music the composition is on the level with some of the most recent developments of cacophony and impotent invention," he added, wondering just how anyone in his right mind could detect an intensification of the pleasures of music from the use of the machine. A few months earlier it might have served to distract the ladies from their knitting, but now it seemed just another one of the empty victories of the bourgeoning machine age.

All in all, at the season's end, it seemed that the year of war had had but slight effect on the world of music. Programs were somewhat curtailed, there were so many refugee musicians in America that salaries and fees seemed to be dropping somewhat, and Mischa Elman had temporarily given up the fiddle because he was "heart-weary" over the war and thought people might better spend the money they normally spent on concerts for charity. Otherwise, it was clear music was going to survive, if in somewhat different circumstances, during the unpleasantness.

There was some fear that the war would have a bad effect on American composition. Very little of it was played, despite the outburst of patriotic nationalism that was giving its first lusty cries in 1915. Pianist-composer-historian Arthur Whiting wrote in a musical journal that "the healthful growth of our music has been retarded, standards have been misplaced, weak men have been given praise, which should have been reserved for strong men, all because certain irresponsible people have the power, simply by uttering two words, 'unpatriotic' and 'disloyal' to silence needful strengthening in the highest sense of friendly criticism." Whiting had to admit, however, that "there is not enough technical finish in the works of many American composers; that they are disposed to dodge the grind which alone can make them masters of their craft."

Writing almost simultaneously with Whiting, Daniel Gregory Mason, the American composer and critic, pointed out the real problem, which had nothing to do with the pressures of those who sought to find an American compositional idiom, wartime nationalism or the lingering effects of genteelism. The problem, as he saw it, was simply lack of interest on the part of the wider public. "Composition," he wrote, "involves a highly complex technique, a freely active imagination—both using up much time and bringing in no money. The American composer, he said, must go hungry for the sake of his art, "but more ominous still, he must go hungry of music." In short, the people who talked the most about the need for developing American music were the least willing to do something about it—that is subsidize the men who were trying to write it.

That situation was due to grow worse instead of better during the war years. But things were so bad anyway that hardly any significant difference could be detected in the status of the composer. Even though the war shut off the flow of new European compositions and conductors, searching for novelties, turned with slightly more frequency to the Americans, a list of new works scheduled for the 1915-1916 season turned up nothing of importance. The list included one Oriental Suite and one Oriental Fantasy, a Prince Hal Overture, Rubin Goldmark's symphonic poem, *Samson*, a revival of MacDowell's *Lancelot and Elaine*, and sundry suites. Like nearly every American work written before the end of the war, none of these pieces, and none of their composers, have passed into the repertory, none are played, even occasionally, today.

The new season offered a number of concerts dedicated to war relief, the first and foremost being an appearance by Paderewski on behalf of the Polish Victims' Relief Fund. He prefaced his performance with a speech on "The Martyrdom of Poland," and a reporter from *Musical America* wrote, "Neither Mr. Paderewski's speech nor his delivery of it will soon pass from the memories of those who heard it. It lasted about an hour and touched upon the glories of Poland—the loftiness of the Polish character, the idealism and humanitarian instincts of the nation's kings and law-givers even in remote centuries, the prowess of its warriors, the higher glories of its poets, painters, scientists, philosophers and musicians; upon the rapacity of its partitioners in past times, and upon the illimitable horrors of its present plight."

Paderewski, in short, covered just about everything, but he made his essential point. Even flowers and programs were auctioned off to eager bidders and at the close of the recital "Mme. Paderewski's famous Polish dolls were auctioned off at dizzy prices." The total take was $16,009.

But all was not routine music and wartime benefits at Carnegie Hall in 1915-1916. Damrosch gave the first American performance of Ravel's second *Daphnis et Chloé* Suite and wonder of wonders, Arnold Schönberg turned up on a Philharmonic program, when Stransky conducted the atonal master's *Pelleas and Melisande*, which the audience not only survived, but also appeared to like rather well. "There is nothing to grow heated about in a discussion of this Schönberg work," said one critic. "It has some harsh moments, but also many agreeable ones. . . . The orchestra performed it magnificently."

Equally well received, a little later, was the First Symphony of the leader of the opposition camp in modern music, Igor Stravinsky. "Those who came prepared to hear a riot of discord and a cubist tone picture must have rubbed their eyes and taken another look at the composer's name . . ." one critic wrote. "This E flat symphony proved to be sane and tuneful, balanced in form and skillfully orchestrated."

Between these two early works by modern masters Carnegie Hall was privileged to hear Fritz Kreisler repay an old debt, when he played the Schumann *Fantasia* in C major for violin and orchestra with the Philharmonic. The work had been written for, and dedicated to, the great nineteenth-century violin master, Joseph Joachim, who played it frequently. One day in 1896 at a table in the *Tonkünstler Verein* (club of artists of the tone) in Vienna, Joachim remarked to Brahms that he was afraid the piece would die when he passed from the scene. Brahms argued that "the best parts of the piece should be saved by eliminating meaningless passages and elaborating the middle passage." "The composition must be stripped of its underbrush," he said. Joachim agreed and made a vague promise to undertake the task. Kreisler and his teacher happened to be at the table and the latter, Joseph Hellmesberger, turned to his pupil and said, "You heard what *Meister* Brahms said. "Don't you ever forget it."

Kreisler never did, and as the years passed he frequently inquired about the revisions. It was not until after Joachim's death that he learned that they had never even been begun.

"When I learned that Joachim had not attempted a revision," Kreisler told his biographer, Louis Lochner, "I was determined that I would. I approached my task with a diffidence, because one does not like to meddle with the work of great artists. But I had to make the choice of meddling or letting the *Fantasia* die. I had only one thought, respectfully and scrupulously to clarify the thought of the master, wherever it seemed perfectly evident what was intended by him."

It was almost twenty years after the Vienna conversation that Kreisler brought forth his revisions; they were extremely well received at his Carnegie Hall concert on December 12, 1915, and the reception convinced Kreisler that he had acted in the spirit of the Vienna meeting. He continued to "fiddle" with the revisions for another twenty years and finally presented them in their final form in 1936 at Carnegie Hall.

The season of 1916-1917 saw war fever reach its highest point since the outbreak of hostilities in 1914. The season began in almost routine fashion. The Philharmonic, celebrating its 75th Anniversary, began its series of concerts with the New York premiere of Richard Strauss's *Alpine* symphony. The composer's great days were now behind him, and those who had disliked the radicalism which had made his early works so important, now were able to dismiss him as a virtual has-been, a thing they proceeded to do with relief and relish. "The work," said Richard Aldrich, "is long, shambling in structure, vague in its impression. The ending is intolerably long drawn out. It is not an achievement that will add lustre to the composer's reputation. It is, on the contrary, one that will increase the force of the description of Strauss as 'a man who was once a genius!' "

This was the only new work of importance which the Philharmonic presented during its anniversary season, a commentary on the qualities of the Stransky leadership rather than on the effects of the war. By the end of the season the running fire which Richard Aldrich and a few other critics had directed at the conductor had precipitated a nice little musical quarrel. The critics conceded that under Stransky's leadership the orchestra's personnel had improved and that with this improvement had come an increase in technical proficiency. Aldrich was pleased to find that "neglected" composers like Brahms, Schumann and Mozart were finding a more prominent place on the orchestra's programs, but he objected to the rather perfunctory readings their works received. The critics even conceded, with Aldrich, that

Stransky was an industrious, hard-working musician, who had made himself popular and well-liked, but those qualities didn't make him a great conductor. In fact, they were the very qualities which doomed much of his work to mediocrity. "The Philharmonic Society has now a large and enthusiastic following," Aldrich concluded. "Its performances ought to be as fine as any that are heard in this country. That they are not is a source of deep regret."

Much more interesting than anything the Philharmonic presented in 1916-1917 was a program of The Society of the Friends of Music at which America received its first long look at the music of Ernest Bloch. The Swiss composer was in this country as a result of the war, and the concert, conducted by Artur Bodansky, who was shortly to become a leading conductorial figure in New York, presented a generous sampling of his works, including the *Schelomo*—the Hebraic rhapsody for cello and orchestra which is still regarded as his masterwork. The critics liked Bloch's work. But many felt that an entire evening of Bloch was too much of a muchness. "In truth," it was written, "this concert of Mr. Bloch's music suffered from the monotony of style and expression inevitable in the work of one man so wholly under the sway of one idea as he is, and especially one whose methods make so heavy demands upon the listener."

Be that as it may, very little else in that wartime season demanded much of the listener. Paderewski gave another concert very much like those he had been giving for years, and so did Teresa Carreño, who died not long after this, her last New York recital. The rest was routine. There were no debuts of significance and there were few radical departures on the part of established favorites.

In a season of "keep out of war meetings," of patriotic meetings, of a riotous mob at a speech by a German soldier, the only speech of any special interest was given by Sir Rabindranath Tagore, the Indian poet who was temporarily living in the United States. The hall was completely filled to hear the 1913 Nobel Prize winner declare himself against nationalism. He hoped that the war would eradicate it; he was certain that it was making the inadequacies of nationalism much clearer than they had ever been before. These, he said, were greed and self-interest, and the subordination of the rights of the individual to the self-imposed rights of the nation.

Just a few months after the poet spoke, however, America was at war. Along with it came a virulent attack of hysteria that was virtually unparalleled in our history. Practically no area of American life was to remain untouched by the superpatriots, the spy mongers, the lunatic fringe. Some of their activities, like the renaming of sauerkraut—it was called victory cabbage—were merely ludicrous, but the roundup of radicals and their imprisonment for daring to dissent from a war in which they did not believe was a violation of the most important principles of democracy, as was the shameful treatment of conscientious objectors. Music, and the world of high culture, was not exempt from the activities of the idiot fringe. Indeed, it was a prime target. For anti-intellectual and anti-artistic attitudes nearly always go hand in hand with an insistence on conformity to nonrationalistic mass values.

Of all the arts, music was the most open to attack. For the German tradition, especially in symphonic music, was the dominant one in America and had been for many years. In the opening days of America's entry into the war, in the spring of 1917, there was little anti-German activity in the musical world. Rather, there was a concentration on the more positive aspects of patriotism. When word reached the Metropolitan that war had been declared, the orchestra deserted the score of Reginald DeKoven's *The Pilgrims of Canterbury* and swung into "The Star-Spangled Banner." In the next few months the national anthem was easily the most popular piece in the repertory. When John McCormack sang it to open a concert made up largely of American songs at Carnegie Hall a few days after the declaration of war, the cheering lasted a full fifteen minutes.

Within a month Carnegie Hall audiences were treated to two speeches by British cousins, urging—as if they needed it—full support for their new allies and for their own army which would soon take its place on the European battleground. Sir Ernest Shackleton, the polar explorer, speaking for charity, "exhorted Americans to stand together with their allies in the 'great adventure' on the European battlefields." The Right Honorable Arthur James Balfour, came to the hall a few weeks later to raise between $50,000 and $100,000 for the British

Red Cross. When a new set of motion pictures showing the actual fighting on the River Ancre in France and the famous tanks in action were thrown on the screen the audience went wild. The films showed allied troops advancing behind a screen of the fantastic new weapons to capture thousands of German prisoners. The film set the proper mood for the reception of Balfour who arrived at the hall at 11:00 P.M. and addressed the crowd from his box.

His speech set off another noisy demonstration. He declared: "America is throwing herself wholeheartedly into this struggle to help us in every way possible on land and sea. America is also giving us something else which in many respects is of even more value and more permanence. I refer to her sympathy and her love. You are struggling with us not only for your own country but for the freedom of the whole world, and in this cause we shall continue fighting until success is achieved."

Sentiments like Balfour's—noble-sounding, well-motivated—dominated the thinking of most Americans during the early days of the war. But they had a mirror image which, on the home front, was to render meaningless the lofty rationales for war offered by orators and editorialists. For if we were busily making the world safe for democracy we were making home-front America exceedingly unsafe for it.

At first the hysteria was kept within bounds. To be sure people like Johanna Gadski, the singer, and her husband were charged with being spies (she had allegedly exulted in the sinking of the *Lusitania*). But it seemed possible that such nonsense would be confined to an unimportant fringe of loud-mouthed fireside warriors, that the larger world could concentrate on important matters—such as winning the war.

This optimistic view failed to reckon with the gnat-like mentality of the super-patriot, and by the time the next musical season began, many of them were raising a general hue and cry against German music. In October the New York Board of Education forbade discussion of German opera in New York public school classrooms and all around the country German operatic titles were hastily being translated into English. The following month the Met's manager Giulio Gatti-Casazza—who didn't like the German repertory anyway—announced that no German operas would be presented at the house. Shortly thereafter, the Philharmonic promised it would perform no works by living German composers; Walter Damrosch extended the same pledge on the part of the Symphony Society, although he pleaded that the ban not be extended to the works of Germans no longer living. In this case, he was acting in his own enlightened self-interest. It would be impossible, even today, to make up a satisfactory year of programs without including the German and Austrian composers.

The situation reached such preposterous heights (*all* German music was actually banned in Pittsburgh) that two guaranteed-100-per-cent-American ladies, Olga Samaroff, the Texas pianist and wife of Stokowski, and Mrs. Ossip Gabrilowitsch, Mark Twain's daughter, were dispatched to Washington to discuss with President Wilson and Colonel House the problem of whether German music should be banned. Both assured the ladies that the war need not be extended to dead composers.

Nevertheless, the husbands of both ladies, along with another outspoken foe of extending the war to music, Leopold Godowsky, found themselves being shadowed by government agents.

During the same year Oswald Garrison Villard, chairman of the Philharmonic's board, who during the anniversary season had boasted that "art and our orchestra were unaffected by prejudice, even in the face of war," was asked to resign. A distinguished pacifist and editor of both the New York *Post* and of *The Nation*, Villard was informed by his fellow board members that "pacifism and music would not mix in wartime." He went quietly, under their pressure, as did Fritz Kreisler, who was feeling less polite pressures. He had continued to concertize but finally could no longer face up ot the opposition he was encountering. On December 1, 1917, he issued the following statement: "Bitter attacks have been made upon me as an Austrian and because at the outbreak of the war I fought as an officer in the Austrian army at the Russian front. I, therefore, am asking all concerned to release me from my obligation under existing contracts. My promise will be kept to play, without compensation, for those charities to which I have already pledged my support. I shall always remain deeply sensible of my debt of gratitude to this country for past kindness and appreciation of my art." Kreisler spent the next couple of years in virtual isolation at his home in Maine.

Yet in this gloomy fall of 1917, with the musical world marking time, and with at least 50 per cent of its standard repertory in jeopardy, there was one brilliant ray of hope. For on October 27 a sixteen-year-old violinist named Jascha Heifetz made his debut in Carnegie Hall.

The house was sold out, for the advance reports on the prodigy had been wildly enthusiastic. It was reported that after hearing him in Berlin four years earlier, Fritz Kreisler had told Efrem Zimbalist, "You and I might as well take our fiddles and break them across our knees." The audience on that Indian Summer Saturday afternoon in Carnegie Hall was a notable one, heavily flavored with Heifetz's fellow professionals, turned out to see if he could possibly be as good as was claimed.

He was. His concert manner was all austerity. Severely elegant in dress, unsmiling and unposturing, with thin, down-drawn lips under a patrician nose, he presented a picture of dedicated musicianship unmarred by showmanship or eccentricity. His appeal was all in his playing, and *that* the audience applauded "relentlessly" from the opening Vitali Chaconne to the final note of the Paganini-Auer Capriccio No. 24.

In the midst of the program came the famous exchange between Mischa Elman and Leopold Godowsky. Dabbing at his forehead with a handkerchief Elman murmured, "Rather warm in here, isn't it?" "Not for pianists," replied the imperturbable Godowsky.

The afternoon was due to grow warmer still, for at the end of the program "there was a mad rush to the stage of an avid, noisy crowd which, with throats tired, waved handkerchiefs and hats. This crowd made the youth, already drooping visibly with weariness, play again and again, and dispersed only when someone resorted to turning off the lights."

The critics were moved to displays of adjectival enthusiasm which occur only once in a generation. Krehbiel said, "He rose above his instrument and the music written for it." Pitts Sanborn of the *Globe* called him "a modern miracle." *The Evening Mail* thought him, "the perfect violinist."

Culver Service

Jascha Heifetz at the time of his debut in 1917 and (below) as he looks today.

RCA Victor

Topping them all was *Musical America*, whose man wrote: "It may not be that the greatest violinists now browsing in these fertile pastures are quite serious in their rumored decision to shut up shop, burn their fiddles and withdraw to distant wastes or sombre forests to invite oblivion because Jascha Heifetz has come upon us. The power and the glory of the newcomer may not be as ruthlessly destructive as all that. Nevertheless, this Russian boy . . . is beyond possibility of cavil a divinely inspired marvel whom advance report has belied only by undervaluation, and the most crushing, the supremest genius of the violin that has confronted us in the past decade or perchance even more."

The "supremest genius" took it all calmly, quietly spending the next day in the warm companionship of his notices. Monday he was back in the hall to hear one of Kreisler's last concerts before his enforced retirement.

Musically, nothing could approach the reception given Heifetz during that wartime season. But there was at least one other event of importance. That was the debut of Ossip Gabrilowitsch as a conductor. His first concert, leading men selected from New York's two major orchestras, for the benefit of Russian refugees was so successful that two more were scheduled during the remainder of the season. His way with the music was Mahler's way—he sacrificed romantic smoothness and grace for force and vitality. Now, however, New York could accept this. The New York *Post* said: "Last night Gabrilowitsch left no doubt whatever that he is one of the greatest conductors of the day. Truth to tell, he achieved more agreeable results with the immature Haydnish First Symphony of Beethoven than Toscanini did with the colossal Beethovenish Ninth by the same composer. Superb, virile and dramatic was Gabrilowitsch's reading of Beethoven's *Egmont* Overture. . . . It was Beethoven rejuvenated, and the audience was wild with delight . . . . the new conductor was overwhelmed with outbursts of enthusiasm such as are seldom heard." The other critics agreed, and a new career had begun for Gabrilowitsch. He was shortly to become the founding conductor of the Detroit Symphony.

But if America gained a conductor that year, it also lost one—and lost him under conditions which even forty years later should cause shame to the nation. Karl Muck was a German and it was well known that he was a friend of the Kaiser's. When war came, and long before America entered it, he submitted his resignation as director of the Boston Symphony Orchestra to Colonel Higginson. Higginson refused to accept it, saying he could not get another conductor of Muck's stature to lead the orchestra, that he would sooner disband the orchestra than let it deteriorate under a new man and that, anyway, it was more important than ever for an artist to continue his work to, in effect, keep alight what candles he could in the encircling gloom. Muck decided to stay on.

From 1917 on, however, his life was miserable. Rumors of the most outlandish sort began to circulate about him. He was in touch with German raiders by wireless, he had been seen signaling to lurking submarines by means of lights, he had stored up dynamite to blow up the Longfellow House and Faneuil Hall even though only a Bostonian could regard such places as prime war targets.

One incident is particularly ridiculous. Performing the third *Leonore* Overture in Cambridge, he sent a trumpet player offstage, as was customary, to sound a call. A lady patriot, observing this, and having no knowledge of the music, reported that "the clarion call of our young soldiers drilling outside confused the traitor Muck to such an extent that he stopped the orchestra more than once and looked as thought he were about to faint."

Such nonsense might have been laughed out of importance had there not been an incident just enough tinged with reality to lend credibility to the vaporings of the fantasists. It was charged that Muck had refused to play "The Star-Spangled Banner" at a concert in Providence. It is true that the anthem was not played, but its absence was the doing of Higginson, not Muck. The Colonel was of the strong opinion that the piece just wasn't appropriate at a concert of symphony music. That, however, was the final outrage as far as the super-patriots were concerned.

During the fall tour of the orchestra there was a mass meeting in Baltimore at which the statesmanlike Governor Warfield of Maryland urged his audience to mob the conductor to death. Back in Boston the D.A.R. and similarly enlightened groups declared a boycott of the orchestra's concerts and newspapers began to openly call Muck a traitor.

The situation reached a head when five cities refused to allow the leader to appear in them. It is to the credit of New York and of the Carnegie Hall audience that it was not among those cities and that there were no incidents when Muck conducted there. When he came to New York on November 8, 1917, the police sent a squad of plain-clothesmen to Carnegie Hall just in case there was trouble. But Muck led the national anthem and the audience was "affected with a desire to be civil to Dr. Karl Muck." But early in the spring of 1918 the mob finally succeeded in getting rid of the conductor. Higginson did his best to stem the tide, publicly declaring that "Dr. Muck is probably German in feeling, but he has done nothing wrong. He has been eminently satisfactory to me as a conductor and as a man." But it was hopeless. He finally announced that Dr. Muck would not return the following season. He did not even get a chance to finish the current one. On March 25 Federal agents arrested the conductor as an "enemy alien." The only charge leveled at him was that he had failed to register as an alien as all German citizens were required to do. Even that charge was untrue, for although a German by birth, Muck was a Swiss citizen. Nevertheless he passed the remainder of the war as prisoner 1337 at Fort Oglethorpe, Georgia. At the war's end, he was secretly deported.

Such was the wartime spirit of America and such were the manifestations of that spirit as they directly affected the musical world. Why did it happen? David Ewen rejects the notion that it was all just another manifestation of the sickness that comes over a nation during wartime. "I strongly believe," he writes, "that an attitude toward great music such as we displayed in 1917 can arise only if a nation has not yet developed its musical tastes fully, if its musical consciousness is not altogether awakened, if music has not yet become an essential part of its cultural life. I feel, therefore, that our violent antagonism toward any music even remotely associated with Germany reflected not so much our hysteria as our musical immaturity at that time."

He points out that in the midst of an air raid a London audience could quietly listen to a performance of *Tristan und Isolde*, that the same city could at the same time sponsor a gigantic Bach-Beethoven festival just as wartime Paris could listen with pleasure to a Schumann festival. America, farther from the war, and still in its cultural adolescence, had to prove that it could be more ruthless, more patriotic than countries suffering far more from the holocaust.

There were to be more immaturities in musical America before World War I ended in the fall of 1918. There was, for example, the business of refusing the directorship of the Philharmonic to Nikolai Sokoloff because someone had heard that he might be a German sympathizer. Happily, this knowledge was not discovered until after he had brought his brand new Cleveland Orchestra to Carnegie Hall for the first time and had received a fine critical reception.

But if the war caused a great deal of nonsense on the concert platform, it also brought one or two rare opportunities to hear refugee artists who might not have come to America except for the dislocations on the continent. One was Leopold Auer, the revered teacher of virtuoso violinists, who made his American debut in Carnegie Hall on March 23, 1918, at the age of seventy-two. In the audience were many of his pupils, among them Heifetz, and the families of such distinguished Auer pupils as Zimbalist and Elman. Also present were others of the professional fraternity—Kreisler, Stransky and Bodansky. Auer played a program of "Old Masters"—Handel, Bach, Vitali, Locatelli and Nardini—his accompanist was his niece Wanda Stein—and the old teacher was received with great warmth and affection by those who knew of his contributions to the musical life and had come to honor him as much as to hear him play.

Such opportunities, however, were rare in wartime. For the most part there was little musical interest in the programs of orchestras and recitalists. Many performers felt compelled to introduce strong elements of patriotism into their activities, as witness the concert Margarete Matzenauer, the Metropolitan contralto, sang at Carnegie Hall to promote the sale of War Savings Stamps. The hall was decorated inside and out with patriotic banners and posters and over the stage was a huge picture of guns and fighting men and the legend:

"These Boys Are Giving Their Lives—Will You Lend Your Quarters?" Since this was a matinee there was a strong feminine slant to the appeal of the posters. One read: "Joan of Arc Saved France—Women of America, Save Your Country." Another showed Uncle Sam beaming at a woman war worker and saying "She's Good Enough for Me."

Mme. Matzenauer's program included songs from all the major allied nations, but she was so moved by the occasion that she interjected a popular war ballad, "Dear Lad of Mine" into the middle of it, then sang "The Star-Spangled Banner." Her performance was typical of the war rallies that abounded in the hall during that season.

Americans also subjected themselves in this period to any number of lectures on life in the trenches, and Carnegie Hall booked its share of them. In September, 1918, just two months before the war ended, Floyd Gibbons, the dashing Chicago *Tribune* correspondent who had been wounded in the pursuit of news at the front, urged his audience to "hold fast at home" and to "finish the fight." He also brought the rather startling intelligence that the soldiers of the A.E.F. were not anxious for peace. They will be "greatly disheartened" he said, "if the people at home convinced themselves that peace with Germany's military power was desirable before that power had been crushed so that it could not rise again."

Happily, it was not necessary to spend the blood, toil and treasure necessary for a vengeful victory. One day in November, the guns fell silent. At home, after the victory celebrations had worn themselves out, another kind of silence fell. It was compounded of profound relief on the one hand and of some slight embarrassment at the excesses of patriotic zeal on the other.

The afternoon armistice was declared Fritz Kreisler and his wife were invited to share the box of friends at a Carnegie Hall concert. But as Mrs. Kreisler remembered the incident and told it to friend and biographer Louis Lochner, the first half of the concert was acutely uncomfortable. "In a box opposite us sat a famous tenor, who pretended not to notice us. Elsewhere sat others, some composers, some pianists, who suddenly developed myopia. The center box, however, was filled with high allied officers in full regalia. During the intermission the door to our box suddenly opened, and in came four allied officers. Such a scene of hugging and hand shaking and mutual demonstrations of affection—the whole house watched breathlessly, and you could have heard a pin drop.. 'Thank God, Kreisler, the war is over,' an English general exclaimed. 'Elgar and Nellie Melba and scores of other friends all send you greetings. And don't you think we stopped playing your music during the war!' I was so deeply stirred I could not utter a word."

After the officers had left Kreisler's box, his friends suddenly regained their eyesight and tried to greet him. But by that time he and his wife were so disgusted by the whole business that they suddenly were unable to see all the waving hands.

That same evening the noise of New York's victory celebration kept Sergei Rachmaninoff awake. He had arrived earlier in the day almost penniless, his money and property confiscated by the Russian revolutionists. He tossed and turned, unable to sleep, sorrowing over his lost homeland, not particularly happy to be in America. But he knew his fortune lay here. No less than three offers to conduct orchestras here had come to him, and although he had turned them all down, they had demonstrated to him the economic possibilities of the musical life in America.

Six weeks of concertizing passed before he gave his first New York recital at Carnegie Hall. "The Rachmaninoff 'fans'—and there were thousands of them in audience—clamored for the favorite piece of Flatbush 'flappers,'" wrote James Gibbons Huneker, substituting at the *Times* for Richard Aldrich, who was in the army. "They surged toward Sergei in serried masses. They clustered about the stage. . . . But the chief thing is that Rachmaninoff did not play it. All Flapperdom sorrowed last night, for there are amiable fanatics who follow the pianist from place to place hoping to hear him in this particular prelude, like the Englishman who attended every performance of the lady lion tamer hoping to see her swallowed by one of her pets."

The "particular prelude" the Rachmaninoff fan club wanted so desperately to hear was the one in C sharp minor. It was much beloved by sentimental hearts and Rachmaninoff came to loathe the day he wrote it, so popular did it prove to be in America. Luckily, Rachmaninoff's compositional gifts as well as his pianistic abilities were of such popularity that he could afford to displease a certain segment of his audience. On the occasion of his return to the New York concert stage, however, he disappointed very few people. Some twenty years of constant concertizing began in triumph.

The rest of the season saw a gradual return to normalcy within the confines of Carnegie Hall. The postwar flood of new artists which would soon reach a peak had not yet begun. But there was promise for the future when Stransky introduced a work by an Italian composer new to America. Ottorino Respighi's *Fountains of Rome* was hardly a sensation when it was played in mid-February, but neither did it cause a violent reaction. Even the reintroduction of Wagner's work by Stransky did not cause that. The most hated of the German composers during the war, his pieces were received routinely when Stransky placed them on a program only months after the war's end. Indeed, there was probably a hidden benefit in the wartime ban on German music. For although the German masters naturally continued to be played with frequency, their dominance of the symphonic and operatic stages was ended by the war. Programs in the Twenties and thereafter became much better balanced as the music of other nations —even America—came to be played more and more frequently. No longer was every symphonist after Beethoven regarded as a radical; no longer were Richard Wagner's music dramas regarded as the ultimate flowering of the operatic art. Musical perspective had been restored in America—although at a bitter price.

Perspective of another sort began to be restored during the season of 1918-1919. The reputation of Stokowski's Philadelphia Orchestra had continued to grow during the war. Some New York music lovers had been so entranced by its sheen and brilliance that they journeyed to Philadelphia to hear it play at Liberty Loan rallies. Its performance of the Mahler "Symphony of a Thousand" at the Metropolitan Opera House in 1918 had ensured its position as the favorite of those who loved dashing innovation. When the orchestra returned to New York in the fall of 1918 to play at Carnegie Hall it was acclaimed. "We know few [orchestras] that have played with such sustained fire as did this particular one," wrote Huneker. "This blond young man has a positive gift as a conductor. . . . And his musicianship is not to be challenged," he said, summing up the impact of Stokowski's reading of the Tchaikovsky Fourth Symphony. It was the beginning of the Golden Era of the Golden One. Indeed, it was the beginning of the greatest era of the virtuoso conductor in America's musical history. Until the war, the great recitalists had attracted the most public interest and had built the largest fan clubs. Now, for reasons one can only guess at, interest in them waned, and the unsophisticated were coming out to watch—not to hear—the conductors as they had once watched the soloists. The days of the Stranskys, for instance, were numbered. The audiences demanded more color—and more ability—than he could offer. Particularly color. Lost in the shuffle were distinguished men who had only musicianship to offer. Bruno Walter, for example, was almost ignored when he first came to this country in the early Twenties to lead the New York Symphony. Henri Rabaud, an excellent musician who succeeded Muck at the helm of the Boston Symphony, suffered the same fate and his tenure lasted but two seasons. "He is," said one critic, "a cerebral conductor. He is sensitive to form . . . a Frenchman, ruled by tact and a fine sense of tonal balance. But cerebral." America was in no mood for cerebration just then. Rabaud's successor, Pierre Monteux, was also discounted. That sensitive and excellent conductor, leading an orchestra suffering evil days in the wake of the Muck scandal, the consequent resignation of Higginson and an attempt to unionize the orchestra, simply did not have the showy qualities the public desired.

Neither did Artur Rubinstein who came back in 1919 to try his luck in the country which had rebuffed him thirteen years before. The general reaction was summed up by Huneker who wrote, "A pianist of charm and technical finesse is Arthur [sic] Rubinstein. . . . He is a trifle old-fashioned in style. . . . It may be said of this Rubinstein that he came, played and was liked. But a miniaturist."

There was, despite this rebuff of a great artist, evidence of a desire for a new musical deal. The dissatisfaction with Stransky, the bourgeoning popularity of Stokowski, evidenced this. So did the formation of a new orchestra, appropriately named The New Symphony Orchestra, which played its first concert at Carnegie Hall on April 11, 1919, under

Edgar Varèse. Once an assistant to Richard Strauss and a composer of some note in his own right, he programmed new works by Debussy, Alfredo Casella, Béla Bartók and Gabriel Dupont. The concert was a failure. His baton, according to Huneker, was "leaden, without fire" and his orchestra sounded "like a wet hen." The orchestra was shortly to dispense with Varèse's services, replace him with Bodansky and begin a short but stimulating career as a virtuoso's instrument which would challenge the primacy of the established bands.

Change was everywhere in the air. Not all of it was for the good, either. Politically, for instance, there was a desire to abandon the nation's hard-won influence on the world scene, to retreat behind the ramparts of the Atlantic and watch the world go by. Eventually Americans were to see that this was impossible. But in the days following the war, heartily sick of the entanglements of European politics, with a powerful Senate cabal focusing the resentments of the nation on the peace treaty and its most important covenant, the one providing for a League of Nations, there was indifference to the responsibilities which were suddenly ours, as well as a desire to remake the nation in the image of the prewar days.

It was to this atmosphere that President Woodrow Wilson returned to the United States on July 8, 1919. He had spent seven months in Europe negotiating a peace, the first American president to leave the country during his term of office. Now, at last, the long hours of debate at Versailles finished, he was home—home to begin an even larger debate, one which was to end in defeat and shattered health.

But that was in the future. As his ship, the transport *George Washington*, steamed up the harbor, accompanied by four battleships and forty destroyers, he exuded confidence and the sheer joy of homecoming. He was well-pleased with his work in Europe, and surely the welcome he was receiving betokened acceptance of his work back home.

In its entire history, the Port of New York has never staged a reception like the one which greeted Wilson. The battleships fired twenty-one gun salutes in welcome, as did the guns at the Battery. Over his ship a blimp hovered protectively, while a squadron of seaplanes,

Culver Service

Woodrow Wilson and his wife on their way to Carnegie Hall where he launched his crusade for the League of Nations—and against the tide of history —on the very day he returned from the Paris peace conference, July 8, 1919.

traveling at the hair-raising speed of 80 miles an hour, whirled and darted like so many welcoming swallows.

The trip up the harbor took two hours longer than anticipated. And along the way, the President and the covey of welcoming ships, loaded to the gunnels with dignitaries, exchanged warm greetings. None was warmer than those exchanged between the President and an excursion steamer full of children on an outing. The kids set up a noisy cry and the President beamed and waved at them.

At the dock at Hoboken his daughters led a welcoming party of relatives and friends and the President didn't stop waving from the moment he spotted them. Later he was to say, "Jerseyman that I am, this is the first time I ever thought Hoboken beautiful."

The presidential party took the ferry across the Hudson, landing at the Twenty-third Street pier. His route through New York led across Twenty-third, up Fifth Avenue to Fifty-seventh Street and across it to Carnegie Hall where he was to make the first speech in his campaign for the League of Nations and the peace treaty into the making of which he had thrown every resource he had.

Wilson's reception on the streets of New York was a triumph. Since eight in the morning welcomers had been gathering along the streets, and by the time the procession began, between three and four hundred thousand New Yorkers, lined the streets. They were an affable and happy group, shouting greetings and encouragement at the President, whose "hat was never on his head for an instant," according to the *Times*. "There was not a time when he was not bowing and smiling to the thousands who joined in the noisy welcome." In front of 324 Fifth Avenue a little girl who was in a second story window threw a carnation at the President. It landed in Mrs. Wilson's lap and she handed it to her husband.

At 5:23 P.M., having been saluted by an honor guard that stretched two blocks along Fifty-seventh Street, Wilson finally entered the hall.

It had never been more lavishly decorated. Behind the speaker's stand American flags were massed, with the presidential standard nestling in the center of them. The rostrum was covered with rambler roses, sweet william, gladioli and clusters of small hollyhocks, and the word *Peace* was spelled out in electric lights over the proscenium arch. Backstage, Wilson was introduced to the captain and first officer of the famous British dirigible, the R-34, which was shortly to come to a tragic end, then listened while the Police Band and Glee Club favored him with such numbers as "For He's a Jolly Good Fellow" and "Over There." Following the national anthem there were three cheers for the President and then a man in the audience proposed "three cheers for Mrs. Wilson, the first lady of the land." These were joined in enthusiastically while Edith Bolling Galt Wilson waited quietly in the center box to hear her husband's speech. She, along with the rest of the assemblage, had first to hear welcoming speeches from New York's Mayor John F. Hylan and the Governor of New York, Al Smith. Then it was Wilson's turn.

"I am not going to try this afternoon to make you a real speech," he began. "I am a bit alarmed to find how many speeches I have in my system undelivered, but they are all speeches that come from the mind, and I want to say to you this afternoon only a few words from the heart."

He spoke first of the homesickness he had felt during his long absence, and he spoke of his pride in the army that America had sent to Europe, "that army of clean men, that army of men devoted to the highest interests of humanity, that army that one was glad to point out and say, 'These are my fellow-countrymen.' "

He spoke too, of that army's effect on the European conception of America, how it had revised the Continent's belief that America was purely isolationist and materialist. "It is a wonderful thing," said Wilson, "for this nation, hitherto isolated from the large affairs of the world, to win not only the universal confidence of the people of the world, but their universal affection."

Now the task was to secure the hard-won peace and back home, "where the great dynamo of national energy" was, "where the great purposes of national action were formed," Woodrow Wilson addressed himself to that task.

"We have had our eyes very close upon our tasks at times," he said, "but whenever we lifted them we were accustomed to lift them to a distant horizon. We were aware that all the peoples of the earth had turned their faces toward us as those who were the friends of freedom and of right, and whenever we thought of national policy and of its reaction upon the affairs of the world we knew we were under bonds to do the large thing and the right thing. It is a privilege, therefore, beyond all computation for a man, whether in a great capacity or a small, to take part in the councils and in the resolutions of a people like this."

But Wilson was afraid that some people did not share his vision and his idealism: "They do not see it," he said. They have looked too much upon the ground. They have thought too much of the interests that were near them and they have not listened to the voices of their neighbors."

Yet he was confident, confident that America "will not disappoint any high hope that has been formed of her. Least of all in this day of new-born liberty all over the world fail to extend her hand of support and assistance to those who had been made free."

"I believe," he concluded, "that if you will study the peace you will see that it is a just peace and a peace which, if it can be preserved, will save the world from unnecessary bloodshed. And now the great task is to preserve it. I have come back with my heart full of enthusiasm for throwing everything that I can, by way of influence or action, in with you to see that the peace is preserved—that when the long reckoning comes men may look back upon this generation of America and say: 'They were true to the visions which they saw. . . .' "

Thus was enacted, one hot July afternoon in Carnegie Hall, the first scene of the final act of a tragedy, one of the few genuine political tragedies ever to afflict the nation. For Woodrow Wilson, burning himself out with his own idealism, failed to see that the day of idealism was finished, that it lay interred in the mud of France with the dead of the army he had taken such pride in. The national mood was one of indifference and cynicism, a mood easily shaped by Wilson's political opponents, stronger and more bitter than he reckoned them, into active opposition to further entanglements with Europe.

America was about to embark on "the gaudiest spree" in its history. At long last its naïve faith in inevitable progress had been shattered, and beneath the gaiety of the next ten years lay a frantic despair over the loss of old values and old ways of behaving. Woodrow Wilson was no longer riding the tide of history. Suddenly he was forced to fight against it, and it was an impossible job.

But if the politics of the next years were to be the dreariest in the nation's history, its culture was to be the most exciting. For there was a sense of discovery in the air, a feeling that comes only at those times in man's intellectual history when a new sensibility is being formed.

Seven

"A Ghostly Rumble . . ."

Our view of the Twenties is obscured by a misty curtain of nostalgia, penetrated by the sounds of a desperate gaiety—the wail of a saxophone, the tap of dancing feet, the muttered exchange at a speakeasy's peephole, the overloud laughter of a party at Jay Gatsby's West Egg estate. Through the curtain we catch a glimpse of a coonskin coat, a painted jalopy, a hip flask raised on high. But most of us cannot—or will not—look long enough and well enough to dispel the mist of memory and false nostalgia, to get a clear view of what was important, to see past the dancing figures in the foreground.

Socially and culturally the Twenties were an important era—the most important ten years of the century thus far. We choose to remember the laughter and to dismiss the disillusion which was the basis of the new creativity. We choose to enshrine the ephemera and reduce the real renaissance that took place in that fleeting time to an adjunct of a big party that happened to last for an entire decade.

It may have been Fitzgerald's decade, but it was also the decade in which the final assaults were made on Babbitt and boobocracy, the decade in which nearly all of the major literary figures of our time and country either made their beginning or reached their apotheosis (sometimes simultaneously). It was a time in which the nation abandoned the simple pieties of progress as well as faith in the established order of things. It was a time when we began to reach gropingly for a more complex code of behavior, at once less repressive and more cynical than the one it replaced. What the American—particularly the artist and the intellectual—sought was freedom; not political freedom, but personal freedom and its corollaries which included freedom from old conventions and old forms of expression. Basically apolitical, if not antipolitical, the artist of the Twenties sought the freedom to see with a fresh eye.

In this search for a creative freedom, he struck a responsive chord in the younger generation that had been alienated by the war from the manners, morals and philosophy of the society which they thought had caused it. They too sought freedom—personal freedom, the freedom to be irresponsible and, most precious of all, the freedom to seek pleasure without guilt.

The young people of the Twenties were no more intelligent than any other mass of young people at any time and much of their rebellion was ludicrous when it was not unspeakably pathetic. Nevertheless their gamy behavior gave the tone to their time, a tone which popular history has carefully preserved with a rueful chuckle and an indulgent wag of the head. And the color and movement of the jazzy Charleston they danced often distract our eye from the solid achievements of the time, which continue to influence us.

For all the antics and wonderful nonsense of that strange decade, it produced social as well as cultural changes of the first magnitude. American society was never quite the same again, never quite so staid, quite so immobile, quite so rigid, once the lost generation had completed its noisy search for a new identity and a new sensibility. Politically and economically it was a period of stasis, but in almost every other way, the express train of history was moving at full throttle. Beneath the gaudy, saucy and endlessly amusing surface of the Twenties a great struggle for power was proceeding relentlessly.

Prohibition, after all, was the last successful attempt of a rural, fundamentalist and rather naïve older generation to keep the world as it was. It was the final stand of puritanism in a society that was discovering the validity of the pleasure principle. This last gasp of the old order became a death rattle when its failure as a panacea for social and moral ills became apparent, and the times made a joke of it.

On other points, however, the old order was less easily defeated. It took the collapse of their economic system to send them reeling in disordered retreat. Before that, however, a good shoemaker and a poor fish peddler had testified with their lives to the tenacity with which the old guard clung to power, as did hundreds of Negroes lynched in the South by a resurgent Ku Klux Klan. A hardly less exacting price was paid for a new social order by dozens of political radicals and by dozens of artists who dared to try the new in a society that clutched with a drowning man's desperation the wreckage of the old. No, the Twenties were a time of struggle, not, primarily, a time of laughter.

The reality of this power struggle was demonstrated in Carnegie Hall in the first year of the decade when Rabbi Stephen Wise dared to criticize Judge Elbert Gary, president of U.S. Steel and industry leader in a heavy-handed attempt to break the steel strike of 1920. Wise called the leaders of the steel industry "Cossackizers of Industry" and "breeders of Bolshevism." Many in his congregation deserted him, others pleaded with him to lay off the men of power. For several months he was a storm center. In the midst of a campaign for a building fund, so that he could have a temple of his own, Wise grimly told a friend that "my synagogue building is going up in smoke today." He was right. The speech cost him the wealthy support he needed.

In music, also, there was a struggle between the old and the new. And it was the new—jazz—that give its name to the decade and George Gershwin who brought jazz to the concert hall. There was opposition to the new music, of course, just as there was to the new art and literature of the age. This war between the old and the new was the basic cultural dialectic of the era. In music, the opposition seemed to represent little more than a new battle in an age-old war. The battle for recognition of Wagner's music had concluded, in the Old World and the New, just before Carnegie Hall was erected. The discounting of Debussy and Strauss, and the eventual acceptance of their quite different newnesses was a part of the story of music in the prewar world. Now it was Stravinsky and Schönberg, as different from one another as they were from their antecedents, who were to be the storm centers of music.

But there are several important factors which must be understood in order to understand the music of the 1920's. One is that, in an age of great social change, the new music was bound to get more involved in the war between social traditionalists and radicals than it had in other times. There were moralists who found in jazz, for example, the causes of the new sexual freedom (or "license" as the publicists for morality put it). There were others who found the new European music to be encouraging to intellectual decadence. In an age pathologically afraid of Bolshevism it was easier to get politics and art mixed up in a cause-effect relationship, than to see that both were the effects of tremendously complicated historical processes.

But there was—and is—some basis for complaint against the music of the time. Most of the new music was not readily approachable by the layman, and failed to communicate with large numbers of people.

It was Stravinsky who started the modern trend toward neoclassicism. He and his contemporaries were attempting to eliminate subjectivism or romantic "feeling" on the part of composer or performer. "Away with emotion or romanticism!" Olin Downes expressed the new war cry of the Twenties. "The essence of music is form; in that is implicit everything music has for humanity." This idea, implemented by many techniques, found expression in almost all the important musical work of the period, including that of Schönberg—in form and in content the opposite and rival of Stravinsky.

The reasons for the revolt of the moderns was clear enough. Romanticism, as we have seen, had reached a dead-end by the beginning of the twentieth century. It was repeating itself and puffing itself up to unrecognizable proportions in an attempt to assert its liveliness as a tradition. To the men involved in composing and performing, it had become a bore. In addition, like most artists, they were increasingly beginning to feel alienated from their time and their society. Instead of fighting their alienation, they decided to accept it, to make an advantage of disadvantage. They began to create for the tiny minority of people capable of appreciating all the nuances of their immense and radical technical virtuosity, preferring to consign the masses to those hacks who were so good at entertaining them and who had found the formulae for popular success but whose work had virtually nothing to do with art.

We are dealing here with one of the most important phenomena of cultural life in the twentieth century. Its beginning could be felt before the war. After the war, the gap between high art and low widened to an unbridgeable point. And it was not limited only to music. In poetry, a revolution led by Pound and Eliot created a virtually new aesthetic, compounded of new verbal techniques and even subject matter which took that once popular art away from the masses and gave it to those intellectuals who had a taste for complexity. In the novel Joyce became the principal hero of an artistic generation that worshiped his austere dedication to his private, intensely personal vision. In the graphic arts, a hundred modern movements lifted painting firmly from the hands of those who liked a picture to tell a story, slapped their wrists and sent them off to the movies.

The cultural revolution, of course, did not begin all of a sudden. In the first seasons of the postwar era there was a concentrated effort, in music, as elsewhere, to return to "normalcy." The first task was to welcome back old favorites, men who for one reason or another, had been forced to be absent from the concert stage during the war years. None of them was more fervently greeted than Fritz Kreisler when he appeared at a charity concert—for the Vienna Children's Milk Relief—at Carnegie Hall. At his entrance, the audience stood and cheered for a good five minutes and the conclusion of each piece was the occasion for a new demonstration. Wreaths were deposited on the stage in profusion and at least 500 people had to be turned away from the auditorium. The critics found his enforced vacation had not harmed his technique, and *Musical America* wrote: "The king has come back into his own. He has come back in the likeness of a conquering hero, midst shoutings and mighty jubilation. He is returned from an exile self-imposed, from needless banishment assumed at the obligatory promptings of a noble nature." The audience demanded encore after encore of him, until at last the lights had to be turned out in order to make them leave.

In that first postwar season, the new men were few and far between. But Benno Moïséwitsch, the young Russian pianist, was a harbinger of things to come, "an artist of uncommon gifts and acquirements, who can deeply interest and engross the listener by a stimulating, even exhilarating vitality and by the perfection, in its kind, of his playing."

The absence of important recital debuts is significant. Although the Twenties were to produce their share of important new individual talents, the chief musical excitement of the era lay elsewhere. For the age of the orchestra was about to begin, and with it, the age of the conductor. It is an age which is not over yet. America had to wait until 1926 for the greatest of them all, Toscanini, to focus this new interest, to become the chief recipient of the adulation which suddenly surrounded the man with the baton. But as early as 1919-1920 one could sense a change in the wind.

Monteux had taken over the Boston Symphony. Although he did not receive his fair share of the general acclaim which his competitors were receiving, a few recognized, with the Boston's historian, Mark A. De Wolfe Howe, that "he made this orchestra the first to reflect the postwar change in creative musical life—a new and important role in which his successor [Koussevitzky] . . . likewise made the most of his opportunities."

Monteux's very first Carnegie Hall program as permanent leader of the Boston Symphony in November, 1919, reflected the cosmopolitanism that is his greatest virtue. It included an obscure Haydn Symphony, a half-forgotten Beethoven overture (*King Stephen*) and Stravinsky's ballet score for *The Firebird*. Works like the latter did not achieve critical recognition easily, but they did find, thanks to men like Monteux, a more and more receptive audience as the Twenties proceeded. The Boston leader, laboring in difficult fields, was a figure symbolic of the era. A mere listing of the composers he introduced to his audiences is an indication of the Twenties' new interest in the new. They included: Bax, Vaughan Williams, Bliss, Gustav Holst, Scott, Goosens, Respighi, Malipiero, Casella, Moussorgsky, Stravinsky, de Falla, Albeniz, Honegger, Milhaud, Lekeu, Aubert, Roussel and a number of Americans.

But Monteux was by no means alone in giving a more prominent place to new compositions, in reflecting musically the cosmopolitanism of an age in which nearly all the artists and intellectuals were heading for the Continent and busily incorporating European influences into their books and poems and paintings.

There was, for example, Bodansky presenting Charles Martin Loeffler's *A Pagan Poem* on the first program of his New Symphony Orchestra in Carnegie Hall and later in the year attempting to interest the audience in Bruckner's Fourth Symphony and, of course, failing. Damrosch, back in Carnegie Hall after lengthy absence from it, found the times congenial or at least a bit more tolerant of the new. He programmed new works by Debussy and d'Indy, invited Percy Grainger to be soloist in his own "Over the Hills and Far Away." Even Stransky was stirred to try something new. He gave a first New York performance of Dvořák's Symphony in F and also debuted a new American piece, Bernard Rogers' dirge, "To the Fallen."

But best of all, there was Stokowski, "Stokowski the scoreless" as some called him, impressed by that trick of memory that so many conductors have since felt compelled to emulate. Stokowski had found in Rachmaninoff a composer almost ideally suited to his lush talents. In January, with Alfred Cortot as soloist, the Philadelphia Orchestra as accompanist and the composer in the audience (he was warmly applauded), he programmed the Third Piano Concerto and scored a great hit. The following month he was back with a new Rachmaninoff piece, *The Bells*, a symphonic setting of Edgar Allan Poe's poem. This huge, pretentious and rather ingenious work, ranging in tonal coloration through the whole orchestral palette, massive in its sonorities and perhaps, in the end, banal, was ideally suited to the instrument Stokowski had built for himself in Philadelphia. It was an organ of an orchestra, and the former organist tended to play it like one. But what excitement he engendered! *The Bells* encountered any number of critical reservations, but for the public this orchestra and its leader were the very embodiment of the brave new, experimental world.

Irving Kolodin has admirably summed up what the Philadelphia Orchestra meant to audiences of the time: "There was a void in the musical life of America at that time, and [Stokowski] filled it fully for more than a decade. Russian music attracted him, likewise French. He had an ear—or an eye—for the asperities of Schönberg . . . he responded to Hindemith; he sought out such American purveyors of the odd and esoteric as Cowell and Eicheim. Not only did he expend much effort to make the unfamiliar sound familiar, and admonish his public when it was unappreciative; as time passed . . . some of the effort also went into making the familiar sound unfamiliar. . . . No one who lived through his time can forget the anticipation that attended each visit to New York of his superb Philadelphia Orchestra, whose members reflected their championship qualities in glossier appearances than the staider Philharmonic or Boston men; the lines that formed on superspecial occasions to buy up the few seats or standing room; the new artists he introduced; the old works he revived; the cascades of tone that engulfed the hall when the work was Rimsky-Korsakov's 'Russian Easter Overture' . . . the 'Venusberg Music' . . . or even the Brahms Fourth or the Beethoven Seventh."

The New York symphonic public has never loved the Philharmonic in the way that it has loved the orchestras of its two sister cities of the eastern seaboard. For years it was the Boston Symphony which received its loving admiration, then during the Twenties, it was the Philadelphia Orchestra. Later, under Koussevitzky, Boston was to regain its warm place in the heart of New York audiences. But never, except perhaps under Toscanini, has the Philharmonic been such a love object. Familiar old friend that it is, it has always been a subject for constant grousing. Never was this sound so audible as during the years when Stokowski commuted to Carnegie Hall to give its habitués a brief and tantalizing vision of the glitter and the glamour which was uniquely his.

But there were other excitements available to the person who bought a Carnegie Hall ticket in this first year of The Wonderful Era. There was, for instance, Al Smith offering to debate William Randolph Hearst on the latter's charge that Smith was the tool of the "milk interests" and was therefore a party to the starvation of poor babies in the city. Smith challenged the Press Lord to a debate in Carnegie Hall. Hearst accepted it, but then didn't show up. Instead, a cheering audience heard Smith rebut the Hearst charges with considerable ease.

And there was the strange case of Maurice Maeterlinck, the Belgian writer, who listened to the beat of a distinctly different drum. He

Culver Service

Leopold Stokowski in his early days with the Philadelphia Orchestra when he was filling "a void in the musical life of America," and his orchestra was undisputedly the champion.

came to America for a lecture tour, which was to begin at Carnegie Hall. What with his libretto for Debussy's *Pelleas and Melisande*, his *The Life of the Bee* and *The Bluebird* he was a well-known figure and his appearance was eagerly awaited. There was only one difficulty. Someone had neglected to inform both his managers and his public that Maeterlinck spoke no English.

He did, however, have an idea. He wrote out his lecture in French, then had it literally translated into English. Then he had each English syllable retranslated into a French syllable. Each English sound was to be rendered by its approximate French equal which the poet undertook to speak to his audience. The result, of course, was chaos. As Alva Johnson reported, "it was equally unintelligible to the French and to the Americans. It was a new literary form; it was not even nonsense, so it topped Gertrude Stein."

The upshot was the hasty cancellation of Maeterlinck's lecture tour. Instead, he embarked for Hollywood—ensconced in nothing less than the railroad car President Wilson had used in his campaign for the League of Nations. He was answering an urgent summons from Samuel Goldwyn, who has always liked a literary name to appear among the credits of his films. Told to make a treatment of one of his own works, the poet decided to translate his biography of the bumblebee for the screen. In due course his work was placed on the producer's desk. He glanced at it, then let loose the patented Goldwyn scream. "My God," he cried, "the hero is a bee."

Maeterlinck, needless to say, was not long for Hollywood either. But Goldwyn, loyal to the last, saw him off at the train. There, it is alleged, he patted the poet fondly on the shoulder and said: "Don't worry, Maurice. You'll make good yet." The intellectual history of the Twenties contains no stranger—and no more typical—odyssey.

But Maurice Maeterlinck was not the only eccentric to invade Carnegie Hall during the first month of the new decade. There was a Duncanish dancer named Lada who "flashed as a ray of sunlight and ran like some fleet-footed wild creature of the woods" in the course of interpreting such works as "Will o' the Wisp," "The Golliwog's Cakewalk" and "The Blue Danube" for her audience.

And there was Sir Oliver Lodge, the oustanding English physicist,

Brown Brothers

Maurice Maeterlinck who made his first—and last—American speech at Carnegie Hall in 1920. His talk was not even nonsense, so it topped Gertrude Stein.

who came to the hall to offer his insights into the spiritual world—and incidentally to predict the wonders of an age in which the power of the atom was harnessed. Sir Oliver, like many in his audience, had lost a son in the war, and he brought his hearers a kind of hope. In the aftermath of war, spiritualism was enjoying a revival. Sir Oliver was a highly intelligent and sensitive man and his vision was an appealing one. He told his audience that the dead were all around them, very little changed from their worldly states. There was, he said, no other world for them to go to. They resided on earth, unseen, but seeing. The problem was merely to get in touch with them. He said that the fault lay not with the spirits but with ourselves. Young children, he said, have a faint recollection of past lives which are blotted from their memories at an early age. "There is an apparent chasm, but love bridges that chasm," Sir Oliver said. "The other life is screened from us, and yet as I think, is not far from us. I think it is all around us and we are screened."

The next season (1920-1921) was similar to its predecessor. There was still a dearth of exciting new recital talents, although Michel Piastro, later to be the Philharmonic's concertmaster and to conduct the Longines Symphonette on radio, made his solo debut, and Erika Morini, the violinist, made her American debut with Bodansky's renamed National Symphony Orchestra, playing the Mendelssohn Concerto and a Vieuxtemps concerto.

A pair of Englishmen, Cyril Scott and Albert Coates, also debuted at Carnegie Hall. Scott, who combined composing with piano playing premiered his Concerto in C with Stokowski's orchestra. He was politely applauded, but it was pointed out by one conservative that his music "is an acquired taste, and that more time is necessary for acquiring it, on the part of most listeners, than was available last evening."

Coates, with a reputation as one of the ablest of the English conductors, was more pleasing. "He immediately disclosed authority, innate musical instinct, a feeling for style and for the finer graces of musical beauty." His program was all-British, including Purcell, Elgar and the first American performance of Ralph Vaughan Williams' *London Symphony*. It was received with only the faintest praise. "The symphony is not, on the whole, pleasing," Richard Aldrich wrote. In Aldrich's attitude, as in the attitude of his colleagues, however, we find a slight shift in emphasis from the prewar days. Most of them, quite honestly, did not like modern music. In general, it was found to be, as Aldrich found the Williams piece, unbeautiful. But the bottles of vitriol had been put away. There was a distinct effort to be fair about the whole disconcerting business. Apparently the critics sensed that the creative tide was running against them, that the cultivation of dissonance was to be the new aesthetic norm. Having no wish to be made fools of in the new era, they adopted an attitude of slightly bewildered politeness to the new musical forms. They were careful to hide signs that they were deeply hurt or offended by the new music.

This is not to imply, however, that there was not some slight broadening of aesthetic horizons. There could not help but be, given the temper of the times. When Willem Mengelberg returned to New York, after a fifteen year absence, to direct the National Symphony (he shared the podium with Bodansky), he found, at his very first concert that Richard Strauss was no longer a *bête noire.* His reading of *Don Juan* was the best received item on his program. The critics, however, could still not accept Berlioz. His *Symphonie Fantastique* was dismissed with the notation that "music so barren, so arid, seldom gains access to concert programs."

Mengelberg was welcomed back as a long-lost friend. His leadership was regarded as "straight-forward and direct, without suggestion of the sensational in his methods or his interpretation." He was one of the growing number of virtuoso conductors who, by the power of their presences, were remaking the symphonic sensibilities of their hearers. Within a short time he was to be co-leader of the Philharmonic, a post he was to hold until his differences with Toscanini ended his American career.

In 1920-1921, New York heard two other fine conductors leading out-of-town orchestras. The first was Gabrilowitsch, and his new Detroit Orchestra in a program of Strauss, Weber, Brahms and Mozart, with the conductor as soloist in one of the latter's piano concertos. "The engrossing feature of the orchestra's playing," wrote one critic, "was the evidence of the training given it by Mr. Grabilowitsch and . . . the intelligence and musicianship of his readings."

Another such figure was Frederick Stock, successor to Thomas at Chicago, who brought his orchestra to Carnegie Hall a month after Gabrilowitsch's appearance there. "He has become one of the most distinguished as well as one of the most unassuming of conductors," wrote a typical critic, "and has put his orchestra in a position second to none in this country." Stock, like nearly everyone else that year, played Strauss. He also presented an English novelty, Arnold Bax's *The Garden of Fand.* "Mr. Bax is modern and adventurous in the midst of subtle dissonances and seeks atmosphere and color more than the clear treatment of theme," wrote a critic. "But he is guided incessantly by a feeling for beauty. His music is pregnant with suggestion."

With the beginning of the 1921-1922 season musical currents had shifted enough so that new directions could be clearly seen. The Philharmonic had merged with the National Symphony and Mengelberg and Bodansky were giving the public blessed respite from Stransky. In addition, the soloists were more than usually interesting. To begin with, Bronislaw Hubermann, the sometime boy genius, he who had been dismissed as "overadvertised and underdressed," returned. Now, twenty-five years after his first Carnegie Hall recital, he was a mature artist, approaching middle age, a talented but still rather crude performer. The faults of his childhood persisted, and although he was technically proficient his tone was labored and heavy, lacking in warmth and appeal. He had his following, and it welcomed him back as it continued to do in later years, but Hubermann simply could not reach the heights to which his natural equipment probably entitled him.

More successful was another former child prodigy who brought his fiddle to Carnegie Hall in the month after Hubermann's recital. Franz von Vecsey had played in the hall (wearing a white sailor suit) fourteen years earlier. Now a dignified young man of twenty-eight he returned with a technique extremely brilliant and accurate and with a "simplicity of demeanor and an unassuming manner" still intact. He was an appealing figure to those members of his audience who valued the unpretentious and the tasteful. But he, like Hubermann, never quite captured the heights.

On Christmas Day a pianist who shared many of the traits of von Vecsey appeared under the management of Sol Hurok. Even that promotional genius must have been hard-pressed to round up an audience for a pianist of Artur Schnabel's rather special gifts. For Schnabel was not even a pianist's pianist. He was a musicologist's pianist, a master of playing music as it was written. Straight-forward in technique, reverent of the composer's intentions, serious in mien and attitude, he was virtually an unpromotable genius. He came, a few heard, but none were conquered, although most of the critics were mildly enthusiastic. It was to be ten years before Schnabel's great Beethoven cycles made his austere artistry commercially valuable. Then it became a mark of musical knowledgeability to worship at the Schnabel temple—preferably with score in hand.

Perhaps the weirdest recital of the season occurred almost simultaneously with Schnabel's debut. That was a joint effort by fifteen of the leading pianists of the day. They banded together to play a concert for the benefit of Moritz Moszkowski, the composer, pianist and teacher who, as an elderly man, was nearly penniless and very ill. The fifteen included Bachaus, Bauer, Casella, Friedman, Gabrilowitsch, Grainger, Hutcheson, Lambert, Lhévinne, Mme. Mérö, Mme. Ney, Ornstein, Schelling, Miss Schnitzer and Stojowski. The idea was a good one, the cause a worthy one, but when all the geniuses assembled to rehearse on the morning of the concert, chaos reigned. For each had his highly individual notions of how each piece should proceed and for an hour there was a good deal more argumentation than playing. Someone finally conceived the notion of getting a conductor and a phone call brought Walter Damrosch to the rescue. He lectured them sternly on the necessity of bowing to his will and on the night of the concert a full house was able to hear more virtuosos play together than any audience before or since has ever heard. Damrosch, surveying the scene as he stood in the wings, observed that the players didn't need a conductor so much as they needed a traffic cop. But they played in twos and threes and all together the Saint-Saëns variations on a theme of Beethoven for two pianos as well as Schubert's "Marche Militaire" and Moszkowski's "Spanish Dances for Four Hands."

Because of the crowded conditions on stage some of the pianists had to share instruments and Damrosch had to conduct from the back of the stage, facing the audience, providing them with a rare glimpse of how a conductor looks to his orchestra. "The concert," wrote one critic, "was an extraordinary success in promoting the object for which it was given, in pleasing a very large audience and in demonstrating the spirit of mutual helpfulness among musical artists."

A little later in the season Damrosch himself was the honored guest at a similar gala, celebrating the 50th Anniversary of his arrival in America. Three orchestras, the New York Philharmonic, the New York Symphony and the Philadelphia Orchestra, 212 players strong, and conducted variously by Stransky, Bodansky, Coates, Mengelberg and Stokowski, combined to play a program of Wagner, Berlioz, Brahms, Beethoven and Liszt. The proceeds were some $18,000 and went toward the establishment of a Walter Damrosch fellowship at the American Academy in Rome. Damrosch received a plaque and also heard some excellent performances in his honor, performances which "offered a magnified conspectus of some of the most characteristic qualities of the several conductors."

The Damrosch fete was not the only orchestrally interesting event of the season. Two composers who had visited the United States during the height of genteelism returned and were welcomed now with great equanimity. They were Richard Strauss and Vincent d'Indy. The Strauss genius had burned itself out early; nothing he wrote after *Salome* had the merit of the early tone poems. So now he came not as a controversialist but as an aging pioneer to be honored rather than argued over. He appeared with the Philadelphia Orchestra on the last day of October, 1921, and was greeted by an enthusiastic audience which filled Carnegie "to at least its legal capacity." He was, an observer observed, "the same tall, slender, upstanding figure that he was seventeen years ago, impassive, immovable in countenance—yet evidently a little moved by the enthusiasm of his greeting—and somewhat grayer at the temples and balder further back." He conducted *Don Juan, Till Eulenspiegel* and the *Sinfonia Domestica* which he had introduced to New York at his 1904 appearances. There were no new insights to be gained from the composer's readings of his own works. The earlier pieces, perhaps the most familiar of the modern additions to the symphonic repertory were received with the enthusiasm that had become customary while the latter piece stirred *its* customary indifference.

The aristocratic and eclectic d'Indy, friend and champion first of Wagner, then of Debussy, received the welcome of a grand old man of music which, at seventy, he was. He led the New York Symphony in a program equally divided between old and new work, all of it unfamiliar. The feature of the evening was the first performance anywhere of his impressionistic tone poem *On the Shores of the Sea.* It was program music, imaginative rather than literally descriptive. It was not cerebral music; rather it was poetic, almost dreamy and audience and critics reacted with mild, but genuine, liking. Like Strauss, d'Indy was a conductor of great simplicity and directness, and his austerity contributed to the warmth which his audience felt for him.

Among the orchestral premieres of the season were Sibelius' Fifth Symphony which Stransky conducted and Mahler's lovely *Das Lied von der Erde*, directed by Bodansky and sponsored by the Friends of Music, a group which was responsible for the presentation of much new and good music during the Twenties.

Mahler was still *persona non grata.* The hall was not full and many people left early when *Das Lied* was performed. "The attitude of all concerned in a costly production was perhaps less that of a musical than of a deeply personal memorial." The performance was praised, but no one committed himself to the music, perhaps the most sheerly beautiful of Mahler's late works.

Of the nonmusical events that year in the hall none was more interesting than the appearance of Sir Arthur Conan Doyle. The creator of Sherlock Holmes, that greatest of all fictional exemplars of the spirit of rationalism, had become, in his dotage, a believer in spiritualism. Like Sir Oliver Lodge, Doyle had lost a son in the war, and his earlier leanings toward belief in the spirit world had been strengthened. He, too, found a ready audience for his belief among the grieving. Unlike Sir Oliver, he could produce photographs of spirits.

In the course of his lectures he told his audience that his lost son had spoken to him at a séance and had begged his pardon for refusing to participate in family séances before the war. He added that after the spirit of his son had received this pardon it placed its hand on Sir Arthur's head, kissed him on the brow and disappeared. Sir Arthur told his audience that the inhabitants of the spirit world "had the same form as on the material plane, exhibited the same character and spoke the same platitudes."

"A devil in the other world," he said, "is a low-down crude bad man who passes over from this world. They do there as they have done here. Then there are mischievous spirits in the other world, just as there are mischievous boys in this world."

He buttressed his statements by producing a spirit message he had received from one of the people who had perished on the *Titanic.* "I will try to keep you posted," the message read.

One who had done more than try to keep her friends posted was Isadora Duncan who returned to the United States the following fall (1922). She had been gone for five years but she had remained excellent copy. The great believer in the spirit of life had spent a couple of years in Russia and she was returning with a Russian "husband," a wild and woolly poet named Sergei Esenin. Inexplicably, Sol Hurok found that the box office was cold. Despite the renewed interest in art, no one apparently wanted to watch Isadora perform the dances that had once been thought so shocking. Perhaps in the era of bobbed hair and short skirts Isadora no longer had the appeal she had in the days when she was virtually alone in her sexual liberation. Happily, the U.S. Government stepped in and, by detaining Isadora at Ellis Island, warmed the box office considerably. Overnight the whole Isadora controversy was reawakened. Heywood Broun called the action of the immigration authorities "blundering boorishness"; there were letters to the papers and protests. Very shortly, Isadora was quit of Ellis Island and regaling a Carnegie Hall crowd with her interpretations of Russian music—including Tchaikovsky's Symphony *Pathetique* and the *Marche Slave.* After her first recital, the lady deemed it necessary to read a little lecture to her audience. She asked the audience why she had to go to Moscow in search of her dreams, when American children could benefit from the liberating force of the dance. "I know the American nervous child," she said, "for I was one myself." She pleaded for a school of the dance where she could free the children from the toils of repression and anxiety.

But Isadora was no longer a lady with only one crusade to carry to her audience. Perhaps she sensed that, in the Twenties, it was not quite as shocking and interesting to be a free spirit as it once had been. Or perhaps she genuinely believed in Bolshevism in a vague sort of way. At any rate, her experiences in Russia had made a convert of her, and in an America which was seeing Reds under every bed, in which the unholy trinity was "communism, atheism and free love" her naïve espousal of Communism was at least as shocking as her continuing career as a free spirit. She told the audience at her last New York recital that "there is a new idea of living now. It is not home life, it isn't family life, it isn't patriotism, but the Internationale."

With that she set off on the most daring concert tour ever undertaken in the United States. It was her wont to whip out a red flag and wave it as the sock climax of her act. When she wasn't doing that she and her lover were setting tongues as well as editorial and ministerial fingers to wagging. The major incident occurred in Boston. There Isadora took it upon herself to lecture the crowd on the nature of beauty which, she claimed, they knew nothing about. In order to demonstrate her theory, she ripped her tunic down to her waist and showed her audience what her idea of beauty was. Boston was not amused—nor did it subscribe to her idea. Sol Hurok, counting the receipts in New York, was delighted financially and worried sick emotionally. He ate up a good chunk of his profits chastising his artiste by telephone. He might as well have saved his nickels.

Within a month of Isadora's return, another artist came back to Carnegie Hall. But Ignace Jan Paderewski returned in glory, not in controversy. He had not played in public for five years, but the interval had placed the finishing touches on the Paderewski legend. After his wartime service as champion of Polish freedom, he had represented his homeland at the Versailles Peace Conference, and had served at the League of Nations as the new nation's first premier. He had finally resigned over the careerist military ventures of Marshal Pilsudski. During his political career there had been many attempts on his life; on one such occasion he had very nearly strangled his assailant to death but refused to allow the police to arrest the man.

Now at sixty-two, the long reddish blond hair turned to silver, a neat mustache and beard enhancing his dignity, he was returning to the relative safety of the concert stage. He returned not merely as a great pianist, not merely as a beloved public figure, but as a giant of a man loved for the rare combination of characteristics that made up his total, commanding personality.

Coincidentally, he was to share the center of the New York stage with an equally commanding colleague, eighty-one-year-old Georges Clemenceau, France's wartime premier, who was in the United States in a fruitless attempt to persuade us to live up to our wartime commitments to internationalism. The two, of course, were friends from the days of the peace conference at Versailles.

On the night before his Carnegie Hall appearance, Paderewski went to the Metropolitan Opera House to hear Clemenceau speak first of his friendship for America, then of his disappointment at her failure to help Europe's postwar recovery. Grizzled, bronzed, his fierce eyes gleaming beneath his beetling brows, he was every inch the legendary tiger on that night, speaking his piece forthrightly, mingling wit, irony and compassion. He singled out two men for his special affectionate attention. One was General John J. Pershing, whom he embraced during his first moment on the platform, their many wartime disagreements momentarily set aside. The other was Paderewski, whom he called "my dear friend," and of whom he said: "He has won honor in the field of art as well as in the political field of his noble country. He is here as a witness to these conditions of peace."

The applause for Paderewski was deafening. It was also upsetting, and when he came on Carnegie's stage the following afternoon to play his concert he was terribly nervous. A wildly cheering audience rose to its feet to welcome him. But several critics noted that in his first pieces the pianist was notably confused and unclear in his interpretations. By the time he had finished, however, he had conquered himself and his audience. "There was re-enacted that scene of maenadic females rushing to the front that first came into fashion in the early days of his New York playing. . . ."

The critics rushed off to their typewriters to vie with one another in the application of encomiums. Some said he was better than he had ever been, detecting a new warmth and a new richness of spirit in his playing. He indeed seemed, as one put it, to have resumed his career "refreshed and inspirited."

But this day of riches was not yet over for Paderewski. Immediately after the three-hour concert he was driven to East Seventy-third Street, to the home of Charles Dana Gibson, for a very special reunion. Gibson was, of course, the fashionable artist, creator of the Gibson Girl. For thirty-three years he had worked in Studio 90 of Carnegie Hall. The studio was aclutter with the mementos of his career and of his art and he steadfastly refused to allow the landlords to repaint its grimy walls. It had, he said, taken years for the place to mellow, like a good briar pipe which it resembled in color, and he would not have that mellowness meddled with. It was at Gibson's home that Clemenceau was staying, and it was there that Paderewski and "the Tiger" were to be reunited.

Clemenceau had missed the concert for he had been paraded through Brooklyn and had delivered another speech in Manhattan. When the two men saw one another they embraced and Paderewski, his voice trembling said, "You are the greatest man I ever knew. You told them the truth," he added, speaking of Clemenceau's Metropolitan speech, "in a splended way of which you alone are capable."

"No, you are the greatest man," said Clemenceau. "At the peace conference you made such a wonderful speech that I was nearly moved to tears."

There was a pause. Then Clemenceau said, "I missed your concert. When will you play for me?"

"Master," the virtuoso replied, " I will do anything for you. I will play for you now."

In the dimly lighted music room, with only the Gibson family and the old statesman present, Paderewski played for an hour. Occasionally Clemenceau, an old man at the end of a very hard day, dozed. But at the end he said, "*merveilleux, merveilleux.* You are not only a great musician and a great statesman, but a great poet also."

Paderewski left the house in tears.

Much later in the season still another beloved figure who had combined art and politics in his career came to Carnegie Hall to speak, not of art, but of the political situation in Europe. He was Hilaire Belloc, English essayist and sometime member of Parliament. He spoke of the need for a tough peace, a peace that could not be broken by a resurgent Germany. Like many another who saw this need, he was not heeded when he said, "Those who talk about peace by understanding, simply mean taking away the security of the victors. Not only must it be an imposed peace, unfortunately, with terms exacted from the unwilling, but it also must be a peace of reparations." These last, he believed, were necessary if peace with justice was to be secured, if the balance of European suffering was somehow to be redressed.

The implications of his message were not unlike those of Clemenceau's. Both men desperately wanted the United States not to turn its back on the world, to continue to act the role of world leader which it had assumed a few years before. There was a responsible minority who agreed with them. But most felt, as Frederick J. Hoffman has summed it up, "victimized by a gross and stupid deception. Nothing genuine had come out of the war." The people—particularly the young—thought they could never equal the folly of their elders, no matter what they did. So they engaged themselves in the minor follies of the decade, and turned away from the pleas for responsibility. In effect, the postwar generation told men like Belloc and Clemenceau (who was widely—and with considerable justice—believed to have sold out America's idealistic war aims for cynical nationalistic goals at the peace conference) that they could clean up their own mess.

The postwar generation was only mildly interested in the small and quasi-comic battles raging within the tiny world of music, although they did manage to raise a faint cheer when, in mid-season, Josef Stransky announced his resignation as director of the Philharmonic. His days, obviously, had been numbered since the coming of Mengelberg, and the scales had been finally tipped against him when even the conservatives tired of his routine ways. He had built a good orchestra, he had played a determinedly conservative repertory well enough and, by his uncontroversial ways, had actually increased the orchestra's audience, but he was simply not a major talent. Richard Aldrich, archconservative critic, had led the attack on him. "It is no discredit to a man that he does not lift himself by his bootstraps to a higher level than that upon which nature put him," he wrote, damning mediocrity by the simple process of naming it.

In his place the Society placed another minor talent, Willem Van Hoogstraten. He came to the post with brave talk of bringing the finest in American music to the concert hall and of generally brightening the programs. But there was no question of his competing with the star of the Philharmonic's podium, his codirector Willem Mengelberg whose very presence on the New York musical scene had focused the musical world's dissatisfaction with mediocrity. He was a conductor of quality, and much admired. After successful concerts he was often mobbed with ladies seeking to embrace him and gentlemen seeking to bestow more manly plaudits. Vincent Sheean recalls that to hear Mengelberg conduct was "a rousing experience. At one bound the Philharmonic, lax and fading, was jerked into life again and delivered itself of some performances which converted one's spine into an electromagnetic field."

Even Mengelberg, however, could not jerk the people into respect for Mahler's work. His performance of the Seventh Symphony late in the season drew forth the usual critical protests and the customary glazed looks from the audience. Stokowski got much the same reaction when he premiered Ernest Schelling's "A Victory Ball," admittedly a minor work by the man who, that very year, took over as conductor of the Philharmonic's children's concerts and thereby made himself a beloved figure to a generation of kids and parents who enjoyed his performances perhaps more than their offspring did.

People at least did Schelling the honor of politeness. They hissed Schönberg's *Kammersinfonie* when Stokowski presented it later in the season and even attempted to suppress the approval of those hardy souls who dared to applaud it.

The same public was politely indifferent to Bruno Walter when he took over Damrosch's orchestra for a series of guest appearances. Walter was a virtuoso all right, but he lacked the crowd-pleasing mannerisms of his competitors, as well as the gimmicks. He played good music exceedingly well, but he would have to wait for proper recognition. Indeed, the only major musician to receive just reward at a debut that season was Myra Hess who, playing with the Damrosch orchestra, received excellent reviews and public reaction for her exquisite pianistic abilities. But it was accidental that the public could recognize her kind of greatness. Bruno Walter and Schönberg were not the only fine artists who were received indifferently that year. Artur Rubinstein had another try at the Carnegie Hall heights he had never fully conquered. Once again an icy wind of ignorance blew him back to those places where his talent was appreciated. As Sol Hurok put it: "It is not infrequently the fate of great men to be first spurned, then worshipped. Their very uniqueness, the qualities which make them memorable frighten conservative folk away from them at first. . . . The battle against conservatism in the new world—paradoxically the New World has always been more conservative than the Old in matters of art—was not to his [Rubinstein's] taste, and he withdrew to the cities which knew how to value him. . . ."

But the musical world, already buffeted by small changes (such as the new interest in the man with the baton), could not long remain aloof from the temper of the times, and the following season (1923-1924) was one in which the old musical times were forever separated from the new. In that year Paul Whiteman brought his orchestra—masters of a diminished sort of jazz—to staid Aeolian Hall and there presented a concert of jazz and pop tunes which shocked many but also pleased a great many. That same year modernist Henry Cowell came to Carnegie Hall for his debut. Cowell wrote music bearing such intriguing titles as "What's This?" and "Antimony" and was a bit of a Dadaist. He was also a bit of a showman. He reached inside his piano to pluck at its wires, he thumped twelve keys at once, he played some chords with his forearms and elbows. But it was not all show. He was a pioneer of the tone cluster technique of composition and the older generation saw in him another busy worker, chipping away at the foundation of their world.

He was by no means the only musician engaged in such labor. Van Hoogstraten and the Philharmonic's assistant conductor, the American composer Henry Hadley, were doing their best to make good their promise to bring new music to its programs. Later in the season Efrem Zimbalist presented a recital of music by American composers with the composers themselves accompanying him. Among the pieces he played were a well-received violin concerto by Schelling and a sonata for violin and piano by John Powell.

But the musical events of the year were the American premieres of two works by Stravinsky. The first was *Le Chant du Rossignol* which Damrosch presented in early November. Most of its listeners found it a barren work, though technically astounding. It was pure music, appealing classically to the mind rather than to the emotions. Its austerity was, paradoxically, too rich for the critical palates. "Does a well-planned, wholesome dinner consist of truffles, lobster, mustard, white pepper, caviar, mince tart, meringue and cognac?" one critic asked. "How the ear longed for a pure, clear and healthy sound—the sound that arises from Beethoven's and Wagner's orchestras."

The audience was thus prepared for the worst when it came to hear Monteux conduct *Rite of Spring* with the Boston Orchestra in February. He had led the 1913 Paris premiere of the work at which the audience had rioted. Times had changed slightly. There was to be no riot in Carnegie Hall on the evening of January 30, 1924. There was, however, hissing at the end of the work's first section, although at the end applause overwhelmed the sounds of dissent. For this was exciting music. Deems Taylor later recalled that he left the hall in a state of "dazed exultation." Olin Downes, having replaced Aldrich as the *Times* music critic, noted that the piece was a logical development of the Stravinsky style, but that the expression was greatly intensified. This, he said, was done "by means of the force and individuality of the counterpoint, and also by rhythms that have at times a well nigh hysterical shock and fury."

He pointed out that it was music of the highest intellectuality. There was not a single accidental effect. Instead, for all its force and fury, the piece was written with exact precision and superb knowledge of the orchestra.

"What stands out technically and emotionally in this work," Downes wrote, "and gives it a place significant . . . in the history of the modern development of an art, is its unprecedented energy, definiteness and power. No orchestra that we have heard throws off such heat, such sonorities, such galvanizing, rhythmical force as this orchestra of Stravinsky."

For better or worse, the die of modern music in America had been cast. No composer who came after Stravinsky was totally uninfluenced by his work. Indeed, nothing less than a new aesthetic was formed out of the Stravinskian revolution. It would be difficult to document it, but it seems obvious that the revolution extended far beyond the writing of music. It came to embrace both performers and listeners. The day of the libertine virtuoso, twisting the shape of the composer's work by his own feelings, was drawing to a close. Now the emphasis was on the precise realization of the composer's intent. Audiences expected this sort of reverence and performers began to vie with one another in an attempt to give them what they wanted.

There was, for instance, the composer and violinist, Georges Enesco, who had played in New York before, but who now found a warmer reception for his technique which contained "never a flamboyant phrase or tone." He was all austerity as he played the Brahms concerto. So was Wanda Landowska whose reputation as a harpsichordist had preceded her to New York. She played with Stokowski's Philadelphia Orchestra and amazed one and all with the amazing tones she could wring from her antique instrument. Her technical accomplishments received the highest praise.

Not that the old order disappeared overnight. In the Stravinsky year such artists as Paderewski, Hubermann, McCormack, Kreisler and Chaliapin came to Carnegie Hall. Stransky was now leading a new orchestra, the State Symphony. And when Monteux gave his farewell concert as leader of the Boston Symphony his soloist was the veteran Moriz Rosenthal. The Oratorio Society celebrated its 50th Anniversary with a routine performance of *Elijah*.

In addition, Vladimir de Pachmann, now in his seventies and quite

Columbia Records Photo

Igor Stravinsky at a rehearsal at Carnegie Hall. His Rite of Spring *was presented there in 1924 by Pierre Monteux who had conducted its riotous world premiere in Paris in 1913.*

mad, was continuing the series of "farewell" recitals that had begun in the late years of the nineteenth century. On occasion he could still muster the old greatness, but most of the time he was a tragic parody of a musician and it is no credit to his audience that they came to enjoy the spectacle of his Lear-like madness as he "chuckled, chortled, explained, admired (himself), grimaced and gesticulated *ad nauseam* the while he played."

However popular the leaders of the old order remained, it was clear that the American aesthetic was beginning to change, that there was a new receptivity to avant-garde ideas. The wind had begun to shift, as we have seen, at the beginning of the decade. Now its velocity began to increase. The leader of the new radicalism in music, Igor Stravinsky, chose the next season, 1924-1925, to visit America and appear in Carnegie Hall. It was a propitious season for his appearance. On every hand there was evidence of heightened interest in radical artistic innovations.

The fact that the staid Philharmonic would open its season by playing Respighi's *Sinfonia Drammatica* which, fashionably enough, was program music masquerading as absolute music, was evidence of this. It was hardly atonal or neoclassic in style. But it was a considerable departure from the society's usual comfortable openings.

Even more significant was the first appearance in New York, on November 27, of Serge Koussevitzky as the new conductor of the Boston Symphony Orchestra. Monteux had departed, his passing unmourned by most. Only a few, like the critic who wrote that he "deserved our gratitude for saving our greatest orchestra," realized what a debt was owed to him. H. T. Parker noted that Monteux's great service was his widening of the repertory, "counting no music, as long as it warranted performance, alien to him or to his hearers." Far from discontinuing this tradition, Koussevitzky, so unlike his predecessor in most ways, broadened it still further. Indeed, it could be said that during the Thirties and Forties, after Stokowski had left the Philadelphia Orchestra, he was the only conductor in America who consistently welcomed the new, devoting himself and much of his personal fortune to the pursuit of new music. This was to be his greatest

Wide World

Serge Koussevitzky who began his twenty-five year tenure with the Boston Symphony in 1925 and who led it back to the pinnacle from which it briefly fell.

Willem Mengelberg, the finicky German drillmaster, who "jerked the Philharmonic back to life" in the early twenties.

Culver Service

service, one which he began immediately upon taking over the Boston Orchestra. He averaged about a hundred new pieces per year, cut down on the number of soloists—particularly singers—and was thus able to give his hearers a solid schedule of works from the classical repertory while championing new music.

His road was not easy. A celebrated master of an obscure instrument, the double bass, Koussevitzky was not in his early years a well-regarded conductor. Some of the men in his orchestra suspected that he could not actually read a score and many a hearer felt that he was, despite his excellent European reputation as a conductor, faking his way through pieces that any journeyman conductor should be able to lead as a matter of course. Koussevitzky himself recognized his defects and he worked devotedly to make himself a better conductor. It was some time before he was to be the catholic, resilient and subtle conductor he was in his great years. By and large he won modest acceptance, though, and some newspapers were at pains to drum up an alleged "war" between Stokowski and Koussevitzky for the attention of musical New York.

If there was such a war, it was fought in terms of new music. Each vied with the other to present the latest sensation. But this was not design. It was merely coincidental that the leaders of the two finest American orchestras happened to be devotees of discovery.

In that first year of their "rivalry" neither conductor presented new music of particularly lasting interest. The high point of the Koussevitzky season was undoubtedly Berlioz' *L'Enfance du Christ*. Stokowski's most interesting concert was a performance of three Hindemith dances. Actually, the most stimulating new work was conducted by Damrosch. In this era of glamour boys he was often ignored, but his devotion to new music was at least the equal of his more publicized contemporaries and it was he who presented the novelty of the year, Arthur Honegger's *Pacific 231*, a witty poem in honor of a locomotive. Diabolically orchestrated to achieve, in the end, a kind of mechanistic ecstasy, it was well received although some critics thought Damrosch not quite the man to bring the piece to life. Under his direction, one critic wrote, Honegger's train "occasionally rushed through the night, but it stopped at local stations."

Symbolic of changing musical values were the reviews that a conductor new to the city received when he stepped off the Carnegie Hall podium after leading the Philharmonic in what might have been a rather routine performance of the Brahms First Symphony. The conductor was William Furtwängler. Tall, scholarly, quick of movement, Furtwängler was a man who plunged deep into a score looking for the composer's meaning. On that occasion, apparently, he found it, for the reviews noted that he did not attempt to storm the heavens with the piece. Rather, the performance "was so charged with musical beauty, so infused with deep and sincere feeling and so clearly and firmly sculptured that . . . the heart . . . dilated." Furtwängler was a classicist of the podium, one of the few conductors whom Toscanini respected (despite later political differences over Nazism). He was very much of the school that was coming into fashion. He was nowhere near as successful with a performance of Stravinsky's *Le Sacre* later in the month; the music was no more congenial to him than it would have been to Toscanini who could not abide modern music. But Furtwängler would return often, in the remaining years of the decade, always to good receptions.

A little later, when Stravinsky played the premiere of his new piano concerto with the Philharmonic, Mengelberg was on the podium and it went off well. A number of critics, however, took the opportunity to point out that Stravinsky seemed currently to be exploring unrewarding paths. Olin Downes went so far as to suggest that like Strauss and Debussy before him, he might be about to burn himself out at the very height of his powers. Downes's review was an important statement by an intelligent opponent of neoclassicism: "Is there really any such thing as music which has no echo of the passions of the human heart? Perhaps. If so, then Stravinsky may really be on the track of a new music, abstract, classic in its conception, a music that derives its existence and its vital force simply by the conflict of the opposing melodic lines and the propulsion of conflicting rhythms. But as an expression of an extraordinary brain and a certain phase of modern temperament this piano concerto is without parallel. . . . He is now in a state of restlessness and transition of which this severe, infertile stuff . . . is a very characteristic symptom. . . . It seems that he has been led into dangerous sidepaths of late, paths as interminable as they are futile. . . ."

The new pieces of Stravinsky and Honegger were not the only evidences of the sudden strength of the new in music. Lawrence Tibbett, fresh from his triumph at the Met (as a hasty substitute in *Falstaff*) sang a well-received Carnegie Hall concert. Ruth St. Denis and Ted Shawn brought their Denishawn dancers to the hall and were told that "few artists in their field show an equal amount of originality." Tibbett was that rarity—an American-trained male singer who made good in opera. St. Denis and Shawn were rarities of another sort—true intellectuals of the dance, from whom much exciting work has stemmed (including that of Martha Graham who began with them, then broke away over their intransigence about innovations other than their own).

These three people were breakers of prejudices. And in this time of rich iconoclasm, they were not alone. Perhaps the most gratifying events of the season were the two appearances of the Negro tenor, Roland Hayes, who sang in concert at Carnegie Hall and who had also appeared with Koussevitzky in Berlioz' *L'Enfance du Christ* mentioned above. He and Paul Robeson were the first of their race to achieve something of a breakthrough into the field of serious musical performance. Hayes's was probably not a great voice, but the critics were so bemused by the freakish fact of his color that they filled their columns with wonder over the fact that there was more to the Hayes talent than the "rhythmic instinct" of his race—that he actually seemed to have an intellectual conception of what he was doing.

His was not the only triumph that season by a member of a discriminated-against minority. On January 9, 1925, the pianist Ethel Leginska got a chance to lead a major symphony orchestra, just like Nadia Boulanger who, at this time, toured the United States, leading among other works her pupil Aaron Copland's First Symphony, later rewritten to exclude the organ part which Boulanger had requested. (She was perhaps the greatest teacher of her day, a magnet who drew most of the young composers of the time to Paris to study with her. It was Copland's symphony which led Walter Damrosch to suggest that if a young man of twenty-five could compose so advanced a work

Culver Service

Ruth St. Denis, co-founder with her husband Ted Shawn of the influential Denishawn Dancers, a group which frequented Carnegie Hall in the twenties.

he could be "capable of murder" in a few more years.) Leginska led Damrosch's orchestra, played the piano and included on her program a composition of her own based on two short poems by Tagore. Unlike Boulanger's, her podium work was a fiasco. Leginska was an energetic time-beater, but as the *Times* pointed out, conducting "involves problems far more delicate and complicated than fall to any singer or instrumentalist." She simply lacked conductorial technique.

A few weeks later, undoubtedly scarred by this experience, she set forth from her home for a concert at Carnegie Hall—and disappeared. When she failed to show up police were notified, but it was three weeks before she was located. She claimed that she had been the victim of intense "mental preoccupation," that she did not come to herself until she found herself wandering around the streets of lower Manhattan. Then she had gone into seclusion with friends, a seclusion from which she did not emerge—except to issue a statement—until she played a concert in Boston in March. It was a simple appearance as a piano soloist.

But despite the preoccupation of the musical world with so much that was excitingly new, there was one terrible lack—a lack of significant work by American composers. In the middle of the season Olin Downes addressed himself to this lack. He noted that "Americans have justified their reputation for resolution and common sense in many fields, but when they adventure in music they suddenly become timorous, imitative and unsure of themselves . . . they show their uncertainty in many ways, some of them bumptious, noisy and self-assertive, but they very seldom show a desire to be, rather than to seem, or a real determination to get at the roots of their art and discover themselves in the process."

Why should this be? Downes thought it might be the laziness of the dilettante. He was willing to admit that the musical tradition built in Germany, France and Italy was not deep-rooted here. But, given the rapid improvement in musical instruction in America since the turn of the century and given America's development politically and in the other arts since that time, as well as the attitude of welcome that greeted the innovator of the Twenties, he (and many of his contemporaries) could not understand why the young composer remained "singularly uncertain, emotionally underdeveloped, intellectually a conglomeration of indeterminate matter." Why, he wondered, did he remain either arrogantly contemptuous of all the knowledge that had preceded him or else complacent, waiting for someone to show him the way?

Olin Downes found no ready answer. But he did not allude to the fact that the soil of musical interest in this country, despite the bourgeoning of the concert business, the broadening of the audience for "culture," was singularly barren for a composer looking for a place to sink roots. There was no machinery, formal or informal, to encourage him. There was no interest on the part of audiences in new American music. Here was an irony. Never before in the history of Carnegie Hall had more new music, and music of quality, at that, been played. Never had performers been caught in such an eager ferment to bring forth novelties; never since the founding of the hall had the basic musical consensus been so thoroughly shaken by the winds of controversy. But, as usual, the Europeans were the moving forces in the revolution (this was true, to a lesser degree, in the other arts as well). What interest there was, was directed toward their work.

Downes could see only one hopeful sign. That was in the modesty and courage of the popular composers. They, he said, "have written music which in some cases is rich in vitality, humor and certain qualities of the people because they wrote it naturally, without affectation or pretending to be something they were not." He urged their methods on the younger Americans. "Their best music," he said, "rings true, stirs the listener and towers high by the side of compositions which discreetly or ostentatiously ape other cultures and other composers' styles."

Undoubtedly he was thinking of what he had heard the previous season at Paul Whiteman's jazz concert. There a popular composer's first serious piece, entitled *Rhapsody in Blue*, had had its first performance. Surrounded by a number of far more pretentious works straining to make something very, very serious out of the popular idiom, this piece, not great music, certainly, but more vital than anything American that had ever been performed on a concert stage, had attracted the ears of many listeners. Whiteman's was hardly the organization to do it justice, but there, for the first time, was evidence of the usefulness of the jazz idiom. Nothing prior to the Rhapsody had demonstrated that usefulness. Perhaps, speculated the intellectuals, America was on the brink of giving something genuinely its own back to the compositional tradition it had been living on parasitically for the length of its musical life. This was an intriguing notion, and although the conservatives were aghast at it, it was the fastest circulating currency in musical circles for the next few years.

The 1924-1925 season came to a sentimental close, one which looked backward instead of toward the future. On April 28, 1925, Jascha Heifetz and Efrem Zimbalist, along with Gabrilowitsch, Josef Hofmann and Rachmaninoff combined forces in a gala concert to celebrate the eightieth birthday of the great master of the violin, Leopold Auer. The evening's high point was a performance by Auer and his two pupils, Heifetz and Zimbalist, of the Vivaldi Concerto for Three Violins. The ending of the piece brought the house to its feet to shout its approval.

Outside Carnegie Hall, the world was preoccupied with a dozen debates between the new and the old. None was of more interest than the question of evolution. In the summer of 1925 the Scopes trial took place at Dayton, Tennessee. It was to end with the legal defeat of the evolutionists but with a crushing defeat for the fundamentalists in the eyes of the public. Six months before that trial the same issues had been debated in Carnegie Hall by two ministers. Rev. Charles Francis Potter spoke for the modernists, Dr. John Roach Straton for the traditionalists. The topic was of sufficient interest to fill the house with vociferous supporters of both positions.

Potter pointed out that if an X-ray photograph of William Jennings Bryan's backside were made, a rudimentary tail would be observed. Dr. Straton asked why it was necessary to bring Bryan, the chief fundamentalist apologist, into the debate. Potter replied that he thought this was more polite than the use of Straton's name in connection with tails. Straton, however, got the last word by declaring some of his remote ancestors might have been hanged by the neck, but that he was certain none of them had ever been hung by the tail.

Straton thereupon launched into a magnificent tirade against evolutionary theory, tracing to it the wave of "animalism" that was engulfing the modern world, "prostrating and destroying the human race." To this indictment he added charges that the theory was causing the degradation of women who now displayed themselves wantonly on the stage, the decline in the quality of literature, the crowds in the divorce courts and the rise of the poodle as a substitute for children in the upper classes.

"Where did the wave of animalism come from?" he inquired. "Why, my friends, it is perfectly obvious that it came from the philosophy . . . which has denied the truth of revelation, thrown the ten commandments on the junk heap, laughed at the principles of Jesus Christ, taken God off the throne and destroyed the safe principles of the past which lie at the very foundations of our modern life."

Straton's moral indignation carried the day and the judges of the debate awarded him a unanimous decision—even though his cause, in the wider sense, was a lost one. His opponent had his revenge a few weeks later when he won a split decision arguing against the virgin birth.

It is probably true that the debate over evolution and, more importantly, over the role of science in the moral life, was the most important intellectual debate of the decade. On it, in this basically apolitical period, more ink and more breath were expended than on anything else. But a large body of Americans was still concerned with political life and the questions raised by leftists, often ignored, were capable of occasionally stirring up a good deal of interest—most of it worried. The Bolshevik Revolution had sent a tremor through the bourgeois western world, and although the frenzy of the early postwar attacks on the left had spent itself, and although the younger generation found left-wing politics to be irrelevant, there were some few who could briefly rekindle the old flames. Chief among them was Eugene Victor Debs, seventy, but still a firebrand. In the fall of 1925 he came to Carnegie Hall to help launch the mayoralty campaign of the Reverend Norman Thomas. Debs had been jailed for his opposition to America's participation in the war; yet, running for President from his cell in the Atlanta penitentiary, he had polled more votes than he ever had before

—close to a million. The majority would never vote for him—but they respected this last representative of the maverick tradition in politics.

Debs was only a year away from death when he came to Carnegie Hall, but his restless energy sent him prowling about the platform, leaning over its edge, his left hand resting on his knee, his right hand extended to shake a bony finger at the evils of capitalism. Here in the hall built by one of his great enemies, from the platform where Wilson, the man who had put him in jail, had had one of his finest moments, he gave capitalism what for.

"I am sorry I can't address you as my fellow citizens," Debs began sardonically. "I shed my American citizenship in Atlanta. It's still down there. I had to come away from Atlanta without it. But I came away with my self-respect. And I'd rather be a man without a country than a man without courage or self-respect."

He spared no one in his indictment of his society's institutions. "Not only the political parties, but the press and churches have become frank agents of capitalism," he thundered. "It is so easy to be for peace now when everyone is for peace," Debs declared, "but just let Wall Street get us into a new war tomorrow and see how every preacher in the country will yell for blood. I scorn to be a patriot as that term is defined in the lexicon of capitalism." He challenged the "masters" of America to fight the next war, but pointed out that they would not do so. "No, our masters don't go to war; they sit at home and wave the flag and talk about patriotism."

A year later Debs was dead of a heart attack. His last act of writing and his last act of love for another human being was to copy off for a fellow patient at a sanitarium the final lines of William Ernest Henley's "Invictus": "It matters not how strait the gate, /How charged with punishments the scroll, /I am the master of my fate: /I am the captain of my soul."

Carnegie Hall opened the 1925-1926 musical season under new management. Andrew Carnegie had died in 1919, and although the board of directors which had been his personal creation continued to run the hall together with the Carnegie estate, it had remained unprofitable. It was finally sold to Robert E. Simon, a prosperous New York realtor. The sales agreement stipulated that he must maintain the hall as a concert hall for at least five years and that he could not demolish it or use it for less exalted purposes before 1930. Simon assured one and all that he would try to keep the hall going much longer than that if he could turn a decent profit on it. But the sale set off a flurry of rumors concerning the future of the hall, the most prominent of which was that Carnegie Hall and the Metropolitan Opera would combine and build a new cultural center. These rumors continued to reappear from time to time throughout the history of the hall. For, although Simon was a responsible citizen, he did not have the resources to absorb incessant deficits the way Carnegie did. He was a businessman—not a philanthropist. Indeed, one of his chief resources during the Depression was musical New York's fear that it would lose its major concert room and he played upon this frequently in an attempt to stir up business for the hall whenever the debts mounted alarmingly.

But in the fall of 1925, in the midst of perhaps the most prosperous decade in American history, the hall looked like a good investment, particularly given the excitement which was stirring the musical world.

The major orchestras began the season with a flourish of novelties. Mengelberg made the first move by adopting the new seating arrangement for orchestra with which Stokowski had been experimenting. He brought the first and second violins together in a body at his left (instead of having them make up two arcs of a semicircle surrounding him) and put the cellos on his right. The effect was interesting but not particularly satisfactory. Stokowski countered by bringing forward a new suite by Gustav Holst. It was less than well received, but as usual, the orchestra's sumptuous tone commanded great respect. A little later the endlessly experimental Stokowski tried out a new piano on his listeners. It was constructed so that its player, Lester Donahue, could play a crescendo on a single note if he wanted to. He did and Stokowski did, but the audience and critics were less than delighted by still another novelty for novelty's sake. More fun was had when Mengelberg brought out some new pieces, two of them by pianist Alfredo Casella and the *Danse de la Sorcière* by the young Polish composer Alexandre Tansman which was wild stuff, leading at least one critic to guess that the audience thought Honegger's locomotive was loose among them for "Tansman danced with quite as much vigor and as many snorts." The Boston Symphony under Koussevitzky was equally ambitious. Among other works it presented Hindemith's Concerto for Orchestra and the first New York performance of an Aaron Copland work, *Music for the Theater.*

Not to be outdone, New York's lesser orchestras threw some novelties in the faces of their subscribers. Stransky had turned the baton of the State Symphony over to Ernö Dohnányi, and he offered two Bartók portraits for orchestra as his opener, following it a month later with Prokofieff's First Violin Concerto, performed in New York for the first time by Lea Luboshutz, who won an ovation for her work with the diabolically difficult piece.

Damrosch, meantime, was concentrating on America compositions. He led off with Charles Martin Loeffler's genteel "Memories of my Childhood" featuring Lawrence Tibbett singing the solo role. Tibbett, still riding his first crest, was well received and the piece, which made use of four harmonicas and some folk tunes Loeffler had overheard during a youthful stay in Russia, was received politely.

There was a good deal more interest in Damrosch's next American offering. It was Deems Taylor's suite based on James Branch Cabell's literary curiosity, *Jurgen.* The piece was judged to be slickly professional, a demonstration of compositional mastery that heartened all who were wondering when American music would grow up.

But all of this activity was prelude, a gradual crescendo to what was hoped would be an event that signaled America's musical coming of age. This was to be the premiere, on December 3, by Walter Damrosch, of George Gershwin's first serious composition of length. After hearing Gershwin's Rhapsody, Walter Damrosch had persuaded his faithful patron, Harry Harkness Flagler, to commission a full-scale work from the young American tunesmith. Ernest Hutcheson gave him a studio at Chautauqua, New York, and there Gershwin wrote most of his Concerto in F during the summer of 1925. The final movement was completed in September and the orchestration on November 10, less than a month before the performance.

Damrosch set the tone for the first performance by commenting that "various composers have been walking around jazz like a cat around a plate of hot soup, waiting for it to cool off so they could

Culver Service

George Gershwin. His Concerto in F *and his one-act blues opera,* 135th Street, *were premiered within a few weeks of one another at Carnegie Hall in 1925.*

enjoy it without burning their tongues," but that it had been reserved for Gershwin to lift jazz to a level enabling it to be received as a respectable member of the musical family. "He is the prince who has taken Cinderella by the hand and openly proclaimed her a princess to the astonished world, no doubt to the fury of her envious sisters," said the conductor.

The Prince himself was not notably nervous on the day of the coronation. A friend had to hustle him out of a hot bath, in which he was luxuriating, in order to get him to Carnegie Hall on time. Once there, he preserved his calm, exhibiting tension only by pacing up and down the artists' room rubbing his fingers (he was to play the solo himself). Said Damrosch, just before they were to go on, "Just play the concerto as well as it deserves, George, and you'll come off with flying banners."

Gershwin played well and the audience, composed of Gershwin's Tin Pan Alley and jazzmen friends as well as dozens of serious musicians, was warmly, if not ecstatically, enthusiastic. It must have been a moment of great triumph for Gershwin. When Gershwin was a boy John Totten, then an usher, and later manager of Carnegie Hall, used to sneak the music-mad child into the hall to hear his favorites perform. Now the ex-gate-crasher was the soloist, and playing his own composition besides.

The critics were divided about the quality of the Concerto. Some thought it banal, conventional, trite. Some thought it nowhere near as exciting—and a good deal more pretentious—than the Rhapsody. But some found it quite the opposite. Samuel Chotzinoff, speaking for Gershwin's contemporaries, said: "He alone of all those writing the music of today . . . expresses us. He is the present with all its audacity, impertinence, its feverish delight in motion, its lapses into rhythmically exotic melancholy. He writes without the smallest hint of self-consciousness. . . . George Gershwin is an instinctive artist who has the talent for the right manipulation of the crude materials he starts out with that a lifelong study of counterpoint and fugue never can give to one who was not born with it."

But whatever the merits of the Concerto—and they are certainly debatable—its effect was to liberate American music from formalism, to give other composers the chance to use the nervous rhythms of jazz to communicate the very essence of the modern American spirit. This did not happen overnight, but in the aftermath of Gershwin's Concerto, men like Maurice Ravel were saying, "I take this 'blues' very seriously," and asking, "why have not more of the important American composers turned to this 'blues' material and to other music of popular origin which has come to you from so many different sources?" Many did, in the years to come, often with greater subtlety and sophistication than Gershwin, but all acknowledged that he was the great pioneer.

A month later Paul Whiteman and his orchestra brought Gershwin's one-act jazz opera, *135th Street,* to Carnegie Hall and set the audience's hands clapping, and feet tapping, in time to the infectious music with which Gershwin limned the tragedy of certain events in one Harlem Mike's saloon. The work featured Benny Fields, Blossom Seeley and Charles Hart as a gambler who "died game" at the climax of the action. "Mr. Gershwin's music, whether or not it proves the 'grandest,' was certainly the first in an opera premiere to be whistled within the hour on Broadway." The whistleable items were the six short, lilting songs of the opera's climax, particularly Fields's big number, "I'm Goin' South in the Morning"; the citizens of the jazz age were humming it, singing it and whistling it as they departed the hall, climbed into their limousines and drove away.

They had been equally excited by Deems Taylor's *Circus Day* which had preceded the Gershwin work. Taylor, however, was less used to public acclaim than the man from Tin Pan Alley, and he was not to be found when it came time to take a curtain call. Said Whiteman, in explanation: "I've no doubt he's just as unhappy and scared as I am."

The Gershwin works were certainly the high point of this season of new works and new performers, but by no means the end of it. Later in December Joseph Szigeti made his first New York appearance, with the Philadelphia Orchestra, which continued to average at least one novelty per concert. Much later in the season Otto Klemperer, guest conducting the Damrosch orchestra, gave the first American performance of Ernst Křenek's Concerto Grosso, while soon afterward Walter Gieseking devoted the first half of his program to the classicists, the second to the moderns, including Hindemith's *Moderne Klavier-*

musik—"music of intensely nervous quality, ironic and of a driving energy."

But in this year of new sounds, perhaps nothing was as touching as some very familiar ones—the tone of a beloved pianist playing with his accustomed excellence, the earthy wisecracks of Will Rogers regaling a Carnegie Hall audience, the sound of a great orchestra under the leadership of an immortal.

The pianist was Ossip Gabrilowitsch returning with the Philadelphia Orchestra early in the season to celebrate a joint silver anniversary. When the Philadelphia Orchestra gave its first public concert on November 16, 1900, its soloist had been Gabrilowitsch and its program had included the Tchaikovsky B Flat minor Piano Concerto, Beethoven's Fifth Symphony, the *Götterdämmerung* Music of Wagner and Goldmark's *Spring* Overture. Now twenty-five years and one day later, the same orchestra and soloist, with Stokowski on the podium, presented the same program in Carnegie Hall. On this occasion the great showman from Philadelphia was content to sublimate his personality to the music and his readings were perhaps more successful than when he was striving for a novel effect. As for Gabrilowitsch, the occasion was a triumph. Of the concerto Olin Downes wrote: "In twenty-five years of orchestral concerts the writer has not heard it presented with the breadth, the fire and the nobility of conception that characterized it last night. . . . Mr. Gabrilowitsch gave it a fabulous interpretation. . . . When many pianists and many concertos have been forgotten this performance will be remembered." The audience agreed. They brought Gabrilowitsch back to the stage time and time again and showered him with approval beyond the dreams of a performer as modest as he.

A little later Gabrilowitsch gave a recital of his own at Carnegie Hall, just to round out the anniversary festivities. He did not look forward to the occasion because he had been a conductor for half-a-dozen years and therefore was out of practice as a recitalist. "My piano playing is ended as far as the press goes," he complained to his wife. "The critics will take it for granted that I must play worse and worse every year as no man can serve two masters."

But the critics surprised him. As far as they were concerned he was getting better and better and Clara chided him gently for his pessimism, which gave him the opportunity for a word of advice: "Expect the worst, then if it comes you'll not be shocked. If it doesn't come surprise will be added to pleasure."

There was no surprise—but a great deal of pleasure—inherent in the reaction to the return of an immortal conductor to New York. Arturo Toscanini had conducted Italian opera and Wagnerian opera at the Met in its golden days before World War I. He had been much loved even then. But absence—and a growing reputation at La Scala whose orchestra he brought here early in the Twenties—had made hearts beat even more fondly for the Maestro. Clarence H. Mackay, president of the Philharmonic, had wanted Toscanini to lead his orchestra for some time. He sensed that Toscanini's aesthetic was precisely right for the new American musical mood, that the conductor might welcome the chance to conduct a symphony orchestra. He was also aware of the Maestro's growing disenchantment with Fascism and he was determined to try to lure him to America. His emissary was Max Smith, critic for the New York *Press* and the *American*, and a friend of Toscanini's. The Maestro liked the idea rather better than anyone had dared hope, and as soon as he was certain that he could arrange a six-week leave of absence from La Scala, he agreed to come.

January 16, 1926, marked his first appearance at the head of the Philharmonic. It was the beginning of an era and a legend. His first program was to include a number of Toscanini favorites, Haydn's *Clock* Symphony, Wagner's "Siegfried's Death" and "Funeral Music," Weber's *Euryanthe* Overture, and as the *pièce de résistance*, the first New York performance of Respighi's *Pines of Rome*. It had been a Respighi year in New York. The composer had been visiting and with Mengelberg had given the first performance anywhere of his piano concerto. Now he would hear his friend Toscanini conduct the piece that was probably his masterwork.

The occasion was in every sense a gala. Italian and American flags draped the hall, the audience, one of the most distinguished of the decade, rose to greet the Maestro, and applauded him wildly at every possible moment. Olin Downes, along with everyone else, was quite swept away by the events of the evening. He described Toscanini as standing before his players, "erect, commanding, pouring a veritable

Pix

P

The Maestro as one of his players photographed him during rehearsals.

Pix

The Bettmann Archive

Caruso's caricature of the Maestro.

fluid of energy from his eyes, his body, his fingers into an orchestra that shakes and reverberates to his commands, and proceeds from climax to climax of tonal splendor."

Of *Pines of Rome*, Downes wrote, "The final pages—a long crescendo which Mr. Toscanini built up with irresistible cumulative power—would be enough to sweep any audience from its feet and part any reviewer from a large part of his judgment."

That night also began the long crescendo of the Toscanini legend. At last the cult of the conductor had found in this fiery little man with the paradoxically austere musical concepts the man on whom to focus all its reverence. Within a few years he was to be *the* conductor, in a class by himself.

By the time of his farewell in mid-February, "the doors of Carnegie Hall had to be held as a fort against the many who pleaded for standing room after the limit of admissions had been reached." Anyone who ventured into the lobby was pounced upon, asked if he was leaving and if so, if he would give his stub to one of the patient ones who waited the whole program through for a chance to hear the Maestro.

But what was Toscanini's secret? It is truly rare for a musician of such fine fiber to attract such adulation. Part of that adulation, of course, was based on his legendary fieriness: the baton breaking, the supply of dollar watches that had to be kept on hand for him to stomp on in a rage. Part of it was the awe-inspiring personal and musical integrity of the man, an integrity that compelled him to refuse to play a Fascist anthem at La Scala, because, "La Scala is not a beer garden."

Both these qualities were abundantly apparent in his interpretations. The first gave his readings a driving pace, a clarity and a sureness of direction which no other conductor equaled. There were no vaporings in a Toscanini performance, no misty wanderings. Each performance was definitive for the moment, although like any fine musician over the course of years he gradually changed his readings of some works as he ferreted out new meanings and nuances. But this is where the integrity came in, for he never interpreted. His job was clear to him —to play the music as the composer intended it to be played. He once told Samuel Antek, a musician who played with him for fifteen years: "Is very simple. Play as written. Is difficult to do, but the only way. Let other *ignoranti*—conductors who think they are greater than God —do as they please. Have courage. Do as written."

Fire and integrity. In a world in revolt against the old ways, here was the perfect musician. The men before the war had been interpreters, products of the romantic movement which had some extremely poetic notions about the role of the conductor. Here was the opposite, and a large segment of the intellectual-musical world welcomed him as a messiah. Their enthusiasm, undoubtedly born of their sympathy for the neoclassic aesthetic which placed "pure" music above all other kinds, was communicated to the rest of the listening world. This, combined with the wonderful color of the Toscanini personality, accounts for his success. He was, historically speaking, the right man in the right place at the right moment in history. Of all performers, he alone came to personify the new aesthetic. Probably the public went to extremes in judging his greatness, however, for one of the paradoxes of Toscanini was that he was a musical conservative. His bouts with modern composers were often disastrous (setting aside his readings of Ravel's *Bolero* and the works of Respighi). And it is a demonstrable fact that his presence on the New York musical scene had a distinctly dampening effect on the experimental, on the search for new modes of musical expression. Although there is no doubt that his firm hand had an excellent effect on the usually erratic Philharmonic, it also emphasized some ongoing bad habits.

Toscanini's conservatism in program-making fell in a little too neatly with the stodgy preferences of the orchestra's subscribers for the routine, the ordinary, the time-tested. The classic repertory was never played better in the orchestra's history, but the Toscanini influence helped keep Carnegie Hall a magnificent museum, rather than allowing it to become the workshop of a living tradition. In the long run, this tendency had already exerted a bad effect on the orchestra. Except for the dreary reign of Stransky, the orchestra had had no permanent conductor with longer than a three-season tenure since the days of Anton Seidl. It had become accustomed to adapting itself to a wide variety of styles and temperaments, but it never originated a style and a temperament of its own. Toscanini was at no time, in any sense of the word, musical director of the orchestra. He came over from Italy for a few months each season, whipped the orchestra into fighting trim, demonstrated its championship abilities for a brief period, then turned it over to preliminary-level trainers during his absences. It is reasonable to suppose that the Philharmonic's board was well satisfied with this arrangement. It prevented a conductor from becoming too powerful a challenge to the board's rule; at the same time it provided the board an opportunity to present any number of conductors who were good box-office in a city that was avid to watch a wide variety of backs and baton styles on the podium.

None of this, of course, was Toscanini's fault. His needs happened to fall in with some rather bad patterns in the orchestra's management. Judged as an event, nearly every appearance on the podium by Toscanini was a high point in the orchestra's history. For he was the king, and whatever the drawbacks of his methods of rule, the fact remains that his were the orchestra's days of glory.

For the rest of the decade his conservatism was rather neatly balanced by the work of the other conductors who regularly plied their craft in New York during the musical season. One is tempted merely to list the new works premiered during the 1926-1927 season to prove the point. Many were unimportant in the long view, but some were not, and all indicated the creative fervor of the times. Mengelberg, for instance, though almost as conservative in taste as Toscanini, did Howard Hanson's *Pan and the Priest*, Johan Wagenaar's overture to *The Taming of the Shrew* and Szymanowski's Third Symphony in which Lauritz Melchior "pitted his most robust and sharpest-edged tones against the Scriabinic orchestra, as thankless a task as any soloist is likely to be called upon to make." The most important debut by a composer during this period was by Darius Milhaud who was piano soloist in his own *Le Carnaval d'Aix*, a frankly amusing, clever, impudent and entertaining piece of work. Among the guest conductors who alternated with Mengelberg during the first part of the season were Georges Enesco and Artur Rodzinski, both making first New York appearances as conductors. Both misled their audiences somewhat. Enesco opened his program with a cautious reading of a Mozart symphony, hiding his naturally energetic personality behind its neatly measured phrases. In a work of his own he opened up a bit, then, with Strauss's *Don Juan*, he suddenly released an extraordinary intensity of temperament that electrified his audience who, shocked out of lethargy, voiced wild acclaim. Rodzinski's deception was based more on his own manner than on music. Facing the audience to take his opening bows he seemed almost shy. But when he turned to face his orchestra —an orchestra which would be his twenty years later—he became all fire and authority, his firm, decisive beat propelling the rhythms of the orchestra with vigor and easy mastery. Here was a man to watch.

The rest of the Philharmonic season was divided between Toscanini, whose engagements were halved because of an attack of the bursitis that plagued him throughout the remainder of his career, and Furtwängler who premiered a new Sibelius overture (*The Tempest*) and Miaskowsky's Seventh Symphony. The event of the orchestra's season was undoubtedly Toscanini's performance of the Beethoven First and Ninth Symphonies, the latter featuring Richard Crooks, the popular tenor who had made his recital debut in Carnegie Hall earlier in the season. Toscanini's reading of the Ninth, fervent, dynamic, exultant, was in sharp contrast to what New York was used to hearing, but where Mahler might have been fired for such "irreverence," Toscanini was cheered to the echo.

Stokowski presented any number of novelties during the Philadelphia's New York season, none more interesting than the spectacle of his conducting with his left arm, while his right reposed in a sling. He called on Rodzinski to help out during the first days of his minor ailment, but once he was used to the new arrangement he carried on in his customary manner. He presented a pair of all-Bach programs, featuring some of his own orchestral transcriptions of the Master's organ music, then went on to offer Rachmaninoff's Fourth Piano Concerto which everyone recognized as belonging to the nineteenth century. This was no longer a recommendation, and the general reaction was summed up by Pitts Sanborn of the *Telegram* who called the piece "long-winded, tiresome, unimportant, in places tawdry."

The day was saved by three Russian songs which Rachmaninoff had arranged for a small chorus and orchestra. Wrote Richard Stokes of the *World*: "Like Napoleon at Marengo, Sergei Rachmaninoff . . . turned the most disastrous rout of his career into decisive victory. The opening attack was made with a new concerto. . . . It came reeling back from the charge in disorder and defeat. After the intermission a chorus . . . proceeded to redeem the catastrophe with Mr. Rachmaninoff's three latest compositions." At best, however, the songs represented only partial redemption. The world had turned over a bit, and Rachmaninoff had not turned with it.

Alas, the world had not turned so much that it was ready to welcome anything as radical as "the 13th sound," an experiment in a new sixteen-tone scale by the Mexican, Julián Carrillo. Stokowski announced himself a convert to it in a speech from the podium and in a program note. But the audience remained mystified and the critics irritable when Carrillo took over to lead a special ensemble in a demonstration concertino.

To end the season, and to begin his first trial separation from his orchestra, Stokowski decided on another new work, Edgar Varèse's "Arcanes," which evoked "hostile sibilations," from the audience and the notation from one critic that "there was no mercy in its disharmony, no pity in its successions of screaming, clashing, clangorous discords." It did, however, avoid dullness, principally by keeping conservative nerves on edge. It was ugly music, but the world was suddenly ugly to many composers, and many were beginning to see that the beauty of the nineteenth century tones had had something to do with the placid, prosperous and harmonious era in which they were formed. Now the world seemed suddenly to be full of anarchy.

Koussevitzky's Carnegie season with the Boston was every bit as interesting as Stokowski's. He gave the New York premiere of Sibelius' Seventh Symphony, followed that with de Falla's Concerto for harpsichord, flute, oboe, clarinet, violin and cello (with Wanda Landowska), then did Respighi's *Church Windows*, Albert Roussel's Suite in F major (dedicated to the conductor) and Edward Burlingame Hill's symphonic setting of Amy Lowell's "Lilacs." The most important Koussevitzky novelty of that season was the New York premiere of Aaron Copland's Piano Concerto, a work that went far beyond Gershwin's attempt to blend jazz and the traditional musical forms. It was dissonant, full of abandonment and a sort of "I don't care" spirit. There were hisses from some, silence from others, but many of the more astute observers found in it a brilliance lacking in most American music and a sophistication. Copland would eventually write more popular music, perhaps better music, but this concerto established him as a truly individual voice working on the pioneering edge of older traditions and forming out of them, through his eclectic genius, uniquely individual works. If there is such a thing as a modern American nonacademic musical tradition, it owes more to Copland than to any other composer.

Copland's Carnegie appearance marked the beginning of his emergence as a major figure on the compositional scene. It came only months after the beginning of the end of an old tradition. In mid-December Walter Damrosch had announced that he was laying down his baton. In recent years his New York Symphony Orchestra had more and more frequently been led by guests, and although Damrosch was to remain an extremely busy toiler in the musical vineyards, particularly as a lecturer on music appreciation for children, this was the end not only of his activity as a full-time musical director, but of his orchestra as well. His first appearance after the announcement was at a concert with Mme. Ernestine Schumann-Heink celebrating her golden anniversary as a public artist. Appropriately, they appeared together in an all-Wagner concert. Inspired by the occasion they gave a memorable concert of the works of their favorite composer. The faithful Flagler was on hand to present the diva with a bit of carefully chosen jewelry to mark the event. Within a year the singer would give her last concert and Damrosch's beloved orchestra would be no more.

The verbal high-points of the season were two debates, the chief attraction of which was Clarence Darrow, upholding, of course, the radical point of view. In the first he took the affirmative side of a discussion titled "Is Man a Machine?" His opponent was Will Durant, already well on his way to becoming the most popular popularizer of philosophy in America. Darrow was a seventy-year-old village atheist and brilliant defender of lost causes. His scathing attack on Bryan at the Scopes trial had probably sent that old man to his death; his defense of Leopold and Loeb had saved them from the electric chair. He was at a loss in his first Carnegie Hall debate, for his was a thankless position. Nevertheless, the hall was packed and hundreds more had to be turned away by police. Both men were frequently interrupted by applause. Darrow, speaking out of his vast knowledge of the squalor of the human condition, growled that he didn't "know so much about the grandeur and nobility of man as my friend seems to think he knows, but . . . I know there are enough facts to warrant concluding that man is a machine and I know that nothing has been proved to the contrary."

He also asserted that "you can buy everything that goes to make a man in a drugstore for ninety cents." From that remark Durant scored his best point. "But you can't put them together to make a man," he replied.

Darrow had a more congenial topic a few months later when he debated Prohibition with a representative of the Anti-Saloon League, a Mr. Wheeler. In this one the audience was solidly on Darrow's side, cheering him while they hissed, booed and jeered the representative of a vanishing kind of morality. Darrow spoke frankly of the solid pleasures of drink and of its virtues. Wheeler cited the ruinous results of alcoholism. A strait-laced type, immaculate in white tie and tails, with a meticulously precise manner of speech and gesture, he was a

Eugene Victor Debs, who left his citizenship in the Atlanta Penitentiary but who emerged to thunder against capitalism in Carnegie Hall in 1925.

Culver Service

splendid contrast to Darrow, in his rumpled tuxedo, the familiar shock of gray hair falling over his forehead. Grizzled, humorous, vigorous in gesture and tone, poor Wheeler didn't have a chance against him, especially after Darrow pointed out the higher morality compelling a citizen to disobey a Prohibition law, with which the majority of the community disagreed. Since the majority of the audience would head for speakeasies as soon as the meeting was over, they were glad to have a mildly sophisticated rationale for so doing. They found Wheeler's counterargument, that this was a call to anarchy, laughable. And they laughed.

The season of 1927-1928 revolved more around personalities than music. Those personalities involved with the New York Symphony Orchestra also were far more interesting than any new music it performed in this, its 50th Anniversary season (and its last as an independent organization). Indeed, at no point in its history had it participated in a debut as exciting as that of Yehudi Menuhin, an eleven-year-old prodigy. He had studied with the best in Europe, had been acclaimed in the many cities of America, and the word was out—this was a genuine phenomenon. Scheduled to debut under Fritz Busch on November 25, he sent word from Europe that he would like, please, to play the Beethoven Concerto. Snorted Busch: "One does not allow Jackie Coogan to play Hamlet." And there the matter rested, with the Mozart A minor Concerto proposed as a compromise selection.

Culver Service

Clarence Darrow debated evolution and prohibition in Carnegie Hall in 1927.

When Yehudi, a modest and well-brought up boy, arrived in New York, there was a terrible clamor over him. Arriving to meet Busch, he was surrounded by newspapermen and photographers and the conductor was distinctly unimpressed. The whole thing seemed to him lacking in taste and in reverence for art. In addition, he had a new work by his brother, Adolph, scheduled for the night of the Menuhin debut and he wanted nothing to detract from that. He had to admit to himself, however, that Yehudi seemed like a nice lad, and, out of respect for Damrosch, he agreed to listen to him play the Beethoven before deciding the question of which concerto they would do together.

Two days later Yehudi came to Busch's hotel suite to play for the Maestro. Damrosch had warned him not to press the point about Beethoven. If he failed with it, his career would be ruined. "But I don't care about a career," the boy had replied. "I just want to have some fun playing with the orchestra."

Yehudi was not strong enough to tune his violin so, as was his custom, he turned it over to his father to do. Busch could scarcely conceal his contempt.

Then, Busch playing the orchestral part on the piano, they launched into the debated concerto. By the second *tutti* Busch was completely won over. "You can play anything with me, anytime, anywhere," he said. Then he and the boy worked together for an hour, discussing various questions of interpretation.

Later, at the first orchestral rehearsal, Yehudi casually mentioned that he could play the Brahms Concerto too. Busch couldn't believe it. "Impossible," he said. "How can your small hands stretch the tenths?" Menuhin proved he could do it and Busch was so effusive in his praise that the boy's father told him to cease for fear he would spoil Yehudi. "No one can spoil him," said Busch, but the elder Menuhin insisted and threatened—at least half-seriously—to make the boy withdraw if Busch didn't stop.

No one could compete with him either. Busch rescheduled the concert's program, putting the soloist last, for he knew that no orchestra and no music could hope to top the sensation Menuhin would cause.

Entering the hall on the night of the concert Yehudi spied a fire

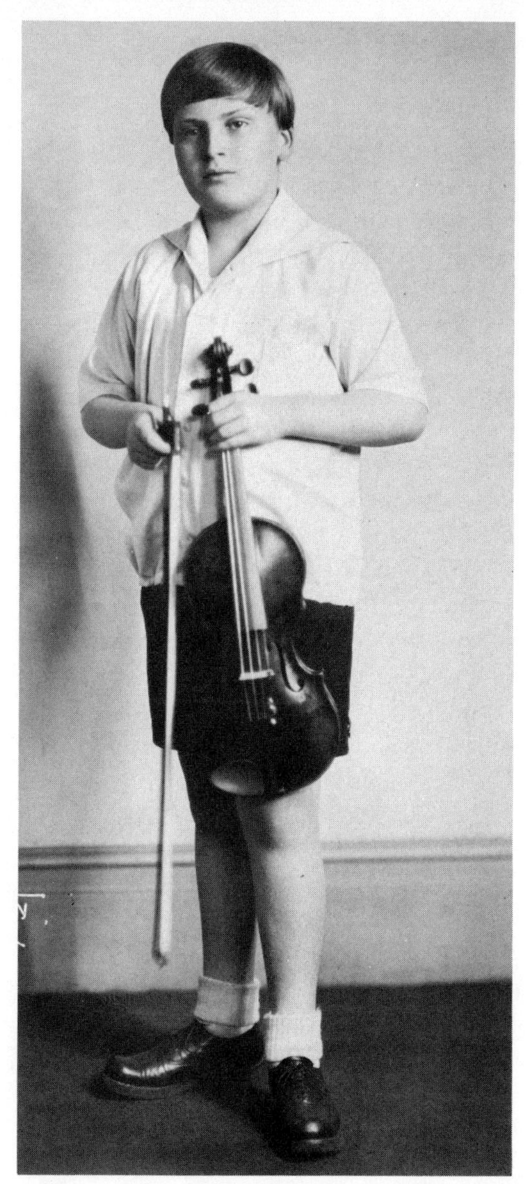

Yehudi Menuhin at the time of his sensational 1927 Carnegie Hall debut. He was eleven—not strong enough to tune his own violin but already "a great artist."

Culver Service

hatchet hanging on the wall and asked the guard what the ax was used for. "To chop heads off soloists who don't play well," was the reply. "And how many heads have you already cut off?" was the next question. "Quite a few," was the answer. Twenty-five years later, at Menuhin's anniversary recital, the same guard nodded at the same hatchet and sagely observed: "Quite a few heads have rolled since then."

That night, however, no heads rolled, although many spun when they heard the sounds produced by the boy in the white silk blouse and the velvet kneepants. After he had finished the Joachim cadenza, applause threatened to halt the performance. When the concerto was ended, the audience rose with a shout and many had tears in their eyes. The men in the orchestra spontaneously rose with them, to applaud and to shout bravos. The crowd simply would not leave. Busch retired and left the stage to the boy, who remained calm and smiling throughout the ovation. Quietly, he insisted on bringing his teacher, Louis Persinger, on stage to share the applause with him. It went on and on—until at last the boy had to appear on stage wearing a coat and cap to signal that the performance was definitely over.

Next day, the reviews were ecstatic. Olin Downes rewrote his notice twice. The first draft was so enthusiastic that he was afraid he would be laughed out of town. The second was not as rhapsodic as he knew the boy deserved. The third, a combination of the first two, still seemed a little too dithyrambic, but Downes let it go with some trepidation. He needn't have worried. His colleagues were as enthused as he was. Later he told Menuhin's biographer, Robert Magidoff, "I had resolved in my indignation at the boy's effrontery to stay just for the first movement, but I simply couldn't tear myself away. I had come to the hall convinced that a child could play the violin no more effectively than a trained seal, and I left with the conviction that there is no such thing as an infant prodigy, but there is such a thing as a great artist who begins at an early age."

A couple of weeks later Menuhin repeated his triumph in recital. The audience overflowed onto the stage and when the concert was over they mobbed him, elbowing, pushing, climbing over chairs in their urge to touch the child. Any number of matrons attempted to crush him to their bosoms. The critics remained in thrall. "One is inclined to doubt Yehudi's mortality," said one. "Well-nigh supernatural," sighed another.

Less wildly emotional, but in many ways as moving was another New York Symphony concert in mid-December. The occasion was the final farewell of Mme. Schumann-Heink and it turned out to be a perfect orgy of sentimentality and patriotism. As the concert ended, the singer was greeted by members of the American Legion, of all organizations, marching up the aisles, then on to the platform, bearing the flag on high. During the war Schumann-Heink had been in the odd position of having a son fighting on each side which, of course, was alluded to during the presentation of the inevitable bouquet by a Legion representative. This, in turn, was the signal for a veritable deluge of floral tributes, one of which, a sheaf of roses, was handed up to the platform by a dignified little lady—Marcella Sembrich. As soon as Schumann-Heink pronounced the name, elongated a velvety *s* as she leaned over to accept the offering, the applause rolled to its highest pitch.

The last rose having been delivered, the singer saluted the flag and spoke of her love of soldiers, an appropriate sentiment given the surprisingly martial nature of the occasion. Whereupon Walter Damrosch materialized from the wings to present her with a book containing greetings from the governor of every state in the Union. He read aloud from the one sent by Al Smith who referred to the "more than fifty years" of Mme. Schumann-Heink's service to art. "There must be some mistake here," said Damrosch gallantly. This earned him a solid, Germanic kiss.

Then, "in a voice that was melody itself," the singer spoke of her gratitude to America for its support, of her love for her hearers. She said she would devote herself to teaching—gratuitously—and that she hoped to find a true contralto voice in the course of her new career. Then she ended the day by singing, as her last encore, "The Star-Spangled Banner."

There would, of course, be other farewells at Carnegie Hall. But this was the last in the old tradition, a sort of last outburst of Victorian sentimentality. In the future, the farewells would be said with more efficiency and fewer flowers—both real and oratorical.

In contrast to the warmth of Schumann-Heink's farewell was the difficult American debut of Béla Bartók who was scheduled to play his new piano concerto with Mengelberg and the Philharmonic. Mengelberg played a great deal of modern music, but his heart was never truly in it. And there was difficulty over the concerto. Some said

Mengelberg just couldn't get the hang of it. Others that he simply loathed the thing, still others that it was too difficult to get ready in the limited rehearsal time available. Whatever the reason, it was cancelled and Bartók played instead his Rhapsody for Piano and Orchestra, Op. 1. But, alas, in the eyes of many critics the orchestra was ill-prepared for the Rhapsody. "A more groping accompaniment has seldom come from the Philharmonic Orchestra," said one critic. Despite these difficulties, however, Bartók captured a number of imaginations with his own playing. Later in the year Fritz Reiner and the Cincinnati Orchestra gave New York a chance to hear the Concerto. Some were horrified, some thought it the finest piece of modern music yet heard.

Trouble of the sort which plagued Mengelberg and Bartók, though more severe, developed shortly thereafter when two greats began to prepare their joint American debut. It was the idea of Sir Thomas Beecham that the Tchaikovsky Concerto should be played at a rather more stately tempo than his soloist, a young man named Vladimir Horowitz, preferred. In the course of a couple of rehearsals they found it impossible to reconcile their differences. Sir Thomas, a short, rounded, bearded gentleman who resembled a toby jug, surveyed the scene of his American debut with calmness, at least as interested in his audience as they were in him. He thereupon launched into the concerto at his own leisurely pace. Horowitz countered with a quickened tempo. "Did this disturb or affect in any way the ideas of Beecham?" Olin Downes asked rhetorically. "Apparently it did not. When the strings entered, over the chords, with the theme, the conductor merely resumed the tempo of his introduction with what could be called, politely, a sturdy British independence of another man's thinking."

The Russian virtuoso, who could—and can—play more notes faster than any other piano player, was not about to have the effect of his debut spoiled by British imperialism. He kept right on playing with blinding speed. Later he recalled, "I played louder, faster and more notes than Tchaikovsky wrote, and there are plenty of notes in the concerto."

The result was less a performance than a rerun of the celebrated encounter between the tortoise and the hare. But, for once, the hare

RCA Victor

Vladimir Horowitz found himself in a race with Sir Thomas Beecham at their joint debut concert in 1928.

won. Observers unanimously agreed that it had been a long time, perhaps not since the early appearances of Paderewski, since New York had given a pianist the reception it accorded Horowitz. Wrote Downes, who was distinctly not amused by the affair, "A mob is a mob, blood is blood; the call of the wild is heard, whether it is a savage beating a drum or a young Russian, mad with excitement and physical speed and power, pounding on a keyboard."

At the next concert, which was a repeat of the same program, Sir Thomas managed to soothe the savage beast. At the concerto's end he simply signaled for silence in his inimitable way and made a speech, thus effectively cutting off Horowitz's curtain calls. The pianist, at that time, suffered one huge disadvantage. He had no English, while Sir Thomas had a great deal of it. Thus the conductor gained at least a draw in the encounter. He also gained enthusiastic notices for his other efforts during the rest of his brief stay with the Philharmonic.

Shortly thereafter Toscanini, fire in his eyes, returned to the Philharmonic podium. He was angry beyond any telling of it at his German co-conductor Mengelberg, who had fallen into the habit of referring patronizingly to Toscanini as "the Italian conductor." In addition, Mengelberg had made several slurring remarks about the nature of the illness which had forced Toscanini to curtail his appearances during the previous year. The implication was that the competition had been too tough for Toscanini to handle. Even worse, Mengelberg was hanging around New York, trying to share Toscanini's limelight, giving him advice on how to conduct.

"Talk, talk, talk, that was Mengelberg," Toscanini said later. "Once he came to me and told me at great length what was the proper German way to conduct Beethoven's *Coriolanus.* He had got it, he said quite seriously, from a conductor who supposedly had got it straight from Beethoven. Bah! I told him I got it straight from Beethoven himself, from the score."

The techniques of the two conductors were as varied as they could be. Mengelberg bored his orchestra into submission with his interminable lectures. Toscanini frightened it into docility. The Philharmonic may not have been the greatest orchestra in the world but it was—and is—the toughest. It delighted in scaring conductors. Some of them tried to appeal to the orchestra's better nature and were greeted with scornful laughter. Others tried to browbeat the men into good behavior. But no orchestra which was used to being dressed down by the Master—Toscanini—was going to accept the same treatment from lesser men.

The demise of Mengelberg came when the well-oiled machine, modeled on German military style and trained to finicky precision by his academic approach, which required pauses for lectures every other measure, was undermined by the Toscanini method. The Maestro never theorized, he simply swept the orchestra through long hours of playing, warmed the air with his angry cries and made each player an extension of his will, incapable of acting on his own. There was no system in the Toscanini method—only sheer charisma. All of Mengelberg's drilling simply broke down. Since he was incapable of operating with the intuitive methods of Toscanini, and since the orchestra had fallen under the spell of the Italian, his academicism resulted in anarchy. The carnage was awful to behold. The final blow to Mengelberg's prestige was the merger of the Philharmonic with the New York Symphony, with Toscanini in full command of the new orchestra. The new orchestra became known as the Philharmonic-Symphony of New York. The hyphen was terribly important. It symbolized that the two orchestras had truly merged, that the Philharmonic had not swallowed up the Flagler-Damrosch organization. Officials recall that Mr. Flagler used to call them up to protest whenever he caught a newspaper referring to the orchestra as the Philharmonic Symphony, *sans* hyphen. The merger resolved the ambiguity in the Mengelberg-Toscanini relationship. It was the latter who received authority to organize the new orchestra out of the members of its two organizations. Mengelberg stayed on as an associate conductor until the end of the 1929-1930 season when he left claiming that Toscanini had intrigued against him.

For all of Mr. Flagler's concern, however, it was hardly a true merger. Only twenty men from the collection of eccentrics which was the New York Symphony got jobs with the combined orchestra. Winthrop Sargeant, who was one of the twenty, and who had been through much with the old New York Symphony, has vividly recalled the last days of the orchestra in his *Geniuses, Goddesses and People.* The orchestra was known in musical circles as "the Foreign Legion" and it included among its personnel a former Bessarabian sheep stealer, a reformed Istanbul white slaver and a man who had once been a cook on a Latvian tramp steamer. It contained a man who carried no money on him but who was never without his cello. Needing subway fare, he would simply unpack his instrument and start playing. Several dollars worth of change nearly always found their way into the innards of the instrument, apparently not affecting its tone in the slightest. Another man dreamed of becoming a conductor. Otherwise an admirable violist, it was his habit to retire to his hotel room to conduct an invisible orchestra for hours. He had signs on each chair indicating the various sections and after a good performance he would confide to his colleagues that "I and my men gave a superb performance of Beethoven's Ninth Symphony—simply superb." He also had his troubles, and wondered aloud if he would have to let his second clarinetist go because his attack was inaccurate. Then there was the great flautist, George Barrère, who, bearded, wearing a broad hat, a Prince Albert coat and pink trousers would stalk into rehearsal, pull an atomizer from his pocket and proceed to disinfect his colleagues who included members of the French Legion of Honor, Algerian longshoremen, ex-wrestlers, Gipsy fiddle players, Ukrainian professors, waiters and failed composers.

It was a motley crew, but perhaps it was just as well. For a Damrosch tour was nearly always chaos. Often the only theater in the towns they played was a burlesque house and the strings would find themselves in the pit, the brasses on stage, the percussion people in the wings, with Damrosch himself out on the runway conducting with the stolid beat that was his hallmark.

The beginning of the end came when that patient patron, Harry Harkness Flagler, appeared one day and presented every man in the orchestra with a pair of solid-gold cufflinks. It became known as "the day we got our cufflinks and lost our shirts." Once the end of the orchestra's career became known its men retreated into gloomy despair or else erupted into hostile fury. Damrosch's last concert contained, as its *pièce de résistance* the Adagio from Beethoven's Ninth Symphony. Let Sargeant tell the tale:

"Seldom, probably, in the history of symphonic music, has the supreme communication of a great composer been so soggily set forth. Damrosch, no doubt, had expected it to be an appropriately sad, dignified, commemorative rite. It was, in effect, the funeral dirge of the New York Symphony. The trouble was that the subject of the funeral was present, still alive and not at all enthusiastic about celebrating its burial. Each man reacted according to his temperament. Some sat back and hacked the notes out of their instruments with vicious deliberateness, as though they were swatting flies on a windowpane. Notes issued from the brasses that subtly suggested . . . the 'Bronx cheer.' Tempos dragged until Damrosch must have felt like a man struggling waist deep in mud. When the last note had subsided, Damrosch turned and bowed gravely to the audience."

Then, a strange thing happened. The public could not have cared less about the quality of the performance. They were there to bid a fond farewell to a beloved orchestral friend. Applause rolled stageward in great, emotional waves. The men in the band could see tears coursing down many cheeks. Damrosch bowed to the orchestra, smiling like the benign old gentleman that he was. Once again, he had beaten his chronically rebellious forces. They rushed off stage, turning the air blue with "scatological expletives ranging . . . from Etonian to Provençal." One of the players told his colleagues the address of a pawn shop where fifteen dollars could be realized on those galling cufflinks and nearly everyone jotted down the information.

Thus ended the New York Symphony, traditionally the second-best orchestra in New York. It is probably just as well that the Philharmonic was obligated to take only twenty of its members into the fold.

In that last season of the New York Symphony nearly every American orchestra was doing something to honor Maurice Ravel who, afflicted by wanderlust after his mother's death, was visiting America. Ravel was, personally, an enigma. A highly nervous insomniac, he hid his natural volatility beneath a mask of dandyism. Small, neat, elegant, he arrived for a comparatively short stay in America with twenty pairs of pajamas, dozens upon dozens of shirts and no less than fifty-seven white ties. Koussevitzky devoted half of his January concert to his works, Toscanini programmed his *Daphnis et Chloé* Suite a little later, but it was the New York Symphony that Ravel himself conducted. He was the last in the long line of great guests who had come to that distinguished podium. But he was not a great conductor. Several critics noted that other men were better interpreters of his music than he was, but the March 8th concert gave New York a chance to pay homage to him. In turn, the opportunity to conduct gave Ravel the chance to sniff appreciatively of the American musical air. He was all over the place, attending jazzy night clubs in Harlem, slipping into rehearsals of the Paul Whiteman orchestra, visiting every odd corner of the city where he might hear a new sound. "How, with his excessively delicate nerves and stomach, did he keep pace with American travel, hospitality, homage?" a musical reporter asked. He had no trouble at all. For like many an artist before him, his love of his craft, his ravenous need to know more about it, enabled him to survive all obstacles imperturbably.

The creative fervor of the musical activity that Ravel was investigating was never more clearly demonstrated than in April, 1928, when two events which virtually spanned the entire history of Western music took place in Carnegie Hall. The first was the presentation by Ossip Gabrilowitsch and the Detroit Symphony Orchestra of the *St. Matthew Passion*, an event which remains one of the great evenings in the history of the hall in the minds of many professionals (like Bruno Walter) who heard it. The performance had its genesis in Detroit in 1926 when Gabrilowitsch conceived the idea of doing the work in full. For this he needed two full orchestras, two large choruses and a boys' chorus, five soloists, an organ and a clavicembalo (a piano adjusted to sound like a harpsichord) which he played to accompany recitatives. The total force had included some four hundred performers and the work was repeated at three concerts. Gabrilowitsch's Detroit patrons, who dearly loved him, finally decided to underwrite the cost of sending the entire production to New York for two performances.

Gabrilowitsch introduced the concert by requesting that there be no applause at any point during or after the performance and he had previously requested that the ladies refrain from wearing brightly colored dresses. "We would like to preserve the dignity and simplicity which prevail whenever Bach's masterpiece is given in church," he said.

It went off beautifully. Gabrilowitsch's wife describes it as "one of those rare events when the cloak of perfection falls on fingers, voices, thoughts, and flashed radiantly that night on the central figure of the performance."

To pass from the sublimities of the *St. Matthew Passion* to a discussion of a blues concert under the direction of W. C. Handy may seem like the rankest kind of apostasy, and it is only by accident of the calendar that the one happens to succeed the other in our consideration. Yet, Handy was, in his way, a dedicated artist, and, peculiarly enough, there is a formality in traditional jazz, a formality as marked as that of the ordered beauty of Bach's work. It might also be noted, as a number of critics did at the time, that there was no "show-off spirit" in Mr. Handy's appearance. He came and he played and his jazz was pure. There were no violins, à la Whiteman, in his arrangements, and there was no tampering with the folkish nature of his material as there was when a more sophisticated musician used the basic figurations of jazz for his own ends.

Handy recruited some fifty jazzmen and singers for his blues concert and they all played and sang "The Birth of Jazz" as they marched onto the stage to begin their demonstration. Occasionally one of the participants would move restlessly about as he played, but by and large the behavior was as decorous as the sounds were authentic. Inevitably, the program included Handy's "St. Louis Blues" as well as such standards as "Memphis Blues," "Beale Street" and "Yellow Dog." The personnel was distinguished, and featured "Fats" Waller, George Jackson, Russell Smith, Sidney Brown, J. Rosamond Johnson, Taylor Gordon, Tom Fletcher, Minnie Brown and W. C. Handy, Jr.

It was the first true jazz concert ever held at Carnegie Hall, preceding by ten years the celebrated Benny Goodman concert that firmly established "Jazz at the Philharmonic" as an institution there. As an event it surely ranked well above Paul Whiteman's concert of jazz for the middle-class which was one of the opening events of the 1928-1929 season. This performance included a fake, jazzy suite by Ferde Grofé, called "Metropolis," as well as a solo by Wilbur Hall on the bicycle pump. The occasion lacked spirit and more than one observer went away convinced that "jazz has lost some of its vitality and in a large measure its *raison d'être* apart from the dance hall." There is no gainsaying the importance of Whiteman as the man who bridged the gap between the basically Negro world of jazz and the middle-class world where it had to find a home if it was to be economically successful, but the hand that waved the violin bow was essentially a dead one, and it is perhaps the irony of Whiteman's career that he was left behind when his audience finally learned the message he had worked so hard to put across.

Indeed, the entire 1928-1929 season was dull. It was as if unconsciously the musical world knew what was coming, and was already beginning to slow down the frantic pace of innovation which had made the immediately preceding seasons very nearly the most interesting and important in Carnegie Hall's history. This dullness is virtually unrelieved. Only one new recitalist of importance appeared, and the disappearance of the New York Symphony was a loss which even the return of Stokowski in all his glory to the Philadelphia podium could not balance. The Philharmonic under Mengelberg and Toscanini was in fine fettle, but those two worthies showed no great interest in bringing anything very radical to their audiences.

The new recitalist was Serge Koussevitsky who appeared in a concert of chamber music. He had still not completely convinced his orchestra that he was musician enough to lead them (it was rumored that he employed a man to play scores for him on the piano because he had trouble reading them). But the previous year he had played two double bass recitals in Boston and his virtuosity had gone a long way toward convincing his men that he was indeed a musician to be reckoned with. Repeating that triumph in New York this season, he erased what lingering doubts there were about his abilities. The high point was his own concerto for double bass. More than a virtuoso piece, it had "form and coherency and clearly stated ideas." The conductor's playing throughout had "finish, taste and high musicianship."

There were a few good orchestral moments as well. One was the premiere of Ernest Bloch's extremely interesting *America* symphony. It had won first prize in a contest for a new American orchestral work sponsored by the magazine *Musical America*. One of the features of the contest was a guaranteed simultaneous premiere of the piece by seven major orchestras. Damrosch directed the Philharmonic-Symphony in the New York premiere. The work was on an epic scale (as is the same composer's *Israel* which Damrosch had programmed earlier in the year) and it was received with respect for its weight if not for its merits. It was not until 1960 that the symphony was finally recorded (it is virtually never played) by Stokowski, who had directed it in the Philadelphia branch of its debut, and a few critics began to take it seriously. It is undoubtedly a major work, but earlier in December of 1928 it was quite overshadowed by a catchy Gershwin tune, "An American in Paris," which everyone thought was a vast improvement over the Concerto in F. Downes said it represented a "material gain in workmanship and structure," while his colleague on the *Herald*, Lawrence Gilman, said it had the "tang of a new and urgent world, engaging, ardent, unpredictable."

After the premiere there was a party at which Otto Kahn, the banker and opera buff, presented Gershwin with a brass humidor on which all his friends had inscribed their names. In his speech Kahn raised a rather interesting point: "There is one note rather conspicuous by its absence," he told the composer. "It is the note that sounds a legacy of sorrow, a note that springs from the deepest stirrings of the soul of the race. . . . Far be it from me to wish any tragedy to come into the life of this nation for the sake of chastening its soul, or into the life of George Gershwin for the sake of deepening his art. But . . . 'the long drip of human tears,' my dear George . . . they fertilize the deepest roots of art. I believe in you with full faith and admiration. . . . And just because of that I could wish for you an experience—not too prolonged—of that driving storm and stress of the emotions, of that solitary wrestling with your own soul, of that aloofness . . . which are the most effective ingredients for the deepening and mellowing . . . of an artist's inner being and spiritual powers."

George Gershwin was not to find that "legacy of sorrow," which Kahn and many of his other friends hoped for. The nation, however, was shortly to feel the full impact of a severe "chastening of its soul." Gershwin would never again write in a nation free of anxiety and free of dread. Since his life was to be cut short, he would never again write even in a prosperous and truly healthy nation.

But there was to be one more moment of greatness in Carnegie Hall before the ten-year party ended. One Sunday afternoon in January, "Music—living, breathing, virile, naked music—came hurtling out of a black-haired young man in an ill-fitting afternoon suit . . . and smote one's jaded senses with the blunting might of Thor's hammer."

The young man was Arthur Honegger. The music was his own *Rugby*, written on a dare made by a Paris journalist, *Pacific 231* and the Concertino for Piano played by his wife, Andrée Vaurabourg. Honegger made music with his bare hands. Disdaining a baton and oblivious to his audience, "he performed imaginary tasks of sinewy prowess that rivaled the achievements of Herculean fable." He was literally breathless and panting by the time he reached the end of his exertions.

His was indeed a performance of music "forged out of human vitals."

And with it, one can honestly end this recital of the saga of the musical Twenties. For Honegger, directing his own exciting and typical creations, after having suffered much in rehearsing the temperamental Philharmonic, is a fitting symbol of the era. In the rest of that season there was only one event of importance, the first Carnegie Hall recital of an obscure singer named Marian Anderson. She was virtually ignored, although her notices were excellent. She, like many another, had to wait her turn. And before the next season could fairly begin, the economic policeman raided the big party and brought it to its sad, guilt-ridden end.

Perhaps the great thing about the Twenties was that so many people did get their turns. The music that followed those years, like the art and the literature, was shaped in new ways by the blast furnace of history. The basic alloy of modernism was forged then. Nearly everything modern in the arts descends from that time and that place—that era of wonderful nonsense and wondrous creation.

The final word must belong to Scott Fitzgerald who says better than anyone else what it all meant, what it meant at the time, what it would mean to those who participated when, at last, they could think about it clearly: "Now once more the belt is tight and we summon the proper expression of horror as we look back at our wasted youth. Sometimes, though, there is a ghostly rumble among the drums, an asthmatic whisper in the trombones that swings me back into the early Twenties when . . . it seemed only a question of a few years before the older people would step aside and let the world be run by those who saw things as they were—and it all seems rosy and romantic to us who were young then, because we will never feel quite so intensely about our surroundings anymore."

Eight

"Audacious Absurdity and Creativeness"

BEFORE THE MUSICAL SEASON OF 1929-1930 GOT UNDER WAY, THE WORLD came tumbling down. True, it had been a paper world all the time, a world of ticker tape, stocks and bonds and folding money, but the weight of a lot of paper, falling from a great height, can crush a man as surely as anything else. And many men were crushed.

There were two major dates in the avalanche. One was Black Thursday, October 24, the climax of a three-day selling spree. On that day something like twelve million shares of stock were traded at the Stock Exchange, and only a bankers' pool of $240 million cushioned the shock of those sales. The market rallied briefly and there was a wave of short-lived optimism that carried the market shakily through the next day. But the weekend was a period in which a lot of people did a lot of thinking, and the consensus was that it would be a good idea to sell some more. This they began to do on Monday. On Tuesday the 29th—Black Tuesday—the bottom really fell out, despite optimistic words from nearly every high place in the worlds of government and business. By the time that awful day had finished values on the big board dropped, in general, about two-thirds. The rest of what happened is history, much of it fast becoming folk history.

What followed, speaking in the broadest terms, was ideological chaos—two decades of peculiarly intense history in which the world witnessed the sharpest depression in history and the most virulent class struggles of all time, the rise of Fascism and an unprecedented race hatred in what had been one of the world's most civilized nations and finally a war of inconceivable destructiveness in which, for the first time, murder was bureaucratized. What immediately followed the crash was a bright flash of revolutionary idealism, a flash that lit up the dirty corners in the house of traditional society.

But this idealism was, in turn, betrayed in a complex fashion. It was betrayed not by the idealists but by the implacable historical forces which men, in their optimism, had thought they could contain and control. History could not be contained, or, more properly, the nature of man could not be changed. Thus, the energetic optimism of the late Thirties and early Forties, born of the feeling that the old ways were wrecked and on that wreckage a new world could be built, gave way, in the Fifties, to despair and cynicism on as grand a scale as the optimism which had preceded it. The optimism was, of course, reflected in the art of the time, as was the desire to satirize and excoriate the powers which had been brought down by their own careless arrogance.

At first the doings in the downtown money market had little effect on the musical world. Schedules, after all, had been made up back in the days when everyone firmly believed, with Professor Irving Fisher of Yale, that the market had reached "a permanently high plateau." They would be kept. Besides, the concentric circles of panic that would widen out from Wall Street until they eventually encircled every citizen and every area of activity, had not yet had time to spread very far. Thus, the awful two weeks in late October and early November, when the end began, were bracketed musically by events which, while interesting, were not in the least untoward. The first was the spectacle of Leopold Stokowski lecturing a Carnegie Hall audience on its manners—or rather its lack of them. His performance of Schönberg's *Variations for Orchestra* had been greeted by some particularly unfriendly noises. Indeed, the hisses were so loud that it sounded as if a flock of geese had been let loose in the auditorium. When the vandalous sibilations had died down sufficiently, Stokowski said, "You have the right to make such noises. We, on our part, have the right to play the things in which we believe. . . ." He thereupon made a plea for more tolerance, more broad-mindedness toward new music. Stokowski took his educator's role seriously. It was neither the first nor the last time that he spoke out as an advocate for new music, and new music has never had a more impassioned advocate than he. Had Stokowski been able to restrain his enthusiasm for the gimmick, which caused him to dissipate much of his force on trivia, his reputation as a champion of the new might today be as secure as that of Koussevitzky who went serenely ahead, seeking out contemporary compositions and bringing them to his audiences without undue fanfare and without going to the fanciful lengths that Stokowski sometimes did.

At least as interesting as the Stokowski lecture was the rediscovery by Arturo Toscanini of Ravel's *Bolero.* Originally written to be danced by Ida Rubinstein, the composer regarded it merely as an interesting technical experiment. So it remained until November 14, 1929, when Toscanini played it. The Maestro did not often fool with contemporary music, but when he did he sometimes discovered, to his astonishment, forms for which he had a natural affinity. His interpretation was a sensation. The Carnegie Hall audience shouted its approval and, as a result of the Toscanini interpretation, the *Bolero* went on to an astounding popularity, one of the few pieces of serious music to attain "hit" status with the mass audience in the twentieth century. Indeed, it was so popular that a movie company under the impression that *Bolero* was an opera, delighted Ravel by making him an offer for the film rights.

This was a season of choice for Toscanini. He was now sixty-two and finding the demands of La Scala excessive. He was tired after eight seasons there and more than ever annoyed by the Fascists. Therefore, he doubled the number of concerts he customarily conducted with the Philharmonic. As one of his biographers, Howard Taubman, put it, he had "an irresistible urge to turn to other forms of musical expression, and he wished to devote himself to the orchestra." This was the first year he led a full season, and was therefore able to offer a far wider range of music than he had in the past. He even offered considerable new music. In addition to the *Bolero*, he played works new to the city by such contemporaries as Tommasini, Busch, Wetzler, Pizzetti, Goosens, Kodály and, of course, Respighi. These men perhaps did not represent the very newest musical trends, but they were certainly Toscanini's contemporaries if not those of the younger and more avant-garde members of his audience. He even flung a few bones at them, in the form of Stravinsky and Honegger, but they carped constantly at his failure to recognize the existence of others—particularly Americans.

But Taubman said, "The public at large did not complain. It found the Toscanini concerts enormously exhilarating . . . it rejoiced at the precision and splendor attained by the orchestra. It felt that New York at last had a conductor and an orchestra that the city's size and pre-eminence deserved."

Meantime, the man who had fought against the predominance of the prima donna in the opera house found himself in the strange position of being one himself. "Many in his audience were not just listeners, but worshippers," Taubman writes. This was not Toscanini's doing at all. He was simply going about his job in his own rather special way. He begged people to remember that the beauty he wrought was due to the composer, that the conductor was only the composer's instrument. Few listened to his pleas.

This was a public eager to make a legend of their demi-god's doings. Once he stopped the orchestra, glared at some late comers hurrying down the aisle and announced in ringing tones, "You are late," a fact of which they were all too painfully conscious.

On another occasion he left the hall precipitately when someone forgot a long standing rule and presented him with a floral tribute. "Flowers," he said, "are for prima donnas and corpses. I am neither." Indeed, it took very little to send the Maestro flying from the concert hall without taking any bows. A photographer's flash bulb could do it. So could a wrong entrance by the brasses in Weber's *Euryanthe*. This sent him on one of the longest dashes of his career, all the way from Carnegie to the Astor Hotel where he was then living. The faithful—and breathless—Bruno Zirato, manager of the Philharmonic, trotted the entire distance in his wake, carrying a coat, afraid that the perspiring and distracted Maestro would either catch his death of cold or be run over by a passing taxi.

For nine glorious seasons the orchestra's librarian would be forced periodically to dash into the wings crying, "lumber, lumber" as the batons snapped simultaneously with the Maestro's temper, but never before had the orchestra reached such heights, and in a day when there was little enough to delight anyone, Toscanini was a purveyor of delights beyond the dreams of the most avaricious culture vulture.

In the last season of "normalcy" before the final fragments of the great crash had drifted to earth around everyone, he received a new tool to work with. This was a $50,000 organ, presented to Carnegie Hall by the Carnegie Foundation. The gift, a replacement for the totally inadequate organ that had been installed shortly after the completion of the hall, was an occasion for genuine rejoicing. On November 4th it was dedicated with appropriately joyous oratory and some rather indifferent music, but its installation assured a number of worriers that Carnegie Hall would survive the crash. There had been a spate of rumors that the hall was about to be torn down (and it might have been had business conditions remained good) but it was now obvious that this was not to be the case, for, everyone reasoned, the foundation would not give such a costly gift to a hall about to be torn down nor would the hall's management go to the trouble and expense of renovating the building to accommodate it if it were due for demolition in the near future.

The rest of the season proceeded without incident and without intrusion from the panic raging in the financial world. Paul Robeson was warmly welcomed back to New York after a lengthy European stay, nine-year-old Ruggerio Ricci made his debut and was proclaimed an authentic genius of the violin, José Iturbi and Gregor Piatigorsky made their New York debuts with the Philharmonic under Mengelberg and both were widely acclaimed. Both repeated their triumphs in recital, with Piatigorsky demonstrating a new truth—"that the cello is by no means a negligible quantity as a solo instrument"—and Iturbi demonstrating that turn of personality, that "nonchalant, happy nature," that was eventually to lead him away from the concert stage and into M-G-M musicals. It would cost him the respect of the musically pure-in-heart, but it would make him a musician with a public far larger than most pianists of his particular quality ever attain.

The Iturbi debut was made with the Mozart Concerto in D (K.

466), and the fact of its selection was interesting. Iturbi was one of three pianists to play a Mozart concerto in New York that season, and Olin Downes thought this constituted "an extraordinary symptom of the return of classicism." The Mozartian vogue was curious, at least on the surface, for it had little obvious connection with the prevailing symphonic modes of the time. Downes thought it for that very reason that the audience exulted in the "very pure Mozart melody, very clean Mozartian form and orchestration." Another segment of the listeners, undoubtedly influenced by the neoclassicists, certainly enjoyed Mozart for precisely the same reasons that they enjoyed the predominant modern compositional idiom. They perceived the connection between Mozart and certain contemporary writers of "pure" music. In one way the two groups came together—both were in reaction against the romanticism that had dominated that concert hall in the days before World War I. And one of the great things about the Twenties and early Thirties was the rediscovery of Bach and Mozart after their long interment beneath the mountains of nineteenth-century sound. Even if the composers who have shaped the modern musical sensibility turn out, in the end, to be only minor figures, we will owe to their aesthetic the rediscovery and the revaluation of Mozart and his predecessors.

There was to be a slight shift in the Thirties away from pure music. In a period when the novelists were rediscovering "the people" and the proletariat was discovered to harbor undreamed of virtues in its simple heart, it was natural for the musicians to become more conscious of folk materials and to make more and more use of the themes to be found in the American past.

The years of greatest interest in this sort of musical material were yet to come, but it is an interesting coincidence that the man whom Koussevitzky brought to New York with the Boston Symphony in February, 1930, was Sergei Prokofieff, erstwhile *enfant terrible*, now nearing the end of his postrevolutionary *wanderjahre*, in which he studiously avoided his native Russia. In 1933 he did return there, finding himself able to suit his music admirably to the rather dreary anti-bourgeois formalism required during the Stalinist years. Prokofieff was an extremely approachable modern composer, who did his best work in the impure musical forms—ballets, suites, film scores, program music of all kinds. His strongest point was an ironic wit and, although he was hardly a folklorist, his music after 1930 represented a distinct turning away from the asperities of the neoclassicists and the atonalists, even though he had gone through his own neoclassic period. The work performed on this occasion was his Second Piano Concerto. It had been written in 1913, then lost when the Bolsheviks confiscated the composer's apartment. He had reconstructed the whole thing from a piano reduction of the score that had turned up in 1923 and now, following a performance of his *Scythian Suite*, he played it with the Boston Symphony under the baton of a long-time friend and champion. Tall, with thinning blond hair and an engaging boyishness of manner, he played, as he had done on his New York visit in 1915, with virtuoso skill. Ironically, the concerto was regarded as more advanced and more absolutely musical than the suite which had been composed a year after it. The suite, however, was the more favorably received of the two for it had a force, a strength of melodic line that the concerto lacked.

In January of that same year Nathan Milstein made his recital debut in Carnegie Hall, and a little later Gabrilowitsch, leading the Philadelphia Orchestra, presented the first New York performance of Abram Chasins' First Piano Concerto, with the composer as soloist. It, too, was approachable music, reminding the critics more of Tchaikovsky and Rachmaninoff than of the work of Chasins' young contemporaries. It was clear, as the sounds of the noisy decade died down, that there was to be a shift in compositional taste, a shift that would temporarily bring to the public music it could receive with less strain than that of the Twenties.

The last important events of the season in the hall were oddly heartening in that year of gathering clouds. One was the appearance of Arturo Toscanini at the final children's concert of Ernest Schelling's season. It represented very nearly the only public speech the Maestro ever made. He said in full: "It is dear to me that my friend, Maestro Ernest Schelling, has wished me to convey the annual prizes to the children. I love and always have loved children. To give them joy is just like giving air and light to flowers. Flowers and children are pretty things, and we are all fond of them. In the heart of children there is always some music to be called out by a touch of sympathy and love. Therefore, I have accepted today this very sweet task."

Whereupon the Maestro presented the red lapel ribbons to those children who had been particularly diligent Saturday morning scholars in Schelling's course. Toscanini himself received one of the prized ribbons, then conducted the last piece on the program, the Prelude to *Die Meistersinger*, a particular favorite of his. Toscanini wore his prize ribbon for days, wherever he went.

Finally, there was Maurice Chevalier, working with nothing more than a black backdrop and his famous personality. Other entertainers shared the program with him, but he so dominated the evening that the audience went away under the impression that they had witnessed a one-man show. He did not seem to do very much. He sang a few songs in English, a few more in French, did imitations of three French comedians, mimicked an apache dancer, but as the *Times* put it, "His gesticulations, changes in gait and physiognomy and his suggestive powers put the songs across and leaped over the language barrier."

Shortly thereafter the Philharmonic embarked on its first European tour, a tour planned before the crash and bravely carried through, despite intervening events. It was a success of the highest magnitude for Toscanini and his men.

But the Depression finally caught up with practically everyone in the musical world in the 1930-1931 season. The Philharmonic, back from its triumphant tour, was a bit out of sorts as the season opened. The conductor was Erich Kleiber, appearing with the orchestra for the first time. A modest and genial gentleman, he led his forces with a minimum of attitudinizing and seemed to some observers to be more of a friend than a field marshal in his conductorial habits. His reign undoubtedly marked a pleasant interregnum for the orchestra, used to Toscanini's more dictatorial ways. The high point of his month on the podium was the presentation, for the first time in America, of some fragments from Alban Berg's *Wozzeck*. Contrary to what one might think, these bits from the story of perhaps the most down-trodden soldier in history were well received by a large segment of the audience and critics. Dorothee Manski was the soprano soloist in two of the fragments, singing the brooding soliloquies of Marie, Wozzeck's mistress. These and some pages from the final tragic scene—"an orchestral effect of bewildering beauty"—moved an audience that was witnessing all around it tragedies as deep as the one Alban Berg wrote about. As one critic put it, "In this music was a depth of mood-painting such as no other atonal composer, not even Berg's master, Arnold Schönberg, has given us." *Wozzeck* appeared now and again, in bits and pieces, on the American concert stage for the next three decades, but it was not until 1959 that the musical world's old curiosity shop, the Metropolitan Opera, finally gave it the full production it deserved. But it was a *succès d'estime,* driving away goodly numbers of that musty museum's patrons, which proves a point: no matter how much our orchestras are criticized for failing to bring forth new works, they are nowhere near as backward along these lines as the country's only major opera company, which has been evading that responsibility for years and failing to educate its public to the new.

After Kleiber's stint, Toscanini wielded the baton briefly, then turned it over to Leopold Stokowski while he journeyed down to Philadelphia to lead that orchestra for a few weeks. It went swimmingly in Philadelphia, but back in New York things went very badly. As so often happened when the Maestro was away, the men of the Philharmonic were in a mood to argue with his replacement. It had reduced such dissimilar types as Damrosch, Gabrilowitsch and Honegger to begging for order and discipline. But Stokowski was having none of that and rehearsals became royal battles of will. The upshot was that several of the players were banished for the two weeks of Stokowski's reign and the concerts were not what they might have been.

Once Toscanini returned, everyone shaped up nicely and, under him, the orchestra presented new works by Kodály, Shostakovich, and Pizzetti, as well as Bruckner's Seventh, Sibelius' Fourth, and some minor works by sundry Italians whom the Maestro favored. Undoubtedly the success of the year was Toscanini's reading of the Verdi *Requiem* and the *Te Deum.* There was even a sop to the Americanophiles—Abram Chasins' "Flirtations in a Chinese Garden" and his "Parade." All in all, an ambitious year for the Maestro.

It was not so for the rest of the musical world. True, the ever-popular Don Cossack Chorus made its American debut that year in a highly theatrical, but none the less pleasing, presentation. The choir had been formed in a prisoner of war camp near Constantinople and had been forced to flee Russia after the revolution. In their black uniforms and boots, with their effective and youthful conductor, Serge Jaroff, they were a highly appealing organization. There were also two new orchestras that year. One, the Manhattan Symphony, only lasted out the season, but under the leadership of Henry Hadley, and featuring a number of his own works, notably the suite *Street Scenes of Peking*, it provided an instrument on which new works could be played. Much longer-lived was Leon Barzin's National Orchestral Association which also presented a good many new works as well as infrequently played pieces from the classical repertory. It must have been, in those hard times, a temptation for financially-pressed musicians to get up an orchestra and try to make a little money. But with the well-established organizations in serious difficulties, it was almost impossible for such ventures to succeed. Even the Philharmonic, with a star attraction like Toscanini, had to weather at least one major financial storm and uncounted minor ones during the Depression decade. Much later in the decade, a WPA orchestra, which did not usually play in Carnegie Hall, was able to provide work for musicians, but it was, of course, subsidized by the government.

For this season, at least, the hub of the musical world was in the Hub of the Universe. It was the Golden Anniversary year of the Boston Symphony Orchestra and for the occasion, Koussevitzky commissioned a number of new works by composers all over the world. Among these were Prokofieff's Fourth Symphony and Roussel's Third Symphony, undoubtedly the strongest of the four written by that fine-fibered, aristocratic French composer. There were also performances of Honegger's new symphony, written especially for the anniversary season, as well as Ernst Křenek's *Little Symphony*. Stravinsky's *Symphonie de Psaumes* (written for the orchestra) as well as his new Capriccio for Piano and Orchestra was heard for the first time in

America that season, as was Hindemith's *Konzertmusik* for string and brass instruments, and Respighi's *Metamorphoseon Modi XII*, both commissioned by the Boston leader. Koussevitzky did not ignore the American composers during this extremely forward-looking season. He commissioned Howard Hanson's *Romantic Symphony* and premiered it along with Edward Burlingame Hill's Second Symphony and his "Ode," also a specially commissioned work.

These were by no means all the new works premiered in Boston that season (there was also a celebratory overture by an "anonymous" composer, obviously Koussevitzky himself), but they were the most important. Nowhere in the history of American music is there a record of a season like it, and comparison to the dreary Centennial of the Philharmonic ten years later reveals the imagination and the appropriateness of Koussevitzky's programming as well as the depth of his devotion to the new. There were, of course, composers of whom he was not fond, notably the loud, the aggressively sensational, the merely fashionable, but by and large his anniversary year was typical of his fastidious taste as well as his enthusiasm for the role of educator and propagandizer.

Sadly enough, Koussevitzky felt it wise to restrict Carnegie Hall's portion of his musical feast to the barest minimum, but he did throw some of the better morsels to the New York audience. Among these were the Stravinsky pieces and the Hill and Roussel symphonies. Through the next few years, however, most of the pieces premiered in Boston did find their way to New York where they were received, for the most part, indifferently.

Despair was rampant in the land now. The economic crisis was reaching its depths and there was a general re-examination of the values which had held sway in the Twenties. The intellectuals, after the years of wonderful irresponsibility, were now in the mood for revolutionary criticism and the bourgeois, who had persistently believed that they had found in the business morality a final ideological resting place, were suddenly homeless, dazed wanderers. When the economic basis of their philosophy was rudely jerked from under them, they were left bereft of a good deal more than financial security. They also lost their faith in the values which had rested on prosperity.

It was therefore no wonder that they turned out in considerable force, in December, 1931, to listen to Bertrand Russell and Rabbi Stephen Wise debate the question: "Is Modern Morality a Failure?" Like most people in trouble and groping for solutions, they hoped for simple answers. Half the audience wanted reassurance from the Rabbi that the nostalgically remembered older values could, given a slight updating, be pressed into service in these new and terrifying times. The other half wanted to hear Russell destroy the entire structure of the old so that something new and splendid could be erected on its ruins. Both groups were slightly disappointed. Russell declared that the new morality of the Twenties had been misunderstood. He said that the traditionalists, in arguing against it, had distorted its basic meaning. They, he said, were "always thinking about sex." But the new freedom which he and so many others had proclaimed meant more than mere sexual freedom. It meant a greater respect for the personality of the individual and a freedom of action in many spheres, freedom from all sorts of institutional suppressions and repressions. Rabbi Wise disagreed only in degree. The very model of a moderate modern minister, he conceded a number of Russell's points, but urged that the new morality come to dominance slowly. Take, for instance, the matter of divorce. Eventually, divorce merely by mutual consent would come about, he thought. But people must be educated toward it. The concept could not be foisted upon them overnight.

Such was the mood of the time. Nearly everyone agreed on the necessity for change. The only strenuous debate was over the timetable. In the musical world, the mood was reflected in a contrast between the music played and the economic conditions of the art. The Carnegie Hall schedule during the worst depression years was notably thin. The number of concerts—particularly those of recitalists—was naturally quite low. Only the biggest names could continue to attract an audience. And, of course, there were fewer debuts by young artists, despite efforts to attract them by lowered rentals and offers of half the house at a cut rate. Orchestral programs generally avoided spectaculars requiring large forces. On the other hand, despite the poverty, the emphasis on the new, begun in the Twenties, continued in the Thirties. It cannot be said that the audiences had suddenly learned to care for new music. It can be said, however, that there was at last a real group of composers at work and composition was finally recognized as a profession in America.

It was hardly a popular or overcrowded profession, but there were at least enough practitioners now so that they could subdivide into rival schools and bicker. More importantly, they could get played, and there were even a few institutions granting prizes and fellowships and performances to them in addition to modest federal recognition, under the WPA, of their existence. Best of all was the fact that the economic elite, which had exercized such heavy influence on the performing musical world, was reeling in retreat under the hammer-blows of the financial upheaval. They had more important things on their mind than the programs of the orchestras they supported, which removed one more albatross from the necks of composers and conductors. In addition, the long years of patient proselytizing by men like Stokowski and Koussevitzky were beginning to pay off. True, not a great many new pieces were sincerely loved by the majority of the audience for serious music, but a large number were tolerated without shrill cries of outrage.

Though the 1931-1932 season heard much new music played at Carnegie Hall, it saw very few first-rate new recitalists, and among them only a few are worth mentioning. One was Lily Pons, who packed the hall to the rafters. The second was a notable trio—Horowitz, Milstein and Piatigorsky—playing crisply and warmly as individuals but failing, as is so often the case with virtuosos assembled, to realize precisely the outlines of the music they were attempting to play together.

Predictably, the Boston Symphony Orchestra brought most of the best of the new to Carnegie Hall. It had a number of works left over from its anniversary season, and these filled the house with new sound. In addition, Dr. Koussevitzky gave Mahler's Ninth Symphony a glowing and lustrous first New York performance and also provided the city with an opportunity to hear Harold Morris in his own piano concerto. Koussevitzky briefly abandoned his policy of not playing the works of composers who had visible means of support to program George Gershwin's rather unsuccessful Second Rhapsody, an expansion of motifs from the score he had written for the movie, *Delicious*. The work had a subtitle—"Rhapsody in Rivets"—and its mood was distinctly mechanistic. It was probably overorchestrated. This is understandable, for like most popular composers Gershwin was not used to doing what serious composers always do—orchestrating his own music. Therefore he was inordinately proud of his late-acquired ability to do his own orchestrations and he tended to prove his point a little heavy-handedly. The last new work offered that season by the Boston Symphony was Ernest Toch's *Bunte* Suite which used the piano integrally with the orchestra and which, in its five short movements, gave an impressive demonstration of an unexpected melodic ability on the part of the composer (who was visiting in the United States that year and heard the performance).

Stokowski, too, was busy with modern music. He gave New York its first hearing of the Stravinsky violin concerto, which one critic regarded as "the apotheosis of nothing" and on the same program played Efrem Zimbalist's tone poem, *Daphne and Chloe* ("graceful and unpretentious"), Darius Milhaud's Concerto for Percussion Instruments ("tedious and empty") and Alexander Mossolov's "Soviet Iron Foundry" which "relieved tedium." Later in the year Stokowski brought the *Metamorphosen Modi XII* of Respighi to the city for the first time, following it with Prokofieff's Third Symphony which also had never been heard in New York before.

Meanwhile things were not going so well with the Philharmonic. Toscanini's bursitis was giving him trouble and whenever he waved his stick he was rewarded by intense, darting pains. He cut short his season, leading only fourteen concerts in four weeks before returning to Italy. His brief tenure was bracketed between Erich Kleiber and Bruno Walter who now achieved something of the acclaim he deserved in the United States. Kleiber again gave his hearers a taste of Berg, three excerpts from the *Lyric Suite*, as well as a bit of Toch (the *Theater Suite*) and three world premieres. These were Wallingford Riegger's Rhapsody for Orchestra, "an original and sincere work, which in portions attains individual poignancy," Křenek's Variations for Orchestra which he wrote especially for Kleiber's Philharmonic appearances, and Henry Joslyn's *Pagan Symphony*. Joslyn was an interesting minor figure. A journalist and businessman, he had composed music in his spare time since he was eight years old. He died in April of 1931, and the *Pagan Symphony* was a memorial on which Kleiber lavished careful attention. The "Pagans" of its title were the denizens of Broadway and the score represented a struggle between jazzy themes and a more sophisticated dissonance. These were resolved, at the end, into a serenity by which the composer proclaimed his spiritual triumph over false gods. The work didn't quite come off, but it had the virtue of being spirited and distinctly not dull.

After the ambitious Kleiber weeks—his programs represented most of the salt in the Philharmonic salad—Vladimir Golschmann and Ossip Gabrilowitsch briefly led the orchestra, then yielded to Bruno Walter, who played the classics with his customary majesty along with some new works, among which were some Křenek and Prokofieff and the second symphony of the American, Daniel Gregory Mason. These appearances, marking Walter's return to New York after an absence of several years, were the first at which his talents received full critical and public recognition and marked the beginning of Walter's long association with the Philharmonic as a frequent guest.

Perhaps the most interesting of the Philharmonic's guest conductors that year was Ottorino Respighi, whose vogue Toscanini had stimulated. The Maestro had been scheduled to lead the world premiere of Respighi's *Maria Eguiziaca* at a pair of pension fund concerts in March, but his bursitis persisted, and the composer himself was invited to substitute. Inspired by Botticelli's triptych, the score is in three scenes corresponding to the three panels of the painting. In the first Maria begs a sailor to take her from Alexandria to Jerusalem so that she may make her confession. In the next she is refused admission to the church there. In the third she finally makes her confession to a priest whom she has met while wandering the desert. Respighi and his rather large cast, which included Nelson Eddy singing the baritone solo, were highly praised for their painstaking preparation of the work, and the colorful score was received as a *tour de force* but condemned for its strange mixture of styles, for its externality, its lack of deeply felt emotion.

Toscanini's failure to return to New York for his scheduled appearances during the second half of the season, and particularly his failure to conduct the premiere of *Maria Eguiziaca*, touched off rumors that he was going to leave the Philharmonic. He laid these to rest by appearing April 28th to conduct a benefit concert for unemployed musicians. This was a great boon to the hard-pressed Philharmonic for it assured subscribers that Toscanini would be able to return the following year. It also reassured the Maestro considerably. He had been afraid that his bad arm might force him to lay down his baton for good. The physically painless preparation of this concert proved to him that he could continue to practice his art. The proceeds of the benefit amounted to $26,000, a whopping amount in those days.

The Toscanini concert was by no means the end of Carnegie Hall's contributions to the alleviation of the year's social dislocations. In mid-July Robert Simon inaugurated a series of free daily noontime organ recitals, a sort of soup kitchen for those who did not live by bread alone. The idea was that the music might provide an inspiring and comforting interlude in the weary rounds of those who were looking for work when there was very little to be had. For the first program Dr. Harry Emerson Fosdick came down from the Riverside Church to make a characteristic Depression speech. Like nearly everyone else, he was full of radical solutions to the economic crisis. "Nothing but a thorough overhauling of our economic processes will ultimately cure the present ills or prevent the future recurrence of them," he declared. "No one supposes," he conceded, "that music is a cure for all this," but he did point out that "many thousands today need to regain their courage. They need their thoughts changed and strengthened by the beauty of music and here we may call the masters of harmony to our help." The good doctor was hopeful that similar plans could be enacted all over the country, for "the provision of recreation where anxious minds can find at least a little refreshment and escape."

Unfortunately, however, the situation had deteriorated to the point where music was of small consolation to the helpless and the hopeless. The concerts continued for some months, but when Simon could not find someone to sponsor the radio broadcasts of them and thus underwrite the project, he was forced to abandon them. Besides, many were not as much interested in the music as they were in the comfortable Carnegie Hall chairs, where they could snooze in the cool dimness, lulled by the same sounds the hall's founder had, in happier times, found to be such an excellent awakener.

Keeping the bums out of Carnegie Hall was the least of Mr. Simon's problem that year. Studio rentals had dropped 30 per cent since 1929. There were 64 fewer rentals of the main hall in 1932-1933 than there had been in the previous year, which had been by no means an active one. A number of notions for keeping the hall operative were entertained by Mr. Simon. He considered opening a beer hall, he announced that he was thinking of turning the main hall into a movie theater. He offered a $100 reduction of the rental fee for the main hall and a plan for renting just the main floor (shutting off the balconies and the dress circle) for only $300. Some of the concert managers tried lowering the price of the cheapest ticket to a quarter. There was, in short, a fine spirit of cooperation among those concerned with the fate of the hall. "If it is at all possible," said Simon, "we are determined to continue Carnegie Hall as a concert hall. Carnegie Hall has grown into a tradition and a symbol . . . and we believe that the public will not let it be turned from its original purposes. The owners of the property prefer to leave it in its present condition, provided the sacrifice is not too great, although investigation has shown that it could produce a much larger income if it could be altered for some other purpose. . . . Whether or not they will do so will depend entirely upon the cooperation they receive from those in whose interest the building was designed."

Simon proceeded to try to cut his losses as much as possible by making many of the building's studios rentable as apartments and doing as much renovation as possible. He even opened an art gallery on the street floor (where the bar now is) and turned it over to the artists who lived and worked in the building as a cooperative gallery.

But as if he did not have enough trouble, there was a fire to contend with. It began in mid-afternoon of a pleasant October day and in a matter of minutes the sidewalks outside were crowded with dancers in diaphanous costumes, painters carrying easels, musicians with half-written scores in their hands. The fire, "of undetermined origin," began on the roof above a jewelry designer's studio. It was quickly contained and only a few of the fifteenth floor studios were damaged, mostly by water. There were no lives lost and no injuries, thanks mainly to a switchboard operator who alerted all the tenants and to two elevator operators who stuck to their posts and carried at least a hundred residents out of the danger zone. Miss Leonora Shier, longtime renting agent of the building, thinks the fire began when a girl who was subletting an apartment threw a lighted cigarette onto the freshly tarred roof. She was the chief sufferer. All her clothes were lost in the blaze. Miss Shier took her home with her, loaned her some clothes and even persuaded a gentleman caller to take the girl along with them on a date that evening. The next morning the girl left and Miss Shier has never seen her again—nor got back the clothes.

The musical season began the day after the fire. Toscanini was back and in fine fettle. He led sixty-five concerts and included among them a brilliant Beethoven cycle, works by Tansman, de Sabata, Respighi, a Schönberg transcription of a Bach piece, works by two Russians, Veprik and Mossolov, and two new American pieces, Howard Hanson's Second Symphony and Bernard Wagenaar's Second.

The latter caused Toscanini no end of anguish. It was full of odd harmonies and strange dissonances. So impatient did he become with it that on the last page of his score he wrote in a thumping C-major chord, circled it in red and wrote, "My chord, Arturo Toscanini." But true to form he played the piece "as written." His final concert of the year marked the beginning of a romance. The soloist was Vladimir Horowitz, and in the course of preparing his performance of the *Emperor* Concerto, Horowitz became friendly with Toscanini's daughter, Wanda. That summer, the pianist came to Toscanini's home in Italy and there asked and received permission to marry the Maestro's daughter.

Besides the new works presented by Toscanini, his associates Bruno Walter and Issay Dobrowen did a few new pieces. With Prokofieff himself at the piano, Walter led his Third Piano Concerto and his suite, *The Gambler*. "One still wonders what on earth Sergei Prokofieff will evolve into," Olin Downes sighed after hearing the concert.

Columbia Records Photo

Bruno Walter finally received the acclaim he deserved when he led the New York Philharmonic in 1932. He has campaigned vigorously for recognition of Mahler's works.

Stokowski continued to be attracted by the rich tones the modern Russians were producing and conducted Shostakovich's *May Day* Symphony. "One is uncertain whether it should be reviewed from an aesthetic or from a political standpoint," one critic said. He settled for the aesthetic, and, like most of his fellows, decided he liked the rhythmic vitality of the piece, but not the superficial clatter which surrounded it. Also to the opulent Stokowski taste was the Ravel G major Piano Concerto which he introduced to New York. The piece was amusing and impudent, combining bits and pieces of the Stravinskian mode with Gershwinesque and Spanish-influenced music.

It was that kind of year in Carnegie Hall. The experiments all ran toward the crudely, the shockingly, modern. Up in the Chapter Room one night Nicholas Slonimsky conducted no less than forty-one percussion instruments in Edgar Varèse's "Ionization," a *tour de force* of instrumentation which, in the words of one observer, "elicited much merriment." On another occasion Paul Whiteman led his forces in a production of Ferde Grofé's *Tabloid*, which was a musical sketch of a night in the life of a newspaper and its staff. As one critic dryly summed up, "the typewriter and solo revolver parts were admirably performed."

Less ostentatious were the works brought down from Boston by Serge Koussevitzky. They included the first all-Sibelius program ever presented in New York, *Patterns*, a light new piece by John Alden Carpenter which the composer performed with the orchestra, and, as the shocker, Igor Markevitch's *Rebus*, an imaginary ballet of noisily experimental proportions. It was in six movements consisting of an introduction and a conclusion and four middle movements, one for each of the words in the French proverb, "Poverty is no vice." Thus, the subtitles included such entrancing items as "Jig of the Noes," and "Fugue of the Vices."

The season began during the crucial presidential campaign of 1932 and ended as the famous "Hundred Days" of the New Deal were beginning. The economic world of the people who were the principal supporters of musical endeavor was being torn asunder, and although many of them were glad that something—anything—was being done, one can

Artur Schnabel's series of concerts in 1933 established his New York reputation, and his survey of Beethoven's piano literature was a triumph of the 1936 season.

RCA Victor

hardly blame them for being just a trifle anxious as they trouped into a concert hall. How easily that anxiety must have been converted into annoyance when the sounds of *May Day* or *Tabloid* or *Rebus* greeted them instead of the soothingly familiar strains of a traditional symphony.

Under the circumstances, these people must have been more than delighted to welcome Artur Schnabel back to Carnegie Hall for a series of recitals in the fall of 1933. For the austere, perfection-seeking artistry of Schnabel was something you could count on, a constant in a world that seemed to be changing with great suddenness. Schnabel was the least showy of pianists. He complained about the action of the piano provided by the Steinway people for the concert. "The instrument," he said, was "terribly loud." "These steeds are of the Paderewski breed," he said, "not made to canter in my paddock." At length he found an instrument suited to his temperament, and proceeded, as Lawrence Gilman put it, to give an example "of what piano playing can be in the hands of a completely self-effacing master." His first appearances were with Walter and the Philharmonic in the Beethoven

Fourth Piano Concerto. He followed these with a series of all-Beethoven recitals. Unlike most recitalists, he refused to crowd *bravura* show pieces into the after-intermission half of his concerts. "The sechand halves of my concerts are as boring as the first halves," he used to say.

But perhaps because musical New York had grown up, or perhaps because Schnabel provided a refreshing contrast to the experiment-laden times, he was acclaimed wildly. After his second set of recitals he said, "It was an exemplary audience . . . and as usual the greatest participation came from the upper balconies, filled with the 'lower' classes."

Once he had called New York a railway station surrounded by a million windows, but now, basking at last in its affection, the city reminded him of ancient Venice and Athens in its power and arrogance, "its audacious absurdity and creativeness."

Shan-Kar, the Indian dancer and his company brought a touch of the exotic to the arrogant and absurd city at about the time Schnabel was reminding it of its European cultural heritage, but more in keeping with the spirit of the times was an otherwise forgettable piece of music by David Stanley Smith, dean of the Yale School of Music. Presented by Walter and the Philharmonic and called "1929–A Satire" it was a perfectly routine academic work, except for one thing—the program notes supplied by the composer. In these he informed the audience that he meant to convey in the work the psychology of the nation, pleasure gutted after the spree of the Twenties but with the possibility of further pleasure ruthlessly taken away by the crash of '29. The work was not quite the "spiced and brisk commentary" the composer thought it was, but if doubts about the American verities had spread even to New Haven what was safe?

Equally characteristic of the times was the Roy Harris symphony, *1933*, which Koussevitzky brought to New York for the first time in February 1934. If any composer was typical of the Depression years it was Harris, Oklahoma born and California reared. Some years earlier, he had hitch-hiked to New York to hear his first major work performed by the Philharmonic. His aim, he said, was to compose music that was "true to his race, to his time, to himself," and it seems apparent from his music that he sought those ideals in about that order. He was the most prominent—in the sense of being the most obvious—user of folk materials. A melodist not much interested in traditional harmonic theory, he created music such as *1933* that was frequently saggy and soggy, lacking in tension, though abounding in good will. A sort of Walt Whitman of music, Harris was also, like many of his fellow artists and intellectuals, a great admirer of the Stalinist vision of social progress. His political feelings, and folk leanings made him an archetypal musical figure of his time, and even at the short remove of fifteen to twenty-five years, his work seems dated and quaint.

Many Americans shared Roy Harris' belief that in the art and heart of the common man they could find strength to meet the troubles of their times. But the world was not going to give them much opportunity to search the nation's soul. On February 27, 1933, the Reichstag fire in Berlin, set by the Nazis and blamed by them on the Communists, did more than gut a government building; it gutted German democracy as well. The diplomatic recognition of Soviet Russia by the Roosevelt Administration in November of the same year amounted to belated recognition that Communism was here to stay—a powerful force which could no longer be ignored.

Of the two revolutions, the one in Russia seemed less immediately dangerous to most Americans. Many in this liberal period hoped that it would ultimately prove friendly to Western democracy, however vague they were about its real aims. So, when the Soviet dancers Vecheslova and Chabukiani came to Carnegie Hall this season, many were delighted to welcome these exemplars of revolutionary culture—and perhaps a little surprised to find them so aesthetically conservative.

There could be no enigma, though, about the aims of the Nazis no matter how much an isolationist and pacifistically inclined nation tried to wish away the threat posed by Hitler's dictatorship. One of the first public manifestations of concern over the pathological qualities of Nazism came in the spring of 1934 when a small army of musicians contributed their services to a charity concert for Jewish refugee children who had been forced to flee from Germany to Palestine. Six thousand dollars were raised on behalf of the children, as were many protesting voices. But Albert Einstein, in whose honor the concert was given, rose from his box to make his observations on the economic holocaust then in progress and on the political holocaust that would shortly develop from it. The physicist-humanitarian found some cause for hope: "It has been mostly in times of peril and need," he declared, "that great works of progress have come into being. Thus the work of emancipation and law giving achieved by Moses was born of the oppression suffered by the Jewish people in Egypt. Thus, too, we may hope that out of the military menace of our time shall grow a system of international law, observed by all; that out of the collapse of our economic organism a more firmly secure, better directed, economic order shall develop."

Einstein was expressing the spirit of the time, for strange as it seems the Thirties represented the last concerted outburst of optimism in this country. Out of the common peril threatening all of society, men were constructing an idealized vision of a future free of fear and poverty. It was a time of mutual sharing and caring and the spirit, once the Roosevelt Revolution had shored up the nation's battered confidence, was one of common striving for what seem now to be almost utopian social goals.

In the very year of Einstein's Carnegie Hall speech, the tide of economic disaster began to lap around the feet of the Philharmonic. It was a good season musically with another Toscanini Beethoven cycle, and his climactic performance of the *Missa Solemnis* as high points, but it was also a year in which the orchestra faced a gigantic $150,000 deficit. The orchestra launched a campaign for $500,000, for the first time in its life going to the general public to insure it against the cost of the seasons to follow as well as to pay off its current debts. Olin Downes offered some consolation by pointing out that the Philharmonic was not alone in its plight, that the Boston and Philadelphia orchestras were in the same perilous state, that there were now "very few who are able or willing" to make up the deficit. There were two courses open to the orchestra. One was to induce the public in some way to pay the entire cost of musical productions, the other was to get governmental support. "Now," Downes wrote, "the wealthy bourgeoisie, as our Russian friends would put it, having lost their wealth, are prone to relinquish their previous positions as patrons of art. The issue must now rest with the general public, which may, and possibly may not, work out for the good of art."

But Downes and others were a little previous in their belief that the bourgeois were about to abandon their patronage. A combination of their gifts—more modest than before—plus those from the wider public saw the orchestra through the crisis. Furthermore, no major American orchestra went under during the Depression. Radio, which had lately came to Carnegie Hall, was of considerable help in rallying people all over the nation to the aid of the beleaguered Philharmonic and in extending the audience for good music. But, although the help of the average man was of great importance to the orchestra, the economic control of music never passed from the hands of the bourgeois. As was so typical of many enterprises of the Thirties, a greater appearance of democracy was affected, but the center of control remained pretty much where it had been during the prosperous decade.

It was not that people didn't try, in the midst of the general upheaval, to wrest control away from the old order for good and all. There was, for example, the case of composer Douglas Moore, certainly no radical, but a man very much concerned with the state of his profession. Speaking at a meeting of the Institute of Arts and Sciences at Columbia University he said, "We are being asked to raise $500,000 . . . and what for? To develop new music? No, but to keep alive a great institution that is a symbol of the past. . . . Certainly it is a great thing to keep alive music of the past, but the Philharmonic and the Metropolitan stand unalterably opposed to any progress in the new principles of music."

Lawrence Gilman of the *Herald Tribune*, a status-quo man, challenged the composer to explain himself more fully. Moore then declared that there was a considerable difference between the patronage music received in the twentieth century and that which it had historically received. Patronage was in some measure responsible for the development of Florentine opera, the instrumental music of

Haydn, the art of Wagner and Beethoven. That was a proper patronage, a support for the new, the different, the pioneering. What music received now was patronage for the old. Moore said he was sorry that he had seemed to come out against the efforts of people who were trying to keep these museums open. They had a valuable historical function, he thought. "But we also need intelligent and widely spread patronage for the living creative spirit of today," he said.

"The Philharmonic may well merit support for other reasons," he declared. "I do, however, state that it is opposed to progress in the new principles of music. . . . When I spoke of it as doomed, I spoke not as a critic, but as a prophet."

He was a false prophet, for of course the orchestra survived without embracing the new. Moore was, alas, whistling upwind, and perhaps today is a bit embarrassed to have his youthful questionings recalled. They are important not so much for themselves but for the attitude they expressed. He was not alone. The trouble was that he and his fellow rebels were without power.

Equally powerless, and far more tragic, was an eight-year-old girl who had come to New York in 1933 and conquered it. Her name was Ruth Slenczynska, and what the public saw was a tiny, chubby child of prodigious talent and uncanny poise. They had not seen such musical temperament in one so young since the debut of Menuhin. Enthusiasm could not be confined in Town Hall where she played her first two New York concerts, in the fall. The third, on January 27, 1934, had to be held in Carnegie Hall. Ruth had amazing strength. At the end of a taxing performance, she played, in honor of *his* anniversary, Mozart's F major Sonata and had enough left over for a Chopin finale. What no one knew at the time was that little Ruth Slenczynska was living under a personal tyranny as brutal as anything the Fascists imposed on masses of humanity. She was the creature of her father's frustrated ambitions as a violinist. He tried to force her, at first, to play his instrument. She threw a small violin that he gave her when she was in her third year, across the room and broke it, all the while screaming for a piano. She got it. The next morning at 6:00 A.M. her father awakened her by pulling the blankets off her bed and told her that he was going to make her into the finest pianist in the world.

Wide World

Culver Service

Two tragic pianists—Paul Wittgenstein who lost an arm in World War I but came back to triumph with the Concerto for Left Hand *that Ravel wrote for him, and Ruth Slencynska who never completely recovered from her "forbidden childhood."*

To that end she was awakened every morning of her "forbidden childhood" to practice. Practice lasted until noon each day, was resumed from three to six and again in the evening. Every time she made a mistake she was slapped across the face. She was not excused from the keyboard even to go to the bathroom. Nor could she wear a dress while working. Her perspiration might ruin it. Therefore she always practiced in her slip. She was allowed to do nothing that could conceivably hurt her hands. On the proscribed list were rope-skipping, playing marbles, going near a dog or closing a car door by herself. Whenever she was given a new piece to learn her father would say, "Let's see if you can learn this without a wallop."

Ruth was not the only person on whom Papa Slenczynska vented his frustrations. He managed to antagonize nearly everyone in the San Francisco area who wanted to help him launch his daughter's career. "Father," Ruth writes in her tremendously moving autobiography, *Forbidden Childhood*, "was always . . . trampling on people's feelings, ridiculing them, cutting them down, thoughtless, crude, loud-mouthed, nursing, deep down in him, a corrosive need to inflict pain." But despite his endearing charms, Ruth found sponsors. They sent her to Berlin to study with Egon Petri. At this point her father began beating her with a stick and forcing her to play for her supper—and for breakfast and lunch, too. If he was dissatisfied with her work, she did not eat. Then, despite explicit instructions to the contrary from her sponsors, Ruth's father arranged a well-paying concert for her in Berlin. It was a triumph and shortly thereafter, the Slenczynskas removed to Paris where they lived, between Ruth's tours, until the outbreak of the war. In 1933 she debuted in New York. The *Herald Tribune* front-paged the review of her debut. Naturally her father pocketed her fees, explaining that they were rightfully his since he had willed her genius (which, of course, he had in his peculiar way). She wound up her first American tour in Carnegie Hall, as noted, and "a great audience was once more astounded by her achievements . . . applauded fervently the talent and the temperament and chuckled delightedly at the manifestations of the poise." What no one could know was that a public performance was the least of the ordeals Ruth had to face. Indeed, they must have been a relief, for her father could hardly wallop her in public if she made a mistake.

Ruth was to return to Carnegie Hall several times during this period before she disappeared for years to seek a normal life and freedom from the psychic bonds imposed on her by her childhood. Her return in 1952, following virtual mental breakdown, demonstrated that only a shadow of her great natural gifts had survived the psychological twistings of her youth.

If her poise was a matter for public praise during these years, the Carnegie Hall audience got a chance to observe, late in the season of her debut, a much more healthily motivated example of poise. On the evening of April 5th the Boston Symphony Orchestra had just launched into the Tchaikovsky Fifth Symphony when members of orchestra and audience noticed smoke curling out over the stage. No one knew how serious it might be, and several members of the audience began to head for the exits. In a moment all was hubbub. Koussevitzky stopped the orchestra, obtained silence from the audience and said curtly: "Just keep quiet. Everything is all right." He thereupon proceeded to lead the orchestra in a faultless reading of the work, while firemen put out the minor, but smoky, blaze in an incinerator. At the end of the symphony the audience cheered itself hoarse, so impressed was it by the orchestra's coolness under fire.

Later, in the Green Room, a friend praised the conductor for his tranquility. Why, he hadn't even speeded up the tempo! "Tempo is tempo," replied the conductor, "but tranquility is tranquility."

The triumphs of the 1934-1935 season were scored by Ossip Gabrilowitsch and Toscanini. Gabrilowitsch undertook a survey of the piano concerto with the National Orchestral Association. He played sixteen concertos in five concerts, and "managed to do equal justice to every period and every composer through his stylistic mastery and all that this implies of mental and imaginative endowment." The survey included works by Bach, Mozart, Beethoven, Brahms, Schumann, Chopin, Tchaikovsky and Rachmaninoff, and represented a feat of unprecedented dimensions, as well as the last major creative act of Gabrilowitsch's life. He died in 1936. It was not until twenty years later that Artur Rubinstein accomplished a similarly varied achievement. No one besides these two great pianists has run this particular course in American musical history.

Toscanini conducted only thirty concerts, but, in a sense, they represented a festive cycle, too, containing almost all the gems of his repertory. He presented a Brahms cycle, two Wagner programs and Beethoven's *Missa Solemnis.* This was music of which Toscanini was the acknowledged master and the public was delighted to hear him conduct "his" classics. Many believed that this season might be their last chance to hear the Maestro conduct his specialties, for rumors of his increasing unhappiness at the Philharmonic were quite true.

He was upset because the Philharmonic had to beg for funds over the radio and he was disgusted because to him this was proof of a lack of support for musical institutions in America. During this period he happened to run into Mayor La Guardia and told him: "Shame on New York. Look at Milan, a small city in comparison. Milan supports La Scala and has a much longer season than New York."

There were other irritations as well. There had been a dispute over an extra rehearsal he thought he needed with the Schola Cantorum. There was the matter of "cheating" on his salary. His contract called for a fee of $102,000 for the season. He received $100,000 and he wondered where the extra $2000 had gone. He was told that he got the $100,000 because it was "a round number." This caused a fracas too, and even an increase to another round number—$110,000—did not totally mollify the Maestro. Then in the summer of 1935 Toscanini decided he could not conduct several weeks of his planned 1935-1936 season. The Philharmonic engaged Sir Thomas Beecham to take over the orchestra in those weeks. They did not consult Toscanini about the choice of Beecham. That broke the camel's back, as far as the Maestro was concerned. He told the board not to count on him for the 1936-1937 season.

Besides the Toscanini concerts, the 1934-1935 Philharmonic season included appearances by Otto Klemperer, recently exiled from Hitler's Germany. Dignified, reserved, unmannered, forthright on the podium, he opened the orchestra's ninety-third season with a reading of Paul

Hindemith's *Mathis der Maler*, the first performance of that large, luscious work in America. Shortly thereafter Werner Janssen became the first native New Yorker to lead the Philharmonic. Possessed of an austere podium manner he revealed himself as one of the most interesting of the younger conductors and at his debut gave the first New York performance of John Alden Carpenter's "Sea Drift," inspired by the Walt Whitman sea poems. Later on in the season he did the young Samuel Barber's *Music for a Scene from Shelley*, a shimmering, broadly melodic and tender evocation of a portion of *Prometheus Unbound*.

It fell to Bruno Walter to lead perhaps the most spectacular of the year's premieres, Rachmaninoff's *Rhapsody on a Theme of Paganini* with the composer as soloist. Robert A. Simon of *The New Yorker* thought the piece might contain at least a partial answer to the financial plight of American orchestras: "It's something for audiences, and what our orchestras need at the moment is more music for audiences. More music for audiences means more audiences for music."

The other important novelties of the season were brought to the city by Koussevitzky and the Boston Symphony. Of these, the most interesting was the Ravel Concerto for the Left Hand which the composer had written especially for Paul Wittgenstein, a pianist who had lost his right arm during the war. It was Wittgenstein who played it with the orchestra, and he demonstrated that the concerto had musical validity and that he, too, was still a pianist of great sensibility. He produced a prodigious tone, was completely musical in his approach to the piece and completely captured an audience which, of course, was more than willing to meet the brave pianist more than half-way but had no need to, such was his artistry. No one, however, was willing to extend himself at all for the composer of the Boston's other major novelty of the season. Alban Berg's severely atonal *Lulu* called forth severely critical notices. "Isn't it time we say 'enough' to music which bluffs itself and will bluff us, too, if we allow it to do so?" asked Olin Downes. He, and many others, found in the work nothing but a tortured attempt to make use of unimportant technical procedures which might or might not have some value to later composers who had something more important to say. Significantly, he thought that in *Lulu* "we are looking back at a past that the world is leaving behind as rapidly as it possibly can, and not into the future."

This, whatever one thinks of the work of Alban Berg, was an astute observation. For the music of the Thirties tended to be less pure than that of the Twenties. The Thirties were a time of rising nationalism, of high political interest, of a much more socially conscious art than that of the Twenties. In the graphic arts realism was the prevalent American style of the period, while in writing the proletarian novel had replaced the art novel in fashionable favor. In music pieces with programs descriptive music often with strong national or folk feeling, were in vogue. The severely private visions of the Twenties, the work of men like Schönberg and Berg and "The Six" of postwar Paris was at a discount. The approachable music of Rachmaninoff, as we have seen, was back in style and the new men, like Harris and Shostakovich, had built a somehow more "realistic" structure out of the materials first used earlier in the century by composers who set greater store by innovation than by communication.

The world of the Thirties was caught in the grip of several conflicting mass ideologies and the social vision rather than the private vision was the one that most interested both the artist and his audience. Private despair was out of fashion, the passionate communication of ideas about the common struggle for a new utopia was very much in fashion, and music was expected to contribute its mite to social awareness. That meant, both in the Soviet Union, where it was formal doctrine, and in the West, where it was certainly the consensus, that music should recall to the hearer past national glories and inspire him to greater commitment to the brave new world which was about to be built. By and large the music of the Thirties seems, from the perspective of the Sixties, rather banal, rather obvious and rather barren. Once again, we tend to appreciate the private vision more highly than we do the social vision. We do not play the Folk-Song Symphony of Roy Harris much any more. We have rediscovered Alban Berg.

By the beginning of the 1935-1936 musical season the nation had recovered much of the confidence it lost at the time of the crash's initial impact. As Arthur Schlesinger, Jr., has put it, "enthusiasm was beginning to bubble everywhere." It seemed that by this mid-point in the Depression decade, the basic political opinions of the country had been reshaped. The long history of liberal reform movements had culminated in the New Deal, and now the reformers finally had power—in quantities they had hardly dared dream of. The first New Deal, wildly eclectic, a battleground between conservatives and radicals, all of whom had the ear of Roosevelt, was over. It was time for part two of the New Deal to begin—a period in which the nation forged ahead on a middle road, one which started from fresh ground.

It had taken but three short years for the reformers to impose their ideas and their morality on the nation. Suddenly the federal government had intervened in every area of the economy, regulating, controlling, even creating new demands as the bureaucracy grew. Moreover, with the enactment of laws ranging from the Wagner Act to Social Security to the creation of the SEC, the government had demonstrated a concern for the average citizen and his social and economic welfare that was unprecedented. At last, it seemed, Washington cared about the ordinary man as much as it did for economic institutions. In the early Depression days a great many people had a great need to feel that someone cared. Once this was demonstrated, confidence bloomed. And with the return of confidence came optimism. The worst was past, people seemed to feel, as 1935 came to a close. The thing to do was to build a new society, to make sure the worst could not happen again and to make the future better than the most glorious of past days. This feeling of solidarity while marching toward a bright tomorrow generated an enthusiasm for the new in art as it did in every area of society. But it was a different sort of newness than that worshipped in the Twenties. There was a new didacticism in art, a new seeking after the functional rather than the merely aesthetic.

Many moderns were encouraged by word that Schönberg had dropped his twelve-tone technique in favor of conventional harmonies and they looked forward eagerly to the premiere of his new Suite for String Orchestra at the October 17th concert of the Philharmonic under Klemperer. They were disappointed, however, as was a critic who reported that "the music sounded as if it might have been written atonally, and then by a rather ingenious shifting of intervals, so transformed as to sound harmonious according to the traditional canons. . . ."

Whatever the technique, this was still cerebral music and cerebral music was still unpopular. In the Twenties Schönberg's music had simply been too radical to be accepted even in those artistically radical times. Now it was out of tune with the prevailing aesthetic harmonies. Not so with Roy Harris' American Overture, *When Johnny Comes Marching Home.* Originally written on order, to fill exactly two sides of a phonograph record, the overture consisted of a number of quotations of and variations on old American tunes. It was loud, absolutely unmeditative and well received. So were other typical-of-their-times works such as William Grant Still's *Afro-American Symphony*, which Hans Lange conducted on a Philharmonic program late in November, and Shostakovich's ballet suite *The Bolt*, which Leon Barzin's National Orchestral Association presented a little later. The ballet suite was full of guffawing trombones, calliope-like woodwinds and booming percussions. The audience liked one part of it so much it had to be repeated.

Three weeks later Eugene List, then only seventeen, made his New York debut with the Philharmonic playing Shostakovich's Piano Concerto (Op. 35), a curious work scored for strings and solo trumpet which List played to perfection but which the gentlemen of the press found rather too circumscribed as a result of its orchestration, and rather too underdeveloped thematically, to merit serious consideration.

The other new music of the year fitted less neatly into the general trends of the time. Stravinsky's *Persephone*, which the Schola Cantorum introduced, contained a fair amount of folk material, and it was certainly approachable enough, but at the same time well within the highly individualistic Stravinsky style. Vaughan Williams' new Symphony in F, on the other hand, represented a departure. Williams had been quite addicted to the folk music of his country back in the days when it was not fashionable, but the new work which Hans Lange and the Philharmonic presented February 6th was dissonant and starkly pure, programless music. Walter Piston's Concerto for Orchestra, performed by Koussevitzky and the Boston Symphony a few days later, was a somewhat academic harking back to the international style of the Twenties. There was an ovation for the composer.

The high point of the recital season was practically reactionary in its austerity. It was Artur Schnabel's Beethoven cycle, including all of the piano sonatas. Single-handed, Schnabel filled Carnegie Hall seven times in January and February and the effect of his playing, the depth of his musical thought, the eloquence of his technique, were such that Olin Downes finally gave up trying to express to his readers the import of the occasions. "Those who were in the audience understood," he said. "For those who were not there words would be futile." The joke of the year was that it didn't make any difference if you had a ticket or not, if you didn't carry a volume of the sonatas under your arm you wouldn't be admitted to the hall. Abram Chasins, "speaking of pianists," writes: "This man was not for this age. Artistic zeal burned within him, doggedness and dedication and pride. He had the will and the power to stir us to the best within us."

The same words could have been applied to Toscanini whose last season with the Philharmonic was an abbreviated one, consisting of only thirty concerts and little that was new and different. As always, he offered the best of the repertory, exactingly played. The big evening of his season was the New York debut concert of Rudolf Serkin, the splendid pianist who joined with the Philharmonic on February 20, 1936, to play a Beethoven and a Mozart piano concerto. The young pianist and the aging conductor were in perfect musical accord and the unheard-of happened—there was applause at the end of the first movement of the Beethoven concerto. There was no faulting the magnificent maturity of Serkin's conceptions and values, the beauty of his tone, the sureness of his technique. As one reviewer wrote, Serkin "established himself as one of the most important pianists of our time."

But nothing so became Toscanini in this last season as his leaving of it—and his orchestra. April 29, 1936 was the date, and the faithful began queueing up at seven in the morning for the 140 standing room tickets that went on sale thirteen hours and fifteen minutes later. Naturally there was an attempt at gate-crashing, but police caught four men who sneaked into the hall to open a fire exit for some 150 fans. The house, of course, was packed and when the Maestro appeared on stage that evening to conduct Beethoven's *Leonore* Overture No. 1, the audience rose and rocked the rafters with cheers and applause. Jascha Heifetz and the Beethoven Violin Concerto were next and it was generally agreed that the sturdy masterpiece has rarely had a more inspired performance. The second half of the program, which was broadcast, was all-Wagner and when the last crashing chord of "The Ride of the Valkyries" resounded the hall went mad. There was a thunder of cheering, whistling and stamping by those who had come to say their affectionate farewell to the Maestro.

The demonstration came to an abrupt halt when a photographer committed the unpardonable sin of flashing a bulb in Toscanini's face. The conductor fled the stage and an announcement was made: "Mr. Toscanini sends his love to you all and begs to be excused from appearing again."

Thus ended the regime. A rumor spread through the city that the photographer's flash had seriously injured Toscanini's eyes, perhaps blinded him permanently. But an inquiring reporter found the Maestro relaxed and happily talking of future plans at the party he was throwing for his men at the Astor Hotel.

He left the country with many gifts, among them a platinum watch from the men and an antique silver service from the board. There was also a letter from Franklin Delano Roosevelt, expressing regret at his departure and adding "my word of appreciation for all that you have done for music during your stay among us."

Toscanini broke a long-standing policy and replied to the letter publicly, calling it "among the most precious of the souvenirs which I shall take from your country, where I have spent so many happy years. I shall never forget with what kindness and true understanding I have been received by the American people. I leave with sadness in my heart but with memories to enrich the years to come."

How shortly he would return was not clear then; since he was already close to seventy it seemed to most people that he would probably never again return.

The Philharmonic baton was turned over to John Barbirolli, then a young English conductor who was virtually unknown in America and to Artur Rodzinski. Their task, particularly that of Barbirolli, as principal conductor, was a thankless one. To follow Toscanini was an impossible assignment.

John Barbirolli. He followed a tough man—Toscanini—to the Philharmonic podium and never completely won the orchestra's—or the public's—approval during his tenure.

Culver Service

It was not that Barbirolli did not get a chance to show what he could do. The 1936-1937 season had progressed little more than a month when he received a three-year contract as musical director of the orchestra with full authority to make artistic decisions. In appointing him the Philharmonic board took cognizance of the criticisms that had been leveled against the recent management of the orchestra. Its statement spoke of "the need for a young conductor of artistic integrity who could build towards the orchestra's future as well as enhance its present," a man who could "mold the orchestra into a consistent personality and technical unity."

The board made the young Englishman the permanent, full-time, one-and-only artistic director rather too hastily. He had conducted only eighteen concerts when he received the appointment. Naturally attendance had risen in that period—curiosity alone accounted for that. Naturally there was a certain enthusiasm for Barbirolli. He was not, by any means, a bad conductor. His first programs were about right for the Philharmonic audience. They were heavy with Wagner, then enjoying a period of high popularity thanks to the presence of such sturdy Wagnerians as Melchior, Flagstad and Marjorie Lawrence (who sang with the orchestra during this period) in New York. They contained a good number of other favorites. They were not radical in the choice of new works presented.

The trouble was that Barbirolli did not wear very well. There were standard works which were then beyond his ken, he was too youthful to be able to discipline the notoriously crotchety orchestra and he was, whatever his manifest virtues, just not in the Old Maestro's league. It is doubtful if anyone could have successfully followed Toscanini to the Philharmonic podium, and there was bound to be a let-down, on the part of audience and orchestra alike, once the good-will of the new man's welcome had worn off. So, although the first half of his season went off extremely well, it was not long before the first droplets of criticism fell, droplets that would swell to a torrent by the time the Philharmonic celebrated its 100th Anniversary and simultaneously let Barbirolli go as sole conductor.

The year in which Barbirolli opened a new and not particularly lustrous period in Philharmonic history was marked, in Carnegie Hall, by the ending of a political career which had been long and distinguished but which now could no longer exist in the party to which Alfred E. Smith had given so much. Defeated as the Democratic presidential nominee in 1928, defeated for the nomination by F.D.R. in 1932 and then left out of the first Democratic Cabinet since the administration of Woodrow Wilson, Al Smith was a bitter man when he came to Carnegie Hall on October 1, 1936, to speak at a meeting of The Independent Coalition of American Women, a sort of ladies auxiliary of the right-wing Liberty League. Here, for the first time in his life, Smith declared himself for a Republican—and Alf Landon at that. It was not, he explained, that he was unhappy at the way his one-time protégé, F.D.R., had turned his back on him. It was rather that the New Deal had proved to be an instigator of what he termed "class-hatred" and a "dismal, dull, dark and dreary failure," which prompted him to support Landon "as the best remedy for all the ills" that beset the nation.

But his bitterness was clearly apparent. He felt that he must defend himself against charges that he had forgotten his days in the Fulton Fish Market and had sold out to the rich. He felt compelled to say that he had never wanted a post in the New Deal anyway because it wasn't really a Democratic Administration but rather a hodge-podge in which "even a Communist with wire whiskers and a torch in his hands is welcome. . . ."

On the whole it was a sad spectacle, not made any happier by a technological mishap which caused Smith to be introduced twice. The first introduction had come three minutes before a radio network was ready to go on the air. Therefore Smith had to suffer an anticlimactic second introduction before speaking. In the end, of course, his defection meant nothing in the Roosevelt landslide of 1936—that is, it meant nothing except to Smith who found himself a man without a party and to those who remembered a brave brown derby and a man who was once called the Happy Warrior.

Musically, there was no scene in Carnegie Hall that season which equaled the emotional impact of Al Smith's political apostasy, but there were good moments, among them a recital by the great Kirsten Flagstad, then at the height of her powers and her popularity, singing the songs of Norway and the German lieder in which she excelled. There was also the recital debut of Serkin who demonstrated the qualities of "penetrating musical insight, structural grasp and appreciation and controlling intelligence" that had marked his orchestral debut with the Philharmonic a year before. Finally, there was the debut of a breakneck pianist named Simon Barere, a soloist of sensational technical accomplishment who played so fast that the ears of some listeners could detect only a blur of sound. Barere never quite made the success he probably deserved, and twenty years later, on the same stage, his career came to a sudden and tragic end in one of the most dramatic moments in the history of Carnegie Hall.

The visiting orchestras in 1936-1937 presented little of note. This year, at any rate, the great moments belonged almost exclusively to the Philharmonic—the Philharmonic as led by Artur Rodzinski, co-conductor for the year, and by a distinquished visitor. Rodzinski revived Deems Taylor's "Through the Looking Glass," an unpretentious, humorous and fantastic piece that, at least to the critics of 1937, seemed as fresh as when it was first presented fourteen years earlier. Rodzinski's great production, however, was Richard Strauss's *Elektra* in concert version. Glowing in its sonorities, played with care, fervor and command, the piece and its production was one of the two pinnacles of the season.

The distinguished visitor was Georges Enesco. Not a particularly ornamental conductor, he restrained himself in the programming of his own works and those of his contemporaries. His novelties were few, but Enesco was such a direct, vigorous and authoritative conductor that audiences and critics alike found a sheen in the Philharmonic's tones which had been lacking under Barbirolli, particularly in the Enesco specialty—Mozart.

The event of the 1937-38 season was the return and—at last—the triumph of Artur Rubinstein in Carnegie Hall. He appeared first with the Philharmonic in a program that included the premiere of Daniel Gregory Mason's *Lincoln Symphony*, an over-programatic evocation of the career of the Great Emancipator that was fashionably folksy in approach. The piece attracted, however, a preponderance of newspaper space and it looked as if, again, Rubinstein was out of luck, even though the reviewers briefly praised the fire and poetry in his reading of the Brahms Second Concerto. On the Sunday Philharmonic broadcast he played the Tchaikovsky Concerto and received more attention. The success of the broadcast in effect prepared the way for him as he set off on a tour in which he played with seven major orchestras. Reports from the tour, in turn, excited critics and public about his Carnegie Hall recitals in January. At these he at last received his due. A cheering audience heard him play the piano suite of *Petrouchka* which Stravinsky had arranged for, and dedicated to, him. The reviews were ecstatic. Wrote Olin Downes: "Mr. Rubinstein must have pos-

RCA Victor

Artur Rubenstein finally conquered the New World, "paradoxically more conservative than the old in matters of art," with his 1938 Carnegie Hall concert.

sessed six hands and thirty fingers on his person, perhaps an orchestra as well, concealed in the vicinity of his sounding board." Seconded Louis Biancolli: "Mr. Rubinstein left his audience cheering and his piano limp."

Perhaps the reception of Rubinstein was the surest indication of the decade that there had been some growth in the musical public's ability to determine the meritorious from the meritricious.

It was also a Menuhin year. He had been absent from the concert platforms for eighteen months, resting and attempting to find his way to a higher level of musical development. His first concert after his return was the first in which the erstwhile *wunderkind* wore tails. It was also the first time in American musical history that Schumann's "lost" violin concerto was played. The piece had a fascinating history. It had been written in one week in 1853, in a white, romantic heat. Schumann had sent it off to the great violinist Joachim for a reading. Three years later Schumann died in madness and Joachim kept the concerto and worked on it intermittently until his death. He found "glorious and wonderful" passages in it, as well as hellish difficulties. When he died he specified in his will that the work be turned over to the Prussian State Archives and kept there until the 100th Anniversary of its composer's death. In 1933, however, a German musician found a copy of the concerto and dispatched it to Menuhin who was wildly excited by it. He thought it the "historically missing link of the violin literature . . . the bridge between the Beethoven and the Brahms concertos." He was determined to play it, but because of difficulties with the Nazi regime which, of course, controlled all material in the Prussian Archives, he had to wait until 1937—and even then wait until a world premiere in Berlin had taken place—before he could present it.

The return of Menuhin bearing such a gift was the occasion for much excitement. "It was indeed a triumphal return," Samuel Chotzinoff wrote, "and enthusiasm was at fever heat throughout the evening." There was considerable controversy over the concerto. One critic thought it should have been left to lie undisturbed in the archives, but others found it "deeply felt, passionate and darkly brilliant" as Chotzinoff did. If the controversy over the concerto's true merit slightly marred Menuhin's comeback, nothing marred the reception he and his sister, Hephzibah, received at their joint recital in February, where "once again the unusual sympathy in dynamics, phrasing and interpretation between the young brother and sister was notable."

The 1937-1938 season was an excellent one for new music at Carnegie Hall. Barbirolli presented the American debut of Bartók's *Music for Strings, Percussion and Celesta,* that remarkable piece of compositional virtuosity which inspired a good deal of awe among the professional observers and which has since become one of the more popular pieces in the modern repertory. Also on the Barbirolli programs that year was a first symphony by the young American

Gardner Read, not so important in itself, but historically important because it was the first winner of a $1000 prize set up by the orchestra to encourage young composers. The award did not continue for many years, but it offered, at least, concrete evidence that the orchestra was giving some attention to its responsibility to foster new music. Also on the Philharmonic agenda were Samuel Barber's delightful overture for *The School for Scandal*, a revised version of William Walton's "Façade" and Abram Chasins' Second Piano Concerto with the composer as soloist.

Perhaps the best received of all the Philharmonic programs in 1937-1938 was the program in which Mme. Flagstad made her first American appearance as a soloist with orchestra. "She seems to have reached a point above the pinnacle of perfection in singing. . . ." wrote one critic summing up the general feeling about the great Wagnerian. The final number on the program alone was worth the journey to the hall for most of the audience. It was a substantial group of excerpts from *Die Götterdämmerung*, played without pause, as one vast symphonic fragment, with "Flagstad's glorious voice riding the orchestral waves of tone." Almost the equal of the Flagstad program was the one in which Georges Enesco turned the orchestra over to concertmaster Michel Piastro while he himself played Saint-Saëns' First Violin Concerto. He played not so much as a virtuoso but as a conductor who heard the work as a whole and was particularly anxious to relate the solo part to its grand design. It was masterful, and no less so was his work when he led the orchestra in a jewel-like performance of the Mozart *Haffner* Symphony. "One page of beauty followed another," Downes wrote, "leaving the listener breathless at the revelation and the spell." He, in turn, left little doubt in the reader's mind that Mr. Enesco would be welcome indeed if he should take over the orchestra on a full time basis, for the men in the orchestra responded to him "as they can when they want to and a really great musician is at the helm."

The Enesco-Philharmonic concert was a Sunday afternoon affair. That same evening, Benny Goodman made history in the hall with a transitory kind of music known as swing, a very good kind of popular music much beloved by a generation now doddering into middle-age and forever associated with the pleasures of its youth.

Goodman had been melancholy about the prospects for the concert. He was convinced that the house would not be filled and had gone so far as to ask Beatrice Lillie to do a turn to relieve the tedium of a night of unrelieved swing. What he had not recognized was the depth of his youthful audience's devotion to a music which they regarded as their own property. They packed the house so tightly that Goodman had to buy tickets for his family from a scalper.

Asked just before he went on how long an intermission he wanted, Goodman made a classic reply. "I dunno," he said, "how much does Toscanini get?" Having thus disposed of details, he went out to face an audience gone mad with joy at the thought of their music penetrating the sacrosanct precincts of Carnegie Hall. The program opened with the big band in full cry. The song was "Don't Be That Way," with solos by Goodman, Babe Russin, Harry James and a beautifully controlled drum break by Gene Krupa. After that they soared through such swing standards as "Sometimes I'm Happy," "One O'Clock Jump," "Life Goes to a Party," "Sing, Sing, Sing," and "Stompin' at the Savoy." In addition there were such bonuses as Twenty Years of Jazz, a historical survey, a jam session based on "Honeysuckle Rose," some work by the Goodman trio and several fine blues numbers. Each piece carried the audience to new heights of ecstasy, their cries often threatening to drown out the band.

Olin Downes was among the doubters about the value of this sort of music. He recorded himself as a Whiteman fan, evidently thinking of Whiteman as some sort of pure ideal from which Goodman had departed. Downes and his fellow moderates found swing unmelodic, a fragmentation of the elements of music. But his newspaper, the *Times*, went on editorial record as favoring the new music, and its statement, appearing the day after the concert, admirably sums up the larger implications of the Goodman concert.

"Swing," it said, "is in harmony with the major movements that are sweeping the world today. . . . Their adherents don't think about them. They feel about them. Like swing, they are strictly a spinal column affair. Yet swing differs from our other great contemporary trends in having nothing repressive about it. It gives free exposure to the player's

Benny Goodman's 1938 Jazz Concert in Carnegie Hall caused The Times *to state that "dictators should be suspicious of swing."*

Columbia Records Photo

The resounding success of the concert opened the way for others—like Duke Ellington.

Columbia Records Photo

individualism. The best things he does are not written in the score at all. . . . Perhaps, after all, it is not so much a doctrine set to music as it is a revolt against doctrine. . . . And if the individual has his unhampered say in music, he may manage to have it in other fields. Dictators should be suspicious of swing."

In a real sense the *Times* was right, and the coming of swing to Carnegie Hall represented much more than an achievement on the part of Goodman and the unprecedented assemblage of great sidemen who joined him. It represented a great outburst of joy on the part of a young generation who had lived through dreary days and saw sunlight ahead. Undoubtedly many of them saw war coming soon, but they were determined to have fun while they could. More important, the victory of swing at Carnegie Hall, the fact that the kids could respond to it with all the healthy animalism at their command, represented a great victory for new manners, new codes of behavior. A great citadel of conservatism had fallen to the postwar generation. It could indeed be said that nothing was sacred any longer. The assault of the Twenties on the old morality and the old genteel sensibility and the assault of the Thirties on the old economics and the old social order might be said to have culminated here in Andrew Carnegie's nineteenth-century hall where 3000 kids barbarically howled their approval of sounds that Old Andrew would have loathed. It was surely a grand moment of triumph. Said Goodman: "I didn't have any idea of putting across a message or anything like that . . . it was the thrill of my life to walk out on that stage . . . and hear the greeting the boys got. We were playing for 'Bix' and the fellows on the river boats, in the honky tonks and ginmills that night."

Nothing else in the season of 1937-1938 quite equalled it. Amparo and José Iturbi in recital, John Charles Thomas and Jan Kiepura in song, even the return of Toscanini to conduct the Verdi *Requiem* did not have the social impact of that group of jazzmen.

The last season of peace, 1938-1939, saw an acceleration in the popular and folk arts in Carnegie Hall. Its defenses breached in recent years, the citadel was firmly occupied this year by various exponents of the new taste of the times. The first of these was Martha Graham who, with her troupe, presented *American Document*, a combination of music, dance and the spoken word recalling, as had so many artists during the Depression decade, the American past. Patterned on a minstrel show, beginning and ending with a stirring "walk-around," the sections of the piece recalled Indian culture, the arrival of the Puritans, the emancipation of the slaves among other aspects of history. Many of the critics felt it was overlong and a trifle pretentious, but they accepted it as valid experimentation. As the *Times* put it, "if, on the whole, the composition is not absolutely top notch Graham, it is unusual, interesting and alive. . . ."

So was the last Copland piece of the decade, the sparkling *El Salón México* which Koussevitzky brought with him from Boston nine days later. Copland had turned his folkloristic talents to the land south of the border and come up with a compendium of themes that skirted the danger of being a patchwork and was a cohesive, witty and brilliant adventure in idiomatic writing which audience and critics alike found enormously entertaining.

Copland later wrote that the piece represented a distinct shift in his point of view about music. It was a shift characteristic of the period. "I began to feel an increasing dissatisfaction with the relations of the music-loving public and the living composer. The old 'special' public of the modern music concerts had fallen away, and the conventional concert public continued apathetic or indifferent to anything but the established classics. It seemed to me that we composers were in danger of working in a vacuum. Moreover, an entire new public for music had grown up around the radio and the phonograph. It made no sense to ignore them and to continue writing as if they did not exist. I felt it was worth the effort to see if I couldn't say what I had to say in the simplest possible ways. My most recent works, in their separate ways, embody this tendency toward an imposed simplicity. . . ."

A day after the premiere of *El Salón México*, Ethel Waters and the Hall Johnson choir appeared in a popular program. Miss Waters, resplendent in a red gown with a handkerchief to match, appeared, flanked by a trumpeter and a vibraphonist, and sang everything from spirituals to "Sleepy Time Down South," to the huge delight of her audience. As one critic put it, "those august shades which may be presumed to lurk in the shadows of Carnegie Hall must have received something of a jolt. . . ."

But if Miss Waters and the choir jolted them, they probably began looking around for a new home a little later when a vast cast, sponsored by the radical publication, *The New Masses*, presented "From Spirituals to Swing." It was a brilliant survey of the Negro folk tradition, including spirituals, holy roller hymns, harmonica playing, boogie-woogie piano, New Orleans jazz and swing, both soft and loud, The personnel was as brilliant as the group of all-stars who had aided and abetted Benny Goodman the previous season. Among those present were Albert Ammons, Meade "Lux" Lewis, Pete Johnson, Sister Tharpe, Sidney Bechet and his New Orleans Feet Warmers, Count Basie, the Kansas City Six, Joe Turner, Big Bill and Jimmy Rushing. The popular favorite was the harmonica player, Sonny Terry. Once a farmhand and laborer in the South, Terry had turned to music when his eyes began to fail him. Now almost totally blind, he had to be led on stage wearing a windbreaker and baggy trousers, then played "as if to do otherwise would be a denial of his nature." His music was literal, dealing with things he had seen at a fox hunt, heard in the sounds of a train passing in the night. His work sent the audience into transports of delight, as indeed, did the whole program which historians of jazz and folk music regard as one of the great events in the history of their art. For this was the entrance of Negro music into the upper-class world, the concert that did for it what the Benny Goodman concert had done for a newer kind of music that was descended from this tradition.

A little later, on Christmas Day, Paul Whiteman returned to the hall and bored those who had recently been hearing the real thing. After him came the Spanish singer Argentinita, who gave American audiences an insight into the Spanish folk traditions. Her work was simple, pure and inimitable, ignoring the clichés of Spanish music which Hollywood and Tin Pan Alley had dinned into American ears.

A little more than a week later Benny Goodman completed his conquest of the heights he had begun to scale the year before. On January 9th he joined forces with Joseph Szigeti and the pianist Endre Petri to present the premiere of Béla Bartók's *Rhapsody for Clarinet and*

Violin. Something no one thought possible occurred that night—a jazzman played serious music in Carnegie Hall, and played it brilliantly. This was devilishly difficult music, sounding to one critic like "a Hungarian jam session," overlaying Hungarian dance rhythm with ingenious dissonances and devices both powerful and amusing. Szigeti snapped a string, necessitating the repetition of the second part of the piece, Goodman played with a dignity which in no way hampered his natural gifts and Petri played the piano brilliantly. The whole evening was a remarkable blending of disparate talents and musical traditions.

There were new voices, too, in Carnegie Hall that season. The fine Swedish tenor Jussi Bjoerling sang for the first time there and received high praise for his beautifully trained talent. Gladys Swarthout followed him by a few days in her first New York recital and demonstrated a voice that had taken on new warmth and color in recent years.

But all was not forward-looking in this year. There were two anniversaries celebrating the fiftieth years in America of two great artists who had begun their careers in the New World together. The first was the anniversary of Moriz Rosenthal. A committee headed by Eleanor Roosevelt arranged the celebration. After the speeches came a program of Rosenthal specials played on a piano painted gold for the occasion. The audience was a distinguished one and it greeted the old pianist, the last pupil of Franz Liszt still appearing in public, with a standing ovation.

In contrast was the Golden Anniversary of Fritz Kreisler, the child prodigy who had accompanied Rosenthal to the New World in 1888. Modest and self-effacing, Kreisler regarded the appearance as nothing more than another of his annual recitals. But word of the anniversary got around, even though the concert was not even placarded. Hundreds had to be turned away from the hall and the audience at this concert by perhaps the most beloved musician of his time was full of sentiment which it succeeded in communicating to the artist. The very modesty of his appearance, the lack of publicity, was characteristic of the man, and contributed a mood suitable to the occasion.

Another sort of special event occurred later in the season when Nadia Boulanger appeared as conductor of the Philharmonic for a part of the program of February 11th. She opened the program with a brisk and engaging overture by one of her pupils. Then, seated at the harpsichord, she led a mixed chorus in a group of madrigals by Monteverdi. Returning to the podium she presented the American premiere of a piano concerto by Jean Françaix, with the composer at the piano. An organ solo by Madame Boulanger in a piece by her sister followed the intermission, and the concert ended with a Mozart concerto for two pianos. All in all, it was a brilliant exhibition by a musician's musician, virtually unknown to the general public but regarded in her profession as one of the most profound influences in music in the twentieth century. As the *Times* commented, "in whatever capacity she exhibited her talents, this amazing artist moved with . . . authority, profound understanding and skill."

But an even more moving example of belated recognition came later in the season. The story begins during the previous year in Paris, where S. Hurok happened to notice a familiar name displayed on a poster. He was on vacation, but his curiosity was aroused. He wondered how this voice had fared in recent years, so he dropped in to hear Marian Anderson, then living in virtual exile in Europe. What he heard electrified him. For here was a great voice, one which had developed marvelously since its indifferent reception in America several years earlier. He signed her, not without difficulty, and arranged a concert in Town Hall for late in the winter of 1939. She broke her leg before the recital and thus had to support herself against the piano, her leg in a cast. The curtain had to be lowered after each song so she could have a moment or two of rest. But her voice was at its greatest. Howard Taubman summed up the meaning of that recital with great simplicity: "Marian Anderson has returned to her native land one of the great singers of our time. . . . It is time for her own country to honor her."

Institutional stupidity forced it to do so in an unprecedented fashion. The Daughters of the American Revolution refused to allow a Negro to sing in their auditorium in Washington. There was a tremendous outcry, in the course of which Mrs. Roosevelt resigned from the DAR and Harold Ickes rose to one of his finer hours. The Secretary of the Interior offered the Lincoln Memorial to Miss Anderson as a platform.

Pix

The Lady from Philadelphia—Marian Anderson—came to Carnegie Hall immediately after her triumphant conquest of bigotry at the Lincoln Memorial in 1939.

And there she sang before an audience of 75,000 who jammed the mall in front of the Memorial to do honor to the lady from Philadelphia.

The emergence of Marian Anderson and her victory over prejudice was the coda to a decade in which, as John Steinbeck said, "our country was modeled, our lives remolded, our government rebuilt, forced to functions, duties and responsibilities it never had before and never can relinquish." One of the things remolded was the attitude of Americans toward minority groups. The political mood rendered prejudice, once an unquestioned part of our attitudes, not only questionable but downright distasteful, at least when expressed in public. Therefore Marian Anderson, singing before an unsegregated audience on government property, performed a symbolic act of the highest significance, symbolic not only of a changed attitude but of a whole decade of the most profound social, political and economic changes. When she returned to Carnegie Hall a week later she received one of the most impressive demonstrations ever heard in that place which had heard many.

Nine

"There Were Shadows"

WORLD WAR II BEGAN ON THE FIRST DAY OF SEPTEMBER, 1939, WHEN Hitler's army invaded Poland. The issue was fully joined two days later when Britain and France declared war on Germany. Several months of "phony war" ensued before Dunkirk, the Fall of France, the Battle of Britain, and finally Hitler's invasion of Russia made it clear to most Americans that it was only a matter of time before their country would be fully involved in the war. During that period and beyond, a great domestic controversy between isolationists and interventionists raged in America. Those were the final hours of the belief that America was secure behind its ocean walls. It was a belief with deep roots in the American past, one which had gained new life in the disillusioned years following World War I and had flowered like an untended weed during the Thirties while the nation occupied itself with pressing economic concerns at home. On December 7, 1941, it was exterminated—forever.

During the two years between the start of the war and America's entrance into it, a curious mood of unreality hung over the nation. Many, of course, were deeply concerned about the events in Europe and found it morally imperative that the United States take an active role in the war against Fascism. They applauded each hesitant step of the Administration toward involvement, toward the building of America's own defenses. Others equally vociferous were doing their best, through such movements as "America First," to hold out against the tide of history. But for most people the issues seemed remote, and if in their hearts there was a sickening certainty that sooner or later America would be involved, they did their best to hide this knowledge from themselves. Thus, the Great Debate continued as if it were an abstraction rather than a life-and-death issue, with only a comparative handful of people deeply concerned about it. Most people hoped against hope that the problems of the rest of the world would solve themselves. Economically these were good times; the industrial effort to prepare for war dealt the final blow to the Depression. Although the nation could hardly be defined as pleasure-mad, it was interested in seizing a few moments of innocent merriment in this interval between Depression and oncoming war.

John Steinbeck has written of the mood of America during this period: "Now war was coming. You didn't have to be an expert to know that. It was patent in every news report, in the clanging steps of goose-stepping Nazis. It had been in the cards since the first German put on his brown-shirted uniform. . . . America knew it was coming even while we didn't believe it. We watched the approach of war as a bird helplessly watches an approaching rattlesnake. And when it came, we were surprised as we always are."

So, despite ominous warnings from every quarter, the world of music, like the rest of the artistic world, went along hopefully on its way in pretty much its customary fashion. The seasons of 1939-1940 and 1940-1941 were very like the seasons which had immediately preceded them—fairly rich in new works and good performances, rich also in works by Americans, for by this time composition seemed almost to be an overcrowded field in this country. The outbreak of the war in Europe had little effect on programs. "War Causes Few Cancellations," headlined a story in one musical paper which stated that most European artists planned to go through with their American tours. For the moment the only effect of the war was to end tours of Europe by American artists.

As the season opened, John Barbirolli was feeling expansive. Everything, in his view, was going very nicely at the Philharmonic. "I am the worst nuisance to rehearse with," he told a reporter. "Long experience as a string player has made me particularly demanding on that section. But the orchestra cooperates with me so perfectly that the other day I became frightened . . . I made a slip. The orchestra actually made the slip with me. I thought it was a high tribute, and at the same time the responsibility of it frightened me. I cannot afford to make mistakes."

The implication was obvious. The orchestra was firmly in hand, all was right in the little world of Carnegie Hall. The only people who were not in hand were the critics and the public. As the year proceeded, they grew increasingly restive under Barbirolli's ministrations. He was not a very colorful or imaginative leader and, his statement to the contrary, not a very forceful one. He tended, in the opinion of more than one critic, to give readings rather than performances, and he never gave the impression of completely possessing the work. He was workmanlike, however, and deformed a piece less than some of his more flamboyant competitors. Probably the most damning thing about him was boredom with the necessity of trying to project an interesting and engaging public personality. No legends, real or imagined, surrounded the Barbirolli personality, and the public did like to make legends of its conductors.

Still and all, Barbirolli managed to present a rather interesting season, again tipped slightly in favor of the English composers. Among the significant new works were Mario Castelnuovo-Tedesco's Piano Concerto and his overture to *Twelfth Night*, the former with the composer as soloist. This was unblushingly melodic music which fell easily on many ears. A short time later Barbirolli and the Philharmonic admitted the solo saxophone to musical respectability by programming Debussy's *Rhapsody for Orchestra and Saxophone* and Ibert's *Chamber Concertino* both with Sigurd Rascher as soloist. "In his hands," the *Times* commented, "the saxophone sheds its nightclub abandon and becomes, in fact, continent and almost reserved." Listeners were amazed to hear that when its natural vibrato was suppressed the instrument could sound almost like a French horn and that it could also make cello-like tones. If hardly a major novelty, the Ibert piece, written especially for Rascher, proved to be an extremely effective exploitation of the instrument's capabilities, and the evening as a whole represented an interesting attempt to bridge the gap between popular and serious musical forms in a new way—by taking an instrument associated primarily with the former and using it with the latter. There was a more important debut at the Philharmonic concert a week later when Zino Francescatti made his first New York appearance with the orchestra, playing the Paganini Violin Concerto in D major. He was recalled a half dozen times after he had revealed superb technique and uncommon interpretative ability. At about the same time Barbirolli invited Arthur Bliss to conduct his own suite from the ballet *Checkmate*, a pleasant, mildly dissonant work that was received fairly well. Perhaps his major novelty of the season was another English work, Benjamin Britten's Violin Concerto in D minor, with Antonio Brosa as soloist. Poetic, satirical and elegiac by turns, there was high praise for the uncommon gifts Britten demonstrated in the piece. It was obviously a substantial work by a composer of genuine substance. The final new work of importance in Barbirolli's season was *Moby Dick*, Bernard Herrmann's cantata for male chorus, soloists and orchestra. The work was hardly a whale of a success. The American composer was a bit overmatched when he attempted to bring Melville's tale within the relatively limited scope of the concert hall, and although many found his intentions both admirable and honorable, it had to be said that his successes in the piece were momentary rather than total.

Perhaps the most important service Barbirolli provided for American artists that season was an all-Wagner program he presented late in October. The soloist he engaged was Miss Helen Traubel, whom Walter Damrosch had discovered in St. Louis where she had attained a good local reputation. Miss Traubel was troubled by insecurity. She simply could not believe her voice was great enough for the big time. Considerable coaxing and coaching, however, encouraged her to try New York. A Town Hall recital excited the musical world, but the Met remained virtually unmoved. Edward Johnson, its manager, continued to offer her a part she felt totally unsuited to her—Venus in *Tannhäuser*. Once again, the old war for equality with Continental artists was being fought out by an American.

In this war, Helen Traubel's Carnegie Hall performance was an important engagement. She sang Brunhilde's immolation aria. Dressed completely in black, wearing no jewelry and refusing to make use of those few gestures with which opera singers attempt to communicate emotion, Miss Traubel stood motionless for sixteen minutes and simply sang—gloriously. "It was my own immolation scene in a sense," she recalls in her autobiography. "It proved that at last I could handle anything in the whole catalogue of music as a *hoch* dramatic soprano—something which I had never *proved* to myself until that moment."

Next day, the reviews communicated a strong desire to hear Traubel in opera. The *Sun* said: "It seems preposterous that there should not be a more important place for so notable a voice and so good a vocal technique than America seems to have found so far for this singer. . . Evidently the hunt for great voices should begin at home."

Johnson came back with the same old offer—that of the Venus role. Traubel bided her time. On December 14th and 15th she sang again with the Philharmonic. Again the reviews were ecstatic. At last the Met capitulated. She got the major role she wanted—Sieglinde in *Die Walküre*. She gives credit for this to the Philharmonic concerts. "Met officials privately admitted," she writes, "that they were 'forced' to take me because of the newspaper reviews and the clamor of the opera buffs."

Things had improved slightly since the turn of the century, but the way of the American artist remained hard. He did not have to bludgeon his way to the top in music, but some well-placed kicks, bites and gouges were more than helpful. The difference between his lot and that of his European colleague probably lies in the fact that the European is sought out by American managers while the American must seek out the managers in his home country.

Even more of a triumph for the American musician than Helen Traubel's breakthrough were two concerts Serge Koussevitzky conducted in November, 1939. Both were comprised exclusively of American works, the first such programs in Carnegie Hall since the days of Karl Muck. Chosen for exhibition by Koussevitzky were Arthur Foote's Suite in E major for string orchestra, Roy Harris' Third Symphony, Randall Thompson's Second Symphony, William Schuman's *American Festival Overture*, Edward Burlingame Hill's Violin Concerto, and Howard Hanson's Third Symphony. Coming almost as the decade turned, Koussevitzky's all-American programs were impressive demonstrations of the fact that American music had at last achieved something like equal status with the music of the rest of the world. Olin Downes summed up the import of these concerts admirably: "The music was full of interesting and suggestive contrasts. Each work was unlike the others, in technique, style, approach and development of subject matter. And each was well written, and some put down with sheer virtuosity. . . . This might not have been the case twenty-five years ago in this country. Certainly, at that time, no program . . . would have demonstrated such craftsmanship and thorough acquaintance with the modern devices of the art. . . . In no case was there technical ineptitude or amateurish orchestration . . . the day is past when any American composer need be told that he doesn't know his business. It means at last that our composers have sharpened their weapons and learned how to use their tools."

Here then was music that was fresh, exciting, invigorating and stimulating—and above all, professional—music. The days of the gentleman composer were at last gone and with them the genteel shibboleths and technical lacks which had marred his own true voice. The long fight to establish a professional groundwork for American composition was over, though the battle for public recognition was another matter and still goes on. In the creation of the new professional ambience no man deserved greater credit than Koussevitzky himself. When the last chord of the last number on his American programs died away, he had conducted a total of 126 new pieces by 47 American composers since taking over the Boston Symphony—a record unequalled by any of his contemporaries.

The American programs, however, represented only part of his contribution to new music that season. He presented Bloch's Violin Concerto, "another major achievement of this outstanding composer." Joseph Szigeti, whose devotion to the new almost equaled Koussevitzky's, was the soloist.

Perhaps the only really disappointing note of the season in Carnegie Hall was the recital of Ted Shawn and a troupe of male dancers which received bad notices. It was with such a troupe that he had scored his first success. The group "is at its best when it is most concerned with vigorous athletic movement and at its least effective when it deals with poetic imagery and symbolism," wrote the *Times*. Others were less kind, finding their work "limited and naïve" and "pretentious." His taste ran toward the exotic, the taste of the times ran toward the homespun moods created by Martha Graham. His work now seemed dated and removed from the mainstream of the dance.

"There was little that could be called festive about the occasion. The menu was routine, the playing ditto." So wrote Virgil Thomson, then music critic for the *Herald Tribune*, of the opening concert of the New York Philharmonic-Symphony Society's 99th season on October 10, 1940. The menu offered Beethoven's *Egmont* Overture, Elgar's *Enigma Variations* and the Second Symphony of Jean Sibelius, "vulgar, self-indulgent and provincial beyond all description." To Thomson's ears, even the performance of "The Star Spangled Banner" sounded "logy and coarse." As he left the hall, a friend remarked to the critic: "I understand now why the Philharmonic is not a part of New York's intellectual life." He meant that the programs and playing of the orchestra provided no stimulation to occupy the leisure of the theory class, those intellectuals who make taste.

Barbirolli's failure lay in his inability to please these people, even though he did present a number of interesting novelties, among them Toch's *Pinocchio* Overture, Villa-Lobos' *Descobrimento do Brasil*, and Benjamin Britten's *Sinfonia da Requiem*. Among the soloists who stirred interest were Vitya Vronsky and Victor Babin playing the latter's new *Concerto for Two Pianos*, and Benny Goodman essaying the Mozart Clarinet Concerto in A.

As had become the rule in recent years, the major excitements of the Philharmonic season were contributed by guest conductors. This time it was Dimitri Mitropoulos, demonstrating a batonless and wildly eccentric podium style which was distinctively effective. He put new life into the old Strauss *Sinfonia Domestica* and gave a memorable interpretation to Nicolas Nabokov's new *Sinfonia Biblica*. Bruno

Walter also returned this season and reached his best moments with the orchestra in his performances of the Bruckner Eighth Symphony and Mahler's *Das Lied von der Erde*, both works by men he had championed through many years of indifference. "As long as I can lift a baton, I shall persist in standing up for the works of Mahler and Bruckner," he has written. "I consider it one of my life's tasks to uncover the sources of exaltation flowing from their music." His earnest—and often lonely—crusade has only recently begun to make a dent in the general musical sensibility.

Walter Damrosch's weeks with the orchestra were relatively routine, except for a sad little incident which occurred during the performance of a revised concerto version of his own opera, *Cyrano*. In the second act members of the audience began leaving, a fact which the conductor noticed. At the act's conclusion he turned to the audience and said, "Please don't go home yet. The best part of the opera is coming." His simple plea won over even the most churlish. They stayed, listened and gave him an ovation, not so much because of the music's quality, but because this grand old man of American music had earned it—and many more.

The most important orchestral event of the season—the fiftieth of Carnegie Hall's history, by the way—was the appearance of the Chicago Symphony led by the revered Frederick Stock. The orchestra sounded to some like a French orchestra, with all the sounds it produced standing out distinctly. "Their harmony is one of juxtaposition, not of absorptive domination," Virgil Thomson noted, and since everyone was dissatisfied with the Philharmonic, the men from Chicago were held up as a sterling example of what an orchestra should sound like. The featured work on the program was Roy Harris' new *American Creed*, a piece which Thomson thought "invites kidding." "One would think, to read his prefaces, that he had been awarded by God, or at least by popular vote, a monopolistic privilege of expressing our nation's deepest ideals and highest aspirations." Nevertheless, Thomson thought Harris had his value, for he seemed to be working seriously on the problem of absorbing all of European musical culture, not just that of Vienna between 1750 and 1850. He seemed to be contributing to the process of selective evolution necessary if America was to mold from the full musical past a musical expression of high quality. Harris' best pages were those which eschewed self-conscious American expression and which had "exactly as much to do with America as mountains or mosquitoes or childbirth have, none of which is anybody's private property and none of which has any ethnic significance whatsoever."

The other visiting orchestras also programmed several new works, Ormandy and the Philadelphians presenting Samuel Barber's Violin Concerto and the Boston Symphony joining forces with Piatigorsky to present Hindemith's Cello Concerto. In addition Koussevitzky favored New York with an interpretation of the Mahler Ninth, "of the beauteous kind that only Boston gives us regularly any more."

But, by and large, the orchestral season was not a highly distinguished one. The better reviews in this last season of American neutrality went to the recitalists. "As long as one keeps to piano concerts, truly the town is teeming with delight," Thomson noted. Among those delighting the critic and his confreres were Rubinstein in an all-Chopin program, Josef Hofmann playing with "a classical beauty scaled to the measure of man," Rudolf Serkin making of each piece "a living and personal expression of his own Sacred Flame," Josef Lhévinne, a trifle remote but reminding Thomson that remoteness was nevertheless "inevitable to those who inhabit Olympus," and Claudio Arrau, demonstrating his fine feeling for color and phrase, pianism that lives and thereby marks the virtuoso.

Thomson could have extended his remarks about pianists to the vocalists who came to Carnegie Hall that season. John Charles Thomas, "gifted so rarely and schooled so soundly," brought sheer beauty to his recital as did the tenor, Jan Peerce. And at the pinnacle was Flagstad, whose greatness Virgil Thomson expressed in just a few short lines: "I doubt if there has existed within the memory of living musicians another singer so gifted as to voice, so satisfying as to taste, and withal such mistress of her vocal instrument as Madame Flagstad."

At the violinistic pinnacle there was, of course, all by himself, Heifetz. That season he chose to enliven his recital with five pieces by Robert Russell Bennett, who has since gone on to fortune if not fame as an arranger of music for Broadway musicals. The Bennett pieces went by the general title of *Hexapoda* (*five studies in Jitteroptera*) and had such lively subtitles as "Gut-Bucket Gus," "Jane Shakes Her Hair," "Betty and Harold Close Their Eyes," "Jim Jives" and "... Till Dawn Sunday." The very names testified to the inroads on stuffiness which had lately been made, and their presence on a Heifetz program was something to wonder at. More importantly, in their small way, they were effective, using swing formulas to communicate the response of youth to the music of its choice, and proved to be the delight of the evening.

On Sunday afternoon, December 7, 1941, the Philharmonic-Symphony Society of New York was presenting its regular concert under the direction of Artur Rodzinski. The first few reports of the Japanese attack on Pearl Harbor did not penetrate the concert hall where Dimitri Shostakovich's First Symphony was played, followed by the Brahms Second Piano Concerto with Artur Rubinstein as soloist. And, in fact, during the musical season which coincided with the first season of war, there is little evidence of wartime curtailment of, or infringement upon, musical activity. It might even be said that musically this was a better war than the last one. It had none of the hysteria which had driven German music and musicians from the platform in World War I and little or none of the extremes of super-patriotism that had so marked its predecessor. The trend of the Thirties toward a more nationalistic American music simply continued, unabated, just as, in a wider sense, the wartime values of America were an extension of its Depression values. This was very much a liberal's war and those Americans who bothered to think at all about war aims considered it more than just another war to end war. To them, it was also a war to end the parody of conservatism which was Fascism, and, just possibly, a war to impose the Depression-born democratic-liberal vision of the good life on the world.

Allowed by the general public to proceed in pretty much its own way, music, although it contributed benefit performances by the score to the war effort, remained generally unaffected. The wartime demand for inspirational music was filled by popular music and those few serious composers who were moved to make musical comment on the war simply extended the techniques they had developed in the Thirties. If anything, with people looking for ways to spend war profits, music benefited economically from the war through increased attendance at concerts.

The first wartime season in New York City was dominated by an exercise in irrelevancy staged by the Philharmonic in celebration of the 100th Anniversary of its founding. The Orchestra's board did not commission any new music, American or otherwise, to mark the occasion. Instead it used the opportunity (*a*) to ease Barbirolli out of his post and (*b*) to announce what amounted to a conductors' tournament in which ten of them, including Stokowski, Walter, Rodzinski, Mitropoulos, Fritz Busch, Eugene Goossens, Koussevitzky, Damrosch, and Toscanini would take over for brief periods. The tenth man was to be Barbirolli, whose tenure on the podium was to be no lengthier than that of his colleagues. This was, as Virgil Thomson pointed out, a nonsensical way for the Philharmonic to celebrate its birthday: "A string of guest conductors, though obviously the first thing the Philharmonic management would think of," he wrote, "is the last thing the Philharmonic musicians need. They have been so thoroughly guest-conducted for twenty years now that they have become temperamental, erratic and difficult as only first-class musicians can become when subjected to every known variety of browbeating and wheedling. The best birthday present the Philharmonic could offer itself and us would be a good permanent full-time conductor, somebody worthy of the job and capable of assuming all its musical responsibilities."

By this time Thomson and a large number of other people were concerned about the Philharmonic. When the Maestro had been around it had been all right to throw the whole weight of the orchestra's prestige against new music. New York may have been robbed of a few pleasures, but it had received in exchange loving renditions of the traditional repertory. But now, with the orchestra very obviously in decline, it was time, in the opinion of many, to start building a real Philharmonic tradition to replace the moribund one of "fine instrumentalism and fancy conducting." Thomson thought it was tempting Providence for the orchestra to go on fooling about with guest conductors when "what she really needs is a lord and master who will take some of the jumpiness out of her and put her to work . . . building something in America's musical life that would be worthy of her history and of the city that loves her and supports her and complains about her."

A lot of people thought that something might well be the building of a real audience for American music as well as a repertory of such music for the audience. However much the American compositional tradition had grown, it had certainly grown despite the orchestra, not because of it, though it still had a long way to go before anyone could proclaim a new golden age of music "made in America." The Philharmonic board did not so much as sniff its disapproval of this radical vision. It just went right ahead with its stodgy plans for the Centennial.

Stokowski batted lead-off and on the first night of the season managed a scratch hit with Henry Cowell's *Tales of Our Countryside*, which made use of the tone cluster technique. He also programmed Roy Harris' *Folk-Song Symphony* and Morton Gould's *Guaracha*. William Grant Still's *Plain-Chant for America* was the major new work of the Barbirolli weeks. Bruno Walter confined himself principally to eighteenth- and nineteenth-century German repertory which is his glory, but he had commissioned a symphonic work by Samuel Barber and programmed it most successfully. Artur Rodzinski's big success was with a "Scenario of Themes" from *Showboat* by Jerome Kern. "No one could hear that music," a critic wrote, "those glorious tunes, without an answering grin, or surreptitious tap of the heel, or even a leap of the heart." It was a night of triumph for Kern who was applauded, cheered, brought back time and time again for an ovation. Mitropoulos concentrated on new music. He managed to prepare a novelty for every one of his concerts, not all of them of equal merit, but all indicating that if the orchestra cared to it could, without great difficulty, increase the dosage of modern music without endangering the patient. Chief among the new works were David Diamond's First Symphony, Hindemith's energetic Symphony in E flat, and Aaron Copland's *Statements for Orchestra*. He also presented a Busoni memorial concert featuring works and transcriptions by the great pianist who had died in 1924.

But the titan of the season was Koussevitzky. The question of how he would fare with a strange orchestra was answered in one word—magnificently. When he took over, the Philharmonic tested him in its time-honored way by deliberately disobeying his instructions to see if he noticed. He did. He laid down his baton and said he would not go on if he were not obeyed explicitly. The orchestra played beyond itself; the critics were agreed on that, and audiences, in turn, agreed with them. Many thought they could detect a change in the Philharmonic's usual sound; the balance and tone seemed to them very like that of the Boston Symphony. Koussevitzky had succeeded, as few men did with this orchestra, in impressing his personality on it. In this tournament of conductors, Koussevitzky was the champion. His work was assured, sensible, eloquent and correct and, as Thomson put it "buying a ticket to one of his concerts was . . . a wholly calculable investment."

The work of the other guest conductors was basically unimportant, with the exception of the Beethoven Festival programmed by Toscanini who was, of course, a known quality and not a "participant" in the tournament. Everyone else, however, was a gamble. Mitropoulos' performances seemed wildly varied in their emotional qualities while Rodzinski's were workmanlike but occasionally unprepared. Fritz Busch was not up to major-league standards, Damrosch was uneven in his interpretation but produced magnificent tone, Walter was great but limited. So the arguments went, and although the season bemused music lovers, it hardly contributed much of lasting significance to American musical history, certainly nothing to compare with the enduring works that had come out of the Boston Symphony's 50th Anniversary season.

The year's recital season was distinguished with Dorothy Maynor, Robert Casadesus, and Efrem Zimbalist, all scoring with the public. The most extraordinary event of the season, though, was a joint recital by Paul Draper, the tap dancer, and Larry Adler, the world's first—and perhaps only—harmonica virtuoso. The program included Vivaldi, Scarlatti, Bach and Brahms as well as Gershwin and boogie-woogie. As the *Times* wonderingly concluded: "Both men are full of music and the dominant impression their performance left was that they got more musical expression than anyone unfamiliar with their work could have expected from such limited instruments as the mouth organ and tap shoes."

That season also marked the Carnegie Hall debut of a very great jazz pianist named "Fats" Waller. He was a great artist, but as John Hammond wrote in his program notes for the concert, "Waller's great talent for the piano has never received the acknowledgment that it deserves in this country. It was easier to exploit him as a buffoon and clown than as the artist he is. . . ."

Success, however, continued to keep its face averted from Fats Waller. On the night that should have been his triumph, all his many friends dropped in to wish him well. A convivial soul, Fats had a drink with each of them and when at last he had been pointed in the direction of the stage and had settled down to work, a curious thing happened. George Gershwin's "Summertime" kept creeping into the spirituals Fats played on the organ and also into a group of improvisations. After the intermission it turned up again in some Tchaikovsky variations. The one place it did not appear was in the Gershwin group.

Oscar Levant, leaving the hall, remarked, "I never realized until I heard Fats tonight how much Tchaikovsky owed to Gershwin." It was a sad and funny occasion—and an almost perfect miniature of the entire benighted but occasionally brilliant career of Fats Waller.

In the early months of the 1942-1943 season, the magazine *Musical America* issued a stern warning against a lowering of musical standards during the war. "Lighter music, since it is believed that during war the public craves lighter music, is available among classical authors. There is in war or peace the same gap between the classical and popular. If taste is lowered for army men they will be disappointed in what they hear, since if they come to a concert hall they expect to hear good music." The voice of musical conservatism, however, failed to mention its real reason for alarm. Since late in the Thirties the gap between popular and high musical art had been narrowing. Every sign, from the Goodman concert to the Kern *Showboat* scenario to the appearances of Larry Adler and Fats Waller, indicated it. In time there would be a slight reversal of this trend, or at least it would come to seem less remarkable, but for the moment it was dispiriting to the musical conservatives who, as always, saw traditional values tumbling all about them. One can only wonder why they could not see that constant change was the very essence of all art.

The way things were heading in American composition during that first full year of war was rather obvious. The Philharmonic, enduring still another season of guest conducting, presented Harl McDonald's *Bataan*, a musical portrait of that most tragic of America's military experiences. It was hardly great music, but because of its frame of reference, it greatly moved the audience when Rodzinski programmed it. So did Tansman's *Polish Rhapsody*, another piece of program music, depicting the anguish of that most unfortunate of nations. Fritz Reiner and the Philharmonic presented William Schuman's *Prayer 1943*, a work which attempted to evoke the higher aspirations of a nation at war.

The Boston Symphony also had timely works. One was Roy Harris' brassy Fifth Symphony, dedicated "to the heroic and freedom-loving people of our great ally, the Union of Soviet Socialist Republics" and regarded by Downes as "a weak symphony, weak in invention, weak in statement, undistinguished by original ideas." A month later Koussevitzky offered another tract for the times, Copland's *A Lincoln Portrait.* With words from the writings of Lincoln woven into the piece (and spoken on this occasion by the admirable Will Geer), the piece seemed to some half-finished. The first part was well-developed; the last section, the portion devoted to Lincoln's words, was flimsy. At the same concert Koussevitzky also programmed Schuman's *A Free Song*, a "secular cantata" with a text derived from Walt Whitman, inspirational in nature and not particularly stimulating in a musical sense.

The contribution of the Philadelphia Orchestra to the times was *The Plow That Broke the Plains*, Virgil Thomson's score for the magnificent documentary Pare Lorentz had written and directed in Depression days for the Farm Security Administration. Thomson himself took over Ormandy's baton as if to the podium born, and it was found that his suite could "stand on its two feet without the benefit of photography."

The work which provided the clearest evidence of the scope of the trend toward American themes was a piece by Ernst Křenek which Dimitri Mitropoulos and the Philharmonic presented for the first time in New York. It was *Variations on a North Carolina Folk Song* in which the severely atonal Křenek, without abandoning his customary style, unbent enough to use an American theme, albeit with some vagueness. The importance of the work lay in the fact that a man like Křenek, European-born and trained, could be seduced into using a theme which was the product of a tradition fundamentally alien to him.

Křenek was working from high art down to low; another man was trying to work from the popular up to the higher levels. He was Duke Ellington who, with Goodman, was the leading "intellectual" of the popular musical world. He chose January 23, 1943 to unveil his most ambitious effort to date, a forty-five minute "symphony" for swing band, *Black, Brown and Beige*, an evocation of the Negro's climb up the social ladder in America. The "Black" section was built around the work songs and spirituals of the slave. "Brown" used themes from the war songs of nineteenth-century conflicts in which Negroes had participated. "Beige" used contemporary themes to discuss musically the Negro's role in the modern world. Many found the piece pretentious, but some, like Irving Kolodin, thought that "the sheer talent that has gone into it, the number, variety and quality of the ideas, certainly affirm again that Ellington is the most creative spirit that has worked this field." At his annual Carnegie Hall concert each year thereafter (until 1950) Ellington premiered a new major work in the popular idiom, including such opuses as *Deep South Suite, New World A-Comin', Liberian Suite, Blue Bells of Harlem, Blutopia,* and *The Tattooed Bride.*

Perhaps the year's most significant cross-fertilization between high and popular art took place that year not on the stage of Carnegie Hall but above it in the famous Studio 61. Once a boy's gymnasium, the studio had gone to become probably the most famous dance studio in America. Isadora Duncan had rehearsed and taught there. So had Mikhail Mordkin, beating out the rhythm with a pogo stick, signaling rests with a Bronx cheer. The names of others who had worked and taught there read like a who's who of American dance—the Fokine family, the Denishawn dancers, Alys Bentley and Aubrey Hitchens,

Columbia Records Photo

Eugene Ormandy rose from the pit of the Roxy Theater to replace Stokowski as conductor of the Philadelphia.

Edward Caton, Anton Dolin, Margaret Croske, Yeichi Nimura (who also taught dance steps to some exceedingly bright Siamese cats he owned), Lisan Kay, Eric Victor and many others. It is safe to say that almost every well-known dancer of recent years has worked in the studio at one time or another.

One day in the winter of 1942-1943 something new, something completely beyond its previous ken, came to Studio 61. In that winter a previously unsuccessful choreographer and dancer named Agnes De Mille began rehearsing the dances she had created for a chancy Broadway musical comedy venture called *Away We Go.* Before it opened in New York on the chilly night of March 31, 1943, after very nearly expiring in New Haven, the show was renamed *Oklahoma!* Before it closed some five years later, nearly everyone connected with it—Rodgers, Hammerstein, Celeste Holm, Alfred Drake and Agnes De Mille—found themselves successful (some of them were already famous) beyond their most avid dreams. The show contributed much to popular culture. It rescued musical comedy from the blind alley down which it had been traveling since the death of George Gershwin (and perhaps sent it down another). It brought the intellectual's preoccupation with folk materials to the great middle-brow audience. It demonstrated the possibilities inherent in the close and careful interweaving of book, lyrics, music and dance to present a well-unified total theatrical experience. But most important of all, it brought real dancing to Broadway.

Here was an excellent example of low art borrowing from high and enhancing itself greatly, for the people responsible for *Oklahoma!* never allowed themselves to become fake or pretentious. Unlike many musical comedies which have followed in its footsteps, this one remained always a very good show, one which never forgot that it was not art, not even folk-art, but popular art, otherwise known as entertainment.

No one has written better about the meaning of Carnegie Hall to the worker in the arts than Agnes De Mille. In her delightful *And Promenade Home* she speaks of the rescue of herself that she effected in Studio 61. She had just married and her husband had gone off to war. Troubled and lonely she "turned, as always, to the practice *barre*,

Culver Service

Agnes DeMille as she appeared in her uncle's movie, Cleopatra. *In 1943 she created the dances for* Oklahoma! *in Carnegie Hall's famed Studio 61.*

and buried myself in Carnegie Hall. There, in the animated decay of that compost heap, amid the rotted, the forlorn and the germinating, once again I warmed my heart."

On one occasion she stayed too close to this warm and warming place. Finishing a class, she stayed on in the Carnegie Hall drugstore writing a letter to her husband. While she was there, he was at her apartment with only a few hours' leave, frantically phoning every place his wife might be. Instead of two hours together they managed to salvage only twenty minutes.

But she could bear no grudge against the place that had caused her to linger too long. Her memories of it are too rich. At one time Leonard Bernstein, a very struggling young artist, lived down the hall from Studio 61. He earned a dollar an hour banging away at a piano for dance classes until an exasperated ballet master fired him because he could not keep strict time. For him, as for Miss De Mille, the very special aura of the place worked its magic. The studios were, as always, full of frauds, sad people hoping the creative atmosphere would somehow transform their small or puffed-up talents, enabling them to create something—anything—worthwhile. But always there was meaningful activity, the sights and sounds of creation. The sounds of scales being practiced, of drama students talking too much and too loudly as is the actor's habit, the wonderful alertness and control which is trained into the very walk of a dancer, all these were here. Here too, on every hand, were the shattered remnants of dreams which had grown too big and the half-finished structures of dreams in the making. Here was decay and renewal, the never-ending, never-changing cycle of art in the making. As Miss De Mille put it: "One could lose oneself here and draw sustenance from the bustle of poverty and from the absolutely unbeaten vegetable strength of the art impulse—pushing, pushing through all people, all barriers, all luck, all turns of fate."

It was therefore natural for her to return to this creative womb when it came time to make the dances for *Oklahoma!* She has told of her emotions as stepped onto the floor of Studio 61: "Floor space is as irresistible to the dancer as cool waters to the thirsty. The sight alone is enough to make one hurry. The room empty, the enclosing walls serenely bare, the mood of reservation protecting as a fortress, it is impossible therein to maintain rage or hate. Sounds cease and fall away. The dancer enters the arena of total, lonely effort and works with spirit and flesh. Pattern is learned here and relationship and law, as communication is worked on the bare air. No dancer comes out of a good practice without exhilaration, and on leaving the room the better self stays behind."

Perhaps no one in recent years has better communicated the essential "why" that underlies the individual's commitment to art.

Agnes De Mille found other satisfactions as well in the dance rehearsals for *Oklahoma!* and she speaks of one that is not obvious to the outsider. For the thing she wrought on the bare air of Studio 61 had social as well as artistic consequences: "The boys and girls with the true ballet look, the erect, brisk and quiet figures . . . began to scurry hatless through the 40's of Times Square during that April. They were to become a familiar figure in the next decade. . . . The chorus girl and the chorus boy of the past, corrupt, sly, ruthless and professionally inept, gradually disappeared. And in their place came singers and dancers, trained and self-respecting. Rehearsal halls began to lose their overtones of boudoir bargaining."

It is one of history's small ironies that in this dismal year, in the midst of the most terrible war the nation had ever seen, creativity of the kind Agnes De Mille described reached one of its highest plateaus in Carnegie Hall. We have seen the evidences of heightened activity on the part of American composers, the results of the work in Studio 61. But they were by no means the total of the year's glories in Carnegie Hall. Early in the season Fritz Kreisler, now an old man, proved again the remarkable capacity of the artist to endure and to prevail. In April, 1942, he had very nearly died as the result of being struck by a car while crossing a street. Almost everyone assumed that his long career was finally finished. But on the last day of October, in the same year, he played again in Carnegie Hall, a place he regarded as "my real home in New York City." The auditorium was packed, there were hundreds seated on the stage. They rose to greet him, fearing the worst, hoping for the best. They heard the best. He played concertos by Bach and Mozart and a number of shorter works, mostly his own transcriptions and arrangements of the masters. There was even a Kreisler original, the *Viennese Rhapsodic Fantasy*, a work he had almost completed at the time of his accident. The *Times* expressed the general reaction: "His enforced rest brought him back to his public with a new strength noticeable even in his physical appearance."

This was also the year of Sergei Rachmaninoff's last appearances in Carnegie Hall. His recital was hardly a triumph. Said one observer: "Lots of argument during the intermission of Rachmaninoff's piano recital. Everyone said there were ups and downs, but few agreed what was up and what was down." As usual, this keyboard emotionalist hit rather too many wrong notes, but in the show pieces, his own études and a Liszt group, he was in top form.

Happily, he did not have to end his fiftieth season of public appearances on an ambivalent note. He helped Mitropoulos prepare his *Symphonic Dances* for a Philharmonic program and they received better notices than they had before, as did his *Rhapsody* which he himself played with the orchestra. A few months later he was dead.

The next season brought the great Bruno Walter performances of the *St. Matthew Passion* of Bach to Carnegie Hall. The conductor had carried guilt feelings about the work around with him for thirty years since his Munich days when he had conducted numerous performances of it in a truncated version. He was ashamed of himself for being a party to this sacrilege and, worse from the creative musician's standpoint, the performance of the shortened version had seemed to prevent him from penetrating to the very heart of the work. Now, after a year of study and meditation, he was prepared to bring forth the work in its entirety. It was a triumph. "Of all the performances in my long life, this was probably the one that made me the most thoroughly happy," he writes in his autobiography. It was not perfect—no performance ever is—but "the performance fulfilled Bach's intentions as far as given circumstances permitted. My vital energy which had threatened to flag at times was renewed by Bach's immortal work, and so I had a personal reason, too, for retaining these performances in my memory."

Once again art had performed its great function of renewal. But it was not only the older men, the Kreislers, Rachmaninoffs and Walters, who found spiritual sustenance in Carnegie Hall that troubled year. A young fiddler named Isaac Stern also found it there. He had made his debut in Town Hall in 1937, at the age of seventeen. He had been no great success, but like Kreisler before him, he had persevered, moving steadily upward in artistic if not public regard. Now, at last, his time had come. On January 8, 1943, he came to Carnegie Hall to play a program of Mozart, Bach, Szymanowski, Brahms and Wieniawski. Nothing, that night, was beyond him, and the young violinist at last joined the select group at the very top of his art. For the knowledgeable, as for Stern, it was an evening of great joy. They had watched him develop, patiently, steadily, unforcedly. The next afternoon Irving Kolodin spoke for them in the *Sun*: "It is a rewarding thing . . . to find a young American artist . . . whose career is marching

S. Hurok Photo

Isaac Stern. His Carnegie Hall Concert in 1943 fully demonstrated his virtuosity. Seventeen years later he was instrumental in saving the Hall from demolition.

steadily toward a splendid maturity. Rewarding? In the case of Isaac Stern, whose playing last night proclaimed him now to be a violinist of superlative abilities, it was downright exhilarating."

Little did anyone know that on that night, and on subsequent nights during this year of his triumph, Isaac Stern acquired a debt—a highly personal debt—to the hall in which his rich tones were first fully appreciated. It was a debt he was to pay back seventeen years later in an unprecedented fashion. Perhaps he felt that he owed his musical life to the acoustics of that place. Whatever his reasons, it was he who set in motion, years later, the forces which were to save the life of Carnegie Hall.

It was a good season, that season of 1942-1943, and it came to an end with a great concert. On April 25, 1943, two magnificant artists, Arturo Toscanini and Vladimir Horowitz, put on what one enthusiast called "the musical event of the century." They played, father and son-in-law, the piece with which Horowitz had debuted so many years before—the Tchaikovsky Piano Concerto in B flat minor. Toscanini's NBC orchestra played without remuneration as did the Maestro and Horowitz. The cause was the sale of warbonds, and $11 million worth of them were sold to those who could not bear to pass up the chance to hear this rare collaboration.

George R. Marek, now head of the RCA Victor record division, speaks very succinctly of the import of that occasion: "None of us who had been in Carnegie Hall that afternoon has ever forgotten that hour. The electricity and excitement always present in a Toscanini or a Horowitz concert were here charged with enormous extra voltage, an emotion which derived from the high purpose of the event."

It was one of those few moments in which all the factors necessary for greatness are present and are somehow simultaneously ignited. The superlatives of the critics the next day pass all description. For, riding once again this warhorse of a concerto, genius found itself inspired, and the ordinary was suddenly transformed into the extraordinary. It was that kind of a year in Carnegie Hall.

The New York Philharmonic began its new season with a new musical director, a conductor with full authority in matters of personnel and programming. His name was Artur Rodzinski and he had a whim of iron. A graduate of the University of Vienna and of the Vienna Conservatory, he had been a familiar figure on the concert stages of the world for many years. For ten years he had been engaged in building the Cleveland Orchestra and he had done his work well, if temperamentally. He upped and left Cleveland in the midst of the 1942-1943 season without even giving his employers notice. He signed with the Philharmonic in January of 1943 and energetically devoted the spring to shaping a new program and to clearing out the dead wood in the Philharmonic. One of the first to feel the vigorous brushings of the new broom was the long-time concertmaster of the orchestra, Michel Piastro. Firing him cost Rodzinski dearly. It got him into a bitter battle with the musicians' union, lost him the friendly regard of many regular Philharmonic customers and, worse, embittered many members of the orchestra.

But Rodzinski was a strong man, a leader whose abilities forced his men to respect him. Not long after he took over, the orchestra that had been whipped and spurred by guest conductors with little sense of responsibility for its future or its relations to the intellectual life of the community and which often sounded like an industrial blast, its good moments almost accidental, "the result of one day's well being in the life of a neurotic," began to sound richer. Thomson, for instance, noted improved tonal transparency, "a faint blush" of health appearing on the string sounds, even improved rhythmic coordination. All in all, there was cause for at least moderate hope at last, although Thomson warned that all those years of bad treatment could not be wiped out in a season. "The Philharmonic," he wrote, "will have to be retrained from the ground up, schooled for dependability and accustomed to being able to count on its conductor."

It was to prove an interesting season for the Philharmonic. There was a great deal of new music on its programs, notably the Bartók Violin Concerto premiered by Rodzinski with Tossy Spivakovsky as soloist. Critical judgment called it "a goldmine of diverting sonorities and figurations," which like many of his other works was somehow disappointing, perhaps more interesting on the surface than it was when you got right down to considering its substance. Rodzinski also premiered Hindemith's sprightly *Symphonic Metamorphoses on Themes of Carl Maria von Weber*, and shared his podium one night with Alexander Tansman who conducted his own rather recondite Fifth Symphony. Under other conductors the Philharmonic presented a number of interesting works. Howard Barlow led *A Christmas Festival* Overture by Nicholai Berezowsky on December 23 and on December 25 turned the baton over to Deems Taylor for the premiere of Taylor's *Christmas* Overture which, fashionably enough, was based on a folk song, "I Wonder as I Wander." In the critical balloting the Berezowsky work won; he was using Ukrainian folk songs for his themes and people seemed to find them much more jolly than the American theme used by Taylor. Guest conductor Wilhelm Steinberg's largest contribution to the season was a premiere of Paul Creston's *Concerto for Saxophone and Orchestra* with Vincent J. Abato as soloist. In the midst of the boomlet that hybrid instrument was enjoying, the piece was found to be quite beautiful in parts, a little too jazzy in others. In that season, New York also had a chance to hear symphonies by Samuel Barber, a revival of his First, characterized by "a Hamlet-like backward yearning toward the womb of German Romanticism," and a premiere performance of his Second Symphony, which Virgil Thomson thought was "Hamlet in modern dress." Whatever else it was, it was certainly modern. Barber was serving in the Air Force as a corporal and he dedicated the work to his service. Into the slow movement he threw a "tone generator" which simulated the sound of the radio beam used as an aid in blind flying. Revising the symphony after the war, Barber eliminated the thing. At the moment, however, it was quite in keeping with the musical mood. During this period the League of Composers commissioned seventeen short orchestral pieces. The Philharmonic played a number of them, which were distinctly of the "occasional" sort but were created by many of the leading composers of the time. Among them were "The Anxious Bugler" by John Alden Carpenter, Berezowsky's humorous "Soldier on the Town," Roy Harris' "March in Time of War," Still's "In Memoriam: The Colored Soldiers Who Died for Democracy" and Darius Milhaud's *Cortège Funèbre*.

Perhaps the best of the war-inspired works was premiered that year by Rodzinski and the Philharmonic at a concert celebrating the 25th Anniversary of the founding of Czechoslovakia. It was Bohuslav Martinu's "Memorial to Lidice," the town which the Germans had wiped out in reprisal for the assassination of Reinhard Heydrich, the brutal "Protector" of the occupied nation. Martinu, an inspired musical journalist (one of his wartime pieces was called "Thunderbolt P-47" and was an ode to an airplane) was also one of the most pleasing modern melodists. He was a deep-feeling Czech nationalist who as a refugee had arrived in this country in 1941 carrying one small suitcase, his many valuable scores and manuscripts left behind. In the midst of flight he had managed to keep working at his music, and once settled in the United States he turned to the larger orchestral forms. There followed a great flow of creativity. The Boston Symphony had presented his First Symphony in November, 1942, and it received an enthusiastic sets of notices. "Just think of it!" Thomson enthused. "An ensemble that sounds like an ensemble playing music that sounds like music! It restores one's faith, it really does." The work was wholly beautiful, folklorish and, although written in the romantic tradition, remarkably fresh and highly personal.

The result was that 1943-1944 was a Martinu year. Each of the major orchestras played a piece by the Czech composer. One was a concerto for two pianos, commissioned by the team of Luboshutz and Nemenoff and played by them with the Philadelphia Orchestra under Ormandy. The piece was experimental-sounding, somewhat of a departure from the usual Martinu style, but it made great playing for the soloists. The same could be said of the concerto he wrote for Mischa Elman who played it with the Boston Orchestra under Koussevitzky, one of the composer's most enthusiastic supporters. The piece was tailor-made for the soloist, and not as well-received as other works by Martinu. There is no doubt, however, that in the war and postwar years, in the midst of a fecund creative period, Martinu was one of the most popular serious composers in America.

But if this season marked the beginning of success for a deserving composer, it was even more notable for the beginning of a purely American musical phenomenon, the end of which is not yet in sight. Early in the season the Philharmonic announced to a world not precisely agog with interest that it had engaged a twenty-five-year-old Harvard graduate as assistant conductor. In the normal course of things that would have been the last anyone heard of Leonard Bernstein for some years, for obscurity is the assistant conductor's lot.

But, on November 13th, Bruno Walter, who was in the midst of one of his guest conducting stints, came down with a stomach ache. That evening Bernstein was informed that he might have to conduct the Sunday afternoon concert, although the management was hoping that Walter would recover in time to conduct. Bernstein did not even own afternoon formal wear in which to lead the orchestra, and a number of the pieces, notably a piece by Miklos Rozsa, *Theme, Variations and Finale,* which he had never conducted.

"I stayed up until about 4:30," Bernstein later told a reporter, "alternately dozing, sipping coffee and studying the scores." He finally fell into a sound sleep about 5:30, fairly well convinced that Walter would probably recover or that a name conductor would be found to substitute for him. But at ten o'clock Sunday morning, Bruno Zirato, the associate manager of the orchestra, told him that he was going to conduct. "My first reaction was one of shock," Bernstein said. "I then became very excited over my unexpected debut and, I may add, not a little frightened. Knowing it would be impossible to assemble the orchestra for a rehearsal on a Sunday, I went over to Mr. Walter's home and went over the scores with him."

That afternoon, with his parents (who happened to be in town) seated in a box, conducting without a baton and wearing an ordinary business suit, Leonard Bernstein conducted the Philharmonic-Symphony Society of New York, with millions listening in over the CBS radio network. His program included Strauss's *Don Quixote*, the *Manfred* Overture of Schumann and as the concluding work, Wagner's *Meistersinger* Prelude.

Bernstein's debut made a front page news story in the next day's *Times*. "He showed immediately," Downes wrote in his review, "though the opening was not his best performance of the afternoon, his brilliant musicianship and his capacity both to release and control the players . . . it was clear at once that whatever the unconventionality and perhaps the technically immature character of his beat, he was conducting the orchestra in his own right and not the orchestra conducting him. . . . He conducted without a baton, justifying this by his instinctively expressive use of his hands and a bodily plastic which, if not always conservative, was to the point, alive and expressive of the music and so understood by the players. Greater reserve will come later."

Downes thought it highly appropriate that the final work, conducted "with glow and splendor," was the *Meistersinger* Prelude, "that apotheosis of youth and art come into their own." On Tuesday the *Times* wrote an editorial about the incident, entitled "A Story Old and Ever New."

The story was by no means over when Bernstein walked off the stage at the end of his debut appearance. In fact, only the first scene of the first act had been played, and it threatens to be at least a five-act drama. Artur Rodzinski arrived at the hall during intermission, having driven down from his Stockbridge, Massachusetts, home just in case he was needed. He told reporters that Bernstein was "a prodigious talent," and that "we wish to give him every opportunity in the future."

The first of these came on December 2, when Bernstein led "Three Jewish Poems" by Bloch. This was his "official" debut and everyone thought he did very well. Conducting from memory, giving his cues with meticulous care, communicating his desires to the orchestra with ease, he infused the performance with the same freshness of spirit that critics had noted in November. A couple of weeks later, when Howard Barlow was suddenly taken ill, Bernstein again substituted at a regular concert and again received good notices, although a few of the more conservative observers noted that his rather choreographic style of leading the band was visually annoying. This criticism plagued Bernstein for years. A naturally exuberant soul, he contended that his swayings and undulations were quite unconscious. When he became co-musical-director of the Philharmonic in 1958 he began using a baton and his podium manner since has become positively decorous by contrast to the days when he was called "our musical Dick Tracy."

His eight appearances with the Philharmonic in the fall of 1943 were not all that Leonard Bernstein contributed to the musical scene that season. In April, 1944, at the Metropolitan Opera House, he conducted the first performance of a new ballet that he and his friend, Jerome Robbins, had gotten up. The name of the work was *Fancy Free* and that rough and tumble, free-wheeling and utterly delightful work burst with explosive force on musical America. With Robbins, John Kriza and Harold Lang in the roles of three sailors on shore leave, it seemed to answer a need for something expressive of the vital energies —even the high spirits—America was pouring into its war effort. Ballet Theatre performed the work 250 times in the first year after the premiere.

A month later it was announced that Bernstein had won the Music Critics' Circle Award for the best new orchestral work by an American that season. The work was his first symphony, the *Jeremiah*. He had led the Philharmonic in the New York premiere of the highly promising work in March, and although a few critics expressed reservations over it—the man from the *Times* thought it did not sustain its symphonic character in the last movement—it too had the electricity of the Bernstein personality. All in all, there has probably never been a debut year like Bernstein's in America's musical history. Nor, as is obvious, did his success prove to be merely transitory.

His, of course, was not the only triumph of the year. Yehudi Menuhin chose that year to premiere in Carnegie Hall the First Violin Sonata of Béla Bartók, who was now, as a result of the war, living in America. The two men took an instant liking to one another. At their first meeting when Menuhin played the sonata for the composer, the shy and gentle Bartók burst out, at the end of the first movement, "I thought works were only played in that way long after the composer was dead." At the concert Menuhin insisted that the composer share the applause, but after a few awkward bows Bartók withdrew—and friends were amazed to see tears in his eyes.

The other recitalists did not fare quite as well as Menuhin that season. Eugene Istomin, seventeen, made his New York debut with the Philharmonic playing the Brahms Second Piano Concerto and although he was certainly not excoriated, the critics left little doubt that he needed a bit of ripening. He, of course, has gone on to have one of the finest of the youthful pianistic careers. An older pianist, Robert Casadesus, was accused of playing either very soft or very loud, but hardly ever with the proper moderation. Marian Anderson was said to be "a lovely icicle" when singing the classic and romantic repertory and was urged to devote herself more to the religious music of her people in which she became "a flame." Even Isaac Stern, so lately elevated to the pantheon, got a reserved critical reception. "In tune, but not with the Infinite" said the headline on one notice.

None of these people, of course, were much hurt by controversy, and the best musical controversy of the year—perhaps of the decade—amused many. It began when Rodzinski, conducting a concert for soldiers at Camp Kilmer, let it be known that he thought popular music was the basic cause of juvenile delinquency and that Frank Sinatra, riding the crest of his original bobby-soxer popularity, was the leading contributor to the delinquency of the nation's minors. Mr. Sinatra's reply was classically brief. "Nuts," he said.

Never one to avoid a fracas, Leopold Stokowski got into the act by declaring that boogie-woogie, then the hottest item in the pops repertory, was really another manifestation of the great creativity of America. "Some foreigners," he sniffed, "do not seem to understand how rich the United States is in folk music." Mr. Stokowski, of course, was defending the house in which he was currently residing. He had left the Philadelphia Orchestra for the fleshpots of Hollywood where he had conducted the music for *Fantasia* (in which he was seen shaking the hand of Mickey Mouse) and for Deanna Durbin's undoubted masterpiece, *One Hundred Men and a Girl.* Having defended the popular taste, he even went so far as to praise Sinatra, whose phrasing he found engagingly "individualistic." It was all a teapot tempest, but a nation fighting a war to defend democracy was pleased to find out that democratic tastes were not as bad as some high-brows seemed to think.

It is fair to say that the musical season of 1944-1945 did not really begin until the night of October 25, when Florence Foster Jenkins, the somewhat different coloratura, made her Carnegie Hall debut—at age seventy-six. Madame Jenkins had long had a large and distinguished following among the musical elite of New York and her annual recital in a hotel ballroom, under her own management (she personally interviewed the purchaser of each ticket) was one of the traditional highpoints of the season. Now at last bowing to popular demand, she booked Carnegie Hall and the minute word of the impending concert got around, the event became the toughest ticket in town. Only a few initiates had been privy to her previous concerts. Now the world at large was to hear the famed voice, to sit at the feet of the famed presence.

There was much in her background and style which commended Madame Jenkins to the attention of the serious devotee of the arts. She had fought her way up the ladder through sheer will. Totally innocent of any musical ability whatsoever, her family and then her husband (whom she divorced early on) had discouraged her musical ambitions. Against all obstacles she had persevered. America has perhaps never known a person more devoted to the musical muse, and America loved a person willing to back her self-convictions by placing name and fame and even money on the line.

In addition, of course, she had a symbolic value. To all the men who had patiently borne the late-blooming cultural pretensions of their wives, she was one kind of symbol. To their wives, to all the people who had dreamed but never dared, she was another kind of symbol. To all who had a need to demonstrate cultural irreverence, she was a sheer delight. Little wonder that the receipts of her Carnegie Hall venture totaled six thousand dollars.

She had a platform manner which more staid singers might well have envied. No concert was complete without at least three changes of costumes, all of which were of her own design. Her masterpiece, in which she delivered "Angel of Inspiration" was a blend of tinsel and tulle, complete with enormous flopping wings. She was no purist, no Helen Traubel standing stock still for sixteen minutes while singing the Immolation scene. No, indeed. Madame Jenkins was wont to act out the drama of her songs. When doing "Clavelitos," for example, she would wear a shawl, a Spanish comb and a red rose in her hair. She marked the cadences of the song by tossing flowers from a pretty basket to delighted groundlings. On one occasion, she forgot herself and let fly with flowers and basket all at once. This number was a favorite of the Jenkins claque and their wild applause often forced her to repeat it—but not before her already overworked accompanist, Cosmo McMoon by name, had passed among them to retrieve the flowers so essential to the total effect.

It is doubtful if Madame Jenkins would ever have attempted the heights of Carnegie Hall, those heights which, as we have seen, have caused so many so much anguish, had it not been for a fortuitous accident. In 1943, a taxi in which she was riding was involved in a collision. Recovering from the attendant bruises and contusions she discovered, to her delight, that she could sing "a higher F than ever before." She rewarded her driver with a box of expensive cigars. The reviews of her Carnegie Hall concert were brilliant. Said the *Herald Tribune*: ". . . the enthusiasm of last night's public can only be compared, both in intensity and unanimity of reaction to that of The Voice, currently drawing the same sort of delighted applause at the Paramount Theatre."

So, on a flower-bedecked stage, a perfect setting for her various and colorful costumes, her manner "an elegant blend of *sang froid* and unstudied simplicity," Florence Foster Jenkins at last reached her apotheosis. The Metropolitan had been denied her, but this pinnacle, happily, was available to anybody with the rental money.

After that, it was as if she had nothing left to live for. She died a month and a day after the concert. Some said it was the result of a broken heart, because her career had been successful only as parody, not as reality. But Robert Bagar of the *World-Telegram*, in his obituary notice, was having none of that. He said: "She was exceedingly happy in her work. It is a pity so few artists are. And the happiness was communicated as if by magic to her hearers. . . ."

No one else in that last wartime season enjoyed a success comparable to Mrs. Jenkins'. But the Philharmonic, once again a tight ship, even though its heavy cargo of guest conductors still caused it to wallow a bit, had an interesting year. Pierre Monteux presented an important new artist, the sixteen-year-old pianist Leon Fleisher, on a program that also included William Grant Still's symphonic poem, *Old California*, a not very exciting evocation of the history of Los Angeles written for that city's 160th Anniversary. Fleisher's interpretations were judged limited by his youth, but his technical equipment boded well for his future. Rodzinski, too, presented a number of new works, including Schönberg's difficult "Ode to Napoleon," Vaughan Williams' Fifth Symphony and John Wooldridge's "A Solemn Hymn to Victory." Behind the performance of the latter there was a tale. Wooldridge was a fighter pilot as well as a composer, and in the previous spring Rodzinski had promised him a performance of one of his works for each five planes he shot down. He was as good as his word and this performance, at which Wing Commander Wooldridge was present, marked his fifth kill. The piece was serious and full of the sincerity of youth; the critics thought greater maturity would bring with it greater music.

On his fifty-first birthday Rodzinski celebrated by leading his orchestra in a "reading rehearsal" of a program of American works, including most notably the Fugue from the Fourth Symphony of Charles Ives, the first of that composer's works to be heard in Carnegie Hall's main auditorium. Afterward, the Philharmonic Women's Club held a surprise birthday party for the conductor. The party symbolized the hold he had managed to gain over his once reluctant orchestra and public. The orchestra was now so fond of him that when his wife gave birth to a son a group of his players appeared at his home to play a serenade to the infant.

Later in the season Rodzinski turned his podium over to the Brazilian composer, Heitor Villa-Lobos, who conducted two of his works. He also invited Virgil Thomson to conduct his own *Symphony on a Hymn Tune* on a program in which Wanda Landowska played two concertos.

Thomson also took over the Philadelphia Orchestra that season to lead the first performance of his *Suite for Orchestra.* One musical journal made a particularly apt comment on Thomson's music on this occasion: "One of the most attractive things about Mr. Thomson as a composer is that he dares to be unoriginal in a highly individual way."

On the popular side, the season was the first in which Richard Dyer-Bennet brought his odd, but esteemed, talents to Carnegie Hall for a recital. The critics found that his ability to project folk material had grown, as had the strength of his rather small voice. Even his diction and phrasing had improved.

Later on, the Spanish dancers, Argentinita, Pilar Lopez and José Greco combined their talents for a joint recital demonstrating another sort of folk tradition. And after them, Mata and Hari came up from Broadway where they were featured in Olsen and Johnson's *Laffing Room Only* to demonstrate their satirical abilities.

For the more high-brow audiences, Ruth St. Denis and Ted Shawn brought a number of their students to the hall to present a Jacob's Pillow Dance Festival, design to attract publicity and financial support to the "dance university" they were starting at Jacob's Pillow in Massachusetts. There was also a return, for charity, of the Toscanini-Horowitz-NBC Symphony team, playing a program of Toscanini stand-bys and featuring a performance of the Brahms Second Concerto.

As the season neared its end, tragedy altered the concert schedule. On April 12, 1945, for the first time since the assassination of Abraham Lincoln, the Philharmonic canceled a concert. On that day, in Warm Springs, Georgia, Franklin D. Roosevelt, thirty-second President of the United States, died of a cerebral hemorrhage. On the following afternoon the Boston Symphony went ahead with its concert, but altered its program to make a musical memorial to the dead leader. It played the Funeral March from Beethoven's *Eroica* Symphony, the first movement of Dimitri Shostakovich's Eighth Symphony and Randall Thompson's war-inspired *Testament of Freedom.*

Thus, the last wartime season of Carnegie Hall came to an end. By the time the musicians reconvened there the following fall, a very different mood would be abroad in the land and the Atomic Age would officially have begun in the sky over a Japanese city most Americans had never heard of.

Of course there was joy on August 14, 1945, the day Japan announced her unconditional surrender to the Allies, but some historians have noted an underlying restraint in America's victory celebrations, a restraint that was not present when the World War I came to an end. Eric F. Goldman put it this way: ". . . always, in the America of V-J, there were shadows. A nation accustomed to the categorical yes and no, to war or peace and prosperity or depression found itself in the nagging realm of maybe. The liberals worried over the conservatives and the conservatives watched the liberals with an uneasiness akin to dread. Conservatives, liberals, and the half of the nation which was not really either asked: Would events follow the same pattern as the last postwar? Was unprecedented boom to bring unprecedented bust? Was peace just a prelude to another war? "The questions broke into conversations as persistently, as much up and down the social scale, as the relish in victory and prosperity and a limitless future. Behind these questions was a further one, often too deeply felt to be expressed. If the pattern held, if history repeated itself, wouldn't another war suck everything into doomsday under those billowing atomic mushrooms?"

The Age of Ambivalence was about to begin. The postwar world was full of technological miracles which distracted Americans from large questions. That was probably a good thing. For the large questions were mostly insoluble and capable of afflicting those who thought too much about them with acute anxiety. America was traditionally an impatient nation, always seeking simple solutions. Now, suddenly, there was a shortage of quick and simple solutions. In a nation beset with the menace of Atomic Energy, the intransigence of the Soviets, the baffling problems raised by the emergence of colonial nations from beneath imperialism, in a time where everything was suddenly too big, in a nation where there were too many cars, too many subdivisions, too much money and too many people, patience, complicated thinking, even craftiness were needed. Fearfully, the nation retreated from considerations of large political realities at an alarming rate.

The retreat continues as this is written. It is true that there is a basic political consensus based on the half-century of economic and social revolution which culminated in the New Deal. It is also true that there is a negative consensus based on opposition to the Soviet Union. But in the first case there seems to be no concrete desire to extend the domestic social gains of the New Deal. In the second, there is no agreement at all about what to do to reverse the bloodless victory trend which the Soviets have enjoyed throughout the world since 1945. There is, instead, a fragmentation of American society, with individuals retreating more and more into themselves, allowing their concerns to extend no farther than the family circle. Ideologies no longer seem to attract or to excite.

Naturally, music and the other arts have reflected this increasing concern with the small and the personal. As in the postwar period of the Twenties, the arts have once again turned inward on themselves; they have been less concerned with the social considerations, more concerned with craft and technique. Once more, art attempts to teach no lessons, preach no moral. That job is left to the mass communicators. The rejection of social aims in art, the retreat to purity after the flirtations with folk and popular traditions did not, of course, occur all at once.

The 1945 season, in fact, began with a work that was perhaps the climactic one in the folkloristic trend. It was Aaron Copland's *Appalachian Spring Suite*. Originally written as a "Ballet for Martha" it was originally scored for a thirteen-piece ballet orchestra. When Martha Graham had first staged the work in 1944 it was a triumph. Descriptive of a pioneer celebration of the spring, it was expanded for full orchestra and premiered October 4, 1945, by the Boston Symphony. It received more critical praise than any American work of the decade and won both the Pulitzer Prize and the Critics' Circle prize.

This was a good year for the older modern composers. Monteux, conducting the Philadelphia Orchestra, gave the first New York performance of the *Suite Symphonique* by Ernest Bloch; George Szell, leading the Philharmonic, presented Schönberg's Theme and Variations in G minor, an impeccably orchestrated work which was highly impressive. Darius Milhaud led the same orchestra, a few weeks later, in his own *Suite Française* which had "the flavor of French conversation, cuisine, landscape and life." Twice in that season the Boston Symphony presented Prokofieff's Fifth Symphony, a remarkably pure work which Olin Downes thought was one of "the most interesting, and probably the best that has come from Russia in the last quarter-century," a judgment which persists today. The Philharmonic's last important premiere of the season was Roy Harris' *Memories of a Child's Sunday*, a frankly programmatic work which was developed at greater length than its thematic materials warranted.

But perhaps the most important premiere of the season took place at a concert of the New York Little Symphony in the recital hall. The work was Charles Ives' Third Symphony which had lain around in a barn in Connecticut for some forty years before it was allowed to make this modest debut conducted by Lou Harrison. This was racy, virile, tremendously original music, remarkable in its modernity even though it had been written at a time when American music as a whole was mired in the ooze of a genteel romanticism.

The first postwar year also saw the debut of Andrés Segovia, the classical guitarist, who had previously confined his work to smaller halls. His finely-spun tones were not lost in those vast reaches and the demand to hear this rather special artist had grown to the point where the hall's large capacity was absolutely essential to him.

One of the most important postwar developments was a growing demand for all kinds of music. After the Depression years, and the pressing distractions of the war years, New York was eager for music. It also had money to spend and a desire for all the pleasures of peace. In October of 1946 the number of concerts in Town Hall and Carnegie Hall was nearly twice that which had been normal since 1930. By the following season, it reached a peak of ninety-five concerts in the opening month. But a downward motion set in after that and the bookings began to drop until, in 1946, the number was once again down to around forty for the month.

This growing interest was reflected in another way. In July of 1946 a whole trainload of equipment was shipped from Hollywood to New York and installed in Carnegie Hall as Boris Morros, the noted counterspy, began production of his film *Carnegie Hall.* Streets were torn up as heavy cable, capable of handling the electrical load imposed by klieg lights and other equipment, was installed. From then until October, something known as a cast of thousands labored in the unairconditioned hall to make the film.

The picture had quite a few firsts to its credit. It was the first feature-length movie in some forty years to be shot in New York and thus started a steadily growing trend back to the city. It was also the first film to use stereophonic sound, with twelve separate tracks, and it was projected on a curved screen. It was also the first film to bring together so much musical talent. Included in the cast were Damrosch,

Rodzinski, Walter, Stokowski and Fritz Reiner. On the set Piatigorsky, Rubinstein and Heifetz, Risë Stevens, Jan Peerce, Ezio Pinza and Lily Pons, rubbed shoulders with Harry James, Vaughan Monroe and his orchestra and hundreds of extras sweltering in dress clothes. There was even a brief appearance by Olin Downes, playing himself. It required two and a quarter hours to show the completed film which opened with premieres quite in keeping with Morros' lavish filming budget in May, 1947.

The only trouble with the whole thing was the plot. Before beginning work on the picture Rubinstein had cracked, "I bet it ends up with Harry James playing the trumpet." Little did he dream how right he was. The plot had Marsha Hunt as a charwoman at the hall taking her son to concert after concert in order to instill in him the desire to be a serious pianist. This was the clothesline to which the musical sequences were pegged. In due course the boy grew up to be William Prince and he tried to be a serious musician—he really did—but his heart wasn't in it. Horror of horrors, he wanted to be a jazzman. Needless to say, he finally got to appear on the great stage—but conducting a performance of something called "57th St. Rhapsody" with none other than Mr. James as soloist. It made for a happy fade-out, but it was something of an anticlimax.

One critic thought the picture "likely to tax the patience of even the hardiest of music lovers, and to drive all others out into the night." Olin Downes disagreed. He observed people staying through it twice and he paid tribute to the high quality of the musical performances and the sound recording. He paid tribute, too, to Morros for "the initiative to prove that fine music, in and for itself, can be purveyed on a grand scale on the screen." He only regretted that the story did not embody, in a first-class way, "all the romance and glamour that Carnegie Hall means to music and America."

In between the filming and the premiere there *was* a real musical season in Carnegie Hall, and a rather good one at that. Early on, Pierre Monteux, leading the Philadelphia Orchestra, produced "the most beautiful orchestral sounds" Virgil Thomson had ever heard as he led that ensemble in readings that were "pure glow and luminosity, loveliness, brightness and sheer auditory incandescence." The featured work was William Pijper's Third Symphony, a piece "thoroughly characteristic of the 1920's" in its contrary harmonies and counterpoint, its masterly uses of dissonance, some of them distinctly jazzy. It was harsh, arbitrary music, and perhaps a harbinger of things to come.

From Russia came Prokofieff's *Ode to the End of the War*, which was commonplace and swollen but stirring to the less sophisticated. On the same Philadelphia Orchestra program was Manuel Rosenthal's *St. Francis of Assisi* which was not unusual but smooth. Dimitri Shostakovich's Ninth Symphony was hugely enjoyed a couple of weeks later when Rodzinski conducted it. Shostakovich had become a genuine favorite in America during the war. The stormy petrel of Russian music had been in and out of grace with the authorities at home, but he had always been able to turn out a piece of "socialist realism" when he needed to regain standing. The average listener in America found socialist realism quite congenial, for it was often programmatic, avoiding like the plague atonalism and the "bourgeois formalism" so offensive, oddly, to the bourgeois. This often produced the awesome dullness noted in the Prokofieff work. Shostakovich, however, had a saving wit which was as baking soda in the heavy dough of party-line music. The Ninth was a perfect example of this. It started out to be a celebration of the Soviet Army's World War II victory, but it ended up a waspish, sprightly bit of burlesque, and a nose-thumbing at musical traditions. It was exceedingly well received here. The Red Army had to wait until the Tenth Symphony for its tribute, and then it turned out to be routine and overblown.

During the next weeks at the Philharmonic, guests took over, with Manuel Rosenthal conducting an all-French program that contained some minor new works and George Szell doing the new Ricercare for Piano and Orchestra with the composer as soloist in this elaborately modern use of a form dating back to the sixteenth century.

During this period the recital season contained a number of delights including a memorable concert by Nathan Milstein, "one of the most distinguished violinists now playing the violin in public," a satirical dance program in which Iva Kitchell did a priceless take-off on Martha Graham and a new work called "Soul in Search" which undermined a whole passel of modern dancers and trends. Miss Graham herself appeared with the Louisville Symphony a month later. Up in the recital hall John Cage's specially prepared pianos, with bits of wood, felt, rubber and metal inserted between the strings in order to change the pitch, were vigorously thumped to the acute discomfiture of traditionalists. This year of 1946 was also the one in which Igor Stravinsky made his debut as a "pop" composer. Woody Herman and his herd brought forward his *Ebony Concerto*. Wrote one critic: "A group of able musicians were so fired . . . that an entirely new kind of jazz eloquence and playing decorum was instituted."

Then came the season's bombshell. Artur Rodzinski left the orchestra, as he had previously left the Cleveland Orchestra, in mid-season. He fired off a twenty-one gun parting salute, in which he charged that Arthur Judson, the orchestra's manager and also head of Columbia Artists Management, was using the orchestra to promote the careers of artists managed by Columbia. This, he said, infringed on his prerogatives as musical director and he was fed up. The Philharmonic board tried to patch things up, offered him a three-year contract with a salary raise. Rodzinski, instead, accepted a contract to lead the Chicago Symphony at something like $30,000 less than he was making in New York. The Philharmonic board ended public discussion of the charges by saying that it, not Judson, was running the show and that they approved his management. The charges, however, hung in the air for a long time and were revived nine years later when the orchestra again was under pressure to improve the quality of its offerings. Then Judson went, but so did the current musical director.

In 1947 the Philharmonic quickly appointed Bruno Walter as "musical advisor" and, following its immemorial custom, engaged a string of guests to engage in another "so you want to lead a band" contest. Among them were Stokowski, Mitropoulos, Szell and Charles Munch. This system persisted until 1949 when Stokowski and Mitropoulos engaged in a sort of semifinal as co-conductors with the latter emerging as the winner in 1949.

Munch made his American debut in the month of Rodzinski's departure leading the American premiere of Arthur Honegger's Third Symphony. "The instant Charles Munch raised his baton," the *Times* commented, ". . . it was evident that we had with us a superb musician and orchestra leader to boot. The beat, the gesture, sometimes very economical, sometimes high, wide and handsome, brought immediate results." The Honegger piece was dramatic, dissonant and perhaps more external than deeply tragic as it had been intended to be.

A February concert by Eugene Istomin produced a telling bit of social commentary by Virgil Thomson. He was enchanted by the young pianist's rendition of Ravel's *Gaspard de la Nuit* and by his work with other modern composers. But he noted that although Istomin played the romantics with "what grace and sentiment he can muster," his heart was not really in it. In this, Thomson thought, he was typical of the other young recitalists. "Their dealings with Romanticism are a child's version of an old wives' tale, or a city boy's dream of the Far West. They are Romanticism's drugstore cowboys, or at best college students who know the heroic days out of books and photographs. But they do know their time, love it, and take it for eternal, just as the Romantics did theirs. That is why they can make beauty of its masterpieces. That part of their work is real and thoroughly grand. The rest is just culture."

Thomson thought this was healthy, much more so than if the reverse were true. The older recitalists, most of whom still dominate the concert stage, of course, are products of the older tradition. They are at home in it and just a bit awkward when confronted by new music which they find uncongenial to them. They are great, many of them destined for immortality, but in the work of the younger players who in a short time will be at the pinnacle, we can see the final triumph of modernity. And when they play Bartók or Schönberg or Stravinsky they will play before audiences to which the scandalous music of the years since 1918 is the ordinary stuff of artistic existence. It began to seem in 1947, and it seems increasingly so now, that the triumph of modern music (meaning that it will receive its fair share of time in the ongoing repertory theater which a concert hall is) is merely a matter of time.

The end of the 1946-1947 season brought two artists back from wartime exile. One was Madame Kirsten Flagstad who had left America to return to German-occupied Norway to be with her husband

Columbia Records Photo

Artur Rodzinski restored the Philharmonic briefly to greatness, then quit in 1948, after a dispute with the management over his conductorial prerogatives.

during the war. He had been accused of collaborating with the Nazis but had died before being brought to trial. No charges were ever lodged against Flagstad and she brought with her a certificate attesting to her patriotism issued by the Norwegian Supreme Court. Nevertheless, there was trouble with the musicians' union, which only grudgingly issued her a temporary card allowing her to sing here. On the night of her return to Carnegie Hall dozens of pickets milled about outside the hall, while inside she received an ovation from a packed house. The pickets were to become a fairly frequent sight outside the hall in the next few years as artists like Gieseking and Furtwängler, who had tried to stay above politics and had gone on plying their art in Hitler's Europe, returned here. It is odd that after its exemplary conduct during the war, remarkably free of the prejudice which had so marred its cultural pursuits during World War I, the nation found itself witnessing this kind of demonstration—something that had not happened after World War I. Most reprehensible of all, it was often the liberal groups, usually the first to defend the freedom of art, who participated in these picketings.

Much less controversial was the debut of a young pianist, Leo Sirota, who should have made his American debut long before. At the outbreak of the war he and his wife had been in the Far East and had been interned by the Japanese. His story was one of remarkable bravery. In the prison camp he had managed to construct a silent keyboard out of scraps of wood and on that he practiced throughout the three and a half years of war. He was received most kindly, but he was not able to have the major career he might have had if there had been no war.

One senses a lack of direction in the musical season of 1947-1948, a sudden break in the continuity with the past. It was not just that the Philharmonic was once again back in the hands of various strangers. It was not just that no new soloists of real distinction appeared on the scene this year. It was not just that this was the year that the beloved old master, Fritz Kreisler, played for the last time in public, breaking one of the musical world's strongest living ties with the nineteenth century. It was more than that. There was a distinct feeling in the air that music was looking around for new directions in which to travel. There was little interest this year in the realistic aesthetic which had so dominated the composers for the last seventeen years. The last ode to victory, the last dirge for the fallen had been written. It would have been ludicrous in the U.S.A., circa 1947, once again to write "proletarian" tone poems. What was good and useful in that tradition had passed into the bloodstream of high art, as had jazz before it. What was ephemeral in the tradition could not survive in an era which was bored with liberalism and suspicious of the left in general because of the increasingly hostile activities of the Soviet Union. The debut at Carnegie Hall of Leonard De Paur's Infantry Chorus, a smartly drilled and well-liked group of Negro veterans, represented a final phase in the prewar and wartime interest in folk and popular music. In the postwar years, music, like all of America, was groping for new answers, new statements to make, new ideas in which to believe.

During this season and the one that followed, there was a return to the fathers of modern music, a replaying of their works, a re-examination of the significance of the pieces which had been written before the Great Crash of 1929.

Thus we find Ormandy and the Philadelphia Orchestra opening their New York season with excerpts from *Wozzek* and we find them being greeted by the following remark: "It is chromatic music of straightforward romantic feeling that should cause no real confusion today twenty-seven years after its completion." When Leon Barzin's National Orchestral Association presented Bartók's Second Piano Concerto with Andor Földes as soloist a month later, another critic wrote, "possibly the most astonishing thing about it is that it should have taken so long to reach New York." And when David Diamond's new Fourth Symphony was presented by the orchestra of the Juilliard School the reaction was that the difficult young American composer had changed his style, made it more simple. The symphony was extremely well-liked. The same reaction greeted Paul Hindemith's *Symphonia Serena*. The work "confirmed suspicions that Hindemith is entering into a phase in which elements of charm, of luminousness in texture, of the broader contrasts in mood are allowed freer reign . . ."

Maybe so. But the truth was that now, after so many years, a sizable number of listeners, who had once found twentieth-century music grating, could accept it. The critics and a steadily growing minority of concert-goers were capable of appreciating it, even occasionally liking it. There even seemed to be a growing discrimination in the criticism of new work. Defenders of the new did not feel compelled to defend everything new. Conservatives seemed to feel no compulsion to discriminate totally against it. There was an increasing realization, at least among the knowledgeable, that a living music demanded real engagement with the work of the creators. Thus, the good new works now had a chance to be appreciated, while the indifferent were likely to be received indifferently. Perhaps Mahler's Sixth Symphony, heard for the first time in a Mitropoulos-Philharmonic performance was too harshly judged, but it is hard to question the judgment passed on Ernst Křenek's Fourth Symphony, an obvious attempt to write a masterpiece. It was dubbed "a pasteboard turkey." The man who applied the adjective, Virgil Thomson, was on the receiving end a little later when his *The Seine at Night* was presented by Stokowski and the Philharmonic. "A musical greeting card," sneered a fellow aisle sitter. Milhaud's Second Symphony presented by Charles Munch lacked "specific gravity." The Boston Symphony tried a new cello concerto by the loudly sensational Khatchaturian in the same April and one critic thought it stood "high on the list of musical works the world could do without." The same was said about the composer's *Russian Fantasy*, also an April offering. "Definitely poor music," said Downes, "noisy, banal, boring." Stravinsky's *Concerto for Strings*, on the same program, was simply "better bred in its clichés," and Walter Piston's Third Symphony was "a labored and fussy score, over-elaborated, of little impulsion and thematic interest."

It was perhaps significant of the new mood that Honegger's "big machine," *Jeanne d'Arc au Bucher*, that immense mélange of patriotic and religious sentiment was greeted with scorn in the more intellectual circles. That group's chief spokesman, Virgil Thomson, one of the few critics with a large view of music and its social functions, and therefore the most useful writer on the subject in this decade, was most astute on this work. While he conceded that the performance by the

Philharmonic, under Munch, with Vera Zorina as Jeanne, was perfection, he nevertheless entered a dissent from popular opinion on the piece. It "aims to please all," he said, "by exploiting religious and patriotic sentiment without doctrinal precision." Therefore it fit well the mood of a nation tired of the niceties of dialectics. "It appeals to the theater instinct in us all by the realistic evocation of horror scenes. It appeases the lover of modern music with bits of polytonal composition. It impresses all by its elaborate mobilization of musical effectives ... [but] the effort to please everybody in every possible way has left the whole effort touched with a flavor of insincerity, that same flavor we know so well from our own 'big machines' of radio and films."

But if *Jeanne d'Arc* created a significant debate, there was no debate about the quality of Vladimir Horowitz's celebration of the twentieth anniversary of his American debut. He played the Tchaikovsky concerto, the work in which he had outraced Beecham. Now, with Walter conducting, there was no race; just simple greatness. The critics vied with one another in the application of adjectives as they attempted to convey their reactions on this occasion, and the audience applauded between each movement.

"Here," said Olin Downes, "is modern virtuosity and romantic passion, meticulous musicianship and the grand manner. This is the freedom that results from years of self-criticism and searching of the artistic conscience. And the realization that the master of an art must first learn to obey before he can command. This is Horowitz at the height of his power ..."

The following season, 1948-1949, Byron Janis, a pupil of Horowitz, made his debut at Carnegie Hall. "Whatever he touched he made significant and fascinating," wrote Downes. It seemed to be the beginning of a great career which has not yet been totally fulfilled. On the other hand, Gary Graffman, having placed second in the second annual Rachmaninoff Piano Prize, was given a "special award" of a recital and played at almost the same time without great success, yet went on to win the coveted Leventritt Piano Competition and to become one of the more highly regarded of the new crop of pianists.

Among the other recital events of the year which attracted more than ordinary attention was the farewell recital of Efrem Zimbalist, who after thirty-eight years on the concert stage could still produce tones of extraordinary beauty with the greatest refinement and ease. Another link with the past was broken that November evening. The first trumpet recital in New York's history a few weeks later—by a woman named Edna White—could hardly ease the pain of parting. Neither could another John Cage recital, this time of a group of sonatas for the specially prepared piano played by Mario Ajemian in the recital hall. The sonatas seemed "gentle almost to the point of gentility" and there was no cry of outrage, for the fabulous ear of John Cage had enabled him to produce "gleaming combinations of overtones such as have never been heard before in Western music." The only trouble was that practically no one was aware of the existence of this exciting—if limited—new kind of music.

The orchestral season, in the middle of which Mitropoulos and Stokowski were announced as co-conductors for the following season—was virtually a duplicate of the preceding one. Again there was a re-examination of the music of the earlier years of the present century, with an early Mitropoulos concert providing the most interesting work—Schönberg's *Five Orchestral Pieces* which, since written in 1909, had received exactly one and three-fifths performances in New York. They were delicate, coloristic pieces, almost impressionistic in nature. Virgil Thomson thought they were "an etherealization of a theme that is at bottom just good old Vienna," and delivered himself of the opinion that they deserved all of their world-wide prestige and none of their world-wide neglect. A little later a reading by the Philharmonic under Walter of Norman Dello Joio's *Variations, Chaconne and Finale* brought that often underestimated composer his best reviews so far and even a hearty round of applause when he was brought to the stage. Mitropoulos conducted the work which probably interested the wider public the most in 1948-1949—the *Rhapsody for Orchestra* by Artur Schnabel. Schnabel's notes for the piece steadfastly insisted that it was atonal music, but to most people it sounded fundamentally lyrical, emotional and dramatic. Not only that, the music was persistently tonal. Schnabel was extremely gratified by the performance and by the warm response he received from the audience. Three weeks later he was stricken with the heart attack from which he never fully recovered.

In many ways Mitropoulos and the man with whom he was to share the Philharmonic podium the next season, Stokowski, were very much alike. Both were at their best in the showier pieces of the late romantic and the modern repertory, both had a love of the dramatic, both were ardent champions of new music. If the effective range of Stokowski was a little wider, if his showmanship was a bit more adroit, if his talents for discipline and organization were greater, it can be said of Mitropoulos that his tastes were more modest, less eccentric than those of the older man. At any rate, Stokowski's Philharmonic programs this season were, as might be expected, at least as adventurous as those of his colleague. He presented the premiere of Hindemith's *Philharmonic Concerto*, which represented that master at his most aridly academic. Vaughan Williams' Sixth Symphony turned out to be far more successful, modern yet somehow recalling the England of the romantic poets. It was lovely and fresh and full of beauty. He also programmed new works by John Alden Carpenter, Benjamin Britten, Sergei Prokofieff and Carl Ruggles, nearly all of them received in *comme ci, comme ça* fashion. If the orchestra was a bit out of sorts again, serving many masters, Mitropoulos and Stokowski were at least keeping it in the twentieth century whence it had been dragged by Rodzinski.

The finest Boston Symphony program of the year was composed entirely of music by Igor Stravinsky and was led by Stravinsky himself. The features were something old and something new. The old were the *Concerto for Piano and Wind Orchestra*, a jazzy, gusty work dating from 1924, and the Concerto in D for Strings, a virtuoso piece of charm and lightness of touch. The new consisted of the concert version of his *Orpheus* ballet, which carefully avoided the vehement and the melodramatic, and the *Ode in Three Parts for Orchestra*. This was a memorial to Serge Koussevitzky's late wife, a tender and elegiac work, very much the product of a modern master who could make something fresh and new from materials which might have been borrowed from him by lesser men seeking to follow the fashion he had set.

The season was the last for Serge Koussevitzky, who had led the

Boston Symphony for a quarter of a century. He was now aging, not totally well, greatly saddened by the death of his wife. He retired full of honors, none of them better considered than the farewell bid him by Virgil Thomson: "No other musical interpreter living has done so much for so many all over the world. . . . He has assumed the music of his time (and it has been a long time) to be worthy of his support, financial, musical and moral. . . . His huge personal talent has been devoted to a cause, that cause the inclusion of the living creator, along with the listener, in the life of art. It is only just that at this time the whole world of music make him aware of its gratitude for services rendered, pay him some outward sign of the deep honor it owes him."

Here was another leading member of the older order passing from the scene, a man who had represented the finest in that tradition, and who had therefore always been mindful of his obligation to the future.

Another man who had fulfilled his obligations to the future also departed that year. Rabbi Stephen Wise died on April 19 at the age of seventy-five. In a letter found in his wallet he suggested that services be held for him in Carnegie Hall "where I preached for thirty years and with which I became associated during the stronger years of my life." Writing of the services, his friend John Haynes Holmes, the noted liberal minister, said: "It seemed at times that Wise would never be understood in the full grandeur of his being. In the crowning years of his heroic struggle against wickedness and wicked men, he was necessarily the fighter with heroic cries upon his lips. Men feared him for his power, but worked with him because of the mighty deeds he did and the public meetings that drew such crowds. But it was these crowds, the common people, who understood him all along, and knew the pitying heart within which was all but smothered by the thundering storm without. It was all at last so clearly disclosed in the funeral services at Carnegie Hall. As I looked about me and saw the great throng of men and women crowding that vast auditorium as a full tide fills the sea, I whispered to my soul, 'They knew him for his greatness.' Then the service was done, and we marched on the rain-swept streets and saw crowds of patient witnesses, waiting, mile after mile, 'through storm and flood,' to pay their last honors to the dead, and again my soul whispered to itself, 'These knew him and loved him for his goodness.'"

The great rabbi had lived long enough to see most of the political reforms he had fought for become reality. He had also, unfortunately, lived long enough to see vicious parodies of liberalism take place both inside and outside the hall where for so long he had lifted his voice in good causes.

A couple of months before he died liberals again picketed a concert of Kirsten Flagstad. A mob prevented the appearance of Gieseking, who had received a visa from the government to appear in America but who less than two hours before his concert was forced to cancel it as the result of pressure group protests. Besides picketing Carnegie Hall, various organizations had managed to apply pressures in Congress. As a result, the pianist was forced to stay in the custody of immigration officials, then given orders to leave the country before 11:00 A.M. on the Sunday following the scheduled concert.

Finally, on March 26th, about sixty protestors bearing placards reading, "Exterminate the Red Rats," "Free Cardinal Mindszenty," "You can't have culture without freedom," "We want freedom, not slavery" and chanting slogans like "Go back to Russia where you belong," and "We don't want you, you're too red for us," milled about outside the hall protesting what was widely regarded as a Communist-inspired "Cultural and Scientific Conference for World Peace."

It was a rowdy group. They booed and shouted at persons entering and leaving the hall, called one clergyman "Fascist" and "traitor" as he left, taunted members of the audience who hesitated to leave the hall by crying, "Come out and get your medicine. Don't be yellow, you Benedict Arnolds."

Some 200 policemen were on hand to keep order, and they kept moving those delegates to the conference who were of a mood to argue with the pickets. The police were given the most trouble by a woman who demonstrated her patriotism by darting out of the picket line to squirt a water pistol at members of the audience. Police finally got her to desist by pointing out that instead of hitting her targets she was managing only to wet the cops' uniforms.

Had the pickets been inside the hall they might have been surprised by at least one speech, that of Harvard astronomer Harlow Shapley. He set out to make it very clear that, as a scientist, he could not abandon his objectivity and that although he could not honestly favor America in all its disputes with Russia he firmly believed "the evidence is clear that at this time . . . individual freedom is sorely restricted in the East." He called upon America to end racial discrimination, to ease curbs on freedom of scientific investigation so that it could enter the propaganda war with the Soviet bloc with clean hands.

He also attempted to inject rationality into the conference by calling on it to remember that "ours is a conference for world peace, not for unilateral or bilateral ill-will. We seek to promote the necessary understanding and good-will, and not to incite further the atmosphere of distrust."

Shapley was a trifle naïve, for the conference was a last gasp attempt by the far left (its Progressive Party led by Henry Wallace had been defeated by Truman in the 1948 election) to make a bid for popular support and to score propaganda points for the Soviets. But his was a voice of reason raised amidst passionate ideological howls by both the radical left and the old guard right. The other speakers of the conference, men like lawyer O. John Rogge and editor Ted Thackrey made speeches referring to the old anti-Capitalist clichés and attacking American aid to Greece and Turkey, the latter an enlightened first step toward a policy of containment of Communism, a precursor of Point Four and the Marshall Plan. These and other speeches of the conference were not subversive; they were simply unrealistic in a nation which was entering a new phase in its history, a phase in which slogans, of left and right, were useless as political tools.

America, as it entered the Fifties, was a sorely confused country. As early as 1946 Dean Acheson had declared, "Our name for problems is significant. We call them headaches. You take a powder and they are gone." But, he said, the new problems of the world were not so easily disposed of. "They . . . will stay with us until death. We have got to understand that all our lives the danger, the uncertainty, the need for alertness, for effort, for discipline, will be upon us. This is new for us. It will be hard for us." The demonstration outside Carnegie Hall was therefore perfectly symbolic of the times. Those on the pavement of Fifty-seventh Street and those inside the hall were seeking in their different ways some simple solution to the perplexities of existence in a period totally unlike anything in past history. The thrust toward progressive and liberal solutions for domestic problems, a thrust which had been one of the chief motive powers in recent American history, was now virtually stopped. The old ways of dealing with the world beyond the oceans were no longer applicable. True ideological debate in the United States was virtually a thing of the past. On every hand there was the hysteria of a nation lost, an hysteria which would shortly lead to the fanatical excesses of McCarthyism on the one hand and "the peculiar war" of Korea, perhaps the most ambivalently conducted war in American history, on the other. The Cultural and Scientific Congress for World Peace was a last attempt to proceed in the old ways; the violent reaction to it was a symbol of the noisy gropings to come.

Ten

"Suddenly There Are Mass Markets . . ."

WE ARE STILL TOO CLOSE TO THE 1950'S TO ASSESS WITH ANY CONFIDENCE their cultural significance. But a few generalizations can be made. The basic one is that it was the decade of the middle-brow. The long-term trend to what is almost universal higher education reached its height in this period and the result is undoubtedly the largest (although certainly not the best) audience for culture in the history of Western Civilization. Art is currently a boom market, and no segment of that market is booming more loudly than music.

By the end of 1959 Americans were spending $425 million a year on phonograph records alone. These were being pressed by 1500 companies at a rate of 500 a week and being sold in 8000 record stores to the occupants of the 26 million American homes which possessed phonographs. In the mid-Thirties, three companies were splitting a seven and one-half million dollar market; in 1948 the market was only $173 million. Much of this increase is the result of the marketing of the long-playing record in 1949. It brought convenience to listening. The days were past when extremely brittle 78-rpm records had to be changed every three minutes. In the Fifties it became possible to put six to eight hours' worth of music on a turntable without having to desert the easy chair more than once in that time to flip the stack of discs. Further, the records were easy to store, the equipment on which to play them became more and more sensitive, until, finally, stereo was able to give a fair approximation of actually having a symphony orchestra in the living room.

Here was a chance to be "cultured"—in the privacy and convenience of your own home. You needed only to have a shelf of records to prove it. Another class line had thus been broken. Carnegie Hall, after all, can hold only 2700 people. Here was a chance to have, with ease and passivity, the status that automatically accrues to the purchaser of a concert ticket. The economic ability to purchase the status symbols had to be present, of course. But in the America of the 1950's that was no problem. Almost everybody had the money to buy the good things. And music is, and traditionally has been, one of the great good things.

There was only one trouble with this process of democratization of culture. Culture itself was cheapened by it.

Way back in 1913 the Italian avant-gardist Luigi Russolo theorized that, scientifically speaking, music consists of sound, that sound is merely noise and that the future of music lay in the production of bigger and better noises. At the higher intellectual level a few musicians have acted on that theory (for example, Varèse) and have produced some interesting works as a result. Most Americans have never heard of Russolo; they merely spend their time listening to music which over and over again seems to demonstrate the pertinency of his theory. We therefore have the noisiest society in human history. Even *Time*, that staunch defender of a nebulous concept known as The American Way of Life, has said that "the music boom sometimes seems less a cultural awakening than a mammoth assault of indiscriminate sounds on a public that no longer has any place to hide. . . . Music in wild profusion volleys forth from phonographs, radios, television sets, jukeboxes. Piped music ushers untold thousands of Americans into the world (hospital delivery rooms), through it (garages, restaurants and hotels) and out of it (mortuary slumber rooms)." As with nearly everything else, we have quantity confused with quality and spend more on music than all the rest of the world put together.

To be sure, this picture of a mass society wallowing indiscriminately in a cacophony of strange sounds is an overly dreary one. In a nation spending upwards of $400 million on records, $685 million on phonographs and component parts, $30 million on sheet music, $55 million on concert admissions, $35 million on performance royalties to publishers and composers, and paying $352 million to the various pipers it listens to, some part of the noise must be meaningful—good music, well performed, attentively and appreciatively listened to.

Music also plays a role as a sort of occupational therapy for members of the lonely crowd. There are now some 70,000 amateur musical organizations in the country which give public concerts. Some 30 million musical instruments are owned by Americans, and in the last twenty years the number of amateur instrumentalists has doubled while the population has increased by only about one-third. The end of stagnation and actual decline in the sale of instruments and sheet music came in 1947. Such sales were only at the $90 million level in 1941; today they are in excess of $500 million. They will continue to grow. Ninety per cent of the nation's schools provide some sort of musical training. These have 68,000 instrumental musical organizations. In addition, there are about 500,000 private music teachers in America and between them, the private and public school music teachers instruct 8,500,000 school-age children in music.

All of this, of course, reflects the increased leisure time Americans now enjoy, a need to escape in some "worthwhile" way from the tensions and anxieties of modern life, the higher income levels which allow Americans to indulge themselves in cultural pursuits, and even improved teaching methods and easier-to-play instruments. It also reflects a snowball effect: the more people making and appreciating music the more their neighbors want to join in the fun and to provide their children with opportunities to learn.

What does it all mean? Bernard De Voto, that great apologist for mass culture, pointed out that "a generation ago most Americans were musical illiterates; today many of them are initiates at the age of twelve and connoisseurs and sophisticates at sixteen." Leonard Bernstein, the quintessential musical figure of our present era says, "Americans have become closer to music, have a deeper appreciation, have become qualitative music lovers."

On the surface it would seem that the wildest dreams of the nineteenth-century exponents of culture for the masses would be pleased beyond measure by the figures just listed, and by the statements of De Voto and Bernstein. Surely Walter Damrosch and Theodore Thomas, were they to glance at the figures, would believe that their labors had not been in vain. Andrew Carnegie, who devoted so much of his fortune to the education of the masses, would be, in that place where the cherubim play the bagpipes and seraphim the organ, a happy man if he could see the balance sheet we have just drawn.

But the figures lie, or rather tell only a partial truth. A few years ago, when a musical organization ran a workshop for community orchestra conductors it was discovered that almost half of them could not beat six-eight time. Vladimir Horowitz in the Fifties blamed the quality of American instruction for the lack of top-flight young recitalists. Where, he wondered aloud, were the Rubinsteins and Heifetzes of tomorrow coming from. Precious few with that potential debuted at Carnegie Hall in the Fifties.

Then there is the matter of the figures within the figures of America's musical participation. Take the 425 million spent annually on records. Only 85 million of it is spent on recordings of unquestionably good music. The rest is spent on show tunes, the perversions of Mantovani and his imitators, popular music which seems to get worse and worse each year, and imitation folk songs ground out by the hacks of Tin Pan Alley and Nashville, Tennessee. This seems to prove an old truth about the wide diffusion of high culture in a mass society. The culture itself tends to become thinned out as it is spread around over a wider area; it becomes weaker. Instead of dragging the large number of people to its plane, it is leveled down. We shall see evidences of this process in the programs of Carnegie Hall during the Fifties.

But, of course, a high musical culture continues to exist. Surrounded and besieged by the bourgeoning mass musical culture, it somehow manages to survive. In the recent history of concert auditoriums like Carnegie Hall we can see its manifestations. But it exists largely because the mass audience is really quite amiably disposed toward *all* music. As Thomson pointed out way back in 1942, "when they can't follow it, their attention merely wanders." Of the whole tradition of fine music, the material the mass audience likes best is that of the melodious nineteenth century. In this, they are very like the segment of the audience which bears the heaviest responsibility for supporting, financially and morally, a living tradition of music—the subscribers to symphony and opera series. As Thomson said, in the same article, the masses are very resistant to new music. "Their ability to analyze music is not, on the average, sufficient to enable them to get hold of it. They feel incompetent and hence inferior in front of it, hating, naturally enough, the cause of their inferiority feeling." The same may be said of the critics who, of course, write mainly for this audience. They will react unfavorably to any piece which is beyond the scope of their technical knowledge, for the same reason that the audience does.

Here is Thomson's analysis of the situation: "Although almost anybody . . . can get some communication out of modern music without half trying merely because its author is alive in the world we all live in, any further penetration of its meaning or estimate of its value to the living musical tradition is dependent on one's acquaintance with the whole tradition, including the living part of it." This poses the key question which all our statistics must answer. How good a job does all the expensive musical training and participation do in acquainting people with the whole musical tradition and thus creating an audience genuinely engaged in the musical life?

The evidence is inconclusive, but seems to weigh on the side of a pessimistic answer. An examination of the professional musical life in America seems to bear this out. Only about one-third of the professionally qualified musicians in America make the bulk of their living by playing. The rest play in their spare time or not at all. Further, it is quite simply impossible for the serious composer to make a living from his art in this country. The average royalty paid for a new piece performed by a major symphony orchestra is fifty dollars, and that must be split evenly with the composer's publisher. Recently, when one of the largest foundations commissioned a group of young composers to write concertos, and a number of recitalists to learn them and to play them with major orchestras, it was the soloists, not the composers, who got the larger fees.

But before one begins to envy the recitalist, he should be aware that there are at the top only two or three dozen recitalists and that hundreds of talented young musicians are doomed to endless toil on what can only be regarded as the original treadmill to oblivion. The careers of these people are controlled by about twenty New York management concerns. Three of them however—Columbia Artists, National Artists, and Sol Hurok—control between them 90 per cent of the recital business in this country. Hurok, for the most part, manages only top names and manages them with great skill and considerable compassion. The first two, which supply artists to the some 1200 towns with community concert series, must bear the heaviest brunt of the responsibility for holding artists in perpetual thralldom. The situation in brief is this: the average civic concert series contains five concerts. But between a third and a half of its budget for artists goes to the single name artist who heads the season's list. Piddling amounts, as low as five hundred dollars, are paid the young artists who pad out the remainder of the list. They may have as few as a dozen concerts a year and by the time they pay their expenses, which are heavy, they are operating their careers at a financial loss. There is only one way for them to get off the treadmill. That is for them to score a New York sensation, preferably at Carnegie Hall. Mere success will not do. Every year a couple of dozen or so of these young artists receive good notices from the New York critics who, whatever their occasional shortcomings, are for the most part respected and intelligent people, fully conscious of the responsibility they carry. These notices may start a bit of a groundswell for the artist, but usually they do not, the general public being as little interested in new artists as they are in new music, and back they go on the community concert circuit. A perfect example of this is Van Cliburn. He won the Leventritt Piano Prize in 1954, which carried with it an appearance with the Philharmonic. He had the bad luck to be on a program with the premiere of a new Roy Harris symphony and that got the bulk of the major review space, although Cliburn's notices were in general very good. He spent the next four years toiling away unnoticed and went off to Russia in search of the Tchaikovsky Prize as a last desperate bid to make a name for himself. He succeeded beyond the wildest dreams of anyone. But he is a distinct exception to the general rule. Each year a surprising number of young artists of comparable ability simply give up the fight. The indifference is too much for them to combat.

It is this indifference to new artists and new music which is the measure of America's failure to create a truly educated musical audience. It is undoubtedly true that a higher percentage of our population can these days identify, after a few measures of listening, the theme of Tchaikovsky's Sixth Symphony. But they will not be a truly good audience for music until they can recognize the merit of a brand new piece they have never heard, be interested in its pure musical statement, judge it in a context of genuine knowledge of the whole musical tradition. It is fair to say that, at the moment, music is "just culture" to the vast majority of the American audience, that they find the deeper thrills of musical discovery irrelevant to their major concerns.

In the face of this indifference, the professional musical world, inhabited by people to whom music is the center of existence, has made a predictable response. It has drawn in upon itself. The patrons of composers these days are conductors and major recitalists. They are commissioning personally, or forcing managements to commission, new works. With the large foundations now in the field, it is the musicians themselves, sitting on boards and commissions, who are passing out to one another the prizes, commissions and fellowships which these quasi-public bodies sponsor. To a lesser extent, the younger recitalists are dependent on their friendships with conductors, who remain the glamour boys of the music field, for the important dates to play concertos. In turn, these tastemakers have worked out an uneasy relationship with their public. They sneak new works onto their programs, and balance them off with old favorites from the basic repertory. The monumental indifference of an audience in Carnegie Hall to a new work has to be seen to be believed (unless the work happens to be by one of the few composers whose status is unquestionable, a Copland or a Stravinsky). It is sort of a tit-for-tat arrangement. A public grateful for good readings of the standard repertory will allow a favorite conductor or soloist to indulge himself by playing a new work which they listen to blankly.

The public cannot be totally blamed for this. The withdrawal of the musicians into their own little world has led to the production of some very curious music, music which cannot help but be offensive and irrelevant to the public. Those tortured sounds, however, represent the agonized yelps and howls of artists who have given up the battle for communication, who, like neurotics, refuse to attempt to face an indifferent and hostile world. One suspects, however, that a search for first causes for the withdrawal of the artists would lead us to the door of the public, for no artist likes to live in a vacuum, and if he thought he could break through this public's armor of indifference, he probably would try. The proof of this can be seen in the musical activities of the Depression and war years. Goaded by the prevailing public philosophies, which stated that there was a basic unity among all peoples, a unity greater than the differences separating individuals, the artists, as we have seen, joined the other discriminated-against minorities and sought *rapprochement* with their society. The postwar years, with their prevailing every-man-for-himself ethic, born of failures of the unifying ideals of the previous decade and a half, have sent the artists scurrying for their storm shelters again. Their eventual emergence depends on whether or not there is again a shift in the national mood. Of that, no one can be certain. There is both hope in some signs, and despair in others. Like almost everything else in our time, the question is surrounded by ambiguities.

The history of the recitalists who appeared in Carnegie Hall in the Fifties is a good case in point. On the one hand, there were grievous losses, and a distinct feeling on the part of many that there was a lack of new talent to replace the losses. On the other hand, there were debuts by talented young people that gave the lie to the gloomy prophesies of an impending lowering of standards.

Certainly no loss was more shocking than the death of Simon Barere, the pianist, who died, on stage, at Carnegie Hall on April 2, 1951. The program, that night, was a benefit for the American Scandinavian Society which was inaugurating a new American-Scandinavian Music Center. The program was intended to be a gala. The orchestra was the Philadelphia under Ormandy. In the last half Set Svanholm was to sing and Erik Tuxen, a director of the Danish State Symphony Orchestra, was to make his American debut conducting Carl Nielsen's Fifth Symphony.

Ormandy began the program with a reading of Sibelius' Seventh Symphony which was received with great enthusiasm. Then Mr. Barere came on, bowed to the applause which greeted him and seated himself at the piano to play the Grieg Concerto. The first half of the first movement was flawless. Then, after he had been playing for about five minutes, his head slowly bowed forward until it was resting on the keyboard after which, "still in what seemed grotesque slow motion," he rolled off the stool to the left and fell to the stage with a thud that could be heard all over the house.

It was at that point that orchestra and conductor became aware that something was wrong. A sudden silence fell. There were gasps from the audience, a rustle of movement as men and women rose from their seats. The silence was only momentary, but it seemed interminable. Ormandy called for a doctor and one clambered over the footlights to minister to the pianist. Again, there was a long moment which seemed suspended in time. Finally the doctor motioned to orchestra players to help him carry Mr. Barere from the stage.

After a slight delay Svanholm came on to sing "King Erik's Songs" by the Swedish composer, Ture Rangström. Then came intermission. As the audience took their seats Lithgow Osborne, president of the American Scandinavian Society came on stage. "It is my sad duty," he said, "to announce that a very great artist has passed away. In respect to his memory Mr. Svanholm and Mr. Tuxen believe that this concert should come to an end here and that the audience will agree with us in paying respect to Mr. Barere."

There was another tense silence and then the audience quietly left the hall. Ormandy, speaking later to the press, described a conversation he had had with Barere just before going on stage. It was the fifty-four-year-old Barere's first performance with Ormandy. The pianist pointed this out to him and asked if he might wish it was not the last time. "I answered, 'Yes, of course,' " said Ormandy. "He was in a wonderful mood." The cause of death was a cerebral hemorrhage. It is the only such death in the history of the hall.

Until the death of Leonard Warren on stage at the Met in 1960, no loss to the music world was quite so dramatic, quite so tragic, as the death of Barere who was at the very height of his powers. But there were other losses. On February 1, 1952, Kirsten Flagstad announced, at the end of her recital, that she had decided, "after long and serious consideration that this is to be my last recital here."

There were shouts of "No!" from the audience, but the great singer continued, pointing out that she had announced her retirement from opera the previous season, but had been tempted into breaking her word by the opportunity to sing in the rivival of Gluck's *Alceste.* She said that she would sing it five more times that season and that she would appear one last time in Carnegie Hall, to sing with the Philharmonic under Bruno Walter. She made it clear that she was making her announcement that day because she wished to bid farewell personally to "this very dear audience" who attended her recitals which, she said were for her "the highlight of every season." When she appeared with the Philharmonic for her farewell appearance applause continued for twenty minutes after the end of her performance. Even her refusal to go on making curtain calls did not cause it to stop, and it was not stilled until concertmaster John Corigliano announced to the audience that Mme. Flagstad had left the auditorium. She reappeared again three years later in recital at Carnegie Hall, delighting everyone with the quality of her voice, but that brief reappearance was her last.

In the late fall of 1953 Roland Hayes, the fine Negro tenor, then sixty-six years old, returned to the hall to sing a 30th Anniversary concert. The occasion was heartwarming, as was the farewell, two years later, of another, greater, tenor, Beniamino Gigli, whose appearance on the stage at the age of sixty-five signaled an outburst at least as great in volume as that which Flagstad had received.

But not all of the older generation of recitalists were giving up their careers in the 1950's. Many were adding new achievements to previous triumphs. Walter Gieseking returned in the spring of 1953 and, despite a raucous collection of pickets outside, played with considerable success. The years had not treated him with great kindness, and "the power and cutting edge of his technique [were] modified to an extent that [forced] him carefully to calculate his effects and to restrain from strenuous tests of virtuosity." He, of course, still commanded great beauty of style, and he continued to play, amidst less violent political reactions, and to increasing veneration, until his death in 1956.

The return of another pianist after an absence of twenty-eight years was greeted with almost universal acclaim. Political questions did not intrude on the reputation of the seventy-year-old Wilhelm Bachaus when he returned to Carnegie Hall in April 1954. Not a great success in his early appearance in America, he was now the possessor of a towering European reputation. He played five Beethoven sonatas. "I left the hall convinced," Winthrop Sargeant wrote, "that I had never in my life heard Beethoven's music so magnificently, sensitively and authoritatively played."

Another venerable artist celebrated his fiftieth year on the concert stage in October 1954. Mischa Elman played the Tchaikovsky Violin Concerto on the same program on which the Shostakovich Tenth Symphony was introduced to America. He performed no longer as a young genius "in the flush of his youth and temperament, but [as] a musician greatly learned through experience and thought." Elman managed another fiftieth-anniversary celebration in January, 1959, this time the celebration of his American debut.

Artur Rubinstein, too, continued his recital activity unabated. In February 1956, he performed a concerto cycle, playing eighteen works in five concerts in two weeks. It was, in effect, the summing up of an artist's life work, and it was a superb summary. Rubinstein himself told Abram Chasins that "it is not really so difficult. After all, I've played these works all my life. Never well enough. Now, before it is too late, I want to play them all together, and perhaps more decently. I won't make a penny of course. But maybe I'll be able to feel that I've accomplished something better than just pounding keys for fifty years." Whatever his feelings, that is certainly what his audiences felt.

The musical world was less entranced by an incident involving another famous recitalist the following year. In December, 1957, Yehudi Menuhin, after playing Ernest Bloch's Violin Concerto with the Philharmonic—and playing it with great dedication and skill—decided to play some Bach as an encore. It was a violation of the Philharmonic's ground rules, rules based on the overtime demands of the musicians' union more than anything else. It caused a mighty tempest in a teapot. Wrote Howard Taubman of the *Times*: "It must be assumed that Mr. Menuhin was responding spontaneously to the warm approval the audience had given him. But the gesture reflected a lack of professional tact. It violated a tradition of an organization whose guest Mr. Menuhin was. What was worse, it disturbed the balance of the program and provided an unwarranted intrusion on the mood left by Bloch. And worst of all, Mr. Menuhin played the encore badly." At the repeat concert the next day he again played the encore. This time the Philharmonic requested that Menuhin please not do it again. At a third concert he gestured for silence, smiled and said, "I am not allowed." Then he added, "I am not at all sure you are allowed to applaud either. I am sure . . . that if Bach could realize what damage even two or three minutes of his music could do to the traditions and budgets of this great orchestra he would be very sorry." He concluded by saying that he and his colleagues on stage loved and were grateful for applause and assured the audience that they could applaud as much as they liked whenever they felt like it.

Later, in a letter to the *Times* he stated that he thought the matter of encores was not the proper concern of management and that he had repeated the encore at the second performance only to uphold his dignity after Taubman's scathing attack. "I fully realize," he wrote, "we all live today in a society that is becoming daily more complicated, and therefore we must all pay tribute to the growing control and organization which are evidently unavoidable. However, it is the moral duty of every individual to protect those rare moments which allow him the liberty of spirit which is his heritage. Art can only flower on this basis." It was a true and ringing statement. One can only wonder at the odd, slightly comic ground on which Menuhin took his stand.

Another artist who decided to make her stand for individualism in the Fifties was Maria Callas. She feuded with most of the opera houses of the Western world, claiming they were indifferent to the demands of art, sacrificing production quality to monetary considerations—and sacrificing proper treatment of singers as well. In 1958 she took on Rudolf Bing and the Metropolitan Opera Company over the number of performances she was to sing in a limited time. The result was the ending of her Met contract.

The situation was tailor-made for the special talents of a young impresario named Allen Oxenburg who, since 1952, had been staging concert versions of obscure operas which the larger companies avoided, first in Town Hall, then, when the demand grew, in Carnegie Hall. His

American Opera Society engaged Callas to sing Bellini's *Il Pirata* late in January. Callas, who is a dedicated singer when she is not scrapping with managers, was delighted. She particularly loves to revive old operas that are rarely heard, and the reputation of the American Opera Society guaranteed a high quality of work. The company had given first American operatic performances of unearthed works by Purcell, Monteverdi, Gluck, Handel and Cherubini. It had brought to America for the first time such foreign stars as Boris Christoff, Elisabeth Schwarzkopf and Giulietta Simionato and had given their first operatic chances to the fine American voices of Eileen Farrell, Rosalind Elias, Laurel Hurley and Albert da Costa.

Il Pirata gave Madame Callas a chance to prove that the rumors of voice failure which had attended her withdrawal from the Met were false. It also gave her impassioned claque an opportunity to cheer its heroine to the echo. They "thronged to see, hear and adore her," an observer reported. "Everything about the evening had the high tension of an event. Tickets were priced at a $25 top for orchestra seats. The gathering was a posh one, inclined largely to be idolatrous."

Callas was not at her best, until the end of the opera. Then with the only light in the hall a single spot shining on her alone she launched into her final aria. Up to them she "had sung with a grasp of the Bellini style and with enormous conviction. At times the voice had been ingratiating; at others it had had an edge. Top notes had been a gamble—either shrill or brilliantly in focus. But now at the end she did not fail. This was Miss Callas living up to her reputation."

The result was a tumult and a shouting, a rush down the aisles by hundreds to stand at the footlights and shout "Brava Maria." They did not leave until the house lights were turned off.

Part of Callas' immense appeal to the audiences of the Fifties was based on the simple fact that she appears to be the last in the great tradition of prima donnas, temperamental, fiery and demanding. Her personality was the stuff of legends, and the musical public was in need of legends.

The younger artists, many of them highly skilled technicians, lacked much of the old-time fire. In an egalitarian age, it is possible to breed skill, of course, but the grand manner seems virtually to have disappeared—perhaps because of its fundamentally undemocratic nature.

One young artist, however, had more than enough temperament and eccentricity to satisfy anyone longing for the good old days. He was Glenn Gould, the youthful pianist who debuted in New York in 1955 and who has returned frequently to receive notices both glowing and exasperated. He has a peculiar manner at the keyboard, rumpled and crumpled, the despair of piano teachers who have been convinced for years that good posture is a prerequisite for genius. Gould carries his own special Poland water with him at all times, has a specially constructed piano stool which accompanies him everywhere, and some highly original notions of how to play the repertory. After his 1957 Carnegie Hall concert, a conservative critic noted that "his touch is sensitive and many colored, his phrasing plastic and varied. . . . With all his turnings and twistings, foot-beatings, arm swoops and head-tossings, he plays with concentration and compels the attention of his audience." Everyone agreed that when he avoided the mannered and the precocious he was a young master, perhaps the finest of the new crop with the capabilities of one who could become a giant of the keyboard.

His only competition in his generation—in the public esteem, at any rate—is of quite a different sort. Van Cliburn is the last of the romantics, attracted to the lush melodies, the sweeping statements of Tchaikovsky and Rachmaninoff. He has yet to prove his versatility and the totality of his musicianship, but there is no denying that he was the phenomenon of the decade. Virtually unknown, he went to Russia in 1958 to compete in and win the Tchaikovsky Piano Competition. Perhaps it was because Americans were tired—in this world of the Cold War—of hearing that their achievements were all in the realm of the material that he was given a hero's welcome when he returned after his Russian triumph. He received a ticker-tape reception in New York, then played, with the Symphony of the Air under Russian conductor Kiril Kondrashin, the pieces that had won him the prize—the Tchaikovsky Piano Concerto and Rachmaninoff's Third Concerto. Scalpers were getting $150 a ticket for the performance and Cliburn did not disappoint those who had paid the price. As Louis Biancolli wrote: "We can all breathe easily now. The Russians were right." Paul Henry

Lang of the *Herald Tribune* thought it a shame that the Cliburn talent was wasted on what he regarded as empty showpieces, but Winthrop Sargeant thought they sounded that way only when played by a mediocre pianist: "Actually they represent a complete command of the instrument and a deep understanding of the psychological purposes of pianistic artistry. . . . Mr. Cliburn's performances . . . gave them all their inherent dignity, fire and romantic tenderness and in listening to him one realized anew what eloquent works they are, and why during their period the piano ranked as the most expressive of musical instruments. . . . I cannot remember a youthful artist who seemed to comprehend the traditions well, or to give comparable promise of becoming a great virtuoso."

Van Cliburn was not the only good thing blown into Carnegie Hall on the ill wind of Cold War. Two Russian virtuosos, pianist Emil Gilels and violinist David Oistrakh, came to America in the fall of 1955 during one of the earliest of the cultural thaws. Gilels had a delightful exuberance if not a particularly fine-spun talent. Oistrakh, on the other hand, quickly proved, as Taubman put it, "that he belongs with the best anywhere." Sargeant was even less reserved: "he is the finest performer on the violin to come to light in the generation or so during which I have been listening to it."

The Fifties were, then, hardly poverty stricken in the matter of new artists. The only doubt raised was whether there was a broad supporting cast of artists beneath the aging virtuosos and beneath the few new people of unquestioned status. There were plenty of talented people around—Michael Rabin, Jorge Bolet, Ruggerio Ricci, to name but three—and it seems likely that some of them will develop into artists who will find room at the very top. We could use more of them, but the American concert management system conspires to keep genius in scarce supply. There is as yet no system by which we develop our younger artists sensibly and without waste. This is still the great shame of the age, musically. It will not be corrected until an educated public demands a change.

Orchestrally, the decade was unquestionably the most interesting in Carnegie Hall's history, with more orchestras playing there than at any other time, with the Philharmonic falling into decline and then

Violinist David Oistrakh proved that "he belongs with the best anywhere" in his 1955 American recital debut at Carnegie Hall.

Columbia Records Photo

making a stimulating beginning on the long process of rejuvenation and, above questions of good and evil, two unique musical institutions —the Boston Symphony and the Philadelphia Orchestra—setting an unparalleled standard for orchestral achievement. Each may occasionally give a bad performance, or program an indifferent work, but basically the two orchestras have maintained for the past twenty years standards so consistently high as to place them outside controversy. The favorite indoor sport of music lovers on the eastern seaboard is arguing which of the two is the greater. Of late years the Philadelphia has had a slight edge in the argument. Its famed precision, its great string section, have seemed to the majority to give it a superiority over the warmer, more adventurous Boston Orchestra. But this is more a question of taste than provable superiority of one over the other. Both orchestras are run with great responsibility. Their conductors have had long tenures (the Philadelphia has had only two since 1920, the Boston just three), and both organizations are conscious of their responsibility to living music and to the broad traditions of the past. As a result they have played unique roles in the cultural life of New York where each year both orchestras play a series of subscription concerts. Their audiences represent an elite, a group more musically knowledgeable than the other audiences. Faced with this kind of audience, neither orchestra needs to pander particularly to popular tastes and both have retained an austere musicality over the years. The memorable concerts of each in the last decade are many, but a few deserve special mention.

In December, 1951, the Philadelphians presented a major new American work, the grim, terrifyingly logical Sixth Symphony of William Schuman, probably the finest work of that composer. A year later, Gian-Carlo Menotti's *Apocalypse*, presented under the direction of Victor de Sabata was a moderately interesting success and the return of Sir Thomas Beecham as guest conductor of the Philadelphians, presenting the delightfully satirical "The Triumph of Neptune" ballet score by Lord Berners, was an unquestioned triumph. "When he twirls his baton delightedly in circles over his head, or thrusts it behind his back, picks a pianissimo delicately from the air, or heaves, most ungracefully, his solid British body at the orchestra for a climax, he is feeling good; and when he is feeling good . . . he is one of the most sensitively gifted and passionately inspired interpreters of this day," one critic wrote.

Virgil Thomson's melodious settings of five William Blake Poems, sung by Mack Harrell, and the Menotti Violin Concerto, which Efrem Zimbalist came out of retirement to play, were the major new works of the following season. In 1953 the orchestra was the New York debut instrument of the great Dutch conductor Eduard von Beinum, who demonstrated his mastery in an impeccable Haydn symphony, then turned to Bruckner's mighty Seventh to demonstrate his versatility. In the spring an all-Brahms program featured William Warfield in the rarely played *Vier ernste Gesänge* of Brahms. He scored a brilliant success. Said the *Times*: "These songs demand more than an accomplished vocalist, they demand a great artist. The fine control of tone, the phrasing, the German diction and the simplicity and nobility of this performance honored alike the interpreter and composer."

In subsequent seasons the orchestra programmed a great number of important new works: Howard Hanson's *Sinfonia Sacra*, Randall Thompson's "A Trip to Nahant," Martinu's Concerto for Violin, Piano and Orchestra, Roy Harris' Seventh Symphony, Vaughan Williams' Eighth Symphony and Carl Orff's "The Triumph of Aphrodite," all of them well received and well played, all of them reflecting the championship qualities of this orchestra.

The Boston Symphony began the decade under guest conductors, but could hardly be said to have deteriorated in the relatively brief period before Charles Munch began his full-time stewardship of the orchestra. Under him the orchestra has demonstrated a propensity for "big machines" of one sort or another, undoubtedly because the French have a proclivity for them and because Munch is at his best with the music of his native land. He has had much to do with the revival of interest in Berlioz in this country, and although some regard him as more limited than his predecessor in Boston, there is no doubt that, like Beecham, when he is feeling at his best he is a conductor of the highest caliber, capable of brilliant performances in almost all the areas of the symphonic repertory.

Among the big Munch productions of recent years have been Honegger's *La Danse des Morts*, like *Jeanne d'Arc* a work for narrator, vocal soloists, chorus and orchestra (1953), Samuel Barber's *Prayers of Kierkegaard* in which Leontyne Price scored one of her early triumphs assisted by the Schola Cantorum (1955), Berlioz' *Damnation of Faust* in which the Harvard Glee Club and the Radcliffe Choral Society sang with the orchestra for the 100th time, and Stravinsky's *Canticum Sacrum*. Under Robert Shaw the orchestra produced, in 1959, Wallingford Riegger's very large Sixth Symphony.

Under Munch the orchestra has continued unabated the policy of encouraging new composition. The foundation set up by Koussevitzky to commission new works and to encourage living music in general, of course, is closely connected with the orchestra and as a result of that, and Munch's own interest in the new, it has continued as one of the leading producers of new music. In the Fifties it presented for the first time in New York such works as Jean Rivier's Violin Concerto, Honegger's masterly though cryptic Fifth Symphony, Walter Piston's romantic and melodious Fourth Symphony, and his light and witty Sixth, Bloch's *Concerto Symphonique*, Toch's Second Symphony, Nabokov's *La Vita Nuova*, the first and second symphonies of the interesting young French composer Henri Dutilleux, Martinu's *Fantaisies Symphoniques*, and his *The Parables*, Roger Sessions' knotty and highly compressed Third Symphony. In December, 1959, the orchestra performed Kabalevsky's Cello Concerto with the composer as conductor and Samuel Mayes as soloist. The work proved to be disarmingly melodious, charming and skillful, whatever one's views of its staying powers.

Somehow, a great soloist rises above nationality, but orchestras, because they are institutions usually with long traditions, do quite the opposite. They seem, to many, to give an insight into national character. In the Cold War years the export of such institutions has risen markedly. The arrival of the Royal Philharmonic in 1950 was the first visit by a foreign orchestra in almost thirty years. Sir Thomas Beecham's orchestra produced, as one might imagine, highly individual tones. It was an orchestra which seemed distinctly British, solid, sonorous, beautifully balanced in the wind and brass choirs, the texture and intonation of the strings very clean. It was as smartly drilled as a Guard's Regiment, and its reviews were highly favorable.

The next foreign orchestra to visit, the Israel Philharmonic, was hardly in a class with the British group. Newly formed, composed of refugees who were now citizens of the new state of Israel, it was conducted in New York by Serge Koussevitzky and it more than made up for its technical shortcomings by playing with a passion and an eloquence that an audience predisposed toward this brave band responded to enthusiastically. Over the years the orchestra has continued to develop, with many American conductors, notably Leonard Bernstein, contributing to its training.

The Danish State Symphony Orchestra under Erik Tuxen and Thomas Jensen came over in 1952 and displayed its dynamic versatility, highly poetic qualities and power by playing a program heavy with modern works. It impressed listeners greatly.

Two years later the great Concertgebouw Orchestra of Amsterdam

RCA Victor

Charles Munch replaced Koussevitzky as conductor of the Boston Symphony Orchestra and under him the orchestra has continued to flourish as one of the nation's best.

came over and taught Americans, in the words of Winthrop Sargeant, "that the lush and vigorous approach to our own American orchestras is by no means the only way to produce fine symphonic music." Man for man he and the other critics thought the orchestra did not quite match the American orchestras in virtuosity and competitive drive, but it had "a mellow quality that our orchestras seldom achieve," and gave an impression of age and maturity. The orchestra brought with it a rather dull novelty, the second symphony of Henk Badings, but more than made up for it with a jewel-like reading of Ravel's Second *Daphnis et Chloé* Suite, Weber's *Der Freischütz* Overture and a very poised reading of the Brahms First.

In 1955 the Berlin Philharmonic arrived amidst political controversy. It was led by Herbert von Karajan, and once again the pickets were out in force, claiming von Karajan was a Nazi collaborator. The reaction of a distinguished journalist and music buff, Vincent Sheean, to this particular sort of hooliganism was significant. His host dropped Sheean and his party off in the midst of a group of hysterical boys and girls carrying banners which screamed "Nazi Go Home" and other similar sentiments. "I found one of these objects being shaken in my face," Sheehan recalls in his *First and Last Love*, "by a girl who had probably been still playing with her dolls when Hitler blew up his . . . bunker. I who had, so to speak, fought, bled and died on every battlefield from Spain to China for twenty years, always and forever against the Nazis . . . I was very nearly seized with palsy and started shouting at the girl: 'Go home yourself! You don't even know what a Nazi is! Go home! Go home!' . . . I suppose she may have thought I was Hitler's ghost." A firm hand on Sheean's shoulder, and some gentle words from a New York cop—"Now you just go along in to your concert, sir. Don't pay any attention to these people"—caused the writer to laugh rather than to argue.

But in his book he speaks the definitive word against this sort of political demonstration. "Performing musicians . . . are far too specialized to have any time for abstract thought; the affairs of the state are not theirs. Sometimes they put the button on and sometimes they take it off, but their reasons in either case are intellectually negligible, morally nil." The one moral crime such people can commit is to allow someone to tell them what they can or cannot play. For the rest they are no more culpable than others of us who raise no protest over those actions of a government which offends us or the decent opinions of mankind.

Whatever the justification, or lack of it, in the political controversy swirling around von Karajan, he made beautiful music. His first program included works by Haydn, Beethoven and Wagner and the critics thought they detected in his orchestra the Germanic virtues of solidity, stolidity, thoroughness and an ability to submit itself to the dictates of its leader without question. The orchestra was neither skittish nor particularly scintillating. It was rather rugged and organ-like and, on the whole, very agreeable. The following fall von Karajan was back with the Philharmonia Orchestra of London, quite a different sort of organization. It had great brilliance and clarity, and like the Royal Philharmonic was smartly drilled and precise. It gave von Karajan a chance to show another side of his musical personality. Playing Mozart, Debussy and Berlioz he showed himself "a consummate master of classical grace and restraint" and he convinced Sargeant that he was one of "the very few really exciting figures in the present generation of symphonic maestros."

In the fall of 1956 it was the Vienna Philharmonic, under the direction of Carl Schuricht, which brought to New York Anton Bruckner's Seventh Symphony. At last, in the Fifties, Bruckner and Mahler were coming to be recognized as the great transitional figures they were, masters of romantic sincerity, highly personal, perhaps even, in the case of Mahler, a little neurotic and withdrawn in their statements, but nevertheless great latter-day practitioners of a great tradition. Under their seventy-six-year-old conductor, the Viennese gave a definitive performance of the Bruckner work. It emerged with a coherence, a warmth, an eloquence which it has rarely received from orchestras which do not have the musical traditions of that city bred in their bones. The men from Vienna presented, in their opening concert, a sort of survey of the musical history of that city, preceding Bruckner with an early Mozart symphony and Beethoven's *Egmont* Overture. The result: "a continuous delight."

In the late years of the decade the parade of foreign orchestras continued, with the Florence Festival Orchestra, the National Symphony Orchestra of Mexico and the Lamoureux Orchestra of Paris, one of the last of the cooperative orchestral societies in existence, but one considerably more successful with that scheme than the Philharmonic was in the early days of the century.

The variety of domestic orchestras appearing in Carnegie Hall almost matched that of the foreign orchestras during the Fifties and the quality of these groups, their obvious professionalism as well as their confident eagerness to display their wares in New York, was one of the few unambivalent signs that America was coming of age. So, too, were the almost universally modern programs which they presented. The first of them to appear in the Fifties was the Louisville Orchestra under the direction of Robert Whitney, with Virgil Thomson as guest conductor and Martha Graham as soloist. The orchestra had an ambitious ongoing program for the commissioning of new works, the most ambitious of any in America, and its appearance demonstrated the scope of the program. The orchestra, which puts out an exciting series of records of new works, played Claude Almond's *Steamboat* Overture, David Diamond's *Timon of Athens*, Martinu's Intermezzo ("the best score of the evening"), Vincent Persichetti's Serenade No. 5 and the moving *Judith*, by William Schuman, danced by Miss Graham.

The appearance of the Cincinnati Orchestra under Thor Johnson, also a man interested in the new, was marked a year later by the beautiful singing of Strauss songs and an aria from Weber's *Oberon* by Eileen Farrell, an American singer who has had an unwarrantedly difficult time getting into the Met. The new work was Roy Harris' *Cumberland* Concerto, a diatonic work, sonorous and coloristic, but like other works by Harris rather monotonous in its rhythm.

Rafael Kubelik's Chicago Symphony put in an appearance in 1953 and it too presented an interesting concert. Kubelik, the son of violinist Jan Kubelik, had taken over the orchestra from Rodzinski (who had had another spat with his management) and was a devotee of new music. Eventually this won him the enmity of Chicago's leading critic and finally cost him his job. It was true that he was weak in the standard repertory, but on this occasion critics found his conducting "distinguished for the integrity of his musical ideas and the clarity with which they were realized." In later years, under the superlative Fritz Reiner, the orchestra has proved itself one of the great orchestras, and Reiner's 1958 concert completely won the New York musical world.

The same sort of reviews greeted the Minneapolis Symphony under Antal Dorati on its trips to New York. It was "an extraordinarily well-drilled and competent orchestra, clearly entitled to a place among the finer organizations in the country." Dorati programmed Bartók's Concerto for Orchestra and gave it a brilliant reading along with an eloquent production of three symphonic pieces from Berg's *Lulu.*

Howard Mitchell's National Symphony Orchestra from Washington also brought a large number of modern works with it on its frequent visits to New York. Particularly notable was its presentation of Paul Creston's Fifth Symphony which stood out on a 1956 program composed almost entirely of contemporary music. The piece had both emotional vitality and a highly developed form and was austere and excellent music. On another memorable occasion the orchestra presented John Vincent's unabashedly joyful Symphony in D, a work the composer said was a sort of thanksgiving for a good and happy life, and John La Montaine's "Songs of the Rose of Sharon" which gave Leontyne Price another opportunity to display her magnificent voice. One critic spoke of the "sheer force of her sinuous musical personality and the incandescence of a great voice" in reviewing the concert.

The Pittsburgh Symphony Orchestra under William Steinberg also appeared frequently and nearly always presented new works, among them a symphony by Paul Hindemith commissioned by the orchestra and, for the first time in New York, those remarkable feats of compression by Anton von Webern, the *Six Orchestra Pieces.* Under Steinberg, a master conductor, this was a continuously improving orchestra, rising to a point where it could truly be said to challenge the Big Three of the East.

Another such group was the Cleveland Orchestra under the admirable George Szell. It now presents an annual series of concerts in New York, nearly always well-balanced between works from the standard repertory and the very new. It is the only orchestra besides the Eastern ones to present an annual series and the knowledgeable await it with considerable eagerness.

But this is by no means the end of the orchestral riches which blessed Carnegie Hall in the Fifties. Leon Barzin's National Orchestral Association continued to program a profusion of new works and there have been such special occasions as the benefit concert of his own works conducted by Alan Hovhaness, the presentation by Stokowski of Hindemith's UNESCO-commissioned *Canticle of Hope*, Carl Orff's *Carmina Burana* with the Boston University chorus and orchestra. That sweeping, gusty and lusty setting of medieval secular songs has become one of the most popular of modern works. As Sargeant put it, it "does something that few compositions of the present era succeed in doing: it speaks from the heart and the viscera instead of from the frontal lobe of the brain."

Nevertheless, this vast creative stirring on the part of the orchestras was not the full story of the Fifties. For in that decade America lost her finest orchestra and her finest conductor. On April 4, 1954, in a sort of grand immolation, the public career of the all-virtuoso orchestra which NBC had created for Toscanini came to an end in Carnegie Hall. The demand for tickets had forced the orchestra more and more in recent years to abandon the famous Studio 8-H in Radio City in favor of the larger Carnegie Hall. It was here that the end came.

There are at least three full scale accounts of the events of the final hours of the NBC Symphony, all of them differing substantially. The one which seems the best, in that it answers more unanswered questions, is that of Irving Kolodin which first appeared in the *Saturday Review*. According to him, trouble began at the Saturday afternoon rehearsal preceding the Sunday concert. There had been a heavy demand for tickets and Socony-Vacuum, the sponsors of the radio program after running out of broadcast tickets, passed out enough rehearsal tickets to almost fill the house. Toscanini did not like to rehearse in public, but knowing, though virtually no one else did, that this was to be his last appearance, he made no objection. It soon became apparent that he was not rehearsing at all; he was giving a full scale performance. It was an all-Wagner program, and everything went beautifully through the *Lohengrin* and *Götterdämmerung* excerpts.

But in "Siegfried's Rhine Journey," at the point where the horn player goes offstage to give the illusion of Siegfried's call receding in the distance, there was trouble. Toscanini abandoned all pretense of giving a performance and the familiar cries of "*ignorante*" and "*vergogna*" (shame) went up. His fury somewhat vented, the Maestro proceeded to give the number of the section of the score where he wanted the orchestra to begin again. There was confusion, perhaps because in his anger Toscanini gave the wrong number. At any rate, he stalked from the stage. The public-address system announcer said, "this concludes the public portion of the rehearsal." It never resumed.

During the broadcast, the trouble did not occur until the "Rhine Journey" had been completed and Toscanini had launched the orchestra in the Overture and Bacchanale from Tannhäuser. Then he seemed to tire. The successive climaxes of the Baccanale have an overpowering fury, and Toscanini often had to rest his left hand on the railing that, in late years, surrounded his podium. It even seemed to some that an extra beat crept into his conducting at one point. But the break did not come until the orchestral furies had subsided. Then, in a slow passage, with less than half the orchestra playing, the Maestro ceased momentarily to beat time. He passed his hand over his eyes as if trying to remember something. For perhaps a dozen bars the orchestra was on its own. The fine first cellist, Frank Miller, tried his best to cue the orchestra, but it wavered badly. Up in the control booth, where the late Guido Cantelli was standing by in case the Maestro could not go on, someone pressed a panic button and over the air came the incongruous strains of Brahms' First Symphony. But the crisis passed. Within thirty seconds Toscanini resumed the beat and the piece proceeded to the end without incident. Immediately Toscanini gave the downbeat for the *Meistersinger* prelude. He continued to beat time, automatically, without attention to detail. The piece finished, amidst thunderous applause, he stepped, almost as if in a daze, from the podium. He dropped his baton. An orchestra member picked it up and handed it to him. But the conductor did not return to take his bows.

We will never know for certain what caused the most famous breakdown in musical history. But certainly the hierarchy of NBC must bear some of the blame. Toscanini's daughter-in-law was seriously ill (she died a few weeks later). The pressure on the Maestro was immense, for he had been forced into retirement. He was angry and worried about the future of the men who had played under him, for he guessed that without him NBC would not continue to support the orchestra.

NBC could have relieved the pressure on him at this last concert of the season by not insisting that the announcement of his retirement be coincident with it. It could have waited a few weeks for that. Instead, when members of the press filed into Carnegie Hall for the broadcast, they were handed copies of two letters. One, from Toscanini, offered his resignation. The photostatic copy revealed that it had been signed with a shaking hand. "No king ever abdicated less willingly or under more duress than Arturo Toscanini," Kolodin comments. The other, a notably bland note from David Sarnoff, NBC board chairman, told the Maestro that he had "fully earned the right to lay down your baton," and went on to recount at great length the contributions of NBC to music.

All of this could have been delayed until a calmer time. Why wasn't it? What did NBC gain? Kolodin is bitter and to the point on the subject. "Toscanini's retirement from the orchestra would have been a front-page story whenever it happened. What would have been lost had it all been withheld for a quieter time, when his season's work was done? So far as I can determine, only one thing: the photo spread in *Life* showing the agony of the ending in all its graphic detail."

This was not, however, Toscanini's last time with the orchestra or his last appearance in Carnegie Hall. The following Wednesday he was scheduled to remake portions of his records of *Aïda* and *The Masked Ball*. The Maestro arrived early, greeted everyone cordially, sprinkled himself liberally with *eau de cologne*, marched briskly to the podium, cried, "*Andiamo*" and with a powerful downbeat launched into the work at hand. He was, in Samuel Chotzinoff's words, "in all respects the autocratic, confident, extraordinary perfectionist the world had known for more than half a century." But that was the end, the last appearance of Toscanini with his great orchestra. A few weeks later NBC announced that it was ceasing sponsorship of the orchestra.

It, however, refused to die. As The Symphony of the Air it opened the 1954-1955 season with an extraordinary feat. It appeared in concert without a conductor, the first time an orchestra of this stature had attempted a conductorless performance. Describing it the next day the *Times* said: "The program was of works that Toscanini had rehearsed and directed with these players. His musicianship and exacting taste in regard to the smallest detail was everywhere in evidence. And yet this was not the mere resurrection of the conceptions of a peerless musician and leader. Imbued with a high tradition, the men had worked out each of the performances for themselves and achieved an intimate understanding of every passage. . . ."

Good training and fine tradition leave their marks on an orchestra, even after the leader who instilled them is gone. An era in symphonic music had ended, but, at least in its first season, the old NBC orchestra continued to live on the solid achievements of the past. The orchestra still exists, although with changed personnel and without a permanent conductor it is not quite the unique instrument it once was. The changes wrought by Toscanini on the symphonic aesthetic and on the tastes of musicians and listeners also live on. Their force has not diminished.

Not only did America lose a great orchestra in the Fifties, it watched another fine orchestra labor in difficulty through most of the decade. That orchestra was the New York Philharmonic. At the start of the decade, it was in good shape. After the several seasons of guest conductors which had followed the departure of Rodzinski, Dimitri Mitropoulos was given the conductorship. He seemed like a wise choice. He was familiar with the orchestra, having guest conducted it many times in the previous decade and having shared its leadership with Stokowski. He had built an excellent orchestra in Minneapolis, was known as a dynamic and dramatic leader, a friend of new music, and had an unexcelled reputation as an opera conductor.

And, for the first few seasons, the orchestra responded well to his leadership. He brought new ideas to Carnegie Hall, a fondness for dramatic performances, large works, operas in concert versions. In April, 1951 there was a concert version of *Wozzeck*, with brilliant performances by Eileen Farrell and Mack Harrell. Said the *Times*:

"It would be easier to find some conspicuous defect in the cast than to find all the desirable words to point out its excellence."

In succeeding seasons there were similar large works. In April, 1952, for instance, there was the first full-length performance of Mendelssohn's *Elijah* ever presented by the Philharmonic in America (it had done it once in Montreal). The Westminster Choir was placed on painters' scaffolds behind the orchestra so they could be seen by the audience and were instructed in dramatic gestures, as were the soloists. It turned out to be a very effective, if radical, performance. Not so successful was a performance of Milhaud's *Christophe Colomb*, with text by Paul Claudel and Mack Harrell in the leading role. It was a big machine, all right, but by the end of the first act at least one-third of the audience had left. The performance demonstrated one of Mitropoulos' troubles; his devotion to the new often far exceeded his audience's ability to appreciate and, sad to say, his taste was not always as good as it might have been. All too many of Mitropoulos' premieres were of unimportant works.

But for all the ephemera he produced, there were also new productions of works which deserved inclusion in the repertory. Among these were Schönberg's Violin Concerto, Alban Berg's three orchestral works, Paul Hindemith's *Die Harmonie der Welt*, Shostakovich's Tenth Symphony, which the composer claimed expressed the thoughts of "people who ardently love peace, who resist the drift to war, who regard man's mission on earth to be creative, not destructive," but which despite this programmatic poppycock was among the best he had ever produced, Peter Mennin's concise and powerful Sixth Symphony, Kabalevsky's Fourth Symphony, and the first New York performance of Mahler's Tenth Symphony as well as a revival of his massive Third. There was also an impressive concert version of Strauss's *Elektra* and a performance of Marc Blitzstein's *Lear: A Study*.

During the Mitropoulos reign there were some impressive debuts. In 1955 the young American conductor Thomas Schippers conducted the orchestra for the first time and impressed observers as "a master of stick technique, a musician of taste and highly believable conceptions, with an artistic approach of sensitivity and seriousness." Two

Columbia Records Photo

Dimitri Mitropoulos had great moments with the Philharmonic, but his years with it were mainly unhappy ones.

years later the fine young pianist Lilian Kallir appeared with Mitropoulos, playing the Mozart Concerto in G major (K. 453). Another young conductor was virtually co-director of the orchestra in the first half of the decade. He was Guido Cantelli, protégé of Toscanini, a dramatic and emotional leader who could be very, very good in the same works that were Mitropoulos' strong points and very, very weak in the classical works which were also the weak spots in the Mitropoulos repertory. On November 23, 1956, Cantelli was killed in a plane crash in Europe and his loss was a great one to the world of music. Six days later Mitropoulos conducted a moving performance of Strauss's *Death and Transfiguration* in his memory.

By this time dissatisfaction with the Philharmonic had reached its zenith. It was apparent that Mitropoulos, excellent musician though he was, was not the man for a permanent conductor's position. He was personally rather erratic, his performances depending greatly on his emotional state at the time of the concert. Winthrop Sargeant once described his podium appearance as that of "a Byzantine monk frantically engaged in shaking Martinis," and this erratic quality extended beyond the on-stage moments. It included his program-making, which followed no coherent pattern, juxtaposing minor works by major composers with ennui-inducing minor works by minor composers. In his enthusiasms he was often carried away, scheduling, for example, three Mozart piano concertos for one concert, thus rather overdoing the celebration of the composer's bicentennial year. On the last day of the 1956 season Howard Taubman of the *Times* came out with a full-page article in criticism of Mitropoulos' leadership. He mentioned his odd programming habits, the decline in the quality of the orchestra's playing based on a lack of discipline, his inability to conduct certain areas of the standard repertory, some anomalies in the policy toward guest artists. They also criticized the management of the orchestra, again raising objections to the two hats worn by co-manager Arthur Judson, who was still connected with Columbia Artists Management. Criticized, too, was the lack of a campaign to build genuine community-wide support for the orchestra, the number of whose subscribers had fallen to its lowest ebb since 1930 and which was now frequently playing to half-empty houses and running up an astronomical deficit. The morale of the audience was almost as low as that of the orchestra itself. Once again, it was obvious that something would have to be done.

Before the next season started, a beginning in the housecleaning operation was made. Judson was retired and his co-manager, Bruno Zirato, was placed in full charge. Taubman, for one, urged patience for a year but insisted that the public had "a right to anticipate marked improvements in 1957-1958." "The paramount issue," he said, "is artistic policy. For too many years the Philharmonic has carried on as though an orchestral season was a fortuitous collection of conductors, soloists and compositions . . . one cannot recall many, if any, seasons in a quarter of a century that had true artistic unity. . . . Only the musical director can do the job, and to do it properly he must be a man of wide-ranging sympathies and the strength of character to fight for his convictions. . . . Hand-in-hand with a revitalized artistic policy must go a re-examination by the Philharmonic of the role it [the orchestra] plays in the community and nation. The old ways of functioning and the established sorts of services need revision. . . ."

In due course, this came to pass. Leonard Bernstein was appointed co-conductor with Mitropoulos for 1957-1958. In 1958 he became sole musical director of the orchestra. He instituted a series of revolutionary reforms which constituted the first real change in the policies of the orchestra since it had passed from its primitive cooperative stage of operation in the first decade of the century. We shall consider the career of Leonard Bernstein in more detail a little later on. For the moment let it be noted that he does have strength of character, wide sympathies and something even more important, something rare in the professional musician—worldliness. He recognizes that an orchestra exists in and of a larger world, that it is not an abstract entity, existing for the pleasure of a few. It must attempt to coexist with a larger society which, frankly, has things on its mind that it considers more pressing than symphonic music. And he wishes to make his orchestra a part of the cultural mainstream of his time.

There are other circumstances which formed part of the musical context of the Fifties in which the Philharmonic was trying to operate. One of these was the increasingly blurred line between serious music, serious culture of all kinds, and the popular, or mass, arts. This represented the culmination of a long-term trend. As we have seen, popular music and folk music began invading Carnegie Hall in the Thirties. Partly this was a response to the political climate of the times. Partly it represented the cultural aspirations of the mass society which resented the inferiority it felt in the presence of high art.

Here there is a premium on individuality, on the expression not of common values, but of extremely uncommon ones. And worse, it is here that the upper economic and social orders have clung most tightly to control. In the Thirties and early Forties there was an attempt made, mostly by the artists themselves, to seek a *rapprochement* between the worlds of mass art and high art. This turned out to be a healthy thing for the latter. It gained vitality and interest as a result. But it had some rather strange side-effects. Musical comedy reached heights of pretension, losing whatever qualities of innocent delight it once had, the Boston Pops' recording of "Jalousie" became the first record by a symphony orchestra to sell a million copies, "The Sabre Dance" and Freddy Martin's awful arrangements of serious music for dance bands became juke box successes and a musical comedy score was constructed out of snippets from Borodin. Eugene O'Neill's *Anna Christie* was subjected in the Fifties to the indignity of transition to the musical stage under the title of *New Girl in Town*, and people laboring under the impression that they were buying real music purchased records by Mantovani and Kostelanetz by the millions. Suddenly, to paraphrase George Orwell, all culture was equal, except some kinds of culture were more equal than others.

Typically, pure folk music, genuine jazz, became cult owned, understood and appreciated by only a few intellectuals and psuedo-intellectuals, just as modern music (not to mention modern art, modern poetry, even the better modern novels) became arts of extremely limited appeal, while a vast gray area of music, neither good popular art nor good serious art, grew in importance. What had started out in the Thirties as a healthy trend toward a broadening of serious musical horizons, a breaking down of the stranglehold of conservative, wealthy music lovers on the higher musical institutions, became a nightmare in which standards and values were genuinely threatened. What occurred in the

Fifties was not a war between the radicals and the conservatives, but a war for the very survival of something like real music.

The jazz concert at Carnegie Hall, a refreshing and exciting and rather rare thing in the Thirties, became a commonplace. And, although the standards of a few of these concerts remained high, most popular-music events in the hall were appalling. On the credit side, there was the great 1950 Jazz at the Philharmonic concert which featured Ella Fitzgerald, the greatest of all popular singers, and men like Charlie Parker, Oscar Peterson, Flip Phillips, Lester Young, Bill Harris and Harry Edison—men who were making a new jazz style by cooling off "Le Jazz Hot." In the same year, The Weavers, popular folk singers who retained standards of taste and quality and who were instrumental in widening the audience for folk music somewhat, appeared. As the *Times* put it, "they enchanted a capacity and wildly partisan audience. And small wonder; they do their kind of repertoire to perfection, with plenty of spirit and enthusiasm." Both The Weavers and the various people connected with JATP continued, through the decade, to conform to high standards in their Carnegie Hall appearances. Many people also appreciate large sections of the midnight folk sing which Alan Lomax organized in 1959 and which featured the admirable Jimmie Driftwood and a collection of blues singers, gospel singers and a boogie-woogie player named Memphis Slim. A "hootenanny" featuring Pete Seeger, Robin Roberts, the New Lost City Ramblers and a steel band also had moments of interest, though it, like the Lomax concert, could not be judged a complete success.

There were also some notable attempts, during the decade, to bring together jazz and symphony orchestras. This was something new. Serious musicians had been using jazz figurations for decades, but putting jazzmen and symphonists together to play what were in effect jazz concertos was something new, and, if a bit crude in concept, interesting.

In March, 1955, Duke Ellington's band shared the stage with the Symphony of the Air and presented a new and extremely ambitious Ellington concert work, *Night Creature*. Ellington called the work "a tone parallel for piano, jazz band and symphony." There was certainly nothing timid about it and, as usual with Ellington's serious work, it stirred considerable controversy. Equally controversial was Rolf Liebermann's "Concerto for Jazz Band and Orchestra" which Dimitri Mitropoulos and the Philharmonic combined with the Sauter-Finegan band to present in the same month. The piece only came to life in the jazz sections, the role of the symphony being largely a passive one. According to the *Times* "the cool Dimitri led the Philharmonic and the Sauter-Finegan band as if the stuff were bread and butter for him. The way he kept the mambo movement taut and flexible suggested that he has not been contemplating Beethoven alone in his spare time. The Philharmonic boys held up their end with spirit." Equally up to the occasion was pianist Leonid Hambro, normally of the long-hair set. He "carried the burdens of a boogie-woogie movement like one to the manner born. His piano playing was authentic and so was the way he pounded out the rhythm with his left foot."

A similar work, a "dialogue for jazz combo and orchestra," run up by Dave Brubeck, was presented by Bernstein and the Philharmonic in December, 1959. The work was not as pretentious as Lieberman's piece, but it was also not quite so impressive. It didn't give Brubeck and his quartet the opportunities many would have liked them to have. It also relegated the Philharmonic to a rather ineffectual role. "All of the movements were too much alike in content. It was neither good jazz nor good concert music."

But the appearance of jazz bands on the stage with symphonies was only one evidence of the breakdown of old lines between the serious and the popular. The celebrated violinist, Jack Benny, got his chance, at long last, to play Carnegie Hall at a pension fund concert of the Philharmonic in October, 1956. Mr. Benny chose for his debut Sarasate's *Zigeunerweisen* and the first movement of the Mendelssohn Violin Concerto. The appearance of the young (39) violinist was marred by several mishaps. For one thing, he forgot his bow and one had to be hastily sought in the wings. For another he had some difficulty getting his instrument, a Stradivarius borrowed from society band leader Meyer Davis, tuned. Harold C. Schonberg of the *Times* thought it "the longest tune up in Carnegie Hall annals. . . . There was more horsing around than in the Louisville stables the morning of the Kentucky Derby." However, once the preliminaries were finally finished, the soloist left no doubt that in matters of intonation and technique, he had a maturity which belied his stated age. As Schonberg summed it up, "he was fine; it merely was that . . . the Philharmonic was out of tune with him." The concert was undoubtedly one of the most successful in the recent history of the hall. In an interview with Jay S. Harrison of the *Herald Tribune* the soloist told why. "There's nothing so funny as humor against a classy background. The laughs come from the fact that I'm so damned highbrow, so haughty and lofty, and so lousy . . . the laughs don't come from my bum playing but from the spot I'm in."

He also pointed out that "bloody awful" as his playing was, he respected his instrument as only a genuinely frustrated artist can. He never attempted to break it over anybody's head or anything like that. "Heifetz," Benny remarked, "doesn't like anyone kidding the violin, but he doesn't mind when I do it."

No one minded, either, when Danny Kaye took over the Philharmonic in November, 1958, to lead a pension fund concert. His entrance into the sacred precincts of Carnegie Hall was described by one observer this way: "He loped onstage carrying twelve batons, shook hands with near half the orchestra, kissed two harpists and a double-bassist and proceeded to test the batons. Finally selecting one—he had flung the others away disdainfully—he launched into his first number, which consisted entirely of a single, simple B-flat chord."

In this opening work the conductor took the opportunity to familiarize his players with his somewhat unorthodox methods. He required the orchestra to play this first number over and over as he demonstrated his method of achieving a diminuendo. He snapped off a bit of his baton each time before giving the downbeat; each time the orchestra played a bit more softly until finally, with the conductor down to the cork grip of the baton, the orchestra rebelled and played a chord that could be heard at the Metropolitan Opera House. This was not the end of Mr. Kaye's unorthodoxy. Subsequently he indicated his desires by "kicking out his foot like a petulant ostrich," sticking out his tongue, shouting "gaboom," barking like a seal, giggling delightedly whenever the orchestra managed to produce anything like a pleasant sound. He also lay down and conducted with his feet, and he demonstrated various methods used by his conductorial competitors to coax good performances from recalcitrant orchestras. These included the coffee-grinder and meat-chopper techniques, the baby-carriage-pusher style and the various gyrations indulged in by maestros with explosive emotions and with allergies. He also faced the audience as he conducted a snippet from *Lohengrin* and gave them an unparalleled opportunity to watch the expressions of a leader as he responds to the music he is conducting. Audience and orchestra alike were helpless with laughter as the evening progressed, and the maestro was finally compelled to inquire of his charges, "Are you always laughing like this?"

The appearances of Jack Benny and Danny Kaye represented good, clean fun and only the stuffiest could have objected to the sacrilege they committed. Their appearances, like those of Anna Russell, the musical satirist, were manifestations of health, representations of a new attitude toward music by many in the audience. They were secure enough now in their tastes, having shed enough of their awe of "culture," to be able to laugh at the pretenses that often accompany it. It is hard to imagine a Carnegie Hall audience of the turn of the century allowing this sort of thing to proceed without cries of outrage. They objected, indeed, to transgressions far more minor.

On the other hand, Carnegie Hall at the turn of the century did not have to encompass the sort of sounds that were bounced off its too, too solid walls in the Fifties. The weird noises produced by Yma Sumac, the foghorn tones of Billy Eckstine, the slushy tones of Mantovani, a program billed as "100 strings and Joni James," the sophomoric sadism of Tom Lehrer, the buttoned-down piano playing of Erroll Garner all invaded the hall in the decade. Worst of all there was a phenomenon known as Harry Belafonte. Wrote the *Times*: "So large a group of musicians for a program made up of simple unpretentious songs lent the occasion an air of pompous formality that, supplemented by Mr. Belafonte's mannered solemnity, raised a wall between the singer and his audience in many selections."

Belafonte exemplified the worst in the musical trends of the Fifties. Dressing up folk music with all sorts of trappings borrowed from what might be regarded as upper-class music and thereby cheapening both and doing honor to neither, is a trend of the times, and it is a dangerous one. The struggle to make music the property of everyone has been, as we have seen, an arduous one, and it would be a shame if it ended not in the wide dissemination of that which is good, whether it be classical music, modern serious music, jazz and folk music, but in the blending of all the forms into a sort of dehydrated instant cultural ready-mix without either distinctive flavor or nourishment. Music, in this country, has been too long the exclusive preserve of a handful of wealthy and not particularly well-educated patrons. They have fought the new, which frightened them, with that particular tenacity reserved to the ignorant. Now with the technological means at hand to make music genuinely a popular art, a new danger arises, the danger that half-educated mass tastes will succeed to the power positions and exercise a different, but equally destructive, tyranny over the art.

There are signs that this new danger can be averted or at least contained. One of them is the advent of Leonard Bernstein to the musical directorship of the Philharmonic.

Bernstein's career during the Fifties was a study of a young musician in search of a character. He tried his hand at almost every musical form—symphonies, musical comedies, opera, small orchestral works. As a public personality he had gained fame as a frequent guest conductor of major orchestras, often conducting while playing the piano solo in concertos.

He opened this pivotal decade of his conductorial career by leading the Philharmonic in the New York premiere performance of his Second Symphony, *The Age of Anxiety*, originally conceived as a ballet score which, in turn, was based on the Auden poem. The reviewers were not particularly ecstatic about the work which seemed exterior and superficial, but one of them asked, "Is not the glitter of this score, its restlessness, its unease, its obvious artificiality, precisely the sincere expression, by a young musician of today, of today's anxiety?" In his music, as in his public personality, Bernstein expressed something fundamental to his moment in history.

As the decade wore on, however, he demonstrated other qualities, qualities that were of considerable value to a musical world faced with new social conditions. Among these, none was more important than his devotion to discovery and rediscovery and his unquestioned talent in communicating his enthusiasms to his audiences. A year after the premiere of *The Age of Anxiety* he presented, for the first time in its complete version, Charles Ives' Second Symphony, an immense work "by turns rudely, tenderly, fantastically and cantankerously Yankee." Ives chose not to be present for the premiere of the work, even though Bernstein offered to conduct a special performance for him alone. Mrs. Ives did come, and as the audience warmly applauded she was heard to exclaim with amazement, "Why they like it!" Ives heard the piece on the radio when it was played the following Sunday. That reserved gentleman demonstrated his approval by dancing a jig in his kitchen. Ives was co-founder of an insurance agency which eventually grew to be the largest in the nation. But his first love was his music which he scrawled, sometimes carelessly in pencil, on weekends, then stuffed into bureau drawers. He knew full well that there was no audience for his kind of music which, prior to Schönberg and Stravinsky, made use of ragtime rhythms and dissonances. The knowledgeable had known of his work for years and in 1946 he finally got a playing of his Third Symphony which received a Pulitzer Prize. A year before that Schönberg himself had informed Americans that "There is a great man living in this country—a composer. He has solved the problem of how to preserve oneself and to learn. He responds to negligence by contempt. He is not forced to accept praise or blame. His name is Ives."

It was typical of Bernstein that, as one critic said, "to his eternal credit," he performed the work. Throughout the Fifties he performed other works of the same sort whenever and wherever he conducted. In the middle of the decade, when he was frequently conducting the Symphony of the Air, he consistently performed such works as Prokofieff's Fifth Symphony, the Hindemith Clarinet Concerto (with Benny Goodman as soloist), Aaron Copland's *Canticle of Freedom.* With the Philharmonic he revived Roy Harris' Third Symphony, probably his best work, as well as Copland's Short Symphony. With the former orchestra he also premiered his own rather charming little piece, the "Serenade for Violin with Strings and Percussion."

In the course of the decade Bernstein endeared himself to a lot of music lovers. There was nothing stuffy about his devotion to the new and he himself was responsible for some distinctly superior musical comedy scores as well as for the projection of a distinctly different sort of musical personality. He happens to live in an era which likes a particular sort of soft-boiled egghead, one who combines obvious talent and intellectuality with an easy manner and nice-guy qualities. Even his players call him "Lenny," and as one observer put it, "No one ever called Toscanini 'Artie.'" The forbidding, remote, austere intellectual or artist is definitely out. Thus, the appeal of the Bernstein image.

The basic personality is combined with a willingness to try something new, to be eclectic in tastes, to persuade rather than to force his audiences into sampling the new or the obscure. To the beleaguered Philharmonic he was obviously the answer to a prayer. And it was a shrewd reading of the nation's musical mood to engage the author of "Wrong Note Rag" as co-director of the orchestra in 1957 and to place him in full command a year later.

Bernstein was totally aware of the problems that went with the job, but unlike his many predecessors, he attempted to meet them rather than to ignore them. As he saw it, the basic difficulty the Philharmonic faced was that it was, in effect, the home-town orchestra of a city that has more music at its disposal than it can possibly digest in a season. To reviewers and audiences alike the Philharmonic was too familiar, too much a predictable quantity in its musical diet. His problem was to make it surprising, to make people realize that it was capable of producing the unexpected delights that the visiting orchestras had been providing. That was the main thing—to make the orchestra interesting again. But there were others. The orchestra had become a slack ship. It needed a fast shape up and shake-up. It also needed the thing which, as we have seen, it has consistently lacked—a unique musical personality. In addition, it had to perform an educational job on its staid and conservative audiences, to make them aware of musical traditions and styles beyond those to which they have remained rather too steadfastly devoted. Once again, under Bernstein, the orchestra has engaged itself in one of its periodic regroupings. What has been his record of success in the two years he has had the Philharmonic?

There is no question that public interest has been stirred as it has never been since the days of Toscanini. Bernstein is one of the few musical figures who, as a result of his excursions into popular music and his appearances on television, is a household name in America. Being attractive both in form and in personality he has won the admiration of the female contingent more or less completely. Observers think that even the audience at the Friday matinees—perhaps the worst in the musical history of the world—have actually been behaving themselves better as they gurgle and coo over Bernstein. He has also begun a long-range music-educational program successfully. His TV appearances in which he has explained, among other things, the intricacies of Bach and Beethoven, jazz, the conductor's art and musical comedy have been distinguished efforts at popular education. He treats his TV audiences as adults capable of understanding something about music and, more than that, capable of making the effort to figure out what he is talking about. Not that his appearances have been painful for viewers. He talks wittily, uses good visual devices to aid him in his explanations. The same may be said about his educational concerts for children, some of which are televised. His preview concerts, at which he lectures his audiences about the form and content of pieces which make up his program have been less consistently successful—although some of them have been quite delightful. The best thing about them is that they prevent reviewers from writing about the first concert of a week's series. One of the great advantages that visiting orchestras have always had over the Philharmonic has been that they bring a piece to New York only after it has been thoroughly tested on the home-town audience. Until the Bernstein era began, the Philharmonic had to give its first public performance of new works on the night the critics were present. This could have a very discouraging effect not only on ticket sales for repeat concerts but on the public's general idea of the quality of the orchestra.

Musically, it is a little harder to determine how the Bernstein regime fares. There seems little doubt that the orchestra is better disciplined than it was under Mitropoulos, more painstakingly prepared, more smartly drilled. It is also clear that Bernstein's programs are more intrinsically interesting than they previously were. He, like Mahler

Columbia Records Photo

Leonard Bernstein, quintessential musical figure of today leads the Philharmonic which he revitalized when he took over in 1958

long before him, has taken the trouble to draw season-long programs that are more than an accidental collection of works. Generally the individual programs are well balanced and the season's schedule has some sort of grand design to it. Like Mahler, Bernstein prefers surveys of various musical forms and festivals of works by a single composer.

In his selection of new works, both in the year he shared the podium with Mitropoulos and in the seasons since, Bernstein has programmed novelties which to many seem more interesting than the choices of his predecessor. Among these have been Shostakovich's catchily tuneful Second Piano Concerto, written as a showpiece for the composer's son and played on this occasion by Bernstein, Igor Markevitch's *Icare*, Copland's *Orchestral Variations*, Roger Sessions' Violin Concerto with Tossy Spivakovsky as soloist, Lukas Foss's impressive *Symphony of Chorales*. Nor has Bernstein skimped in the matter of large works or in the matter of engaging stimulating soloists.

All of this has helped to make the Philharmonic once again an interesting orchestra, an orchestra engaged in the musical currents of its time, an orchestra performing a large educational function, an orchestra, almost for the first time in its career, playing a part in the intellectual life of its community. The question now is whether it can be kept up.

To know the answer to this, one would have to be privy to the psyches of its board of directors, which has traditionally shown a liking for leaders considerably more passive than Bernstein. One would also have to be privy to the enigmatic feelings of its traditionally stodgy subscribers who up to now have been titillated by Bernstein but who are quite capable of becoming frightened and defensive if he pushes their limited tastes too far too quickly. One would have to know, too, how long the critics will retain their rather cautious attitude toward Bernstein. Most of them have applauded his efforts to drag the resisting orchestra, board and subscribers into the musical mainstream. Critics have been calling for that for some time, and they can hardly back away from the position now. The trouble is that they have their doubts about Bernstein's purely conductorial abilities. They all concede that his way with the moderns and the late romantics is unexcelled. But they have wondered about his abilities with works composed in the eighteenth century and the first part of the nineteenth. Here it has to be conceded that they have a point, though one cannot help wondering if it is not healthy for the orchestra to be led by a man who does the living music of his time superbly. The opposite has been true too long, and, in any case, Bernstein is usually at least adequate in the traditional repertory.

Finally, a great deal depends on Bernstein himself. He is quite capable of being a very great conductor if he sets his mind to it. As he himself said a couple of years ago, "Up to now I've been hedging. . . . I should know more about myself than I do." His facility in a number of musical areas has prevented him from digging very deeply into any of them. If, as his first three years as a full-time conductor come to an end, he has found what he wants in it, and if he is allowed to develop further in this career, he could become one of the finest conductors of the time. If he continues with the Philharmonic he might even be able to turn that notorious collection of rugged individualists into something it has practically never been—an orchestra with a personality of its own, expressing something unique in the musical dialogue of the age.

Be that as it may, there is no doubt that Bernstein is one of the finest bridgers of the gap between popular taste and high art ever to come along. He has a unique talent for speaking to both camps, of overcoming the mutual suspicions which keep mass and class apart. He has an almost uncanny ability to keep standards of taste high while trudging back and forth between the two camps on a tightrope, bearing gifts from one to the other. In an age in which popularization is too often synonymous with cheapening, he is a remarkable figure who deserves applause for his genuine achievements and understanding for the occasional misstep he makes, the occasional shortcomings that result from the regrettably limited number of hours in the day.

It is just barely possible that, as Carnegie Hall enters its eighth decade, he is operating in a climate of opinion better than any which has ever preceded it in the musical history of America. We have seen that technology and increased money and leisure have made music a boom industry. We have also seen some of the dangers attendant on this bull market. It is therefore particularly fortuitous that we can close our history of Carnegie Hall with an example of intelligent concern for the future of music, a concern illustrating an appreciation of the fact that music is something more than mere "culture."

This was the citizens' effort to save Carnegie Hall when it was threatened with demolition at the end of the 1959 season. After the death, in 1935, of Robert Simon who had headed the corporation which had purchased the hall from the Carnegie estate, his son, Robert, Jr., became the head. The Hall enjoyed generally good economic conditions for most of the years he headed it, and in recent years profits averaged in the neighborhood of $100,000 per year.

In the meantime, however, Carnegie Hall's appearance was declining. Its exterior was soot-encrusted, its dusty interior became more dingy with each passing year. Its last general clean-up occurred in 1948.

When plans were announced for the erection of the Lincoln Center for the Performing Arts, and when, in the middle Fifties, it became clear that the Philharmonic, the steadiest renter of the main hall, was going to move to the new center, Simon announced that the hall would necessarily be torn down. A syndicate was formed which publicized a new red skyscraper costing $22,000,000 and rising 44 stories from stilts. There was a howl of outrage from music lovers, but, by and large, New York quietly accepted the inevitability of the building's destruction. New York is a city constantly tearing itself down and starting over again, and its citizens are inured to the loss of landmarks in this pervasive atmosphere of restless reconstruction.

As time passed, it seemed clear that the new building would not rise on the site. It called for enormous financing. The corporation proceeded with demolition plans, and the Philharmonic was required to make temporary arrangements for concerts at the Hunter College Auditorium to fill the time gap until Lincoln Center could be completed, an expected period of at least two years. Meanwhile, Mr. Simon and the tenants engaged in a serio-comic war of pronouncements and retaliatory claims, and in the tenants' slightly eccentric attempts to save the hall one lady suggested they all parade in sackcloth and ashes to dramatize their plight.

Mr. Simon did, however, let it be known that "if there's a program for its use that makes sense, then we'd see what could be done. And we'd . . . sell it at a financial sacrifice, as our contribution to the effort." But, he added, he didn't believe there was a practical plan for saving the hall. "After all," he told a reporter from *Cue*, "competing Carnegie Hall against Lincoln Center would be a very un-civic thing to do."

All over New York people were wagging their heads sadly, saying that it was a darn shame something couldn't be done about saving the Hall, and going on about their business. Happily, however, one citizen did more about the impending disaster than wag his head. He was Isaac Stern, the violinst. Mr. Stern decided to try to do something about it before leaving on a long concert tour and approached his friends Alice and Jacob M. Kaplan about rescuing Carnegie Hall from the hands of those who have made New York into what one apoplectic writer of a letter to the *Times* called "this barbarous real-estate-mad city."

Mrs. Kaplan has been active and influential in New York musical activities, and Mr. Kaplan, a merchant, supports a modest philanthropic foundation which bears his name. Mr. Kaplan believed that support for a venture of this kind should not come from only one foundation but should be more broadly representative. The J. M. Kaplan Fund is administered by an imaginative and energetic gentleman named Raymond S. Rubinow, who has had considerable experience in organizing such civic rescue missions as closing Washington Square Park to traffic and supporting the performance of Shakespeare in Central Park. Mr. Kaplan asked him to devote time to figuring out ways and means of saving the Hall. Rubinow, Stern and Kaplan immediately rounded up people who could help, as well as ideas for saving the hall in the few months before the wreckers were scheduled to go to work. These recruits included Frederick W. Richmond, who later played a key role in the project, and Colonel Harold Riegelman, who was to activate the program to save Carnegie Hall.

They saw three possible avenues of approach to the problem. One was aid from a number of foundations; another was the launching of a wide-scale public appeal for funds to buy the hall; the third was solicitation of some sort of governmental aid: federal, state, or city.

The first method was abandoned after a few approaches to some of the larger foundations proved fruitless. The second was considered possible but not feasible in the short time available. The third method looked to be the only remaining practicable one.

Hasty exploration revealed that federal aid was unlikely; that state assistance, at best, would only be permissive; and the main hope was to convince the City. The final plan which was evolved was simple enough but involved considerable delicate political maneuvering since it meant dealing with both a Republican State administration and a Democratic City administration. For this purpose a bi-partisan Citizens Committee for Carnegie Hall was organized at a meeting at Mr. Kaplan's home on February 7, 1960.

The Committee's proposal was for New York City to acquire the hall, then lease it to The Carnegie Hall Corporation which they would organize to operate the hall. Under the plan the City would issue bonds to pay for the purchase and renovation of the hall, the bonded indebtedness to be paid off by the Corporation. Once the bonds were retired the hall would become the property of the Corporation running the hall on behalf of all the citizens of New York. Mayor Wagner was approached by the Committee and indicated his personal sympathy with their plans and his willingness to have the City undertake to save the hall.

In order for the City to do all this, enabling legislation by the State was necessary. The Committee's counsel, Colonel Harold Riegelman, drafted such a bill, which the city presented, while State Senator MacNeil Mitchell, whose district encompasses Carnegie Hall, presented a more general bill which gave all New York municipalities the right to acquire historical sites in order to prevent them from being destroyed.

Both bills were signed by Governor Nelson Rockefeller on Saturday, April 16, little more than six weeks before the announced date of the beginning of demolition of the hall.

When the news that the bill had been signed was flashed to Carnegie Hall, where Leopold Stokowski was conducting the Symphony of the Air in a children's concert, there was jubilation. When Stokowski, who was active in the rescue operation, announced the signing the orchestra played a fanfare and the children raised a three-minute ovation.

By early June a purchase price of $5,000,000 was negotiated between Carnegie Hall, Inc., and the City, and on the last day of the month Frederick Richmond, as chairman of the board of trustees of the Carnegie Hall Corporation, signed a lease for the property. Shortly thereafter, renovations on the hall began. By the end of the summer, under the direction of Robert W. Dowling, chairman of the Corporation's Executive Committee, its exterior had been sandblasted, the dreary reddish color of the main hall had been repainted a sparkling white and Carnegie Hall was ready to begin its eighth decade of service with a new lease on life.

So pleased was she by this rescue from the edge of the grave that poet Marianne Moore, who occasionally takes it upon herself to be poet laureate of the city, published a work in praise of Mr. Stern, the prime-mover in the whole business, which ended:

> . . . We hunt
> you down, Saint Diogenes—
>   are thanking you for glittering,
> for rushing to the rescue
>   as if you'd heard yourself performing.

Mr. Stern himself has talked of using the hall as a headquarters for developing new musical talent. Just when the "golden age of music," to which Mr. Stern and many other people are looking forward, will become a reality cannot be certain.

But this much is certain; its chances of arriving are considerably enhanced by the passing of Carnegie Hall from private to public hands. In January, 1960, when it looked as if the city was about to be deprived of Carnegie Hall, Howard Taubman, music critic of the *Times*, wrote that "Carnegie Hall should never have been private property at all. . . . When Andrew Carnegie built the hall . . . he meant it as a public monument. His was the first blunder, for he should have deeded the building to a civic agency." He pointed out that in the Twenties the

Philharmonic could have acquired the place as a permanent home, that at one point negotiations to this end had begun, but had broken down simply because there was lack of real interest in it, a lack of foresight into the cultural needs of the community. The same indifference was the rule of conduct until Stern finally sparked his fellow citizens into a determined effort to save the hall. It took near disaster to awaken the community to the value of Carnegie Hall.

But in fairness it must be pointed out that it is only in the last twenty years that public opinion has been conditioned to accept the fact that the intellectual and cultural welfare of its citizens is as proper a concern for a government as is their social and economic welfare. It would also be fair to say that this concept is still more arguable than are other aspects of the modern welfare state. But the construction of the quasi-public Lincoln Square Center and the acquisition of Carnegie Hall by the city are strong indications that a wealthy and powerful nation is at last ready to concede the importance of art. If the Lincoln Center project and the reborn Carnegie Hall are signs that the wide public, operating through its governmental agencies, is at last ready to commit itself to the support of cultural and intellectual activities, not as isolated individuals but on a community-wide basis, then we may, indeed, be about to begin a golden age.

It is true that you cannot legislate cultural interests into existence. But it is to be hoped that the passage of legislation like that which saved Carnegie Hall will create an atmosphere in which cultural activity is increasingly easy to support. Legislation in a democracy is traditionally the result of the pressure of an informed minority exerting itself to counterbalance a heavy weight of indifference. The same may be said of the creation of public opinion. Generally speaking, legislation or the agitation for legislation is one of the first manifestations of the creation of a new consensus on the part of opinion makers. It is a supreme tool in the molding of a society-wide consensus. The entire history of social welfare legislation proves this. It is possible that the public activity on behalf of culture which we have witnessed in recent years betokens a new birth of interest in art, an interest based not on the social prestige inherent in its ostentatious appreciation, but on a vital concern and involvement in art as the last ideological hope of man, one from which he can gain the solace he sought and failed to find in the many ideologies he has abandoned in the indifferent decade of the Fifties.

At the moment, of course, only a few activists possess this belief. But if they should prevail over the indifference of the mass society then we may be about to witness a renaissance. We have the money for it, and we have the leisure. We need only find the desire. If that is forthcoming it would be a logical conclusion to the trends set in motion in the nineteenth century when wealthy men decided it was time to devote some of their time and money to the raising up of their fellow men. It would be an especially logical conclusion to the trend set by the man who created a Music Hall, a platform for good causes, which eventually bore his name.

Andrew Carnegie's stated desire was to provide for other men the tools by which they could help themselves to richer, fuller lives. As it turned out, he and the wealthy men who followed his lead, needed help, eventually, from public sources. Three generations of liberal reformers have forced the creation of governmental agencies to extend the nation's welfare activities far beyond the limits set by the very nature of private philanthropy. Only in the cultural area has the job been left to individuals. It now seems probable that the task of providing for the cultural needs of a nation as large as this one is too great for them to manage without governmental aid. If this is true, and our mass society genuinely wants to enrich its cultural diet, then it is only a matter of time before we, like most of the rest of the Western World, begin a wide-scale program of subsidization of the arts.

The rebirth of Carnegie Hall, in large part due to the cooperation of public bodies and public officials seems to be a start in this direction. It is, at the very least, a cause for hope. The future is uncertain, the difficulties high art must surmount if it is to survive in a mass society are seemingly insurmountable, but there is at least a chance for survival. And a chance is all art, that bravest of all chronic individuals, has ever needed.

Index

Abato, Vincent J., 340
Abbott, William, 46
Abel, Walter, 74
Academy of Music, N.Y.C., 18, 22
Acheson, Dean, 366
Acropolis (Athens), 151
Adler, Larry, 327, 328
Advertiser, 77-78
Aeolian Hall, 216
Afro-American Symphony, Sill, 296
Age of Ambivalence, 350
Age of Anxiety, The (Second Symphony), Bernstein, 405-406
Aïda, Verdi, 394
Ajemian, Mario, 362
Alaskan boundary dispute, 84
Albeniz, 198
Albert, Eugene d', 77, 114
Alceste, Gluck, 377
Aldrich, Richard, 99-101, 105, 110-111, 112, 115, 129, 138, 156, 157, 164, 169, 173-174, 185, 204-205, 215, 217. *See also Times*
Almond, Claude, 390
Alpine symphony, Strauss, 173
Also sprach Zarathustra, Strauss, 111. *See also Thus Spake Zarathustra*
Altschuler, Modeste, 114-115, 129, 169
Alves, Mrs. Carl, 53
"America," 49, 63, 64
America symphony, Bloch, 260
American, New York, 161, 237
American Academy, Rome, 208
American Academy of Dramatic Arts, N.Y.C., 73-76
American Creed, Harris, 322
American Document, 309
American Festival Overture, Schuman, 319
"American in Paris, An," Gershwin, 260-261
American Opera Society, 380
American Scandinavia Society, 375-376
A minor Concerto, Schumann, 60, 142; Mozart, 246
Ammons, Albert, 310
Amparo, 308
Amsterdam Concertgebouw Orchestra. *See* Concertgebouw Orchestra
Amundsen, Roald, 163
Anderson, Marian, 262, 312-314, 345
And Promenade Home, Agnes De Mille, 332-335
"Angel of Inspiration," 346
Anna Christie, O'Neill, 400
Antek, Samuel, 240
"Antimony," Cowell, 216
"Anvil Chorus," Verdi, 17
"Anxious Bugler, The," Carpenter, 340
Apocalypse, Menotti, 384
Apostles, The, Elgar, 103, 123
Appalachian Spring Suite, Copland, 351
"Arcanes," Varèse, 243-244
Argentinita, 310, 349
Arion Society, 19-20
Armistice, 184
Arnold, Richard, 132
Arrau, Claudio, 323
Arriola, Pepito, 138-139
Astor Hotel, 266, 298
Atomic Age, 349
Aubert, 198
Auden, W. H., 405
Auer, Leopold, 178, 183, 228
Autobiography, Mark Twain, 117-118
Away we Go, 332. *See also Oklahoma!*

Babin, Victor, 321
Bacall, Lauren, 74
Bacchanale, from *Tannhäuser,* Wagner, 152
Bach, 7, 9, 65, 108, 144, 151, 168, 183, 243, 258, 268, 280, 291, 292, 327, 335, 336, 378, 379, 408
Bachaus, Wilhelm, 160, 161, 207, 377-378
Backus, Jim, 74
Badings, Henk, 388
Bagar, Robert, 347
Balfour, Arthur James, 175-176
"Ballet for Martha," Copland, 351
Baltimore, 55, 181
Bancroft, Anne, 74
Barber, Samuel, 293, 305, 323, 326, 340, 385

Barbirolli, John, 298-300, 304-305, 316-318, 321, 325, 326
Barere, Simon, 301, 375-376
Barlow, Howard, 340, 343
Barnum, P. T., 16, 57, 64
Barrère, George, 256
Bartered Bride, The, 130
Bartók, Béla, 188, 232, 251-252, 304, 310-311, 339, 344, 356, 359, 391
Barzin, Leon, 272, 296, 359, 392
Basie, Count, 310
Bataan, McDonald, 329
Bauer, Harold, 4-5, 160, 169, 207
Bax, Arnold, 198
"Beale Street," Handy, 259
Bechet, Sidney, 310
Beecham, Sir Thomas, 252-253, 292, 361, 384, 385, 386
Beethoven, 7, 9, 10, 16, 37, 40, 49, 50, 53, 65, 66, 98, 100, 103, 110, 112, 120, 122, 127, 129, 130-131, 132, 138, 139, 140, 141, 144, 146, 148, 161, 180, 183, 186, 198, 200, 207, 208, 217, 236, 242, 246, 248, 254, 256, 280, 283-284, 286, 288, 291, 292, 297, 304, 321, 327, 349, 378, 389, 390, 408
Beinum, Eduard von, 384
Belafonte, Harry, 404
Bellini, 380
Belloc, Hilaire, 214
Bells, The, Rachmaninoff, 199
Belmont, August, 131
Belmont, Mrs. O. H. P., 135
Ben Greet Players, 131
Bennett, Robert Russell, 323-324
Benny, Jack, 402-403, 404
Bentley, Alys, 330
Berceuse Elégiaque, Busoni, 147
Berezowsky, Nicholas, 340
Berg, Alban, 270-271, 276, 293-294, 391, 396
Bergmann, Carl, 18
Berlin, 62, 151, 178, 285, 290, 304
Berlin Philharmonic Orchestra, 388-389
Berlioz, Hector, 9, 21, 49, 66, 80, 86, 110, 146, 158, 205, 208, 222, 224, 385, 389
Berners, Lord, 384
Bernstein, Leonard, 69, 333-334, 342-344, 370, 386, 399-400, 402, 405-412
"Betty and Harold Close Their Eyes." *See Hexapoda*
B Flat minor Piano Concerto, Tchaikovsky, 236, 338
Biancolli, Louis, 303, 381
Big Bill, 310
Bing, Rudolf, 379
"Birth of Jazz, The," Handy, 259
Bispham, David, 111, 126
Bizet, Georges, 1, 146
Bjoerling, Jussi, 311
Black, Brown and Beige, Ellington, 330
Blaine, James G., 29, 46, 48
Blaine, Margaret, 29. *See also* Damrosch, Mrs. Walter
Blake, William, Poems, settings by Thomson, 384
Bliss, Arthur, 198, 318
Blitzstein, Marc, 398
Bloch, Ernest, 174, 260, 320, 343, 351, 378, 379, 386
"Blue Bell," MacDowell, 126
Blue Bells of Harlem, Ellington, 330
"Blue Danube, The," 17, 202
Bluebird, The, Maeterlinck, 202
Blutopia, Ellington, 330
B minor Sonata, Chopin, 82
Bodansky, Artur, 174, 183, 188, 199, 204, 205, 206, 208, 209
Boer War, 84, 95-96
Bolero, Ravel, 240, 265
Bolet, Jorge, 382
Bolshevik Revolution, 139, 229, 269
Bolt, The, Shostakovich, 296
Borodin, 400
Boston, 17, 181-182, 211, 226, 260, 309
Boston Pops Orchestra, 400
Boston Symphony Orchestra. *See sub* Symphony Orchestra
Boston University chorus and orchestra, 392
Botticelli, 277
Boulanger, Nadia, 224-226, 312
Brahms, 7, 9, 21, 39, 61, 101, 112, 115, 120, 161, 163, 164, 172, 173, 200, 205, 208, 218, 223, 248, 291, 292, 302, 304, 324, 327, 336, 344, 349, 384, 388, 393
Breslau, Germany, 19
Britten, Benjamin, 318, 321, 363
Brodsky string quartet, 61
Brooklyn music societies, 35
Brosa, Antonio, 318
Broun, Heywood, 210
Brown, Minnie, 259

Brown, Sidney, 259
Brubeck, Dave, 402
Bruckner, Anton, 7, 122, 129, 144, 148, 157, 163, 199, 271, 322, 384, 389-390
Bruder Lustig, S. Wagner, 158
Bryan, William Jennings, 78-79, 228, 245
Budapest, 151
Bülow, Hans von, 17, 24
Bunte Suite, Toch, 276
Busch, Adolph, 248, 265
Busch, Fritz, 246-248, 250, 325, 327
Busoni, 143-144, 147, 169, 326
Butler, Nicholas Murray, 125

Cabell, James Branch, 232
Cadenza, Joachim, 250
Cage, John, 355, 362
Cakewalk, Gottschalk, 17
Callas, Maria, 379, 380
Calvé, 70
Canada, 84
Cantelli, Guido, 393, 398
Canticle of Freedom, Copland, 406
Canticle of Hope, Hindemith, 392
Canticum Sacrum, Stravinsky, 385
Capriccio for Piano and Orchestra, Stravinsky, 272
Capriccio No. 24, Paganini, 178
Captivity, The, Vogrich, 41
Carmina Burana, Orff, 392
Carnaval d'Aix, Le, Milhaud, 242
Carnegie, Andrew, 3, 4, 20, 24-31, 33, 35-36, 41, 46, 47, 48, 49, 50, 51, 54, 56, 70, 123-124, 132, 230, 308, 371, 416, 417
Carnegie, Dale, 76
Carnegie Foundation, 267
Carnegie Hall, location, 3, 32-33; architecture, 4, 33-34; passes to public ownership, 12-13, 415-418 *passim;* beginnings, 20, 29, 31ff.; financing of, 28, 29-30, 31; cornerstone laid, 34-36; inaugural concerts, 36, 38; Philharmonic first concerts in, 65; acquires its name, 71-72; major additions constructed, 72; first dramatic performance in, 132.
Under new management, 230-231, 412; economic crisis, 273, 278-279; fires, 279-280, 291; fiftieth anniversary season, 321ff.; Studio 61, 330-335; recent profits, 412; demolition plans, 412-413; rescued from destruction, 413-418 *passim*
Carnegie Hall (film), 351-353
Carnegie, Mrs. Andrew, 24, 30, 35, 46
Carnegie peace conference (April-May, 1907), 123-124
Carpenter, John Alden, 282, 293, 340, 363
Carreño, Teresa, 77-78, 114, 126, 174
Carrillo, Julián, 241
Casadesus, Robert, 327, 344-345
Casals, Pablo, 108, 169
Casella, Alfredo, 188, 198, 207, 231
Castelnuovo-Tedesco, Mario, 317
Caton, Edward, 332
Cederström, Baronesse. *See* Patti, Adelina
Cello Concerto, Hindemith, 323; Kabalevsky, 386
Central Trust Company, N.Y.C., 42-43
Chabrier, 146
Chabukiani, 285
Chaconne, Vitali, 178
Chadwick, George, 122, 146
Chaliapin, 218
Chamber Concertino, Ibert, 317
Chant du Rossignol, Le, Stravinsky, 217
Chasins, Abram, 269, 272, 297, 305, 378
Chautauqua, N.Y., 232
Checkmate, Bliss suite from, 318
Cherubini, 380
Chevalier, Maurice, 270
Chew, Otie, 115-116
Chicago Symphony Orchestra. *See sub* Symphony Orchestra
Chicago *Tribune,* 184
Chickering, Charles F., 31, 32
Chickering Hall, 24, 32
Chopin, 37, 60, 82, 120, 138, 288, 291, 323
Chotzinoff, Samuel, 234, 304, 394
Christian Catholic Church, 104
Christmas Festival, A, Overture, Berezowsky, 340
Christmas Overture, Taylor, 340
Christoff, Boris, 380
Christophe Colomb, Milhaud, 396
Church Windows, Respighi, 244
Churchill, Winston, 95
Cincinnati, 18-19
Cincinnati Symphony Orchestra. *See sub* Symphony Orchestra

Circus Day, Taylor, 235
Civil War, 4, 15, 16, 17, 18
"Clair de Lune," MacDowell, 126
Clarinet Concerto, Hindemith, 406
Clarinet Concerto in A, Mozart, 321
Claudel, Paul, 396
"Clavelitos," 346-347
Clemenceau, Georges, 212, 213-214
Clemens, Clara, 92-94, *See also* Gabrilowitsch, Mrs. Ossip
Cleopatra, Chadwick, 122
Cleveland Symphony Orchestra. *See sub* Symphony Orchestra
Cliburn, Van, 17, 373, 381-382
Clock Symphony, Haydn, 237
C minor Concerto, Saint-Saëns, 60
Coates, Albert, 204-205, 208
Cockran, W. Bourke, 84, 106
Colonne, Edouard, 110
Columbia Artists Management, 355, 372-373, 398
Columbia University, 125, 287
Comédie Française, 73
"Comin' Through the Rye," 106
Communism, 285
Concert Etude, MacDowell, 126
Concertgebouw Orchestra, Amsterdam, 386
Concertino for Piano, Honegger, 261-262
CONCERTO. See below, also by keys *e.g.,* A minor), instruments, titles, and ordinal numbers (First, Second, etc.)
Concerto for Harpsichord, Flute, Oboe, Clarinet, Violin and Cello, Falla, 244
Concerto for Jazz Band and Orchestra, Liebermann, 402
Concerto for Orchestra, Hindemith, 232; Piston, 296; Bartók, 391
Concerto for Percussion Instruments, Milhaud, 276
Concerto for Piano, Grieg, 375
Concerto for Piano and Wind Orchestra, Stravinsky, 363
Concerto for Saxophone, Creston, 340
Concerto for Strings, Stravinsky, 360
Concerto for the Left Hand, Ravel, 293
Concerto for Three Violins, Vivaldi, 228
Concerto for Violin, Beethoven, 246; Brahms, 248, 250
Concerto for Violin, Piano and Orchestra, Martinu, 385
Concerto Grosso, Křenek, 235
Concerto in C, Coates, 204
Concerto in D (K. 466), Mozart, 267-268
Concerto in D for Strings, Stravinsky, 363
Concerto in F, Gershwin, 232-235, 260
Concerto in G major (K. 453), Mozart, 398
Concerto Symphonique, Bloch, 386
Connecticut Yankee, A, Mark Twain, 125
Consecration of the House Overture, Beethoven, 138
Converse, Frederick S., 124
Cook, Frederick, 163
Copland, Aaron, 224, 232, 244, 309, 326, 329, 351, 374, 406, 410
Corigliano, John, 377
Coriolanus, Beethoven, 120, 130, 254
Cortège Funèbre, Milhaud, 340
Cortot, Alfred, 199
Costa, Albert da, 380
Court Opera Company, Vienna, 130
Cowell, Henry, 200, 216-217, 326
Craig, Edward Gordon, 151
Crash, Great, of 1929. *See* Stock Exchange crash
Creston, Paul, 340, 391
Critics' Circle. *See sub* Music
Cronyn, Hume, 74
Crooks, Richard, 242
Croske, Margaret, 332
C Sharp minor Prelude, Rachmaninoff, 185-186
Cue, 413
Cultural and Scientific Congress for World Peace, 365-367
Cumberland Concerto, Harris, 390
Cummings, Robert, 74
Cyrano de Bergerac, Damrosch, 322
Czechoslovakia, 341

Damnation of Faust, Berlioz, 385
Damrosch, Frank, 82, 103, 131, 161
Damrosch, Leopold, 19-22, 26, 28, 52
Damrosch, Mrs. Walter, 29, 40, 49
Damrosch, Walter, 20, 21-22, 24, 26, 28-29, 30, 32, 35, 36, 40-41, 42, 44, 47, 49, 50, 53, 60, 70-72, 79, 81, 82-83, 92, 99-100, 101-102, 112, 113, 119-120, 126-127, 128, 130, 131, 151, 152, 161, 169, 171-172, 177, 199,

207-208, 216, 217, 222, 224, 232-234, 244-245, 248, 251, 255, 256-257, 260, 271, 318, 322, 325, 327, 352, 370
Danish State Symphony Orchestra, 375, 386
Danse de la Sorcière, Tansman, 231
Danse des Morts, La, Honegger, 385
Daphne and Chloe (tone poem), Zimbalist, 276
Daphnis et Chloé Suite, Ravel, 171-172, 257, 388
DAR, 312
Darrow, Clarence, 245-246
Daughter of the Regiment, The, Donizetti, 70
Davis, Meyer, 402
Davis, Richard Harding, 95
Dayton, Tenn., Scopes trial at, 228
"Dear Lad of Mine," 184
Death and Transfiguration, Strauss, 398
"Death of Adonis," Ted Shawn, 154
Debs, Eugene Victor, 220, 229-230
Debussy, 7, 9, 146, 188, 195, 199, 202, 209, 223, 317, 389
Deep South Suite, Ellington, 330
DeKoven, Reginald, 128, 129, 152, 175. *See also World*
Delicious (film), 276
Delius, Frederick, 158
Dello Joio, Norman, 362
Delsarte, François, 73, 74
De Mille, Agnes, 332-335
DeMille, Cecil B., 74
Denishawn dancers, 154, 224, 330
Descobrimento do Brasil, Villa-Lobos, 321
Detroit Symphony Orchestra. *See sub* Symphony Orchestra
"Devil's Trill" sonata, 168
DeVoto, Bernard, 370
Dewey, Admiral, 82-83
Diamond, David, 326, 359, 390
"Dixie," 129
D minor Cello Concerto, Rubinstein, 100, 120
Dobrowen, Issay, 280
Dohnányi, Ernö, 92, 232
Dolin, Anton, 332
Don Cossack Chorus, 272
Don Giovanni, 82
Don Juan, Strauss, 205, 208, 242
Don Quixote, Strauss, 111, 342
Donahue, Lester, 231
"Don't Be That Way," 306
Dorati, Antal, 391
Dos Passos, John, 152
Dostoevski, 54
Douglas, Kirk, 74
Dowie, John, 104-105
Dowling, Robert W., 415
Downes, Olin, 91, 125, 196, 217-218, 223, 226-227, 236, 237-239, 250, 252, 253, 260, 268, 280, 286-287, 293-294, 297, 302-303, 305, 306, 320, 329, 342-343, 351, 353, 360, 361. *See also Times*
Doyle, Sir Arthur Conan, 209-210
Drake, Alfred, 332
Draper, Paul, 327
Dream of Gerontius, The, Elgar, 103
Dreiser, Theodore, 127
Driftwood, Jimmie, 401
Dukas, 116
Duncan, Isadora, 150-154, 210-211, 330
Dupont, Gabriel, 188
Durant, Will, 245
Durbin, Deanna, 345
Dutilleux, Henri, 386
Dvořák, Antonin, 9, 63-64, 66-68, 69, 70, 72, 76, 94, 199
Dyer-Bennet, Richard, 348

Eames, Emma, 71
Ebony Concerto, Stravinsky, 355
Eckstine, Billy, 404
Eddy, Nelson, 277
Edison, Harry, 401
Egmont Overture, Beethoven, 180, 321, 389
Eicheim, 200
Eighth Symphony, Schubert, 110; Bruckner, 129, 322; Mahler, 165. *See also* "Symphony of a Thousand"; Shostakovich, 349; Williams, 385
Einstein, Albert, 286
Elektra, Strauss, 302, 396
Elgar, Edward, 103, 114, 123, 160, 185, 204, 321
Elias, Rosalind, 380
Elijah, Mendelssohn, 51, 218, 396
Eliot, T. S., 197
Ellington, Duke, 330, 401
Elman, Mischa, 114, 129, 178, 183, 341, 378
Emanu-El, Temple, N.Y.C., 134-135

Emperor Concerto, Beethoven, 60, 143, 280
Enesco, Georges, 146, 218, 242, 302, 305
Enfance du Christ, L', 222, 224
England, 70, 95, 96, 103. *See also* Great Britain
Enigma Variations, Elgar, 321
Enoch Arden, Strauss, 111
Episodes Amoureuses, Herbert, 86
Eroica Symphony, Beethoven, 72, 126, 138, 349
Essenine, Sergei, 210, 211
Eugene Onegin, Tchaikovsky, 39, 126
Euryanthe Overture, C. Weber, 237, 266
Evening Mail, 178
Ewen, David, 18, 182-183

"Façade," Walton, 305
Falla, Manuel de, 198, 244
"False Spring," MacDowell, 126
Falstaff, Verdi, 224
Fancy Free, Kern-Robbins, 344
Fantaisies Symphoniques, Martinu, 386
Fantasia (film), 345
Fantasia in C major, Schumann, 172-173
Fantastic Suite for Piano and Orchestra, Schelling, 129
Farrar, Geraldine, 119
Farrell, Eileen, 380, 390, 395, 396
Fascism, 237, 240, 264, 265, 315, 324. *See also* Nazism
Fauré, 116
Faust, Schumann, 61
Fiedler, Max, 128, 139
Field, Betty, 74
Fields, Benny, 235
Fifth Piano Concerto, Saint-Saëns, 80
Fifth Symphony, Beethoven, 40, 53, 103, 120, 130-131, 140, 236; Dvořák, 66-68; Glazunov, 79; Tchaikovsky, 86, 120, 291; Mahler 118; Bruckner, 157-158; Sibelius, 209; Harris, 329; Tansman, 340; Williams, 348; Prokofieff, 351, 406; Nielsen, 375; Honegger, 385; Creston, 391
Finck, Henry T., 86, 117, 138, 158 *See also Post*
Firebird, The, Stravinsky, 198
First and Last Love, Sheean, 388-389
First Piano Concerto, Tchaikovsky, 44, 53; Paderewski, 60; Brahms, 101; Chasins, 269
First Symphony, Beethoven, 7, 180, 242; Brahms, 21, 223, 388, 393; Dvorák, 66; Tchaikovsky, 72; Suk, 94; Mahler, 140; Stravinsky, 172; Copland, 224; Shostakovich, 324; Diamond, 326; Barber, 340; Martinu, 341; Bernstein, 344; Dutilleux, 386
First Violin Concerto, Prokofieff, 232; Saint-Saëns, 305
First Violin Sonata, Bartók, 344
Fisher, Prof. Irving, 264
Fitzgerald, Ella, 401
Fitzgerald, F. Scott, 193, 262
Five Orchestral Pieces, Schönberg, 362
Flagler, Harry Harkness, 24, 102, 232, 245, 255, 256
Flagstad, Kirsten, 300, 301, 305, 323, 356-358, 365, 376-377
Fleisher, Leon, 347-348
Fletcher, Tom, 259
"Flirtations in a Chinese Garden," Chasins, 272
Florence Festival Orchestra, 390
Florentine Opera, 287
F major Sonata, Mozart, 288
Foch, Nina, 74
Fokine family, 330
Földes, Andor, 359
Folk-Song Symphony, Harris, 294, 326
Forbidden Childhood, Slenczynska, 290
Forest Stillness, MacDowell, 125
Fort Oglethorpe, Ga., 182
Fosdick, Dr. Harry Emerson, 278
Foss, Lukas, 410
Foote, Arthur, 319
Fountains of Rome, Respighi, 186
Fourth Piano Concerto, Beethoven, 100, 284; Rachmaninoff, 243
Fourth Symphony, Glazunov, 108; Mahler, 114; Schumann, 115; Tchaikovsky, 187; Bruckner, 199; Brahms, 200; Sibelius, 271; Prokofieff, 272; Ives, 348; Diamond, 359; Křenek, 360; Piston, 386; Kabalevsky, 396
Françaix, Jean, 312
France, 17, 176, 192, 212, 226, 315
Francescatti, Zino, 318
Franck, 80
"Fraternity and Charity" (speech), 37
Free Song, A, Schuman, 329

Free Synagogue, N.Y.C., 134
Freischütz, Der, Weber, 388
Frick, W. C., 46
Friedheim, Arthur, 37-38
Friedman, 207
Friends of Music, 174, 209
Friml, Rudolf, 112
"From Chaos to Man" (lecture), 62
"From Spirituals to Swing" (survey), 310
From the New World, Dvořák, 66-68
Fry, Roger, 25-26
"Fugue of the Vices," Markevitch. *See Rebus*
Funeral March from *Eroica,* Beethoven, 349
"Funeral Music," Wagner, 237. *See also* "Siegfried Idyl," *Götterdämmerung*
Furtwängler, 223, 242, 358

Gabel, Martin, 74
Gabrilowitsch, Clara (Mrs. Ossip), 92-94, 177, 236-237, 258
Gabrilowitsch, Ossip, 92-94, 100, 122, 149, 177, 180, 205-206, 207, 228, 236-237, 258, 269, 271, 277, 291-292
Gadski, Johanna, 156, 176
Gallico, Paolo, 143
Gamble, The, Prokofieff, 280
Garden, Mary, 90, 119, 128, 154-156
Garden of Fand, The, Bax, 206
Garner, Erroll, 404
Gary, Judge Elbert, 195
Gaspard de la Nuit, Ravel, 356
Gatti-Casazza, Giulio, 176-177
Geer, Will, 329
Geniuses, Goddesses, and People, Sargeant, 255-257
Gerardy, Jean, 80, 98, 164
Gericke, Wilhelm, 80, 101, 115, 116, 118
German Requiem, Brahms, 61, 161
Germania Orchestra, 16
Germany, 18, 19, 124, 142, 184, 214, 226, 286, 292, 301, 315
Gershwin, George, 195, 232-235, 244, 260-261, 273-276, 327, 328, 332
Gibbons, Floyd, 184
Gibson, Charles Dana, 213
Gieseking, Walter, 235-236, 358, 365, 377
Gigli, Beniamino, 377
Gilels, Emil, 382
Gillmore, Margalo, 74
Gilman, Lawrence, 260, 283, 287. *See also Herald* and *Herald Tribune*
Gilson, Paul, 66
Girl of the Golden West, The, 119
Glazunov, Alexander, 79, 108, 110, 156
Glinka, 115
Globe, 178
Gluck, Alma, 164
Gluck, Christophe W., 377, 380
G major Piano Concerto, Ravel, 282
"God Save the Queen," 64
Godowsky, Leopold, 38, 163, 164, 177, 178
Goldman, Eric F., 349-350
Goldmark, Rubin, 171, 236
Goldwyn, Samuel, 202
"Golliwog's Cakewalk, The," 202
Golschmann, Vladimir, 277
Goodman, Benny, 259, 305-306, 308, 310-311, 321, 328, 330, 406
Goodson, 160
Goosens, Eugene, 198, 265, 325
Gordon, Taylor, 259
Götterdämmerung, Wagner, 70, 236, 305, 392. *See also* "Funeral Music"
Gottschalk, Louis, 17
Gould, Glenn, 381
Gould, Morton, 326
Graffman, Gary, 361
Graham, Martha, 154, 224, 308-309, 321, 351, 354-355, 390
Grainger, Percy, 199, 207
Grand Army of the Republic, 37
Great Britain, 84, 96, 315. *See also* England
Greco, José, 349
Grieg, 375
Grofé Ferde, 259, 282
Guaracha, Gould, 326
"Gut-Bucket Gus." *See Hexapoda*

Hadley, Henry, 146, 217, 272
Haffner Symphony, Mozart, 305
Hall Johnson, choir, 309-310
Hall, Wilbur, 259
Hambourg, Mark, 85, 101
Hambro, Leonid, 402
Hamlet and Ophelia, MacDowell, 125
Hammerstein, Oscar I, 118-119, 128
Hammerstein, Oscar II, 332
Hammond, John, 328
Handel, 17, 53, 183, 380

Handy, W. C., 258-259
Handy, W. C., Jr., 259
Hänsel und Gretel, 119
Hanson, Howard, 242, 273, 280, 319, 385
Harmonie der Welt, Die, Hindemith, 396
Harold in Italy, Berlioz, 158
Harrell, Mack, 384, 395, 396
Harris, Bill, 401
Harris, Roy, 284-285, 294, 296, 319, 322-323, 326, 329, 340, 351, 373, 385, 390, 406
Harrison, Jay S., 403
Harrison, Lou, 352
Hart, Charles, 235
Hartford, Conn., 94
Hartmann, Arthur, 128
Harvard Glee Club, 385
Hawthorne, 71
Haydn, 198, 237, 288, 384, 389
Hayes, Roland, 224, 377
Hearst, William Randolph, 200
Heifetz, Jascha, 178-179, 183, 228, 297-298, 323-324, 353, 371
Heldenleben, Ein, Strauss, 85, 111, 115
Hellmesberger, Joseph, 172
Henderson, W. J., 138, 140, 142, 156-157
Henley, William Ernest, 230
Herald, New York, 46, 48, 52, 62, 64, 78, 156, 260
Herald Tribune, New York, 287, 290, 321, 347, 382, 398, 403. *See also* Gilman, Lang (Paul Henry), Harrison (Jay S.), etc.
Herbert, Victor, 68, 86, 102, 103, 110
Herman, Woody, 355
Hero and Leander Suite, Herbert, 110
Herrman, Bernard, 318
Hess, Myra, 216
Hexapoda (five studies in Jitteroptera), 324
Heydrich, Reinhard, 341
Higginson, Col. Henry Lee, 22, 63, 64, 103, 118, 181, 182, 187
Hill, Edward Burlingame, 244, 273, 319
Hindemith, Paul, 199, 222, 232, 235-236, 273, 292-293, 323, 326, 339, 359, 363, 391, 392, 396, 406
Hinkle, Florence, 161
Hippodrome, N.Y.C., 136
Hitchens, Aubrey, 330
Hitler, Adolf, 292, 315, 358, 388
Hoffman, Frederick J., 214
Hofmann, Josef, 79, 98, 112, 127, 160, 166, 228, 323
Hofmann, Mrs. Joseph, 166. *See also* Sembrich, Marcella
Hofstadter, Richard, 6
Hollywood, 202, 352
Holm, Celeste, 332
Holm, Hanya, 154
Holmes, John Haynes, 364
Holst, Gustav, 198, 231
"Home Sweet Home," 105
Honegger, Arthur, 198, 222, 223, 231, 261-262, 266, 271, 272, 355, 360-361, 385
Honegger Mrs. Arthur, 261
"Honeysuckle Rose," 306
Hoogstraten, Willem Van. *See* Van Hoogstraten
Horowitz, Mrs. Vladimir, 280
Horowitz, Vladimir, 252-253, 275, 280, 338, 349, 361, 371
House, Colonel, 177
Hovhaness, Alan, 392
Howe, Mark A. de Wolfe, 80, 198
Hubermann, Bronislaw, 76-77, 206, 207, 218
Huckleberry Finn, Mark Twain, 125
Humphrey, Doris, 154
Huneker, James Gibbons, 64-65, 82, 83-84, 86, 185-186, 188
Hungarian Fantasia, Liszt, 60, 76
Hunt, Marsha, 353
Hunter College, N.Y.C., 412
Hurley, Laurel, 380
Hurok, Sol, 157, 207, 210, 211, 216, 312, 373
Hutcheson, Ernest, 207, 232
Hyde, E. Francis, 35, 39, 42, 49
Hylan, Mayor John F., N.Y.C., 190

Iberian Suite, Debussy, 146
Ibert, 317
Icare, Markevitch, 410
Ickes, Harold, 312
"I'm Goin' South in the Morning," 235
In Autumn, MacDowell, 125
"In a Summer Garden," Delius, 158
In the South, Elgar, 114
Independent Coalition of American Women, The, 300
Indian Suite, MacDowell, 79, 124

Indy, Vincent D', 90-91, 116, 126, 199, 208, 209
Infantry Chorus (Negro veterans), 359
"Influence of the G.A.R. on the Future of the Republic" (speech), 37
"In Memoriam: The Colored Soldiers Who Died for Democracy," Still, 340
Intermezzo, Martinu, 390
International Society for Contemporary Music, 30
"Invictus," Henley, 230
"Ionization," Varèse, 282
Ireland, 108
"Is Man a Machine?" (debate), 245
"Is Modern Morality a Failure?" (debate), 274
Israel, Bloch, 260
Israel in Egypt, Handel, 53
Israel Philharmonic Orchestra, 386-388
Istonien, Eugene, 344, 356
Italian repertory, 119
Italy, 84, 226
Iturbi, José, 267-268, 308
Ives, Charles, 68-69, 348, 352, 406
"I Wonder as I Wander." *See Christmas* Overture

Jackson, George, 259
Jacob's Pillow Dance Festival, 349
"Jalousie," 400
James, Harry, 306, 353
James, Joni, 404
"Jane Shakes Her Hair." *See Hexapoda*
Janis, Byron, 361
Janssen, Werner, 293
Japan surrenders, 349
Jaroff, Serge, 272
JATP, 401
Jeanne d'Arc au Bucher, Honegger, 360-361, 385
Jehlinger, Charles, 74
Jenkins, Florence Foster, 345-347
Jensen, Thomas, 386
Jeremiah Symphony, Bernstein, 344
Jewish refugees, 285
"Jig of the Noes," Markevitch. *See Rebus*
"Jim Jines." *See Hexapoda*
Joachim, Joseph, 72, 172, 250, 303
Johnson, Alva, 202
Johnson, Edward, 318, 319
Johnson, J. Rosamond, 259
Johnson, Pete, 310
Johnson, Thor, 390
Johnston, Robert E., 139
Jones, Jennifer, 74
Joseffy, Rafael, 72-73
Joslyn, Henry, 276-277
Jour d'été à la Montagne, D'Indy, 126
Joyce, James, 197
Judith, Schuman, 390
Judson, Arthur, 355, 398, 399
Juilliard School, 359
Jullien, 16, 18
Jurgen, Taylor-Cabell, 232

Kabalevsky, 386, 396
Kahn, Otto, 261
Kallir, Lilian, 398
Kammersymphonie, Schönberg, 215
Kanin, Garson, 74
Kansas City Six, 310
Kaplan, Alice (Mrs. Jacob M.), 413
Kaplan, Jacob M., 413
Kaplan, J. M., Fund, 413
Karajan, Herbert von, 388-389
Kay, Hershy, 17
Kay, Lisan, 332
Kaye, Danny, 403-404
Kelly, Grace, 74
Kern, Jerome, 326, 328
Khatchaturian, 360
Kiepura, Jan, 308
Kilgraston castle, Scotland, 24, 28, 29
Kindertotenlieder, Mahler, 142
"King Erik's Songs," Rangström, 376
King Lear, Weingartner, 110
King Stephen Overture, Beethoven, 198
Kingdom, The, Elgar, 123
Kitchell, Iva, 354
Kleiber, Erich, 270-271, 276, 277
Kleine Nachtmusik, Eine, Mozart, 120
Klemperer, Otto, 235, 292-293, 295-296
Knabe Piano Company, 39, 55
Kneisel, Franz, 103-104, 146
Knickerbocker, Cholly, 42
Kodály, 265, 271
Kolodin, Irving, 199-200, 330, 336-338, 392-394
Konzertmusik, Hindemith, 273
Korean War, 367
Kostelanetz, 400
Koussevitzky, Serge, 198, 200, 220-222, 224, 232, 244, 257, 260, 265, 268, 272-273, 275-276, 282, 284, 291, 293,

296, 309, 319-320, 323, 325, 327, 329, 341, 363-364, 385, 386
Krehbiel, Henry E., 36, 82, 86, 118, 119, 127, 138, 146, 149, 152, 158, 160, 162, 178. *See also Tribune*
Kreisler, Fritz, 94, 98, 112, 122, 166-169, 172-173, 177-178, 180, 183, 184-185, 197, 218, 311, 335, 336, 358
Kreisler, Mrs. Fritz, 167, 168, 184-185
Křenek, Ernst, 235, 276, 277, 330, 360
Kreutzer Sonata, Beethoven, 114
Kriza, John, 344
Krupa, Gene, 306
Kubelik, Jan, 96-98, 108, 112, 116, 391
Kubelik, Rafael, 390

Lada (dancer), 202
Lafayette Camp, G.A.R., 37
Laffing Room Only, Olsen and Johnson, 349
La Follette, Robert M., Sr., 149-151
La Guardia, Fiorello, 292
Lambert, Alexander, 79
La Montaine, John, 391
Lamoureux Orchestra, Paris, 390
Lancelot and Elaine, MacDowell, 125, 171
Landon, Alfred, 300-301
Landowska, Wanda, 218, 244, 348
Lang, Harold, 344
Lang, Paul Henry, 381-382
Lange, Hans, 296
LaScala, Milan, 119, 237, 240, 265, 292
"Last Farewell, The," 105
"Last Rose of Summer, The," 105
Laurents, Pare, 329
Lawrence, Marjorie, 300
League of Composers, 340
League of Nations, 188, 189, 202, 211, 212
Lear: A Study, Blitzstein, 396
"Legend," Tchaikovsky, 52
Leginska, Ethel, 224-226
Lehmann, Lilli, 78, 83, 118
Lehrer, Tom, 404
Lekeu, 198
Lenore Symphony, Raff, 102
Leoncavallo, Ruggiero, 119
Leonore Overture No. 1, Beethoven, 297; *No. 3,* 49, 50, 181
Levant, Oscar, 328
Levene, Sam, 74
Leventritt Piano Competition, 361, 373
Lewis, Meade "Lux," 310
Lhévinne, Josef, 114, 117, 120, 160, 207, 323
Liberian Suite, Ellington, 330
Liberty League, 300
Liebermann, Rolf, 402
"Liebestod," from *Tristan,* Wagner, 152
Lied von der Erde, Das, Mahler, 144, 148, 209, 322
Liederkranz Society, N.Y.C., 72
Life (magazine), 394
Life for the Czar, A, Glinka, 115
"Life Goes to a Party," 306
Life of the Bee, The, Maeterlinck, 202
"Lilacs," Hill-Lowell, 244
Lillie, Beatrice, 306
Lincoln, Abraham, 85, 329, 349
Lincoln Center for the Performing Arts, N. Y. C., 12, 412, 416
Lincoln Memorial, 312-314
Lincoln Portrait, A, Copland, 329
Lincoln Symphony, Mason, 302
Lind, Jenny, 16, 17
Lindsay, Howard, 74
List, Eugene, 296
Liszt, Franz, 9, 18, 19, 39, 60, 65, 66, 82, 86, 102, 110, 120, 138, 208, 311, 335
Little Symphony, Křenek, 272
Little Symphony Orchestra, N. Y. C., 351-352
Locatelli, 183
Lochner, Louis, 172, 184-185
Lodge, Sir Oliver, 202-204, 209
Loeffler, Charles Martin, 124, 146, 199, 232
Lohengrin, Wagner, 392, 404
Lomax, Alan, 401
Lombroso, 76
London, 58, 182-183, 389
London Symphony, Williams, 204-205
London Symphony Orchestra, 162
"Long Ago," MacDowell, 126
Longines Symphonette, 204
Lopez, Pilar, 349
Los Angeles, Calif., 347
"Lost" Violin Concerto, Schumann, 304
Louisville Symphony Orchestra. *See sub* Symphony Orchestra
Lowell, Amy, 244
Luboshutz, Lea, 232
Luboshutz and Nemonoff, 341

Lucia di Lammermoor, 96, 106
Lulu, Berg, 293-294, 391
Lyric Suite, Berg, 276

MacDowell, Edward, 68, 72, 77, 79, 124-126, 146, 171
Mackay, Clarence H., 237
MacKaye, Steele, 73
McCarthyism, 367
McClellan, Mayor G. B., N. Y. C., 123
McClintic, Guthrie, 74
McCormack, John, 168-169, 175, 218
McDonald, Harl, 329
McKinley, William, 78
McMoon, Cosmo, 347

Madison Square Garden, N. Y. C., 32, 61, 104
Maeterlinck, Maurice, 200-202
Magidoff, Robert, 250
Mahler, Alma (Mrs. Gustav), 146, 148
Mahler, Gustav, 7, 65, 89-90, 103, 114, 118, 130-131, 132, 133, 138, 139-149, 163, 165, 180, 186, 209, 215, 242, 275, 322, 323, 360, 389, 396-398, 410
Mahler Memorial Concert, 157
"Maid Sings Light, A," MacDowell, 126
Malipiero, 198
Manfred Overture, Schumann, 132, 342
Manhattan Club, 53
Manhattan Opera Company, 118-119, 128
Manhattan Symphony Orchestra, 272
Manila Te Deum, W. Damrosch, 82-83
Mann, Thomas, 117
Manski, Dorothea, 271
Mantovani, 371, 400, 404
"March in Time of War," Harris, 340
"Marche Militaire," Schubert, 208
Marche Slave, Tchaikovsky, 210
Marche Solennelle, Tchaikovsky, 44, 49
Marchesi, Blanche, 83-84
"Marching Through Georgia," 37
Marek, George R., 338
Maria Eguiziaca, Respighi, 277-278
Markevitch, Igor, 282, 410
"Marseillaise," 136
Marshall Plan, 366
Martin, Freddy, 400
Martinu, Bohuslav, 341, 385, 386, 390
"Martyrdom of Poland, The" (speech), Paderewski, 171
Masked Ball, The, Verdi, 394
Mason, Daniel Gregory, 170, 277, 302
Massenet, 102
Mata and Hari, 349
Mathis der Maler, Hindemith, 293
Matzenauer, Margarete, 183-184
May Day Symphony, Shostakovich, 282, 283
Mayer, Ferdinand, 39, 42, 55
Mayes, Samuel, 386
Maynor, Dorothy, 327
Mazeppa, Liszt, 138
Meck, Nadejda von, 39
Meistersinger, Die, Wagner, 86, 130, 270, 342, 343, 393
Melba, Nellie, 70, 105, 106, 118, 185
Melchior, Lauritz, 242, 300
Melody in F, Rubinstein, 103
Melpomene, Chadwick, 146
Meltzer, Charles Henry, 148, 161
Melville, Herman, 318
"Memorial to Lidice," Martinu, 341
Memories of a Child's Sunday, Harris, 351
"Memories of My Childhood," Loeffler, 232
"Memphis Blues," Handy, 259
Mendelssohn, 9, 51, 76, 131, 132, 204, 218, 396, 402-403
Mendelssohn Choir of Montreal, 122
Mengelberg, Willem, 115, 205, 206, 208, 214, 215, 223, 231, 237, 242, 251-252, 254-255, 260, 267
Mennin, Peter, 396
Menotti, Gian Carlo, 384
Menuhin, Hephzibah, 304
Menuhin, Yehudi, 246-250, 288, 303-304, 344, 378-379
"Mephisto Waltz, The," Liszt, 18, 86
Mérö, Yolanda, 143, 207
"Merry Maiden Spring," MacDowell, 126
"Merry Song and a Chorus Brave, A, MacDowell, 126
Messiah, The, Handel, 17
Metamorphoseon Modi XII, Respighi, 273, 276
"Metropolis," Grofé, 259
Metropolitan Opera, 22, 24, 32, 35, 41, 46, 55, 61, 65, 70, 79, 85, 89, 92, 118, 119, 127-128, 129, 130, 165, 175, 176, 183, 186, 212, 213, 224, 231, 237, 271, 287, 318, 319, 343-344, 376, 379, 390

Mexico, National Symphony Orchestra of, 390
Miaskowsky, 242
Midsummer Night's Dream, A, Mendelssohn incidental music for, 131
Milan, 292
Miles, Gwilym, 161
Milhaud, Darius, 198, 242, 276, 340, 351, 360, 396
Miller, Frank, 393
Milstein, Nathan, 269, 275, 354
Mindszenty, Cardinal, 365
Minneapolis Symphony Orchestra. *See sub* Symphony Orchestra
Missa Solemnis, Beethoven, 286, 292
Mitchell, Howard, 391
Mitchell, MacNeil, 414
Mitropoulos, Dimitri, 321, 325, 326, 327, 330, 336, 355, 360, 362, 363, 395-399, 402, 410
Moby Dick (cantata), Herrman, 318
Moderne Klaviermusik, Hindemith, 235-236
Moïséiwitsch, Benno, 197-198
Monroe, Vaughan, 353
Monteux, Pierre, 187, 198, 217, 218, 220, 347, 351, 353-354
Monteverdi, 312, 380
Montreal, 122, 396
Moody, Dwight L., memorial service for, 84-85
Moore, Douglas, 287-288
Moore, Marianne, 415
Moorehead, Agnes, 74
Mordkin, Mikhail, 330
Morgan, J. P., 20, 25-26, 131
Morini, Erika, 204
Morning Journal, 42
Morris, Harold, 275
Morros, Boris, 352-353
Moscow, 41, 55, 110, 211
Mossolov, Alexander, 276, 280
Moszkowski, Moritz, 207, 208
Moussorgsky, 39, 198
Mowry, George, 6
Mozart, 7, 9, 65, 120, 164, 173, 205, 242, 246, 267-268, 288, 291, 297, 302, 305, 312, 321, 335, 336, 389, 390, 398
Muck, Karl, 119, 122, 124, 129, 162, 164, 167, 181-182, 187, 319
Muckle, May, 126
Munch, Charles, 355-356, 360, 361, 385-386
Munich, 144, 151, 166
Murray, Don, 74
Music Critics' Circle Award, 344, 351
Music for a Scene from Shelley, Barber, 293
Music for Strings, Percussion and Celesta, Bartók, 304
Music for the Theater, Copland, 232
Music Hall, N. Y. C., 3, 29, 31-36, 40 ff., 71-72, 416. *See also* Carnegie Hall
Musical America, 81, 118, 128, 166, 167, 171, 180, 197, 260, 328
Musical Courier, 50, 78

Nabokov, Nicolas, 321, 386
Nardini, 183
Nation, The, 177
National Artists Management, 372-373
National Conservatory of Music, 63, 64
National Geographic Society, 163
National Orchestral Association, 272, 291, 296, 359, 392
National Symphony Orchestra, 204, 205, 206, 391. *See also* New Symphony Orchestra
National Symphony Orchestra of Mexico, 390
"Nature, Life and Love" (triple overture), Dvořák, 64
Nazism, 9, 223, 285-286, 304, 316, 358, 388. *See also* Fascism
NBC Symphony Orchestra, 338, 349, 392-395
Neapolitan Scenes, Massenet, 102
Neilson, Mrs. James, 21
Nemenoff and Luboschutz, 341
New Deal, 282-283, 295, 300-301, 350
New Girl in Town. See Anna Christie
New Haven, Conn., 332
New Jersey music societies, 35
New Lost City Ramblers, 401
New Masses, The, 310
New Orleans Feet Warmers, 310
New Symphony Orchestra, The, 187-188, 199. *See also* National Symphony Orchestra
New World A-Comin,' Ellington, 330
New Yorker, The, 293
New York Philharmonic Orchestra. *See* Philharmonic Orchestra
New York Symphony Orchestra. *See sub* Symphony Orchestra
New York Times, The. See Times

New Zealand, franchise in, 136
Ney, Mme., 207
Nielsen, Carl, 375
Night Creature, Ellington, 401
Nikisch, Arthur, 80, 140, 162
Nimura, Yeichi, 332
1933 Symphony, Harris, 284, 285
Ninth Symphony, Beethoven, 122, 144, 148, 180, 242, 256; Bruckner, 148; Mahler, 275, 323; Shostakovich, 354
Nordica, Lillian, 71, 88, 91
Normandie, Hotel, N. Y. C., 40, 41
Norway, 301, 356-358
Nutcracker Suite, Tchaikovsky, 115

Oberhoffer, Emil, 161
Oberon, Weber, 390
O'Brien, Pat, 74
"Ode," Hill, 273
Ode in Three Parts for Orchestra, Stravinsky, 363
"Ode to Music," Chabrier, 146
"Ode to Napoleon," Schönberg, 348
Ode to the End of the War, Prokofieff, 354
Oedipus Rex, Schelling-Sophocles, 98
Ohe, Adele Aus der, 44, 53
Oistrakh, David, 382
Oklahoma! 332, 334
Old California, 347
"Old Hundred," 47-48
Olsen and Johnson, 349
On the Shores of the Sea, 209
One Hundred Men and a Girl (film), 345
"100 strings and Joni James," 404
135th Street, Gershwin, 235
"One O'Clock Jump," 306
O'Neill, Eugene, 400
Oratorio Society, N.Y.C., 20, 21, 22, 24, 26, 28, 30, 34, 61, 82, 103, 122, 161, 218
Orchestral Variations, Copland, 410
Orff, Carl, 385, 392
Ormandy, 323, 329, 341, 359, 375, 376
Ornstein, 207
Orpheus (ballet), Stravinsky, 363
Orwell, George, 400
Osborne, Lithgow, 376
Ostrovsky, Alexander, 41
"Our Father," Tchaikovsky, 52
"Over the Hills and Far Away," 199
Oxenburg, Allen, 379-380

Pachmann, Vladimir de, 85, 108, 160, 218-220
Pacific 231, Honegger, 224, 261-262
Paderewski, Ignace Jan, 56-61, 85, 92, 108, 112, 163-164, 166, 171, 174, 211-214, 218, 253, 283
Paderewski, Mme. Ignace Jan, 171
Pagan Poem, A, Loeffler, 199
Pagan Symphony, Joslyn, 276, 277
Paganini, 178, 318
Palestine, 286
Pan and the Priest, Hanson, 242
Pankhurst, Emmeline, 135-138
Parables, The, Martinu, 386
"Parade," Chasins, 272
Paris, 40, 41, 44, 58, 148, 183, 224, 290, 294, 312, 390
Parker, Charlie 401
Parker, H. T., 220
Parliament, British, 95; House of Commons, 136
Parsifal, Wagner, 7, 30, 53
Pathetique Symphony, Tchaikovsky, 210. *See also sub* Sixth Symphony
Patterns, Carpenter, 282
Patti, Adelina, 104
Paur, Emil, 80-81, 85, 94, 99, 122
Paur, Leonard De, 359
Peace Conference. *See* Carnegie peace conference
Pearl Harbor, 324
Peerce, Jan, 323, 353
Pelleas and Melisande, Schönberg, 172
Pelléas et Mélisande, Debussy, 202
Persephone, Stravinsky, 296
Pershing, Gen. John J., 212
Persichetti, Vincent, 390
Persinger, Louis, 250
Peterson, Oscar, 401
Petri, Egon, 290
Petri, Endre, 310-311
Petrouchka, Stravinsky, 302-303
Petschnikoff, Alexander, 85
Pfitzner, 144
Philadelphia Centennial Exposition, 17
Philadelphia Symphony Orchestra. *See sub* Symphony Orchestra
Philharmonia Orchestra, London, 389
Philharmonic Concerto, Hindemith, 363
Philharmonic Orchestra, N.Y.C., 18, 21, 24, 31, 34-35, 42, 53, 61, 63, 64-65, 66, 71, 72, 76-77, 79, 80-81, 85, 98, 99-102, 110-111, 114, 115, 118, 120,

128, 129, 130-132, 133-134, 138, 139 ff., 156, 157-160, 163, 169, 172, 173-174, 177, 183, 200, 204, 205, 206, 208, 214-215, 217, 220, 222-223, 231, 237-241, 242, 251-255, 257, 258. *See also* Philharmonic-Symphony Orchestra
Philharmonic - Symphony Orchestra, N.Y.C., 255, 259, 260, 262, 265-268, 270-272, 273, 276-279, 280, 283-284, 286-287, 288, 292-293, 295-300, 301, 302, 304-305, 311-312, 316-319, 321-322, 324, 325-327, 329, 330, 336, 338-343, 344, 347, 349, 351, 354, 355-356, 358-359, 360-361, 362-363, 377, 378-379, 382-383, 386, 390, 395-400, 401, 402, 403-404, 405-413; children's concerts, 98, 215, 269-270, 408, 415
Philharmonic Women's Club, 348
Phillips, Flip, 401
Piano Concerto in E, Dohnányi, 92
122, 236, 252, 253, 302, 338, 361, 381; Scriabin, 122; Sauer, 128; Brahms, 163; Copland, 244; Bartók, 251, 252; Shostakovich (Op. 35), 296; Castelnuovo-Tedesco, 317
Piano Concerto in E, Dohnányi, 92
Piastro Michel, 204, 305, 339
Piatigorsky, Gregor, 267, 275, 323, 353
Pijper, William, 354
Pilgrims of Canterbury, The, DeKoven 175
Pilsudski, Marshal, 212
Pinchot, Gifford, 150
Pines of Rome, The, Respighi, 237, 239
Pinocchio Overture, Toch, 321
Pinza, Ezio, 353
Pirata, Il, Bellini, 380
Piston, Walter, 296, 360, 385-386
Pittsburgh, 18-19, 177
Pittsburgh Symphony Orchestra. *See sub* Symphony Orchestra
Pizzetti, 265, 271
Plain-Chant for America, Still, 326
Plow That Broke the Plains, The Thomson-Laurents, 329
Poe, Edgar Allan, 199
Poet and Peasant, Suppé, 102
Poland, 211-212, 315
Polish Rhapsody, Tansman, 329
Polish Victims' Relief Fund, 171
Political Equality League for Self-Supporting Women, 135
Pons, Lily, 275, 353
"Pop" music, 355. *See also* Boston Pops Orchestra; composers and singers by name, etc.
Portland, Ore., 134
Post (New York), 86, 117, 138, 168, 177, 180
Poston, Tom, 74
Potter, Bishop Henry Codman, 48-49
Potter, Rev. Charles Francis, 228, 229
Pound, Ezra, 197
Powell, John, 217
Powell, William, 74
Prayer 1943, Schuman, 329
Prayers of Kierkegaard, Barber, 385
Press (New York), 237
Price, Leontyne, 385, 391
Prince and the Pauper, The, Mark Twain, 125
Prince Hal Overture, 170
Prokofieff, Sergei, 232, 268-269, 272, 276, 277, 280, 351, 354, 363, 406
Prometheus, Scriabin, 169-170
Prometheus Unbound, Shelley, 293
Prussian State Archives, 304
Prynne, Hester, sung by Nordica, 71
Pugno, Raoul, 80
Pulitzer, Joseph, 131, 158-160
Pulitzer Prize, 351, 406
Purcell, 204, 380

Rabaud, Henri, 187
Rabin, Michael, 382
Rachmaninoff, Sergei, 9, 114-115, 129, 139-140, 185-186, 199, 228, 243, 269, 291, 293, 294, 335-336, 381
Rachmaninoff Piano Prize, 361
Radcliffe Choral Society, 385
Radio sponsorship of music, 278, 287, 292, 298, 302
Raff, Joseph, 102, 125
Rainy Day Club, 98
Rangström, Ture, 376
Rascher, Sigurd, 317
Ravel, Maurice, 9, 171-172, 235, 240, 257-258, 265, 282, 293, 356, 388
RCA, 338
Read, Gardner, 304-305
Rebus, Markevitch, 282, 283
Reiner, Fritz, 252, 329, 353, 391
Reisenauer, Alfred, 110
Reno, Alice, 39, 40, 45, 49

Reno, Morris, 30, 35, 39, 41-42, 45, 48, 49, 62
Reno, Mrs. Morris, 51
Requiem, Brahms. *See German Requiem;* Verdi, 271, 308
Respighi, Ottorino, 186, 198, 220, 237, 240, 244, 265, 273, 276, 277-278, 280
Reszke, Edouard de, 118
Rhapsody for Clarinet and Violin, Bartók, 310
Rhapsody for Orchestra, Riegger, 276; Schnabel, 362
Rhapsody for Orchestra and Saxophone, Debussy, 317
Rhapsody for Piano and Orchestra (Op. 1), Bartók, 252
Rhapsody in Blue, Gershwin, 227, 232, 234
"Rhapsody in Rivets," Gershwin. *See* Second Rhapsody
Rhapsody on a Theme of Paganini, Rachmaninoff, 293, 336
Rheingold, Das, Wagner, 35
Ricci, Ruggerio, 267, 382
Richmond, Frederick W., 413-414
"Ride of the Valkyries, The," Wagner, 298. *See also Walküre*
Rider-Kelsey, Corinne, 126
Riegelman, Harold, 413-414
Riegger, Wallingford, 276, 385
Rimsky-Korsakov, 200
Rite of Spring, The, Stravinsky, 217
Ritter, Thelma, 74
Rivier, Jean, 385
Robards, Jason, Jr., 74
Robards, Jason, Sr., 74
Robbins, Jerome, 344
Roberts, Robin, 401
Robeson, Paul, 224, 267
Robinson, Edward G., 74
Rockefeller, John D., 20, 25, 46
Rockefeller, Nelson, 414-415
Rodgers, Richard, 332
Rodzinski, Artur, 242, 243, 298, 302, 324, 326, 327, 329, 339-341, 343, 345, 348, 353, 354, 355, 363, 390, 395
Rogers, Bernard, 199
Rogers, Will, 236
Rogge, O. John, 366
Roman Carnival, Berlioz, 86
Romantic Symphony, Hanson, 273
Rome, American Academy in, 208
Roosevelt, Eleanor (Mrs. Franklin Delano), 311, 312
Roosevelt, Franklin Delano, 285, 295, 298, 300-301, 349. *See also* New Deal, WPA
Roosevelt, Theodore, 6, 13, 83, 95, 123-124, 127, 135, 149-150
Rosenthal, Manuel, 354
Rosenthal, Moriz, 76, 82, 120-122, 218, 311
Rosh Hashana services (1909), 134
Ross, Ivy, 42
Roussel, 198, 244, 272, 273
Royal Philharmonic Orchestra, 386, 389
Rozsa, Miklos, 342
Rubinow Raymond S., 413ff.
Rubinstein, Anton, 17, 20, 60, 61, 76, 77, 98, 100, 102, 110, 120, 160
Rubinstein, Artur (Arthur), 116-117, 160, 187, 216, 292, 302-303, 323, 324, 353, 371, 378
Rubinstein, Ida, 265
Ruegger, Elsa, 100
Rugby, Honegger, 261-262
Ruggles, Carl, 363
Rummel, Franz, 37, 45
Rushing, Jimmy, 310
Russell, Anna, 404
Russell, Bertrand, 274
Russell, Lillian, 70
Russell, Rosalind, 74
Russia, 39, 40, 41, 53, 118, 139, 151, 180, 210-211, 232, 268, 272, 285, 315, 373, 381. *See also* Moscow, World War I and II, Soviet Union
"Russian Easter Overture," Rimsky-Korsakov, 200
Russian Fantasy, Khatchaturian, 360
Russian Symphony Orchestra, 101, 114-115, 117, 122, 126, 169
Russin, Babe, 306
Russolo, Luigi, 369

Sabata, Victor de, 280, 384
"Sabre Dance, The," 400
Sacre Le, Stravinsky, 223
Safonoff, Wassily, 110-111, 114, 115, 118, 120, 121, 126, 128, 132
St. Bartholomew's Church N.Y.C., 164
St. Denis, Ruth (Mrs. Ted Shawn), 154, 224, 349

St. Francis of Assisi, Rosenthal, 354
St. Louis, 18-19, 103, 318
"St. Louis Blues," Handy, 259
St. Matthew Passion, Bach, 258, 336
Saint-Saëns, Camille, 60, 66, 80, 119, 128, 161, 207, 305
Salome, Strauss, 85, 127-128, 208
Salome legend, Schmitt's suite based on, 164
Salón México, El, Copland, 309
Samaroff, Olga, 114, 166, 177
Samson, R. Goldmark, 171
Sanborn, Pitts, 178, 243. *See also Globe* and *Telegram*
San Francisco, 290
Sarasate, 402
Sargeant, Winthrop, 255-256, 256-257, 378, 382, 388, 389, 392, 398
Sargent, Franklin Haven, 73
Sarnoff, David, 394
Sarony, Napoleon, 41
"Satire, A," Stanley, 284
Saturday Review, 392-394
Sauer, Emil, 128
Sauter-Finegan band, 402
Scala, La. *See* La Scala
Scarlatti, 327
Scarlet Letter, The, Damrosch-Hawthorne, 71
"Scenario of Themes" from *Showboat,* Kern, 326
Scheel, Fritz, 101
Schelling, Ernest, 98, 129, 207, 215, 217, 269-270
Schelomo, Bodansky, 174
Schildkraut, Joseph, 74
Schippers, Thomas, 396
Schirmer's music store, N.Y.C., 121
Schlesinger, Arthur, 294
Schmitt, Florent, 164
Schnabel, Artur, 207, 283-284, 297, 362
Schnitzer, 207
Schola Cantorum, 292, 296, 385
Schönberg, Arnold, 7, 172, 195, 196, 199, 215, 216, 264, 271, 280, 294, 295-296, 348, 351, 356, 362, 396, 406
Schonberg, Harold C., 402
School for Scandal, The (Overture), Barber, 305
Schubert, 110, 144, 208
Schuman, William, 319, 329, 384, 390
Schumann, Robert, 60, 61, 101, 115, 130, 132, 138, 142, 146, 172, 173, 183, 291, 303-304, 342
Schumann-Heink, Ernestine, 88, 106, 244-245, 250-251
Schuricht, Carl, 389-390
Schurz, Carl, 53-54
Schütz, Henrich, 52
Schwarzkopf, Elisabeth, 380
Scopes trial, on evolutionary theory, 228-229, 245
Scotland, 24, 28
Scott, Cyril, 198, 204
Scriabin, Alexander, 114, 122, 169-170
Scythian Suite, Prokofieff, 269
"Sea, The," Gilson, 66
"Sea Drift," Carpenter, 293
Second Cello Concerto, Herbert, 69
Second Hungarian Rhapsody, Liszt, 102
Second Piano Concerto, MacDowell, 72, 126; Rubinstein, Anton, 77; Liszt, 110; Rachmaninoff, 139; Prokofieff, 269; Brahms, 302, 324, 344, 349; Chasins, 305; Bartók, 359; Shostakovich, 410
Second Rhapsody, Gershwin, 275-276
Second Symphony, Strong, 66; D'Indy, 116; Rachmaninoff, 129; Mahler, 131; Hill, 273; Mason, 277; Hanson, 280; Wagenaar, B., 280; Thompson, 319; Sibelius, 321; Barber, 340; Milhaud, 360; Toch, 386; Dutilleux, 386; Bodings, 388; Bernstein, 405-406; Ives, 406
Seeger, Pete, 401
Seeley, Blossom, 235
Segovia, Andrés, 352
Sehnsucht, Siegfried Wagner, 79
Seidl, Anton, 53, 63, 65-68, 69, 70, 76, 79, 80, 241
Seidl, Mrs. Anton, 53. *See also* Ohe, Adele Aus der
Seine at Night, The, Thomson, 360
Sembrich, Marcella, 79, 98, 105-106, 156, 166, 251
"Serenade for Violin with Strings and Percussion," Bernstein, 406
Serenade No. 5, Persichetti, 390
Serkin, Rudolf, 297, 301, 323
Servios, Garrett P., 62
Sessions, Roger, 386, 410
Seven Words of Our Savior, The, Schutz, 52

Seventh Symphony, Bruckner, 122, 271, 384, 389-390; Beethoven, 132, 146, 200; Mahler, 215; Miaskovsky, 242; Sibelius, 244, 375; Harris, 385
Shackleton, Sir Ernest, 175
Shakespeare, 132
Shan-Kar, 284
Shapley, Harlow, 366
Shattuck, 160
Shaw, Robert, 385
Shawn, Ted, 154, 224, 320, 349
Sheean, Vincent, 215, 388-389
Sheldon, Mrs. George R., 129, 138, 147-148
Shier, Leonora, 280
Shiloh, story of (speech), 37
Short Symphony, Copland, 406
Shostakovich, Dimitri, 271, 282, 294, 296, 324, 349, 354, 378, 396, 410
Showboat, Kern, 326, 328
Sibelius, Jean, 126, 209, 242, 244, 271, 282, 321, 375
Siegfried, Wagner, 21
"Siegfried Idyl," Wagner, 132. *See also* "Funeral Music," *Götterdämmerung*
"Siegfried's Death," Wagner, 237
"Siegfried's Rhine Journey," 393
Sieverking, Marius, 77
Simionato, Giulietta, 380
Simon, Robert A., 293
Simon, Robert E., 230-231, 278-279, 412
Simon, Robert E., Jr., 412
Sinatra, Frank, 345
Sinfonia Biblica, Nabokov, 321
Sinfonia da Requiem, Britten, 321
Sinfonia Domestica, Strauss, 111-112, 208-209, 321
Sinfonia Drammatica, Respighi, 220
Sinfonia Sacra, Hanson, 385
"Sing, Sing, Sing," 306
Singer, Paris, 151
Sirota, Leo, 358
Six Orchestra Pieces, Von Webern, 391
Sixth Symphony, Tchaikovsky, 39, 70, 142, 374. (*See also Pathetique*); Bruckner, 163; Mahler, 360; Williams, 363; Schuman, 384; Riegger, 385; Piston, 386; Mennin, 396
"Sleepy Time Down South," 309
Slenczynska, Ruth, 288-291
Slim, Memphis, 401
Sloan, William, 46
Slonimsky, Nicholas, 282
Smith, Alfred E., 190, 200, 251, 300-301
Smith, Max, 237. *See also Press* and *American*
Smith, Russell, 259
Social and Political Union, 136
Society for the Publication of American Music, 30
Society of the Friends of Music, The, 174. *See also* Friends of Music
Sokoloff, Nikolai, 183
"Soldier of the Town," Berezowsky, 340
"Solemn Hymn to Victory, A," 348
"Sometimes I'm Happy," 306
Sonata in D minor, Bach, 168
"Songs of the Rose of Sharon," La Montaine, 391
Sophocles, 98
"Soul in Search," 354-355
South Africa, 84
South Pole, 163
"Soviet Iron Foundry," Mossolov, 276
Soviet Union, 285, 294, 329, 350, 359, 366. *See also* Russia
Spalding, Albert, 128, 160
Spanish-American War, 6
"Spanish Dances for Four Hands," Moszkowski, 208
Spectre's Bride, The, Dvořák, 66
Spiering, Theodore, 147
Spivakovski, Tossy, 339, 410
Spring Overture, Goldmark, 236
Spring Symphony, Schumann, 130
Stanislavski, 74
Stanley, David, 284
Stark, Waldemar, 42
"Star Spangled Banner, The," 83, 175, 181, 182, 184, 251, 321
Statement for Orchestra, Copland, 326
State Symphony Orchestra, 218, 232
Steamboat Overture, Almond, 390
Stein, Gertrude, 202
Stein, Wanda, 183
Steinbeck, John, 314, 316
Steinberg, William, 340, 391-392
Steinway, William, 31-32
Steinway booking agency, 58, 61
Steinway Hall, 21, 24, 32
Steinway pianos, 55, 60, 283
Stern, Isaac, 336-338, 345, 413-416 *passim*
Stevens, Risë, 353

Still, William Grant, 296, 326, 340, 347
Stock, Frederick, 160, 206, 322
Stock Exchange crash, 263, 294, 359
Stojowski, 207
Stokes, Richard, 243
Stokowski, Leopold, 114, 164-165, 166, 177, 186-187, 199-200, 204, 207, 208, 215, 218, 220, 221, 231, 236, 243, 244, 260, 264-265, 271, 275, 276, 282, 325, 326, 345, 353, 355, 360, 362, 363, 392, 395, 413
Stokowski, Mrs. Leopold. *See* Samaroff, Olga
"Stompin' at the Savoy," 306
Stone, Ezra, 74
"Story Old and Ever New, A," (*Times* editorial), 343
Stransky, Josef, 148, 156, 157-158, 163, 166, 167, 169, 172, 173-174, 183, 186, 187, 199, 206, 208, 209, 214-215, 218, 232, 241
Straton, John Roach, 228-229
Strauss, Johann, the younger, 17
Strauss, Mrs. Richard, 111
Strauss, Richard, 7, 9, 66, 81, 85, 94-95, 100, 103, 111-112, 115, 116, 144, 146, 164, 173, 188, 195, 205, 206, 208-209, 223, 242, 302, 321, 342, 390, 396
Stravinsky, Igor, 7, 9, 172, 195, 196, 198, 217-218, 220, 223, 266, 272, 273, 276, 296, 302, 355, 356, 360, 363, 374, 385, 406
Street Scenes of Peking, Hadley, 272
Strong, Templeton, 66
Studio 61 (Carnegie Hall), 330-335
Suite for Orchestra, Thomson, 348
Suite for String Orchestra, Schönberg, 295-296
Suite Française, Milhaud, 351
Suite in D, Bach, 151
Suite in E major, Foote, 319
Suite in F major, Roussel, 244
Suite Symphonique, Bloch, 351
Suk, Joseph, 94
Sulamith, Leopold Damrosch, 52
Sumac, Yma, 404
"Summertime," Gershwin, 328
Sun, 45, 49, 60, 138, 142, 319, 336-338
Suppé, 102
Svanholm, Set, 375, 376
"Swanee River," 129
Swarthout, Gladys, 311
Switzerland, 167
Symphonia Serena, Hindemith, 359
Symphonic Dances, Rachmaninoff, 336
Symphonic Metamorphoses on Themes of Carl Maria von Weber, 340
Symphonie de Psaumes, Stravinsky, 272
Symphonie Fantastique, Berlioz, 110, 205
Symphony of the Air, 381, 395, 402, 406, 413
SYMPHONY. See below and by ordinal number or title
Symphony in C major, Schubert, 144
Symphony in D, Vincent, 391
Symphony in E flat, Hindemith, 326
Symphony in F, Dvořák, 199; Vaughan Williams, 296
"Symphony of a Thousand," Mahler, 186. *See also* Eighth Symphony
Symphony of Chorales, Foss, 410
Symphony on a Hymn Tune, Thomson, 348
Symphony Orchestra, Chicago, 19, 80, 86, 99, 160, 206, 322-323, 355, 390; New York, 20, 21, 22, 24, 53, 60, 61, 86, 119, 120, 151, 161, 208, 209, 216, 235, 244-245, 246-251, 255, 257, 260; Boston, 22-24, 63, 80-82, 86, 92, 98, 99, 101, 108, 115, 116, 118, 120, 122, 124, 128, 139, 162, 167, 169, 181, 187, 198, 200, 217, 218, 222, 232, 244, 268, 269, 272-273, 275-276, 282-283, 286, 291, 293-294, 296, 319-320, 323, 327, 329, 341, 349, 351, 360, 363-364, 383-384, 385-386; Pittsburgh, 85-86, 122, 391-392; Cincinnati, 86, 99, 164, 252, 390; Philadelphia, 101, 116, 128, 164, 186-187, 199-200, 208, 218, 220, 235, 236, 243, 260, 269, 271, 276, 280-282, 286, 323, 329, 341, 345, 348, 351, 353-354, 359, 375, 383-384, 386; Minneapolis, 160-161, 391, 395; Detroit, 180, 205, 258; Cleveland, 183, 339, 355, 391; Louisville, 355, 390. *See also* New, National, State orchestras, etc., and foreign orchestras by country or city
Symphony Society, N.Y.C., reorganization, 101-102, 130-131, 177
Szell, George, 351, 354, 355, 391
Szigeti, Joseph, 235, 310-311, 320
Szymanowski, 242, 336

Tabloid, Grofé, 282, 283
Taft, William Howard, 135, 150
Tagore, Sir Rabindranath, 174-175, 226
Tales of Our Countryside, Cowell, 326
Taming of the Shrew, The, Wagenaar, 242
Tannhäuser, Wagner, 132, 152, 318, 319, 393. *See also* "Venusberg Music"
Tansman, Alexander, 231-232, 280, 329, 340
Tarrytown, N.Y., 72
Tattooed Bride, The, Ellington, 330
Taubman, Howard, 265, 266, 312, 378-379, 382, 398, 399, 416. *See also Times*
Taylor, Deems, 217, 232, 235, 302, 340
Tchaikovsky, Peter Ilyitch, 9, 36, 38-45, 49-55, 65, 66, 70, 72, 86, 92, 100, 101, 110, 120, 122, 127, 142, 187, 210, 236, 252-253, 269, 291, 302, 328, 338, 361, 373, 374, 378, 381
Tchaikovsky Piano Competition, 373, 381
Te Deum, Berlioz, 49; Dvořák, 64; Verdi, 271
Telegram, 243
Tempest, Marie, 70
Tempest, The, Sibelius, 242
Tenth Symphony, Mahler, 133, 396-398; Shostakovich, 354, 378, 396
Terry, Sonny, 310
Terry, Walter, 154
Testament of Freedom, Thompson, 349
Tetrazzini, 118
Texas, 114
Thackrey, Ted, 366
Tharpe, Sister, 310
Theater Suite, Toch, 276
Theme, Variations and Finale, Rozsa, 342
Theme and Variations, Joachim, 72
Theme and Variations in G minor, Schönberg, 351
Thibaud, Jacques, 108
Third *Leonore* Overture. *See sub Leonore*
Third Piano Concerto, Hofmann, 127; Rachmaninoff, 139, 199, 381; Prokofieff, 280
Third Suite, Tchaikovsky, 40, 44, 51, 52
Third Symphony, Sibelius, 126; Saint-Saëns, 119; Schumann, 146; Weingartner, 158; Szymanowski, 242; Roussel, 272; Prokofieff, 276; Harris, 319, 406; Hanson, 319; Ives, 352, 406; Pijper, 354; Honegger, 355; Piston, 360; Sessions, 386; Mahler, 396-398
Thomas, John Charles, 308, 323
Thomas, Norman, 229
Thomas, Theodore, 18-19, 20, 21, 22, 24, 32, 36, 65, 70, 80, 206, 370
Thompson, Randall, 319, 349, 385
Thomson, Virgil, 321, 322-323, 325-326, 327, 329, 339, 340, 341, 348, 353-354, 356, 360-361, 362, 364, 371-372, 384, 390
"Three Jewish Poems," Bloch
"Through the Looking Glass," Taylor, 302
"Thunderbolt P-47," Martinu, 341
Thurber, Jeanette, 63
Thus Spake Zarathustra, 111, 128, 144
Tibbett, Lawrence, 224, 232
Till Eulenspiegel, 138, 208
". . .Till Dawn Sunday." *See Hexapoda*
Time (magazine), 369
Times, 19, 31, 34-35, 36, 37, 38, 46, 50, 52, 60, 62, 64, 69, 72, 76, 82, 86, 92, 96, 100, 105-106, 129, 138, 151, 168, 185, 190, 217, 226, 270, 306-308, 309, 312, 317, 321, 327-328, 335, 342-343, 344, 355-356, 378-379, 384, 395, 396, 398, 401, 402, 403, 404, 413, 416. *See also* Aldrich, Downes, Huneker, Taubman
Timon of Athens, Diamond, 390
Tin Pan Alley, 235, 310, 371
"To the Fallen," Rogers, 199
Toch, Ernest, 276, 321, 386
Tolstoi, 54
Tommasini, 265
Toscanini, Arturo, 66, 141, 180, 198, 200, 205, 223, 237-241, 242, 253-255, 257, 260, 265-267, 269-270, 271-272, 276, 277-278, 280, 286, 291, 292, 297-298, 300, 308, 325, 327, 338, 349, 392-395, 398, 408
Toscanini, Wanda, 280
Totten, John, 234
Town Hall, N.Y.C., 288, 312, 318, 336, 352, 379
Tracy, Spencer, 74
Traubel, Helen, 318-319, 346
Tribune, Chicago, 184

Tribune, 36, 84, 96-98, 105. *See also Herald Tribune,* Krehbiel
Trio in B flat, Beethoven, 98
"Trip to Nahant, A," 385
"Trip to the Moon, A" (lecture), 62
Tristan und Isolde, Wagner, 152, 183
"Triumph of Aphrodite, The," Orff, 385
"Triumph of Neptune, The" (ballet score), Berners, 384
Truman, Harry, 366
Turgenev, 54
Turner, Joe, 310
Tuskegee Institute, 117
Tuthill, William Burnet, 30-31, 34, 42, 46-47
Tuxen, Erik, 375, 376, 386
Twain, Mark, 92, 117-118, 125, 177
Twelfth Night Overture, Castelnuovo-Tedesco, 317
"Twenty Years of Jazz" (historical survey), 306
"Two New Worlds—The New World of Columbus and the New World of Music" (lecture), 63
"Tyrant's Love," MacDowell, 126

U.S.A., Dos Passos, 152
U. S. Steel, 195

Vanderbilt, reply of Rosenthal *re* money of, 82
Van Hoogstraten, Willem, 215, 217
Van Vechten, Carl, 151, 152
Varèse, Edgar, 188, 243, 282, 369
Variations, Chaconne and Finale, Dello Joio, 362
Variations for Orchestra, Křenek, 276; Schönberg, 264
Variations on a North Carolina Folk Song, Křenek, 329-330
Vaurabourg, Andrée, 261
Vecheslova, 285
Vecsey, Franz von, 206-207
"Venusberg Music," Wagner, 200. *See also Tannhäuser*
Veprik, 280
Verdi, 271, 308
Versailles Peace Conference, 188, 211, 212
Victor, Eric, 332
"Victory Ball, A," Schelling, 215
Vienna, 92, 130, 133, 148, 151, 172, 173, 322
Vienna Children's Milk Relief, 197
Vienna Conservatory, 339
Vienna Opera, 157
Vienna Philharmonic Orchestra, 389-390
Viennese Rhapsodic Fantasy, Kreisler, 335
Vier ernste Gesänge, Brahms, 384
Vieuxtemps, 204
Villa-Lobos, Heitor, 321, 348
Villard, Oswald Garrison, 177
Vincent, John, 391
Violin Concerto, Dvořák, 70; Mendelssohn, 76, 402-403; Brahms, 115; Beethoven, 129, 297-298; Elgar, 160; Stravinsky, 276; Hill, 319; Bloch, 320, 378; Barber, 323; Bartók, 339; Tchaikovsky, 378; Menotti, 384; Rivier, 385; Schönberg, 396; Sessions, 410
Violin Concerto in A minor, Glazunov, 156
Violin Concerto in D major, Paganini, 318
Violin Concerto in D minor, Britten, 318
Vitali, 178, 183
Vita Nuova, La, Nabokov, 386
Vivaldi, 228, 327
Vogrich, Max, 41
Von Hugo Musical Society, 157
Vronsky, Vitya, 321

Wagenaar, Bernard, 280
Wagenaar, Johan, 242
Wagner, Richard, 7, 9, 10, 19, 21, 22, 39, 65, 66, 70, 79, 104, 119, 120, 132, 151-152, 157, 161, 186, 195, 208, 209, 217, 236, 237, 245, 288, 292, 298, 300, 305, 318-319, 342, 343, 389, 392
Wagner, Robert F., Jr., 414
Wagner, Siegfried, 79, 158
Walküre, Die, Wagner, 319. *See also* "Ride of the Valkyries"
Wall, Joseph, 25, 26-28
Wallace, Henry, 366
Waller, "Fats," 259, 328
Walter, Bruno, 141, 187, 215-216, 258, 276, 277, 280, 283, 284, 293, 322, 325, 326, 327, 336, 342, 353, 361, 362, 377

Walter Damrosch Fellowship, 208
Walton, William, 305
Warfield, William, 384
Warren, Leonard, 376
Washington, Booker T., 117
Washington, D.C., 55, 123-124, 312-314, 391
Waters, Ethel, 309-310
Weavers, The, 401
Weber, Carl Maria von, 205, 237, 266, 388, 390
Webern, Anton von, 391
Weimar, Germany, 19
Weingarten, Felix, 110, 114, 158
Weiss, Joseph, 142-143
Westminster Choir, 396
Wetzler, Hermann Hans, 100-101, 108, 111, 265
"What's This?", Cowell, 216
Wheeler, Mr. (prohibitionist), 245-246
"When Johnny Comes Marching Home" (American Overture), Harris, 296
White, Edna, 362
Whiteman, Paul, 216, 227, 235, 257, 258, 259, 282, 306, 310
Whitfield Louise 24. *See also* Carnegie, Mrs. Andrew
Whitman, Walt, 285, 293, 329
Whitney, Arthur, 170
Whitney, Mr. & Mrs. William C., 46
Whitney, Robert, 390
Wienawski, 336
"Will o' the Wisp" (ballet), 202
Williams, Ralph Vaughan, 198, 204-205, 296, 348, 363, 385
Wilson, Edith Bolling Galt (Mrs. Woodrow), 190
Wilson, Woodrow, 127, 135, 150, 177, 188-192, 202, 230, 300
Windsor Hotel, N.Y.C., 58, 60
Winter Journey, A, Tchaikovsky, 72
Wise, Rabbi Stephen, 134-135, 195, 274, 364
Wittgenstein, Paul, 293
Woodland Suite, MacDowell, 126
Wooldridge, John, 348
World, 46, 50, 77, 128, 243
World-Telegram, 347
World War I, 7, 120, 150, 165, 166ff., 214, 237, 268, 315, 324, 349, 358. *See also* Versailles Peace Conference, League of Nations, etc.
World War II, 10, 11, 51, 160, 264, 308, 315-316, 324-349 *passim*, 354
Wozzeck, Berg, 270-271, 359, 395, 396
WPA, 275; orchestra, 272
"Wrong Note Rag," Bernstein, 407
Wüllner, Ludwig, 142

Yale, 264, 284
"Yankee Doodle," 17
Yeats, William Butler, 106-108
"Yellow Dog," Handy, 259
YMCA, 95
Young, Lester, 401
Ysaÿe, Eugène, 72, 79, 80, 112, 114, 129, 162, 164

Zeldenrust, Eduard, 98
Zigeunerweisen, 402
Zimbalist, Efrem, 156-157, 161, 178, 183, 217, 228, 276, 327, 362, 384
Zirato, Bruno, 266, 342, 399
Zorina, Vera, 361